JN451529

IAFICO Book Project No.1

An International Comparison of Financial Consumer Protection

An International Comparison of
Financial Consumer Protection

초판인쇄 2018년 8월 25일
초판발행 2018년 8월 31일

지은이 사단법인 국제금융소비자학회(IAFICO)
편 집 Tsai-Jyh Chen
펴낸이 박노일
총괄기획 김중용 · 최준규
펴낸곳 pnc publishing and culture 피앤씨미디어
경기도 고양시 일산동구 강송로 153 310-1501
등록 제396-2012-000203호
전 화 070)7550-3758 팩 스 02)718-8554
홈페이지 www.pncmedia.co.kr 이메일 pnc@pncmedia.co.kr
ISBN 979-11-5730-571-1 93320

※ 무단복사 및 전재를 금합니다. 파본 및 낙장본은 교환하여 드립니다.

정 가 28,000원

IAFICO Book Project No.1

IAFICO THE INTERNATIONAL ACADEMY OF FINANCIAL CONSUMERS

An International Comparison of Financial Consumer Protection

사단법인 국제금융소비자학회
(International Academy of Financial Consumers)

publishing and culture
피앤씨미디어

Preface

Financial consumer protection has been an important issue for the modern society where people cannot live without financial products and services, such as mortgage and insurance. The development of financial market has made a great contribution to the quality of life and the economic growth of a society. On the other hand, being strongly dependent on financial services may drive people into a disaster when the financial industries run out of order. The suffering experience of the financial crisis of 2008 has called for the advocacy of financial consumer protection. Consumer protection traditionally is a local issue because of the societal differences in each country. However, financial consumer protection involves both international and domestic factors. Due to the globalization and liberalization of financial services, the systemic risk caused by one financial institution in one country may influence the consumers in other countries because the regulations and business practices in the domestic market must change frequently to keep up with the international trend. Therefore, communication and cooperation among countries are essential for financial consumer protection.

The newly established organization International Academy of Financial Consumers (IAFICO) aims to be a global platform for sharing knowledge and insights about financial consumer protection through forums and publications. This first book of IAFICO intends to explore consumer protections in the global financial markets. With the contribution of scholars from 13 countries, this book provides an international comparison of financial consumer protection among countries with different cultural background and economic development. It intends to share knowledge regarding the major issues of financial consumption and the efforts to counter those issues in the selected countries. The innovations in financial institutions and public policies for consumer protection presented in this book hopefully can provide insights for the future development of global financial markets.

Finally, I wish to acknowledge Hongjoo Jung, the Chairman of IAFICO, and William Achauer, the Executive Editor of Springer, for their support to the preparation and publication of this book. Many thanks are also addressed to all the authors as shown in the list of contributors for their voluntary contribution of the article and great patience in collaboration for this writing project.

Taipei, Taiwan Tsai-Jyh Chen

Contents

Contributors

Wardatul Adawiyah Universitas Indonesia, Jakarta, Indonesia

Idris Ademuyiwa Centre for International Governance Innovation (CIGI), Waterloo, Canada

Patricia Born Florida State University, Tallahassee, FL, USA

Tsai-Jyh Chen National Chengchi University, Taipei, Taiwan

Misoo Choi Seoul Digital University, Seoul, South Korea

Ida Ayu Agung Faradynawati Universitas Indonesia, Jakarta, Indonesia

Montserrat Guillen University of Barcelona, Barcelona, Spain

Youkyung Huh University of Virginia, Charlottesville, USA

Hongjoo Jung SungKyunKwan University, Seoul, South Korea

Robert R. Kerton University of Waterloo, Waterloo, Canada

Ahcene Lahsasna Malaysian Financial Planning Council, Kuala Lumpur, Malaysia

Hongmu Lee Waseda University, Tokyo, Japan

Jan-juy Lin National Chengchi University, Taipei, Taiwan

Jean-Paul A. Louisot Institut Catholique de Lille, Lille, France

Muhammad Ziaulhaq Mamun University of Dhaka, Dhaka, Bangladesh

Satoshi Nakaide Waseda University, Tokyo, Japan

James O'Hara Minter Ellison Law Office, Sydney, Australia

Rofikoh Rokhim Universitas Indonesia, Jakarta, Indonesia

Andrew D. Schmulow University of Western Australia, Crawley, Australia

Vincenzo Senatore GSA Law Firm, Rome, Italy

Jorge M. Uribe University of Barcelona, Barcelona, Spain

Xian Xu Fudan University, Shanghai, China

Chapter 1
Introduction and Overview of This Book

Tsai-Jyh Chen

1 Motivation to Write This Book

Consumer protection has been an important issue for the society and extensively discussed by the academics since 1950s (Devaney 2016). The subjects for discussion include a full range of products and innumerable types of consumer complaints. Traditionally the manufactured products, such as cars and food, are the focus of consumer protection. However, the financial crisis of 2008 which caused many people incurring disastrous loss in wealth has attracted attention to financial consumer protection. The creation of the Consumer Financial Protection Bureau (CFBP) in the US in 2010 could be regarded as a significant movement for the trend.

Financial sectors, including banks, securities firms, insurance companies, etc., are closely related to everyone's daily life. In the modern society people shop with credit card, invest in securities, and plan estate through insurance. A critical element in consuming financial products is "trust". A customer will not save her money in a bank if she cannot trust that bank. Kennedy et al. (2001) indicate that customer's trust is an essential ingredient to achieve long-term relationship for business. Although people all agree that trust is a crucial factor, the concept of trust is subjective and not precisely defined. Consequently there is no unanimous approach to win customer's trust. Banks and insurance companies spend huge costs to train their salespersons or perform many corporate social responsibilities (CSR) in order to raise consumer's trust.

The financial crisis of 2008 inflicted financial consumers heavily, and how to restore their trust in financial sectors became a challenge to the financial institutions and the policy makers. Legislation seems a commonly used approach in such situation, according to Sharon (2016). de Jager (2017) indicates European Union (EU) attempts to pursue the trust of investors by way of legislation. However,

T.-J. Chen (✉)
National Chengchi University, Taipei, Taiwan
e-mail: tjchen@nccu.edu.tw

© Springer Nature Singapore Pte Ltd. 2018
T.-J. Chen (ed.), *An International Comparison of Financial Consumer Protection*,
https://doi.org/10.1007/978-981-10-8441-6_1

whether laws and regulations can reach the target effect is unknown according to previous literature. Guiso (2010) suggests that legislation has little impact on raising consumer trust, but Reich (2008) considers legislation is a suitable method to restore consumer trust in financial industries. Creutzfeldt (2016) empirically compares people's expectation of ombudsman model for justice based on the consumers in Germany and the UK, and finds that there is common identification about ombudsman except for some national specificities.

In general, most people in the world still rely on their government to protect them from disastrous financial losses although the level of reliance may differ. Due to the specific economic and societal environments in each country, the measures for financial consumer protection adopted in practice are quite diverse among countries. On the other hand, the international capitals and investors enter almost every financial market in the world under the trend of globalization. The interests of local consumers may be affected by foreign investors and international financial markets. For example, the financial crisis of 2008 initially ignited in the US but then influenced many other countries in the world. The systemic risk in the global financial markets becomes an important issue to local financial consumers as well as international investors.

As the financial institutions in the world are connected to one another through the potential systemic risk in the future, it is expected that consumers, investors, and regulators will be interested in understanding the protection mechanisms in other countries. Therefore, the newly established organization International Academy of Financial Consumers (IAFICO) aims to serve as a global platform for sharing information (Jung 2016), which invites distinguished scholars in the world to contribute their knowledge and insights in financial consumer protection, by way of annual conference and research publications.

2 Contents of This Book

This book explores consumer protections in the major financial markets in the world, and provides an international comparison among the countries of different cultural background and economic development. Each chapter describes the major issues of financial consumption in the selected country. Then the efforts and legislative measures to counteract current problems of financial consumption are investigated. The innovation and renovation in the financial institutions and the public policies for consumer protection are also analyzed for their potential impacts on the future development of financial markets.

In order to provide a comprehensive understanding of financial protection mechanisms in the global financial markets, the countries are selected based on the consideration of their economic development and societal environment, such as cultural and demographic factors. Because some of the invited authors cannot finish the writing for their countries by the deadline, finally there are 13 countries included in this book as follows:

(1) Australia: Australia;
(2) East Asia: China, Japan, Korea, and Taiwan;
(3) South Asia: Bangladesh, Indonesia, and Malaysia;
(4) Europe: France, Italy, and Spain;
(5) North America: Canada and the US.

These countries can represent most of the important financial markets in the world. In addition to the familiar and well developed markets such as Japan and the US, this book also includes the countries of emerging market and Islamic economy. The consumers of France, Italy and Spain are protected by the legislation of European Union but with their own market conditions. Australia and Canada have their own regulatory systems for financial sectors even though they also belong to the western culture.

Bangladesh is an emerging market but her growth in economy is fast. Besides, her cultural environment is distinguished and unfamiliar to most of the readers. Indonesia and Malaysia are prominent countries of Islamic economy in the south Asia and have great potential in economic development due to their rich natural resources. People in China, Korea, and Taiwan all live under Confucian culture but with different political environments and financial markets. Through the essays in this book, we can obtain knowledge of various systems of financial consumer protection in the world.

3 Structure and Organization of Paragraphs in Each Chapter

In order to make a comparison of the financial consumer protection (FCP) systems across the countries, a framework was proposed for the authors to write their chapter. Some of the items in the framework may be missed in certain chapters because those countries probably do not publish the statistics or establish the systems/institutes. However, the authors have made their efforts in writing the article based on this framework. The framework includes five sections to discuss the issues related to financial consumer protection, which is outlined in Table 1 and described as follows.

(1) Financial Consumer

The first section provides the background of financial consumer protection in the selected country, including (a) the legal meaning of financial consumer and (b) the economic situation. Some countries may formally define "financial consumer" through legislation to provide a clear scope of protection, but others simply regard it as consumer shopping/using financial products. The description for the economic situation of financial consumer includes the total population, age structure, income distribution in each country, and the social security system if available. Additionally, the statistics of total number of bank deposit holders and bank

Table 1 Structure and organization of the paragraphs in each chapter

Section	Items
(1) Financial Consumer	a. Legal Meaning of Financial Consumer b. Economic Situation of Financial Consumer
(2) FCP System (Software)	a. Relevant Laws and Rules b. Rationale and Direction of FCP c. Ex-Ante Protection d. Ex-Post Protection
(3) FCP Institution (Hardware)	a. Financial Supervision Organization b. Deposit Insurance Corporation c. Dispute Settlement Organization
(4) Special FCP Systems	a. For the Elderly Group b. For the Poor Group c. For the Young Group
(5) Market Issues	a. Product Complexity b. Price Dispersion c. Governance

accounts, total number of insurance policyholders, total number of insurers and total number of insurance salespersons are reported if the data are available. The market structure of financial industries may also be discussed in this introductory section.

(2) Financial Consumer Protection System (FCP Software)

The second section is to introduce the software of financial consumer protection system, such as the relevant laws and regulations, the rationale and direction of FCP. The authors may discuss the ex-ante protection system, including the consumer literacy and education for financial products, or the product/price regulations. The laws and regulations for salesperson qualification, legal/contractual authority of salesperson, and information disclosure may be also referred. The rules for appropriateness principle, good faith and fair treatment, and anti-trust competition may be included if they are available in that country. Additionally, the authors may discuss the mechanisms for ex-post protection, such as emergence prohibition of problematic products, complaints and dispute settlement, and deposit insurance scheme/insurance guarantee funds.

(3) Financial Consumer Protection Institution (FCP Hardware)

In the third section, the authors discuss the hardware of financial consumer protection in their countries. The financial supervision organization is usually the first and the most important hardware for FCP. The basic structure and the number of employees of the organization are provided, together with its authorities and relationship with financial consumers. The potential issues of supervision are discussed and the number of attorneys and experts may be provided. Secondly, the deposit insurance corporation and the organization of insurance guarantee funds are introduced, including their structure, scale, authorities and issues, if that country has established these institutions. Furthermore, some countries have set up the dispute settlement organization (or ombudsman bureau) to help financial consumers, and thus may be indicated by the authors about its organizational structure, authorities and contribution.

(4) Special Financial Consumer Protection Systems

Since demographic and societal environments are crucial factors, in addition to economic environment, for developing the public policies of financial consumer protection, the authors try to describe the updated FCP programs for special groups of consumers in their countries, including the senior, the poor, and the young. The special programs may include separate products and service counters for the elder and the young people. For the poor people, some countries have developed the assigned risk plans to solve the availability problem of auto insurance. Micro insurance and micro finance are popular approaches in some countries to help their poor people deal with financial problems.

(5) Market Issues

In the final section, the authors discuss the current issues in the market related to FCP and provide their comments and suggestions for the FCP policies to be implemented in the near future. The common market issues may include product complexity, price dispersion, and governance. Financial products become more and more complex due to the advanced technology of financial engineering. How to enhance product simplicity and consumer literacy in finance can be an important topic for FCP. Price dispersion is another issue for financial products due to information asymmetry in the market. How to reduce price dispersion but uphold price-quality competition must be seriously studied. Adequate disclosure of information may be required for certain financial products. Finally, governance also plays an important role in FCP because people usually rely on the government. How to ensure the integrity of the supervision agencies and avoid the corruption of the authorities is definitely a critical issue for FCP.

The market issues may be quite diverse among the countries due to the differentiated development in economic and societal environments. Therefore the market issues referred in each chapter are not all the same. Besides, the authors may provide their own comments on the current issues or policies and propose their suggestions for FCP in the future.

4 Summary of This Book

From the 13 chapters of this book, we can find some common protection mechanisms among the countries as well as some specific issues in certain countries. A summary of these chapters is provided as follows.

Australia is one of the few countries which have a legal definition of "financial consumers." Most households in Australia have bank deposits, life insurance, and annuity fund. A "Twin Peaks" model is adopted for consumer protection. The FCP software in Australia can be categorized into two areas: (1) general protections to consumers of financial products and financial services, and (2) industry specific regimes such as licensing, conduct and disclosure. The hardware for FCP includes (1) Financial Supervision Organizations with three corporate regulators, (2) Deposit Insurance Corporation for bank accounts and insurance policies, and (3) Dispute Settlement Organization with internal and external schemes. The Australian Law Reform has considered the protection for the elder against abuse of their rights as financial consumers, but at this moment does not specifically target at the protection for the poor and the young. The performance of Australia's consumer protection agency (ASIC) seems not satisfactory yet, and the author provides several suggestions for improvement.

Bangladesh is a country with a literacy rate around 60%, and thus financial consumers may incur huge loss in wealth due to lack of knowledge. The population of Bangladesh has been increasing at a high rate, and its economy is also improving. There has been a positive trend in the growth of personal wealth for the citizens in Bangladesh in the recent years. Bangladesh has only limited number of banks, but the member-based Microfinance Institutions (MFIs) constitute a rapidly growing segment, especially for the rural market. Customers' right and protection is mainly supervised by the central bank Bangladesh Bank (BB). In addition to set up the guidelines for financial consumer service policies such as financing limit and pricing strategy, BB also strengthens financial education initiatives. In Bangladesh, the financial institutions offer extra protections and hold relevant activities for the elderly. For the poor group, micro finance has experienced for more than ten years, and micro insurance keeps on developing. The current issues of financial markets in Bangladesh are many and complicated as the country is fast-growing these days, where new products and services are being introduced every year. The author gives his comments on those issues and proposes suggestions for future FCP in Bangladesh.

In Canada, a financial firm can be incorporated either under federal laws or under provincial legislation, which implies at least fourteen agencies regulating financial services. Canada was relatively early (in year 2001) in establishing a specific agency to protect financial consumers because its financial sector is very important to the economy, about 7% of GDP. The soundness of banking industry is highly ranked in the world and none of the Canada's banks needed to be rescued during the crisis of 2008. The FCP system in Canada includes the measures taken by the financial institutions, the regulations to guide these institutions, and the supervision of the governmental agencies. The ex-ante FCP mechanisms include improving financial literacy, simplifying documents, enhancing information disclosure, etc. The ex-post FCP mechanisms include the agency for complaints and dispute settlement, deposit insurance, and customer compensation schemes for insurance and securities. The author also discusses two current issues of FCP in Canada: the effect of the digital technology (FinTech) on financial service, and the impact of financial service globalization.

At this moment China has no specific law to protect the rights of financial consumers, but there is a general law for consumer rights and interests in any industry. As a country of socialism, the social security system is important in China to guarantee a minimum allowance for living, but the trend of capitalization also keeps private insurers increasing. Regarding FCP, laws and regulations are the fundamental mechanisms, but the commissioned authorities are even more directly connected with the protection for financial consumers. The protection mechanisms are emphasized on consumer literacy and education, and salesperson qualification control. Deposit insurance scheme and insurance guarantee funds are also available in China to provide protection for the depositors and the insured. There are three agencies which regulate banking, securities, and insurance respectively, in addition to the central bank of China. For dispute settlement, there are Financial Consumption Mediation Center and local arbitration institutions to help consumers. Extra protections are offered for the elderly, and microfinance is available for the poor. Finally, the author discusses how to enhance simplicity of products from five viewpoints: issuer, buyer, product duration, price and yield, and risk. He also suggests the concept of risk management for improving asset quality and enhancing competitive power.

Financial consumer is not legally defined in France either, but usually inferred to an individual who engages in purchasing a financial product or service. The savings rate of French citizens is considered high among the EU members and only a few people do not have a bank account. Banking on line is growing in both credit and insurance business, which becomes a competitor for traditional banks. The FCP in France is applicable in a number of areas, such as withdrawal period and obligation of information for financial contracts. In case of dispute, the burden of proof is on the financial services provider. French government has been aware of the importance of consumer literacy on financial products for the soundness of capital market. The increasing number of international litigation concerning investments causes the French courts to integrate some legal principles from Common Law. For the complaints and dispute settlement, most insurers have adopted the insurance mediator (ombudsman) whereas banks still relies more on their internal solutions. In the final section the author provides his comments on product complexity and risk management of financial institutions. Additionally, an appendix for French inspired insurance system in Africa is attached.

Indonesian financial system has experienced five phases of development since 1966. Currently the government pays more attention to consumer protection in financial industry than before. The financial service sector in Indonesia can be divided into three main subsectors: banking industry, capital market and nonbank financial industry, but banking dominates the other subsectors. The authority to supervise FCP is mainly held by OJK (Otoritas Jasa Keuangan, i.e., Indonesia Financial Services Authority). In 2013, OJK issued the first regulation concerning consumer protection in the financial services sector. In Indonesia, the disclosure requirements are not well emphasized yet, but the education plans for financial literacy are concerned and must be submitted with annual business plans to the supervisory board of OJK now. There are six agencies to manage mediation in financial services and two mechanisms to handle the complaints from financial consumers. Indonesia already has a deposit insurance corporation to protect depositors, and a protection fund for securities investors.

The chapter of Italy provides many European Union (EU) legislations and directives as the background to understand the development of FCP in the European countries in addition to Italy. The author greatly emphasizes the importance of financial literacy for FCP, and considers Italy should do more in this aspect. In 2015 a law has launched financial education programs for public schools in Italy to help students develop the necessary financial knowledge. The FCP mechanisms in Italy are mainly based on around 90 EU directives related to consumer protection issues, which aim to protect consumers and promote fair and efficient financial markets. Additionally, there is an alternative dispute resolution (ADR) for consumers to resolve their contractual disputes, and an online dispute resolution (ODR) platform is set up to help the contractual disputes of online shopping. Consumer complaints and disputes may be resolved through arbitration and mediation. Besides, a no-fault indemnification fund is available for unlawful brokerage activities, and the Banking and Financial Ombudsman has been set up since 1993 to resolve disputes with banks and financial intermediaries. In the final section the author provides suggestions for restoring consumer confidence after the global financial crisis.

In Japan there is no law specific for FCP, but a variety of laws regulating financial services can provide protection for financial consumers, such as the Banking Act and the Consumer Contract Act. Besides, the Financial Services Agency (FSA) is responsible for supervising financial services, which also contributes to protecting financial consumers. A significant demographic issue in Japan is the rapid aging society. The aged people rely on financial products (e.g., savings and pension) for living much more than others, which implies that financial services are especially important in the aging society. On the other hand, the aged people are more vulnerable to frauds than others, which urges the strengthening of financial protection system. The FCP software in Japan mainly depends on the innovation or renovation of certain laws and acts related to financial service. The hardware of FCP in Japan includes the Consumer Affairs Agency (CAA) to strengthen the consumer protection, and the Financial Services Agency (FSA) to ensure the stability of financial system. Additionally, each financial sector establishes its own Alternative Dispute Resolution (ADR) institution to settle disputes with customers. The mechanisms of protection for consumers in case of bankruptcy of financial institutions are also available in Japan.

In Korea, a recent bill proposed by the government formally introduces a statutory definition of financial consumer and stipulates the basic rights of financial consumer. The very low birth rate in Korea, together with the increasing longevity, has changed a number of public policies there. The financial innovation is especially influenced by the progress in information technology such as internet and mobile phones. The Korean financial industries can be characterized as an oligopolistic system due to regulatory control on new entry. Regarding the FCP software, currently there is no single law overseeing all aspects of financial consumer protection, but the regulations related to FCP are scattered in various sector-based statutes, such as the Banking Act. In Korea the market conduct regulations have not been as popular as the prudence regulations. The financial institutions are somewhat against strengthening consumer protection because they consider consumers also have certain responsibility in using the financial products. The consumer literacy programs have been developed by financial institutions as well as governmental agencies. In 2012 a new agency, the Financial Consumer Protection Bureau (FCPB), was established to enhance financial consumer protection.

Malaysia is well known for being the center of Islamic finance in the global financial markets. Currently it has a stable GDP growth rate and a sound financial system supported with strong supervision and regulation. Malaysia is stepping to a high-income country through Islamic finance and high technology industries. Recently two new acts, FSA 2013 and IFSA 2013, were enacted to further strengthen the country's financial system. The bank's lending structure has evolved from corporate loans towards retail loans such as household consumers and small-and-medium enterprises. Therefore the call for customer protection becomes a top priority. The Malaysian government now is committed to improve financial consumer protection and financial literacy due to the increased sophistication in the Malaysian financial markets and the advancements in information technology. The financial education has been incorporated into the school curriculum since 2013. The new regulations intend to provide a sound FCP through specific provisions which safeguard the consumer's right. It is expected that Malaysia will continue to evolve in FCP as the country is ambitious on paving its way into a well-developed and high-income nation.

Spain is also facing the trend of aging society due to the reduction in both fertility and mortality, which may threaten the solvency of annuities and lifetime mortgages and impose huge challenges for financial industries and policy makers. The global financial crisis of 2008 and the European debt crisis of 2010 have a great impact on the Spanish economy and consequent evolution for financial markets. The regulations for financial institutions in Spain usually follow the guidelines of the European Union (EU). The Bank of Spain acts as a supervisor for the three markets: banking, insurance, and securities. For the banking industry, a Single Resolution Mechanism (SRM) has been approved to ensure an orderly resolution of failing banks. A supervisory framework (Solvency II) for insurance companies in the EU has been established recently and applicable in Spain, which will enhance the consumer protection of insurance products. Besides, there is a national fund to help insurance consumers in case of insolvency. For the securities market, the law MiFID emphasizes market transparency and information disclosure, and there also exists a guarantee fund to compensate clients of insolvent securities firms.

The term "financial consumer" was legally defined in the Financial Consumer Protection Act (FCPA 2011) in Taiwan after the global financial crisis of 2008. The FCPA 2011 was enacted specifically for the rules of protection, dispute resolution, and financial education. Other financial laws and regulations, such as the

Banking Act and the Insurance Act, can also provide protections supplementally. The FCP institutions in Taiwan may include governmental agencies such as the Financial Supervisory Commission (FSC), and special institutions such as the Financial Ombudsman Institution (FOI), the Securities and Futures Investors Protection Fund (SFIPF), the Central Deposit Insurance Corporation (CDIC), and the Taiwan Insurance Guarantee Fund (TIGF). In addition to handling financial disputes, the ombudsman FOI also conducts education programs for financial institutions and financial consumers. Nowadays the FSC is steering several tasks to enhance financial consumer protection, including research on protection policies and data analysis of financial disputes.

The FCP in the U.S. is available through a wide range of regulations and activities at all levels of government. However, the complex structure of financial products, the variability in suppliers and distributors, and the federal-state regulation system all make the FCP even more challenging in the U.S. financial markets. The ex-ante protections include agent licensing requirements, disclosure requirements, and education to promote financial literacy. Information disclosure is especially emphasized these days because it has many important consequent effects. A new commission FLEC has developed a national strategy for financial literacy. For the ex-post protections, the new law Dodd–Frank Act provides revised measures to investors and establishes new rules for customers-dealers relationship. The accrediting agencies, Better Business Bureaus (BBB), intend to enhance ethical business behavior. Disputes are usually settled by the financial firms themselves through customer service lines. For the special groups, most states have financial exploitation laws designed to protect the seniors, and require high school students to take a course in economics or personal finance. Finally the author provides her comments on certain market issues such as Bitcoin and marketing of debt.

5 Concluding Remarks

Financial consumer protection becomes an important subject in public policies and academic research after the financial crisis of 2008. Although some of the protection mechanisms, such as deposit insurance and guarantee funds, have been established for a long time, they are probably insufficient for the new challenges in the financial industries today. The challenges come from (1) more knowledge required to consume the new and complicated financial products, (2) systemic risk caused by other financial institutions in the domestic and global markets, and (3) revolution in business transactions through FinTech with computerized operation. The potential problems of financial consumption in the future are expected to be larger in scale and scope, which will require more educational programs to enhance financial literacy and more legislative mechanisms to maintain operational soundness in the financial sectors. Furthermore, experience-sharing and communication among countries are necessary to facilitate the development and stability of the global financial markets.

References

Creutzfeldt, N. (2016) 'What do we expect from an ombudsman? Narratives of everyday engagement with the informal justice system in Germany and the UK', *International Journal of law in Context*, 12(4): 437–452.

Devaney, S. A. (2016) 'Fifty years of consumer issues in the Journal of Consumer Affairs', *The Journal of Consumer Affairs*, 50(3): 505–514.

Guiso, L. (2010) 'A trust-driven financial crisis. Implications for the future of financial markets (EUI Working Paper)' http://cadmus.eui.eu/bitstream/handle/1814/13657/ECO_2010_07.pdf?sequence=3&isAllowed=y.

de Jager, C. E. (2017) 'A question of trust: The pursuit of consumer trust in the financial sector by means of EU legislation', *Journal of Consumer Policy*, 40(1): 25–49.

Jung, H. J. (2016) 'Chairperson's Address', *The International Review of Financial Consumers*, 1 (1).

Kennedy, M., Ferrell, L., and LeClair, D. (2001) 'Consumers' trust of salesperson and manufacturer: An empirical study', *Journal of Business Research*, 51(1): 73–86.

Reich, R. (2008) 'Government needs to rebuild trust in markets', *U.S. News & World Report*, https://www.usnews.com/opinion/articles/2008/09/16.

Sharon, T. (2016) 'Can Regulations Improve Financial Information and Advice?', *The International Review of Financial Consumers*, 1(1): 1–8.

Tsai-Jyh Chen is a professor of risk management and insurance at the National Chengchi University (NCCU) in Taiwan. She received her Ph.D. from the Wharton School, University of Pennsylvania. She was the chairman of the Department of Risk Management and Insurance and the director of the Graduate Institute of Insurance at the NCCU. In addition to the academia, she provided services for the governmental and professional organizations, such as Ministry of Finance, National Health Insurance Administration, and Taiwan Insurance Institute. Dr. Chen has authored several textbooks of insurance and risk management, translated an insurance dictionary, and published many articles in academic and professional journals.

Chapter 2
Protection of Financial Consumers in Australia

Andrew D. Schmulow and James O'Hara

1 Financial Consumers in Australia

1.1 Legal Meaning of Financial Consumer

Financial consumers are defined by s 12BC of the *ASIC Act* [1] as consumers of services worth less than AUD 40,000.00,[2] or if worth more, then 'of a kind ordinarily acquired for personal, domestic or household use or consumption'[3]; or if the services are for use or consumption in connection with a small business,[4] and cost more than AUD 40,000.00, ordinarily acquired for business use or consumption.[5]

1.2 Economic Situation of Financial Consumers

Australia's population is approximately 24 million,[6] with a median age of 37.4 years.[7] The average net worth for all Australian households in 2013–14 was $809,900.[8] In real terms, average equivalised disposable household income was AUD 998 per week in 2013–14.[9] Over 70% of households had debt of some level in 2013–14.[10] Twenty-six per cent of such households were servicing a total debt that was three or more times their annualised disposable income.[11] Of 8.8 million households in 2014,[12] almost 36% had a mortgage over their primary residence.[13]

A. D. Schmulow (✉)
University of Western Australia, Crawley, Australia
e-mail: Andy.Schmulow@uwa.edu.au

J. O'Hara
Minter Ellison Law Office, Sydney, Australia

© Springer Nature Singapore Pte Ltd. 2018

T.-J. Chen (ed.), *An International Comparison of Financial Consumer Protection*,
https://doi.org/10.1007/978-981-10-8441-6_2

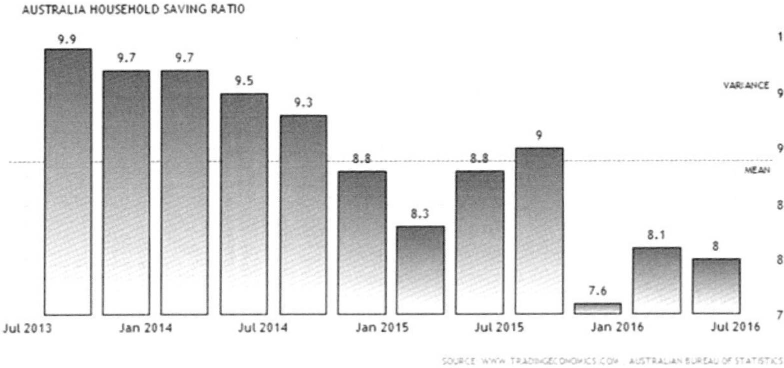

Trading Economics, "1959–2016", in *Australia Household Saving Ratio*, published by Trading Economics, 2016, accessed: 8 December, 2016

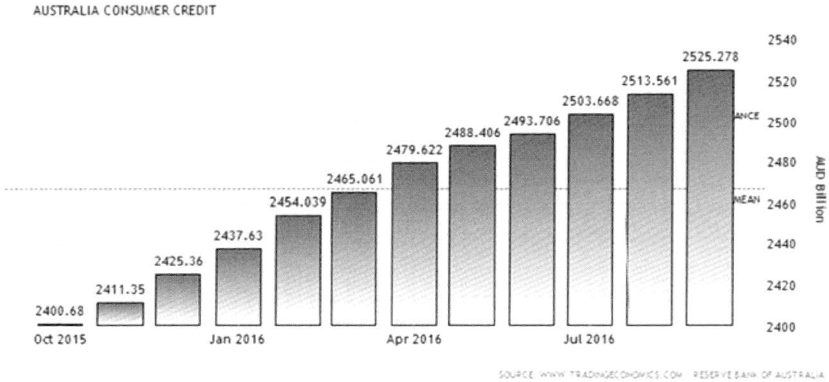

Trading Economics, "1976–2016 ", in *Australia Consumer Credit*, published by Trading Economics, 2016, accessed: 8 December, 2016

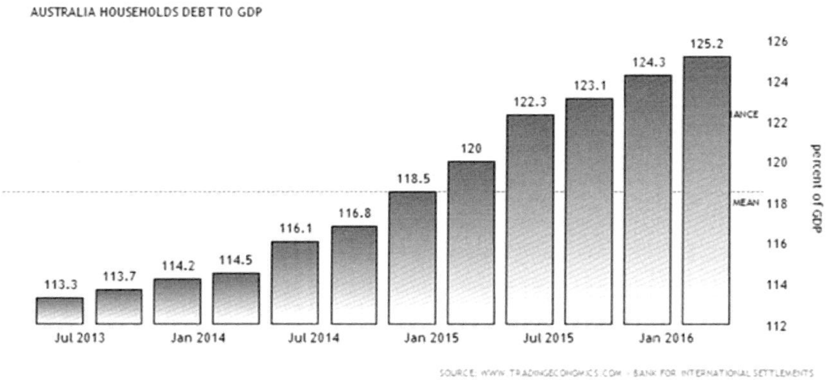

Trading Economics, "1977–2016", in *Australia Households Debt To Gdp*, published by Trading Economics, 2016, accessed: 8 December, 2016

As at October 2016 the total value of bank deposits held by Australian households was AUD 815,708 million.[14] Almost 14 million working-age Australians had some form of life insurance as at late 2013,[15] and 24% had some form of credit card debt.[16] Superannuation assets totalled AUD 2.1 trillion as at the end of the June 2016 quarter,[17] and over 14.8 million Australians had a super fund account.[18]

Total employment in the Financial and Insurance Services sector numbered 444,400 in February 2016.[19] Australia's largest bank, Commonwealth Bank, had total assets in 2016 of AUD 933,078 million, and total liabilities of AUD 872,322 million. Its net asset position was AUD 60,756 million.[20] The bank's Common Equity Tier 1 Basel III capital buffer was 14.4% on an international comparable basis, and 10.6% using the APRA definition.[21]

According to the IMF, across the entire Australian banking sector, regulatory tier 1 capital to risk-weighted assets averages out at 12%, which places Australian banks 69th in the world.[22] In terms of tier 1 and 2 capital to risk-weighted assets, the same report places Australia 70th in the world.[23]

There are a total of 94 insurers authorised to write new or reinsurance in Australia,[24] of which 29 are life insurers,[25] and 18 are not-for-profit/mutual health insurers.[26]

In terms of financial literacy, Australia ranks first in the Asia-Pacific region, and ninth in the world.[27]

Australians enjoy access to a comprehensive social welfare system, the primary purpose of which is to provide individuals with a 'minimum adequate standard of living'.[28] The principle forms of social welfare include income support payments and payments to families, including age and other pensions, the 'Newstart Allowance', and the Family Tax Benefit and supplementary payments schemes.[29]

Income support payments are made to those identified as unable to support themselves, with their need for support measured by means-testing of income and assets.[30] According to the most recent figures available, as at 2013, approximately 5.1 million Australians received some form of social security.[31] During 2015/2016 the Australian government spent AUD 154 billion on social security.[32]

According to the Financial Ombudsman Service, of those seeking assistance in relation to financial consumer protection, 50% were male, 32% female and 18% joint applicants.[33] Forty-seven percent were between the ages of 40 and 59, and 22% were between the ages of 30 and 39.[34]

Research conducted under the National Financial Literacy Strategy found that only 25% of Australians reported having a long-term financial plan in place (15–20 years).[35] Eighty-eight per cent of those surveyed had at least one insurance policy,[36] and 78% indicated that they have a retirement policy (superannuation fund).[37] Around 10% of Australians surveyed maintain a self-managed superannuation fund.[38] Of those surveyed, 40% did not understand the risk/return trade-off principle,[39] and 34% were unaware of the diversification principle.[40]

2 Financial Consumer Protection System (Software)

The framework for the protection of financial consumers can be categorised into two main areas. First, there are general protections afforded to consumers of financial products[41] and financial services,[42] and secondly, there are industry specific regimes covering matters such as licensing, conduct and disclosure.[43]

The first category, consumer regulation, is contained across an array of Statutes.[44] From the perspective of generic financial consumer legislative protection —that is to say protections that are not contained in legislation that covers specific products, like insurance—the most important provisions are contained in the *Australian Securities and Investments Commission Act 2001 (ASIC Act).*[45] This Act covers all financial products and services, including credit. The provisions of the ASIC Act mirror the relevant provisions of the *Australian Consumer Law*,[46] and empower ASIC to administer these provisions.

The second category, industry-specific consumer regulation, includes licensing, conduct and disclosure regimes, as contained in the *Corporations Act 2001*,[47] and the *National Consumer Credit Protection Act 2009*[48]—the most notable of which address responsible lending, hardship and unjust transactions.

It is not within the scope of this chapter to address every aspect of these protections. Analysis will be confined to the most salient elements overall of consumer protection.

2.1 Generic Consumer Regulation Provisions

The general protections for consumers of financial products and services are contained in the *ASIC Act*,[49] and include: unconscionable conduct[50]; misleading or deceptive conduct[51]; unfair contract terms[52]; bait advertising[53]; referral selling[54]; harassment or coercion[55]; pyramid schemes[56]; and offering gifts and prizes.[57] An analysis of the first three categories follows below.

2.1.1 Unconscionable Conduct

A person must not, in relation to financial services, engage in unconscionable conduct.[58] 'Unconscionability' has a particular meaning in Australian law which, within the context of financial services, is informed by its meaning as developed in the context of consumer law generally, and one that has been developed over many years. Unconscionability has, therefore, a technical legal meaning, but broadly refers to the exploitation of a 'special disadvantage'.[59]

2.1.2 Misleading or Deceptive Conduct

There is a general prohibition against conduct that is misleading or deceptive or likely to mislead or deceive.[60] There are also specific prohibitions relating to particular representations, for example, a person cannot make a false or misleading statement that the financial services are of a particular standard or price.[61] False or misleading testimonials in relation to financial services are also prohibited.[62]

2.1.3 Unfair Contract Terms

Terms of consumer contracts for financial services and financial products which are unfair are void.[63] Some common examples where this protection is invoked are contracts for banking services, loan or credit card contracts.[64] This protection does not, however, extend to insurance contracts, which are regulated under other legislation.[65]

Three common situations giving rise to unfair terms include: a significant imbalance between the parties[66]; the term is not necessary to protect the legitimate interests of the party advantaged by the term[67] or, thirdly; the term causes detriment.[68]

2.2 *Industry Specific Regulations*

2.2.1 Responsible Lending

The principle consumer protections in this area are contained in Schedule 1, *The National Credit Code.*[69] All credit providers must be licensed,[70] are required to lend responsibly,[71] and must be a member of an external, approved, dispute resolution scheme,[72] the aim of which is to ensure access to justice for consumers. Briefly, by way of overview, the provisions apply to natural persons[73] obtaining credit for personal, domestic or household purposes, which includes a mortgage to buy a house,[74] provided a charge is levied for the service.[75] Also covered are instalment sale agreements[76] and pay-day loans (unless they attract interest and charges below a threshold, in which case they are exempt from the Act).[77]

Credit licensees must conduct reasonable inquiries about the consumer's financial situation.[78] Second, they must conduct reasonable inquiries into the consumer's requirements and objectives in using that credit product.[79] Third, credit licensees must take reasonable steps to verify the consumer's financial situation.[80] In that respect, licensees should ask for documents such as payslips, employment documents, tax returns, bank statements, and the like.[81] Fourth, the credit licensee must make an assessment as to whether the credit contract is 'not unsuitable'.[82] There are prohibitions on suggesting or assisting credit under an unsuitable credit contract,[83] or on entering into, or increasing credit, under an unsuitable credit contracts.[84]

2.2.2 Hardship and Unjust Transactions

The *National Credit Code* (NCC)[85] contains rules relating to hardship and unjust transactions.[86] The NCC applies to debtors, credit providers, and credit contracts.[87] A debtor includes a prospective debtor.[88]

If a debtor considers they are unable to meet their obligations under a credit contract, they may give a 'hardship notice' to the creditor.[89] The creditor may then vary the terms of the contract to help the debtor.[90] The creditor may refuse to vary the terms if there is no reasonable cause, or where the creditor reasonably believes the debtor would not be able to meet their obligations under the contract even if it were changed.[91] Where a debtor is in default, the credit provider must give a default notice and allow 30 days for the debtor to remedy the default.[92]

A debtor may apply to the court to reopen a transaction if it was unjust.[93] 'Unjust' means conduct which is unconscionable, harsh or oppressive,[94] and is therefor wider than unconscionable conduct. In making such a determination, a Court must have regard to the public interest,[95] and may use an extensive array of factors. These include the consequences of compliance; the relative bargaining power of the parties; whether the contract's terms were negotiated and could be altered; whether there are terms that are unreasonably difficult to comply with, or are not reasonably necessary; whether the debtor was adequately represented in negotiations; the accessibility of the contract document; whether the debtor received independent advice; the extent to which the contract was explained, and the extent to which the debtor understood the contract; whether the debtor was subjected to unfair influence, pressure or tactics; whether the credit provider took steps to ensure the debtor understood the transaction; whether the credit provider knew or could reasonably have known that the debtor would be unable to repay, or would face substantial hardship in repaying; whether the terms or the conduct of the credit provider are justified, in light of the risk to the credit provider, of the transaction; in the case of a mortgage, whether there are terms of the contract rendered void by the NCC; whether comparable contracts have comparable terms or rates of interest; any other factor a Court deems relevant[96]; unforeseen circumstances giving rise to an unjust outcome[97]; and the conduct of the parties.[98]

Along with the catch-all provision of 'any other factor', it is clear therefore that the NCC provides an extensive list of factors that a Court may rely upon to give relief to consumers.

2.2.3 Small Amount Credit Contracts

A Small Amount Credit Contract (SACC or pay-day loan) is a credit contract of AUD 2000 or less, with a term between 16 days and one year, that is unsecured, has only a single advance of monies, and where the credit provider is not an authorised deposit-taking institution (ADI—usually an ADI is a bank).[99] An SACC is prohibited where a consumer receives at least 50% of their gross income as social security payments.[100] Additionally, an SACC is prohibited if the repayments would exceed 20% of the consumer's gross income in an income cycle.[101]

There are additional responsible lending obligations which apply to an SACC. For example, a credit provider must obtain an applicant's bank account statements for the preceding 90 days, when verifying their financial position.[102] Moreover, there is a presumption that an SACC is unsuitable where a consumer is either already in default under another SACC, or has had 2 or more SACCs in the previous 90 days.[103] The credit provider must also prominently display warnings to potential debtors on their premises,[104] their website[105] or during telephone contact.[106] In these warnings consumers must be reminded that they can request payment plans from utility providers; a toll-free number for financial counselling, and; the availability of social welfare loans.

2.2.4 Short Term Credit Contracts

A Short Term Credit Contract (STCC) means a credit contract of AUD 2000 or less, with a term of 15 days or less, has only a single advance of monies, and where the credit provider is not an ADI.[107] Credit providers who hold an Australian Credit Licence (with the exception of an ADI) are prohibited from offering STCCs, and if they contravene this prohibition, or fail to adhere to the requirements for the granting of an SACC, they may be liable for both civil and criminal consequences.[108] Similarly, credit assistance in relation to an STCC is prohibited.[109]

2.2.5 Analysis

Despite the protections outlined above, the results have been mixed. Persistent problems remain in the short-term and small amount credit industry, despite the increased regulatory burden.

Evidence put forward to the Treasury's Review of the small amount credit contract laws by the Financial Rights Legal Centre indicates that the SACC regime has failed to protect consumers, and is inadequate to the task of preventing financial damage to the most vulnerable consumers.[110] Despite the 2013 amendments, harmful repeat borrowing has increased, and is spreading to other demographics, thereby undermining efforts at financial literacy.[111] The same submission asserts that the payday lending industry has a culture of avoiding its legal obligations, relies upon repeat borrowing, and has a systemic culture of non-compliance with responsible lending laws.[112] Despite concerted attempts to reign in this industry, there has been a 20-fold increase in the demand for short-term credit over the last decade.[113] According to the Financial Rights Legal Centre:

> We have no confidence that the industry will ever comply with the law in any meaningful way ... the only effective way to protect consumers is to ban the industry.[114]

Having said that, the same submission does point to improvements effected under the current regime, particularly as compared to the pre-2013 position. These include limits on the amounts recoverable under an SACC, reductions in direct re-financing, and effective caps on costs.[115] However, evidence suggests the results of these reforms have been patchy. Payday lending to financially distressed households has suffered a modest decrease of approximately 5%,[116] but in respect of financially stressed households—that is to say households that are in less serious financial predicaments than those of financially distressed households—small amount and short term credit has exploded.[117] Moreover, several of the most prominent national payday lenders in Australia charge the maximum interest permissible—at times in excess of 240 per cent per annum—indicating that price competition in this market has failed.[118] As argued further by the Financial Rights Legal Centre:

> Worse, we have a more or less effective system of responsible lending for most of the population and a completely ineffective one for those most in need of protection.[119]

Evidence from the United States and Canada points strongly to the need for inviolable interest rate caps on small and short term loans, prohibitions on multiple loans from one lender, and bans on rollover loans.[120]

3 Financial Consumer Protection Institutions (Hardware)

3.1 Financial Supervision Organizations

In Australia, there are three corporate regulators: the Australian Competition and Consumer Commission (ACCC), the Australian Securities and Investments Commission (ASIC), and the Australian Prudential Regulation Authority (APRA).

While the ACCC has wide general consumer protection powers, including competition law,[121] ASIC, the national regulator of corporations, was vested with the power to protect financial consumers,[122] as of 1 July 1998.[123] ASIC may delegate its power to the ACCC[124] and vice versa,[125] although such instances are rare. APRA, as the national regulator of prudential institutions, is responsible for the soundness of the financial system, and its powers extend to authorised deposit takers (banks), insurance companies, and superannuation funds.[126]

The financial products over which ASIC has jurisdiction to enforce consumer protection include: deposit-taking activities[127]; general insurance[128] (except health insurance[129]); life-insurance[130]; superannuation[131]; retirement savings accounts[132]; managed investment schemes[133]; securities[134]; derivatives[135]; debenture stock or bond issued by a government[136]; foreign exchange contracts[137]; and credit.[138] These powers, however, are *ex post*, and do not extend to ASIC taking proactive steps against product issuers unless and until a breach of the law has occurred. It has been argued that this is a serious flaw in ASIC's powers, and should be remedied.[139]

Currently, ASIC's consumer protection powers in respect of financial products include information disclosure; prohibitions against misleading or deceptive conduct and unconscionable conduct, and other unfair practices; licensing of financial advisors and product issuers; conduct requirements for financial services providers; and the approval of alternative dispute resolution schemes and industry codes.[140]

3.2 *Deposit Insurance Corporation*

In 2008 the Australian Government created the Financial Claims Scheme.[141] This scheme covers account holders in banks, building societies and credit unions, and policy-holders with general insurers.[142] The scheme may only be activated by the Australian Government if one of the covered institutions becomes insolvent.[143] Once activated, it is administered by the Australian Prudential Regulation Authority.[144]

Under this scheme individual account holders' funds are guaranteed up to AUD$ 250,000.[145] This guarantee does not extend to foreign banks, and is limited per account holder, not per account.[146] An account holder with multiple accounts at one failed bank will, therefore be protected up to $250,000 in total, not $250,000 for each separate account.[147] This limitation extends to accounts held at banks that operate under different trading names, but are all part of the same holding company.[148] Put differently, if a consumer has multiple accounts at one bank, or multiple accounts at different banks all of which are part of the same group, and together those accounts are worth more than $250,000, the consumer will only be able to receive a maximum of $250,000, in total. APRA undertakes to compensate consumers within seven calendar days.[149]

In addition, Australia is one of the few countries[150] where depositors enjoy preference as against any other claimants, in the event that an Australian bank is wound-up.[151] Evidence to date suggests that at current levels of capitalisation, all Australian banks would be able to repay all preferred—that is to say domestic - depositors, without becoming insolvent.[152]

3.3 *Dispute Settlement Organization*

Currently the financial system's dispute resolution framework consists of government, which sets the framework and appoints members to the Board of the Superannuation Complaints Tribunal (SCT) and funds the SCT; ASIC, which approves and oversees industry ombud schemes and staffs the SCT; internal dispute resolution schemes (IDR), which are required to be established by providers of financial products and services to consumers[153]; external dispute resolution (EDR) bodies[154] to be available free to consumers when disputes lodged with IDR fail to be resolved, and finally; the courts.[155]

3.3.1 Internal Dispute Resolution

As a first option to resolving a complaint, consumers may have recourse to internal dispute resolution (IDR) facilities. These are designed to make dispute resolution quick and easy.[156] As indicated, such arrangements are required by law.[157] Firms have 45 days to resolve a complaint before external dispute arrangements are triggered.[158] Superannuation funds have 90 days.[159]

3.3.2 External Dispute Resolution

If IDR processes fail to resolve a consumer's complaint, the next step is external dispute resolution (EDR). These processes are designed to be quicker and easier than court processes, and at much lower cost.[160]

In Australia, EDR takes the form of independent Ombuds, membership of which is a legal requirement.[161] These are the Financial Ombudsman Service (FOS), the Credit and Investments Ombudsman (CIO), and the Superannuation Complaints Tribunal (SCT), all of which are industry funded, but must maintain independence from the entities that provide that funding.[162] Establishment must be approved by ASIC,[163] which maintains limited oversight of their operations.[164] They are free to access by consumers, and while banks and insurers are bound by the decisions of these ombuds, consumers are not.[165]

FOS is responsible for complaints in relation to financial and credit products and services. That includes complaints against banks; insurers (including life and general insurers); credit providers; credit unions; financial advisers and planners; brokers; debt collection agencies; and other businesses that provide financial products and services.[166]

The CIO deals with complaints concerning lenders (residential and commercial mortgage providers, personal loan and credit card providers, small amount lenders and pawn brokers); mutual banks, credit unions and building societies; finance brokers; securitisers; debt purchasers and collectors; timeshare providers; financial planners; accountants; and credit reporting schemes.[167]

Since the establishment of FOS in 2008, there has been a dramatic increase in the number of disputes, attributable to the global financial crisis, the expansion of the FOS's jurisdiction, and the impact of natural disasters suffered in Australia.[168]

The SCT is a statutory tribunal, governed by Statute,[169] and not by ASIC. It is responsible for resolving complaints concerning the conduct of trustees, insurers, retirement savings account (RSA) providers, superannuation providers (excluding self-managed superannuation funds), approved deposit funds, life policy funds, annuity policies and RSAs.[170]

3.3.3 Courts

If all other avenues of dispute resolution fail, the option of last resort for financial consumers is litigation. In Australia, however, this option is costly to the point of being prohibitive for most consumers.[171] Litigation is also typically complex, time-consuming[172] and stressful, and there are no guarantees as to the outcome. However, the court's powers in terms of remedies are wide.

3.3.4 Analysis

The current arrangements, particularly in respect of EDR, have been found to be confusing[173] and unnecessarily complex.[174] There is evidence that outcomes tend to differ between various EDR schemes.[175] There are also significant gaps in the current schema, including out-dated monetary limits, lack of EDR for consumers of debt management firms' services, and a lack of a compensation scheme as a last resort.[176] Delays in respect of actions brought before the SCT are 'unacceptable.'[177] Its handling of complaints is inhibited by Statute, and transparency and accountability are lacking.[178] As the Interim Report of the EDR Review found:

> The existence of multiple schemes that have overlapping jurisdictions contributes to consumer confusion and makes it more challenging to achieve and be seen to achieve comparable outcomes for consumers with similar complaints.[179]
>
> IDR schemes lack adequate reporting,[180] suffer from inconsistent time-frames,[181] and some schemes are inaccessible to consumers.[182]

As a result, one recommendation is that:

> There should be a single industry ombudsman scheme for financial, credit and investment disputes (other than superannuation disputes) to replace FOS and CIO.[183]
>
> SCT should transition into an industry ombudsman scheme for superannuation disputes.[184]

The same Inquiry recommends an assessor to review Schemes' complaints handling,[185] while enhancing ASIC's powers to compel remedial action where Schemes fail to do so.[186] Finally the Inquiry recommends the establishment of a compensation scheme of last resort, to provide compensation where firms are incapable of doing so.[187]

4 Special FCP Systems

4.1 For the Elderly Group

The Australian Law Reform Commission was recently called upon to investigate the protection of older Australians against abuse, including in respect of their rights as financial consumers.[188] The Report identifies elder abuse as one of the most common types of abuse that older Australians suffer.[189] In particular this involves asset theft, and abuse of powers of attorney.[190]

The principal recommendations in respect of the protection of older Australian as financial consumers involve addressing enduring powers of attorney, and banking services. In respect of the former, the Commission's main recommendations were as follows:

- the establishment of a national online registration scheme for enduring documents;
- the provision of significant safeguards in a national legal framework for enduring documents; and
- the replacement of current forms of enduring documentation with a single 'representatives agreement.'[191]

In respect of the latter, the Commission's main recommendations were:

- The *Code of Banking Practice* should provide that banks will take reasonable steps to prevent the financial abuse of older customers.[192]
- The *Code of Banking Practice* should increase the witnessing requirements for arrangements that allow people to authorise third parties to access their bank accounts.[193]

4.2 For the Poor Group

Australia does not enjoy protections specifically targeted at protecting the poor. However it does regulate small amount and short term credit (typically payday lenders), which most often are used by, and targeted at, the poor.[194]

Analysis of these types of products and the regulations that restrict them is provided *supra*, at pp. 12 and at 13.

4.3 For the Young Group

As with protections aimed at the poor, Australia does not provide protection tailored to the young. However, one study makes a compelling argument that a close connection exists between higher levels of financial literacy amongst the young, and their ability to protect themselves as financial consumers.

> Financial literacy is increasingly recognised as an essential part of consumer protection, complementing traditional consumer protection mechanisms such as disclosure.[195]

Further:

> Effective consumer protection frameworks and institutional structures are necessary but not sufficient conditions for effective protection of the interests of the consumer of financial

> services. Only informed and educated users of financial services can be fully empowered by the opportunities the modern financial system provides.[196]

The study finds disparities in the overall level of financial literacy amongst the young related to demographics, such as location (urban or rural), parental income and education levels and the like, and argues in favour of national policies aimed at improving financial literacy amongst the young.[197]

5 Conclusion

5.1 Regulatory Failure

Australia's consumer protection agency, ASIC, has performed poorly.[198] There have been numerous and extensive scandals in Australia over the past nine years.[199] These have included serious and persistent instances of fraud[200] and malpractice in the financial advice industry,[201] (which is substantially owned by Australia's four major banks); allegations of bench-mark rate rigging,[202] which in turn affects the price of finance paid by consumers; consumer abuse in the life insurance industry[203]; and charging fees to bank clients, for services that were never provided, in amounts that are eye-watering.[204] The severity of these scandals cannot be underestimated. They have involved somewhere between hundreds of thousands of consumers,[205] and 1.3 million consumers,[206] and have caused damage to consumers running into hundreds of millions of dollars.[207]

What makes the position worse is that these scandals were not uncovered by ASIC. They were uncovered by the media. It then became apparent in some cases that ASIC had been provided with evidence at least six years prior to the first news reports,[208] yet failed to pursue the wrongdoers, until media attention[209] and the public outcry[210] forced their hand.

> ASIC has limited powers and resources but even so appears to miss or ignore clear and persistent early warning signs of corporate wrongdoing or troubling trends that pose a risk to consumers.[211]

As a result, ASIC's conduct was examined by Australia's Parliament, and was subjected to extensive and withering criticism.

> …it showed ASIC as a timid, hesitant regulator, too ready and willing to accept uncritically the assurances of a large institution that there were no grounds for ASIC's concerns or intervention. ASIC concedes that its trust in this institution was misplaced.[212]

This issue is of relevance for reasons beyond straightforward consumer protection, as ASIC has, in addition, a market conduct remit,[213] and is one of two peaks in the Twin Peaks model of financial regulation.[214]

The subprime disaster in the United States in 2007/2008, which then metastasised into the Global Financial Crisis, was precipitated by rampant market misconduct in the subprime housing industry.[215] Consequently, the market conduct function is also, at least in part, a consumer protection function. ASIC's failures as an effective consumer protector do not bode well for its ability to enforce market conduct and, therefore, that potentially poses a risk to overall financial system stability too.

As the Twin Peaks model is gaining traction internationally,[216] the serious failings that ASIC has evidenced is of great, and should be regarded as being of international, concern.

5.2 *Fixing the Problem/Regulating the Regulator*

ASIC can and should preform better,[217] and any improvements to ASIC's performance will include improvements to the overall state of consumer protection in Australia. That would be positive for investor/consumer confidence.[218] The importance of the task cannot, therefore, be underestimated.

There are four areas of reform that should be investigated or implemented, with a view to improving the performance of the regulator. These are:

(1) the establishment of a *Financial Regulator Assessment Board*, in line with the recommendation of the Financial System Inquiry,[219] the purpose of which would be to independently assess the performance of the regulators (ASIC and APRA), on an on-going basis. This could include comparative analysis of world's best practice, ASIC enforcement strategies, ASIC's allocation of resources and the like[220];
(2) a user pays system, like that employed by APRA,[221] to ensure that ASIC's funding is not permanently at the mercy of government, and to ensure also that those entities that consume disproportionally large quantities of ASIC's time and money, pay their fair share;
(3) allow ASIC to retain a percentage of whatever fines and court-imposed penalties they levy on firms found guilty of malpractice. This too would contribute to greater budget certainty for ASIC, while at the same time incentivise the regulator to impose the largest penalties and fines possible. One of the current and persistent criticisms levelled at ASIC is that it imposes penalties that are too small[222] to effect improvements in firm behaviour, or create credible deterrence,[223] and finally;
(4) the establishment of a disgorgement penalties regime, like that in force in the United States, the purpose of which would be to ensure that fines and penalties are not simply seen as an operational cost. Disgorgement damages would ensure that, at a minimum, firms do not profit from their malpractices; thereby further bolstering credible deterrence.

Overall, however, Australia's regime for the protection of financial consumers is sophisticated and advanced, as would be expected of a developed, representative democracy. Its legal system is possessed of a rich commercial jurisprudence, and there exist an array of protections, from legislation to alternative dispute resolution to education initiatives to frequent and independent formal inquiries. This is, no doubt, a contributing factor to the comparatively high levels of asset ownership and personal wealth.[224]

That said, there is also doubtless room for improvement: some of which, as should be expected, involves the ordinary, run-of the mill reforms that will always be necessary to adapt to changing conditions, and keep existing structures up-to date and fit for purpose. But some issues—one in particular—ASIC—represent an out-of the ordinary set of problems, and a critical challenge to the overall goal of the protection of consumers of financial products and services.

For Australia to continue to progress as a developed economy, with a strong foundation in the rule of law, and with the fair and equitable treatment of consumers, that issue should be tackled immediately, and with courage and foresight.

Notes

1. *Australian Securities and Investments Commission Act (Cth)*, No. 51 of 2001, (Australia).
2. S 12BC (1)(a).
3. S 12BC (1)(b).
4. Defined in s 12BC (2) as employing less than 100 people if it engages in manufacturing, or otherwise less than 20 people.
5. S 12BC (1)(c).
6. Australian Bureau of Statistics, "March Key Figures", in *3101.0—Australian Demographic Statistics, Mar 2016*, published by Australian Bureau of Statistics, 22 September, 2016, accessed: 5 December, 2016; Anonymous, "Population of Australia 2016", in *Australia2016 Population*, published by Australia2016 Population, 2016, accessed: 5 December, 2016.
7. Australian Bureau of Statistics, "Summary", in *3235.0—Population by Age and Sex, Regions of Australia, 2015*, published by Australian Bureau of Statistics, 18 August, 2016, accessed: 5 December, 2016.
8. Australian Bureau of Statistics, "Key Findings", in *6523.0—Household Income and Wealth, Australia, 2013–14*, published by Australian Bureau of Statistics, 4 September, 2015, accessed: 5 December, 2016.
9. Ibid.
10. Ibid.
11. Ibid.
12. Roger Wilkins, *The Household, Income and Labour Dynamics in Australia Survey: Selected Findings from Waves 1 to 14, The 11th Annual Statistical Report of the HILDA Survey*, in 'The Household, Income and Labour Dynamics in Australia (HILDA) Survey', The University of Melbourne, 2016, p. 26.
13. Ibid, p. 59.
14. Australian Prudential Regulation Authority, *Monthly banking statistics*, in 'Statistics', Australian Prudential Regulation Authority, October, 2016, p. 16.

15. Australian Securities and Investments Commission, *Submission by the Australian Securities and Investments Commission*, Australian Securities and Investments Commission, October, 2016, p. 4.
16. Reserve Bank of Australia, "Household Debt—Distribution—E7", in *Statistical Tables*, published by Reserve Bank of Australia, 2001–2017, accessed: 10 January, 2017.
17. Australian Prudential Regulation Authority, *Quarterly Superannuation Performance*, in 'Statistics', Australian Prudential Regulation Authority, June, 2016, p. 5.
18. Australian Taxation Office, "Super accounts data overview", in *Research and statistics*, published by Australian Taxation Office, 15 August, 2016, accessed: 11 January, 2017.
19. Penny Vandenbroek, *Employment by industry statistics: a quick guide*, in 'Parliamentary Library Quick Guide', Research Paper Series, 2015–16, Parliament of Australia, 14 April, 2016, p. 3.
20. Commonwealth Bank, *Annual Report*, in 'Annual Reports', Commonwealth Bank, 2016, p. 77.
21. Ibid, p. 11.
22. International Monetary Fund, "Financial Soundness Indicators (FSIs): At a Glance", in *Access to Macroeconomic & Financial Data*, published by International Monetary Fund, 12 July, 2016, accessed: 9 December, 2016.
23. Ibid.
24. Australian Prudential Regulation Authority, "Insurers Authorised to Conduct New or Renewal Insurance Business in Australia", in *General Insurance*, series edited by Australian Prudential Regulation Authority, published by Australian Prudential Regulation Authority, accessed: 8 December, 2016.
25. Australian Prudential Regulation Authority, "Registered Life Insurance Companies", in *Life Insurance & Friendly Societies*, series edited by Australian Prudential Regulation Authority, published by Australian Prudential Regulation Authority, accessed: 8 December, 2016.
26. Members Own Health Funds, "Members Own Health Funds", in *Home*, published by Members Own Health Funds, 2016, accessed: 8 December, 2016.
27. Leora Klapper, Annamaria Lusardi & Peter van Oudheusden, *Insights From The Standard & Poor's Ratings Services Global Financial Literacy Survey*, in 'Financial Literacy Around the World', Global Financial Literary Excellence Center (GFLEC), 18 November, 2015, pp. 7; 23–25.
28. The Treasury, *Part Two: Detailed analysis*, in 'Australia's future tax system, Report to the Treasurer', Vol. 2 of 2, Commonwealth Government of Australia, December, 2009, p. 485.
29. The Treasury, *Architecture of Australia's tax and transfer system*, Commonwealth Government of Australia, August, 2008, p. xiii.
30. Professor Rosalind Croucher (President and Commissioner in Charge), Justice Berna Collier (part-time Commissioner) & The Hon Susan Ryan AO, Age Discrimination Commissioner (part-time Commissioner), *Grey Areas—Age*

Barriers to Work in Commonwealth Laws (DP 78), in 'Publications', no. 78, Vol. Chapter 5, 'Social Security', Australian Law Reform Commission, 2 October, 2012, p. 114.
31. Department of Social Services, *Income support customers: a statistical overview 2013*, in 'Statistical Paper Series', Statistical Paper No. 12, Department of Social Services, January, 2015, p. 2.
32. Don Arthur, *What counts as welfare spending?*, in 'Parliamentary Library Research Paper', Research Paper Series, 2015–16, Parliament of Australia, 21 December, 2015, p. 3.
33. Financial Ombudsman Service, *Financial System Inquiry—Financial Ombudsman Service Submission*, in 'Submissions', Financial Ombudsman Service, April, 2014, p. 25.
34. Ibid, p. 25.
35. Australian Securities and Investments Commission, *Australian Financial Attitudes and Behaviour Tracker: Wave 4: September 2015—February 2016*, in 'National Financial Literacy Strategy', ASIC report 481, Australian Securities and Investments Commission, December, 2016, p. 24.
36. Ibid., p. 26.
37. Ibid., p. 27.
38. Ibid., p. 29.
39. Ibid., p. 34.
40. Ibid., p. 35.
41. Defined by s 12BAA, *Australian Securities and Investments Commission Act (Cth),* No. 51 of 2001, and Chapter 7, *Corporations Act (Cth)*, No. 50 of 2001, (Australia). Generally these are defined to include making a financial investment; managing a financial risk, or; making payments, other than in cash, to acquire a facility.
42. Defined by s 12BAB, *Australian Securities and Investments Commission Act (Cth),* No. 51 of 2001, and Chapter 7, *Corporations Act (Cth),* No. 50 of 2001. Generally these are defined to include: providing financial product advice; dealing in a financial product; making a market for a financial product; operating a registered scheme; providing a custodial or depository service; operating a financial market or clearing and settlement facility; providing a service that is otherwise supplied in relation to a financial product; engaging in conduct of a kind prescribed in regulations, or; providing a traditional trustee company service.
43. Financial System Inquiry, *Financial System Inquiry Interim Report*, Commonwealth Government of Australia, July, 2014, pp. 3–51.
44. *Banking Act (Cth)*, No. 6 of 1959, (Australia); *Corporations Act (Cth),* No. 50 of 2001; *Financial System Legislation Amendment (Financial Claims Scheme and Other Measures) Act (Cth)*, No. 105 of 2008, (Australia); *Insurance Contracts Act (Cth)*, No. 80 of 1984 as amended, (Australia); *Life Insurance Act (Cth)*, No. 4 of 1995 as amended, (Australia); *National Consumer Credit Protection Act (Cth)*, No. 134 of 2009, (Australia); *Retirement Savings Accounts Act (Cth)*, No. 61 of 1997 as amended,

(Australia); *Superannuation (Resolution of Complaints) Act (Cth)*, No. 80 of 1993 as amended, (Australia); *Superannuation Industry (Supervision) Act (Cth)*, No. 78 of 1993 as amended, (Australia).
45. *Australian Securities and Investments Commission Act (Cth),* No. 51 of 2001.
46. *Competition And Consumer Act (Cth), Schedule 2, The Australian Consumer Law*, No. 51 of 2010, (Australia).
47. *Corporations Act (Cth),* No. 50 of 2001.
48. *National Consumer Credit Protection Act (Cth),* No. 134 of 2009.
49. *Australian Securities and Investments Commission Act (Cth),* No. 51 of 2001.
50. SS 12CA-12CC, ibid. Section 12CA captures judicial decisions that relate to unconscionable conduct, such as that handed down in *Commercial Bank of Australia Ltd v Amadio,* HCA, 1983, (151, CLR (12 May, 1983), 447. Section 12CC captures concepts such as undue influence (s12CC 1(d)).
51. S 12DA, *Australian Securities and Investments Commission Act (Cth),* No. 51 of 2001. For an outline of how misleading or deceptive conduct is interpreted in the context of insurance, see further: Stanley Drummond, "Misleading or deceptive conduct in insurance", *Insurance Law Journal*, Vol. 14, no. 1 (2002).
52. SS 12BF-12BM, *Australian Securities and Investments Commission Act (Cth),* No. 51 of 2001.
53. S 12DG, ibid.
54. S 12DH, ibid.
55. S 12DJ, ibid.
56. S 12DK, ibid.
57. S 12DE, ibid.
58. SS 12CA-12CC, ibid.
59. *Louth v Diprose,* HCA, 1992, (175, CLR (2 December, 1992), 621 at 637 per Deane J; *Blomley v Ryan,* HCA, 1956, (99, CLR (28 March, 1956), 362 at 385; *Commercial Bank of Australia Ltd v Amadio*, op cit. See further: Stanley Drummond, "Unconscionable Conduct in Insurance", *Insurance Law Journal*, Vol. 14, no. 2 (2003), pp. 105–6; Pelma Rajapakse and Jodi Gardner, "The Unconscionable Conduct and Consumer Protection in Subprime Lending in Australia", *Banking & Finance Law Review*, Vol. 29, no. 3 (2014), p. 485.
60. S 12DA, *Australian Securities and Investments Commission Act (Cth),* No. 51 of 2001.
61. S 12 DB, ibid.
62. S 12 DB, ibid.
63. S 12BF, ibid.
64. Stephen Corones & Philip Clarke, *Australian Consumer Law, Commentary and Materials*, 4th ed., 2011, p. 619.
65. S 15(1), *Insurance Contracts Act (Cth),* No. 80 of 1984 as amended.
66. S 12BG(1)(a), *Australian Securities and Investments Commission Act (Cth),* No. 51 of 2001.

67. S 12BG(1)(b), ibid.
68. S 12BG(1)(c). An inexhaustive list of examples of unfair terms is contained in s 12BH(1), ibid.
69. *National Consumer Credit Protection Act (Cth)*, No. 134 of 2009.
70. "Chapter 2—Licensing of persons who engage in credit activities", ibid.
71. "Chapter 3—Responsible lending conduct", ibid.
72. S 47 (i), ibid.
73. S 5, ibid.
74. Schedule 1, s 5, ibid.
75. Schedule 1, s 5(1)(c), ibid.
76. Schedule 1, s 11, ibid.
77. Schedule 1, s 6, ibid.
78. SS 117(1)(b) & 130(1)(b), ibid.
79. SS 117(1)(a) & 130(1)(a), ibid.
80. SS 117(1)(c) & 130(1)(c), ibid.
81. Australian Securities and Investments Commission, "*Credit licensing: Responsible lending conduct*", Regulatory Guide 209, published by Australian Securities and Investments Commission, November, 2014, p. 21/22.
82. SS 115; 116; 128; 129, *National Consumer Credit Protection Act (Cth),* No. 134 of 2009.
83. S 123, ibid.
84. S 133, ibid.
85. Schedule 1, ibid.
86. Schedule 1, Part 4, Division 3, ibid.
87. Legal Services Commission of South Australia, "What credit contracts are regulated by the NCC?", *Law Handbook*, (20 June, 2013), (accessed: 14 December, 2016), published electronically.
88. S 204, Schedule 1, *National Consumer Credit Protection Act (Cth)*, No. 134 of 2009.
89. S 72(1), Schedule 1, ibid.
90. S 73(1), Schedule 1, ibid.
91. S 72(3), Schedule 1, ibid.
92. S 88, Schedule 1, ibid.
93. S 76, Schedule 1, ibid.
94. S 204, Schedule 1, ibid.
95. S 76(2), Schedule 1, ibid.
96. S 76(2)(a)–(p), Schedule 1, ibid.
97. S 76(4), Schedule 1, ibid.
98. S 76(5), Schedule 1, ibid.
99. S 5(1), ibid.
100. S 133CC, ibid.; s 28S(2), *National Consumer Credit Protection Regulations (Cth)*, Select Legislative Instrument No. 44 of 2010 as amended, (enacted: 13 June, 2014), (Australia).

101. S 28S(3), *National Consumer Credit Protection Regulations (Cth),* Select Legislative Instrument No. 44 of 2010 as amended.
102. SS 117(1A); 130(1A), *National Consumer Credit Protection Act (Cth),* No. 134 of 2009.
103. The so-called "presumption of unsuitability", contained in ss 118(3A); 123 (3A); 131(3A) and 133(3A), ibid.
104. S 28XXA, *National Consumer Credit Protection Regulations (Cth)*, Select Legislative Instrument No. 44 of 2010 as amended.
105. S 28XXB, ibid.
106. S 28XXD, ibid.
107. S 5(1), *National Consumer Credit Protection Act (Cth)*, No. 134 of 2009.
108. S 133CA(1) and Chapter 6, ibid.
109. S 124A(1), ibid.
110. Financial Rights Legal Centre, *Review of the small amount credit contract laws, September 2015*, in 'Submission by the Financial Rights Legal Centre', Financial Rights Legal Centre, October, 2015, p. 3.
111. Ibid, p. 3.
112. Ibid, p. 4/6. See also: Australian Securities and Investments Commission, "*Payday lenders and the new small amount lending provisions*", Report 426, published by Australian Securities and Investments Commission, March, 2015, § 11, p. 6.
113. Marcus Banks, Ashton De Silva & Roslyn Russell, *Trends in the Australian small loan market*, in 'Commissioned Paper Series', Australian Centre for Financial Studies and School of Economics, Finance and Marketing, RMIT University, October, 2015, p. 5; Jasmine Ali & Marcus Banks, "Into the Mainstream: The Australian Payday Loans Industry on the Move", *JASSA, The Finsia Journal of Applied Finance*, no. 3 (2014), p. 36.
114. Financial Rights Legal Centre, op cit, October, 2015, p. 4.
115. Ibid, p. 5.
116. From 395,297 households in 2010 to 376,206 in 2015. Martin North & Gill North, *The Stressed Finance Landscape Data Analysis*, in 'Digital Finance Analytics, Reports', Digital Finance Analytics and the Centre for Commercial Law and Regulatory Studies, Monash University, October, 2015, p. 15.
117. From 20,805 households in 2010 to 266,881 in 2015. Ibid, p. 15.
118. Financial Rights Legal Centre, op cit, October, 2015, p. 11.
119. Ibid, p. 13.
120. Ibid, p. 12.
121. Established under s 6A, Part II, 'The Australian Competition and Consumer Commission', *Competition And Consumer Act (Cth)*, No. 51 of 2010 as amended, (Australia), and responsible for the enforcement of, *inter* alia, Part IV, 'Restrictive Trade Practices', ibid.
122. Part 2, 'Australian Securities and Investments Commission and Consumer Protection in Relation to Financial Services', Division 2, Subdivision A to H, s 12AB to s 12HD, *Australian Securities and Investments Commission Act (Cth)*, No. 51 of 2001.

123. Australian Securities and Investments Commission, *Annual Report 1998/99*, Australian Securities and Investments Commission, 18 October, 1999, pp. 2/3/30/60.
124. S 102(2)(e), *Australian Securities and Investments Commission Act (Cth)*, No. 51 of 2001.
125. S 26, *Competition And Consumer Act (Cth)*, No. 51 of 2010 as amended.
126. S 8, *Australian Prudential Regulation Authority Act (Cth)*, No. 50 of 1998, (Australia). See also: Financial System Inquiry, *Financial System Inquiry Final Report*, Commonwealth Government of Australia, November, 2014, p 241.
127. SS 12A(3); 12BAA(7)(h); *Australian Securities and Investments Commission Act (Cth)*, No. 51 of 2001; Stephen Corones & Philip Clarke, op cit, p. 624.
128. S 12A(1); s 12BAA(7)(d), *Australian Securities and Investments Commission Act (Cth)*, No. 51 of 2001; SS 11A & 11B; *National Consumer Credit Protection Regulations (Cth)*, Select Legislative Instrument No. 44 of 2010 as amended; Stephen Corones & Philip Clarke, op cit, p. 624.
129. S 12BAA(7)(d)(i) & (ii); s 12(8)(b) & (ba), *Australian Securities and Investments Commission Act (Cth)*, No. 51 of 2001; Stephen Corones & Philip Clarke, op cit, p. 624.
130. S 12A(1); s 12BAA(7)(e), *Australian Securities and Investments Commission Act (Cth)*, No. 51 of 2001; s 7(1)(b), (2) & (3), *Life Insurance Act (Cth)*, No. 4 of 1995 as amended; Stephen Corones & Philip Clarke, op cit, p. 624.
131. S 12A(1); s 12BAA(7)(f), *Australian Securities and Investments Commission Act (Cth)*, No. 51 of 2001; s 6, *Superannuation Industry (Supervision) Act (Cth)*, No. 78 of 1993 as amended; ss 64 & 64A, *Superannuation (Resolution of Complaints) Act (Cth)*, No. 80 of 1993 as amended; Stephen Corones & Philip Clarke, op cit, p. 624.
132. S 12A(1); s 12BAA(7)(g), *Australian Securities and Investments Commission Act (Cth)*, No. 51 of 2001; s 3, *Retirement Savings Accounts Act (Cth)*, No. 61 of 1997 as amended; Stephen Corones & Philip Clarke, op cit, p. 624.
133. S 12BAA(7)(b), *Australian Securities and Investments Commission Act (Cth)*, No. 51 of 2001; Stephen Corones & Philip Clarke, op cit, p. 624.
134. S 764A(1)(a), *Corporations Act (Cth)*, No. 50 of 2001; s 12BAA(7)(a), *Australian Securities and Investments Commission Act (Cth)*, No. 51 of 2001; Stephen Corones & Philip Clarke, op cit, p. 624.
135. S 901A, *Corporations Act (Cth)*, No. 50 of 2001; s 12BAA(7)(c), *Australian Securities and Investments Commission Act (Cth)*, No. 51 of 2001; Stephen Corones & Philip Clarke, op cit, p. 624.
136. S 764A(1)(j), *Corporations Act (Cth)*, No. 50 of 2001; s 12BAA(7)(i), *Australian Securities and Investments Commission Act (Cth)*, No. 51 of 2001; Stephen Corones & Philip Clarke, op cit, p. 624.
137. S 12BAA(7)(j), *Australian Securities and Investments Commission Act (Cth)*, No. 51 of 2001; Stephen Corones & Philip Clarke, op cit, p. 624.

138. S 12BAA(7)(k), *Australian Securities and Investments Commission Act (Cth)*, No. 51 of 2001; Stephen Corones & Philip Clarke, op cit, p. 624.
139. See: Financial System Inquiry, op cit, November, 2014, p 206ff.
140. Stephen Corones & Philip Clarke, op cit, p. 625.
141. *Financial System Legislation Amendment (Financial Claims Scheme and Other Measures) Act (Cth)*, No. 105 of 2008; Australian Prudential Regulation Authority, "About the Financial Claims Scheme", in *Home*, series edited by Australian Prudential Regulation Authority, published by Australian Prudential Regulation Authority, accessed: 8 January, 2017; Australian Prudential Regulation Authority, "Financial Claims Scheme for banks, building societies and credit unions", in *Cross Industry*, series edited by Australian Prudential Regulation Authority, published by Australian Prudential Regulation Authority, accessed: 9 January, 2017.
142. S 16AD read with s 5(1), *Banking Act (Cth)*, No. 6 of 1959; Australian Prudential Regulation Authority, "About the Financial Claims Scheme", op cit; Australian Prudential Regulation Authority, "Financial Claims Scheme for banks, building societies and credit unions", op cit.
143. SS 14F & 16AB, *Banking Act (Cth)*, No. 6 of 1959; Australian Prudential Regulation Authority, "About the Financial Claims Scheme", op cit; Australian Prudential Regulation Authority, "Financial Claims Scheme for banks, building societies and credit unions", op cit.
144. S 16AC, *Banking Act (Cth)*, No. 6 of 1959; Australian Prudential Regulation Authority, "About the Financial Claims Scheme", op cit; Australian Prudential Regulation Authority, "Financial Claims Scheme for banks, building societies and credit unions", op cit.
145. Australian Prudential Regulation Authority, "About the Financial Claims Scheme", op cit; Australian Prudential Regulation Authority, "Financial Claims Scheme", in *Cross Industry*, series edited by Australian Prudential Regulation Authority, published by Australian Prudential Regulation Authority, accessed: 9 January, 2017; Australian Prudential Regulation Authority, "Financial Claims Scheme for banks, building societies and credit unions", op cit.
146. Australian Prudential Regulation Authority, "Financial Claims Scheme", op cit; Australian Prudential Regulation Authority, "Financial Claims Scheme for banks, building societies and credit unions", op cit.
147. Australian Prudential Regulation Authority, "Financial Claims Scheme for banks, building societies and credit unions", op cit.
148. Ibid.
149. Australian Prudential Regulation Authority, "About the Financial Claims Scheme", op cit; Australian Prudential Regulation Authority, "Financial Claims Scheme for banks, building societies and credit unions", op cit.
150. Grant Turner, *Depositor Protection in Australia*, in 'Bulletin', Reserve Bank of Australia, December Quarter, 2011, p. 54.

151. S 13A, *Banking Act (Cth),* No. 6 of 1959.
152. Kevin Davis, *Depositor Preference, Bail-in, and Deposit Insurance Pricing and Design*, Department of Finance, University of Melbourne, and Australian Centre of Financial Studies and Monash University, 14 September, 2015, p. 11.
153. S 912A, *Corporations Act (Cth),* No. 50 of 2001, and s 47, *National Consumer Credit Protection Act (Cth),* No. 134 of 2009, and regulated by: Australian Securities and Investments Commission, "*Licensing: Internal and external dispute resolution*", Regulatory Guide 165, published by Australian Securities and Investments Commission, July, 2015 and Australian Securities and Investments Commission, "*Approval and oversight of external dispute resolution schemes*", Regulatory Guide 139, published by Australian Securities and Investments Commission, June, 2013. See also: Australian Securities and Investments Commission, op cit, October, 2016, p. 8.
154. The Financial Ombudsman Service (FOS), Credit and Investments Ombudsman (CIO), and Superannuation Complaints Tribunal (SCT).
155. Ian Ramsay, Julie Abramson & Alan Kirkland, *Review of the financial system external dispute resolution and complaints framework, Interim Report*, in 'EDR Review', The Treasury, Commonwealth Government, 6 December, 2016, p. 39.
156. Ian Ramsay, Julie Abramson & Alan Kirkland, *Review of the financial system external dispute resolution framework, Issues Paper*, in 'Consultation on the financial system external dispute resolution framework', The Treasury, Commonwealth Government, 9 September, 2016, § 14, p. 4.
157. Australian Securities and Investments Commission, "*Licensing: Internal and external dispute resolution*", Regulatory Guide 165, op cit.
158. RG 165.88(b), ibid.
159. S 101(b), *Superannuation Industry (Supervision) Act (Cth),* No. 78 of 1993 as amended.
160. Ian Ramsay, Julie Abramson & Alan Kirkland, op cit, 9 September, 2016, § 19, p. 6.
161. S 912AA, *Corporations Act (Cth),* No. 50 of 2001.
162. Australian Securities and Investments Commission, "*Approval and oversight of external dispute resolution schemes*", Regulatory Guide 139, op cit, RG 139.88ff, p. 22ff.
163. S 912A(2)(b)(ii), *Corporations Act (Cth),* No. 50 of 2001 and s 47, *National Consumer Credit Protection Act (Cth),* No. 134 of 2009, and regulated by: Australian Securities and Investments Commission, "*Approval and oversight of external dispute resolution schemes*", Regulatory Guide 139, op cit.
164. Ian Ramsay, Julie Abramson & Alan Kirkland, op cit, 6 December, 2016, § 3.24, p. 48.
165. Ibid., p. 43/44.
166. Ian Ramsay, Julie Abramson & Alan Kirkland, op cit, 9 September, 2016, § 31, p. 8.

167. Ibid., § 35, p. 9.
168. Financial Ombudsman Service, op cit, April, 2014, p. 9.
169. S 6, *Superannuation (Resolution of Complaints) Act (Cth),* No. 80 of 1993 as amended.
170. Ian Ramsay, Julie Abramson & Alan Kirkland, op cit, 9 September, 2016, § 64, p. 14.
171. Louis Schetzer, Joanna Mullins & Roberto Buonamano, *Access to Justice & Legal Needs, A project to identify legal needs, pathways and barriers for disadvantaged people in NSW*, in 'Background Paper', Law & Justice Foundation of New South Wales, August, 2002, p. 10. See further: Community Law Australia, *Unaffordable and out of reach: the problem of access to the Australian legal system*, National Association of Community Legal Centres, July, 2012.
172. Mr Justice Joe Harman, "From Alternate to Primary Dispute Resolution: The pivotal role of mediation in (and in avoiding) litigation", *Paper presented at the National Mediation Conference*, Melbourne, 2014, p. 1.
173. Law Council of Australia, *Review of the Financial System External Dispute Resolution Framework*, Law Council of Australia, 7 October, 2016, § 62, p. 14.
174. Ian Ramsay, Julie Abramson & Alan Kirkland, op cit, 6 December, 2016, p. 96.
175. Ibid., § 5.11, p. 97.
176. Ibid., § 5.45, p. 103/4.
177. Ibid., § 5.104, p. 120.
178. Ibid, § 5.117, p. 122.
179. Ibid., § 5.19, p. 98.
180. Ibid., p. 137.
181. Ibid, p. 138.
182. Ibid., p. 139.
183. Ibid., § 6.8, p. 144.
184. Ibid., § 6.22, p. 149.
185. Ibid., § 6.58, p. 159.
186. Ibid., § 6.64, p. 160.
187. Ibid., § 7.17, p. 168.
188. Professor Rosalind Croucher (President), The Hon Justice John Middleton, Federal Court of Australia (part-time Commissioner), & The Hon Justice Nye Perram, Federal Court of Australia (part-time Commissioner), *Elder Abuse - Discussion Paper 83*, in 'Publications', (DP 83), Australian Law Reform Commission, December, 2016, p. 3.
189. Ibid., § 1.19, p. 18.
190. Ibid.
191. Ibid., § 5.3, p. 86.
192. Ibid., Proposal 7.1, p. 129.

193. Ibid., Proposal 7.2, p. 134.
194. Chris Field, "Pay day lending: an exploitative market practice", *Alternative Law Journal*, Vol. 27, no. 1 (February, 2002), p. 36ff, and p. 413.
195. Paul Ali, Malcolm Anderson, Cosima McRae & Ian Ramsay, "The financial literacy of young Australians: An empirical study and implications for consumer protection and ASIC's National Financial Literacy Strategy", *Company and Securities Law Journal*, Vol. 32, no. 5 (2014), p. 334.
196. Nataliya Mylenko, Adetola Adenuga, Roziah Baba, Elizabeth Davidson, Ros Grady, Johanna Jaeger & Valentina Saltane, *Global Survey on Consumer Protection and Financial Literacy: Results Brief—Regulatory Practices in 114 Economies*, in 'Publications', The World Bank, 2013, p. 22.
197. Paul Ali, Malcolm Anderson, Cosima McRae & Ian Ramsay, *Company and Securities Law Journal*, op cit, p. 352.
198. Adele Ferguson, "Royal commission: not a populist whinge for burned bank customers", 'Comment', *The Sydney Morning Herald*, 13 August, 2016; Gail Pearson, "Failure in corporate governance: financial planning and greed", Chap. 8, in *Handbook on Corporate Governance in Financial Institutions*, edited by Christine A. Mallin, in 'Business', 27 May, 2016, p. 185/190/197/198; Ruth Williams, "'Tough cop' ASIC too timid on enforcement: Allan Fels", 'News & Views/Banking', *The Sydney Morning Herald*, 15 April, 2016.
199. See: Gail Pearson, op cit, p. 203, fn 6; Adele Ferguson, "Hearing into ASIC's failure to investigate CBA's Financial Wisdom", 'Business Day', *The Sydney Morning Herald*, 3 June, 2014; Adele Ferguson & Deb Masters, "Banking Bad", in Four Corners, *Audiovisual Material*, Documentary, 5 May, 2014; Adele Ferguson & Ben Butler, "Commonwealth Bank facing royal commission call after Senate financial planning inquiry", 'Banking and Finance', *The Sydney Morning Herald*, Business Day ed., 26 June, 2014; Adele Ferguson, "A banking royal commission couldn't make the sector's reputation any worse", 'Business/Banking & Finance/Financial Services/Opinion', *The Australian Financial Review*, AFR Weekend ed., 11 April, 2016 at 08:46 am. See also: Denise Brailey, *Australia's 'Banking Cartel Scandal' - The Rise of White-Collar Crime*, in 'Senate Economics Standing Committee, 2016 Inquiry into 'Penalties for White-Collar Crime'', Submission 23, Banking and Finance Consumers Support Association (Inc.), 29 March, 2016.
200. Senate Economics References Committee, *The Performance of The Australian Securities and Investments Commission*, in 'Executive summary', Parliament of Australia, 26 June, 2014, Executive Summary, p xviii.
201. Gail Pearson, op cit, p. 185.
202. André Dao, Andrew Godwin & Ian Ramsay, "From enforcement to prevention: international cooperation and financial benchmark reform", *Law and Financial Markets Review*, Vol. 10, no. 2 (1 June, 2016), p. 90; Australian Securities and Investments Commission, "16-060MR ASIC commences civil penalty proceedings against ANZ for BBSW conduct", published by Australian Securities and Investments Commission, Sydney, NSW, Friday, 4

March, 2016; Australian Securities and Investments Commission, *Annual Report 2015–2016*, Australian Securities and Investments Commission, 14 October, 2016, p. 73; Pat McConnell, "ASIC finally pulls the BBSW trigger on ANZ", 'Business & Economy', *The Conversation*, 4 March, 2016 5.52 pm AEST; Pat McConnell, "Market manipulation—ASIC better get it right, first time", 'Business & Economy', *The Conversation*, 9 February, 2016 1.54 pm AEDT; Chris Wright, "Regulation: Banking's dark side reaches Australia", *Euromoney*, 6 April, 2016; Mario Christodoulou, "ASIC: $20 trillion worth of financial products may be affected by BBSW rigging", in *News*, series edited by Australian Broadcasting Corporation, published by Australian Broadcasting Corporation, 29 July 2016, 3:16 pm, accessed: 16 October, 2016; Andrew Schmulow, "Why rigging of the bank bill swap rate hurts everyone", 'Business & Economy', *The Conversation*, 9 March, 2016 2.29 pm AEDT.

203. Pat McConnell, "CommInsure case shows it's time to target reckless misconduct in banking", ibid, 8 March, 2016 9.38 am AEDT; David Jacobson, "Life insurance claims handling inquiry", *Bright Law*, (4 April, 2016), (accessed: 16 May, 2016), published electronically; Darren Snyder, "Senate to investigate life industry", 'News/Insurance, Regulatory', *Financial Standard*, Tuesday, 8 March, 2016 12:21 pm; Anna Henderson & Dan Conifer, "Commonwealth Bank boss Ian Narev says no-one sacked over CommInsure scandals", in *Breaking News*, series edited by Australian Broadcasting Corporation, published by Australian Broadcasting Corporation, 4 October, 2016, 11:17 pm, accessed: 30 January, 2017.
204. Georgia Wilkins, "Big banks to refund $178 million to financial advice customers", 'Business', *The Sydney Morning Herald*, 27 October, 2016; Stephen Letts, "Banks facing $180 million compensation payments for gouging fees without advice", in *Breaking News*, series edited by Australian Broadcasting Corporation, published by Australian Broadcasting Corporation, 27 October, 2016, 1:02 pm, accessed: 30 January, 2017; Misa Han, "Big four banks, AMP charged $178 m for no financial advice", 'Business/Banking & Finance', *The Australian Financial Review*, 27 October, 2016 at 11:37 am.
205. Gail Pearson, op cit, p. 202.
206. Adele Ferguson, "Financial misconduct costs a fortune", 'Business/Comment', *The Sydney Morning Herald*, Business Day ed., 17 September, 2016.
207. Gail Pearson, op cit, p. 202.
208. For a timeline see: Senate Economics References Committee, op cit, 26 June, 2014, pp. 110 and 114.
209. Gail Pearson, op cit, p. 186.
210. A. Odysseus Patrick, "Flush and Dominant, Australia's Banks Come Under Pressure", 'Dealbook', *New York Times*, New York ed., 14 October, 2016.
211. Senate Economics References Committee, op cit, 26 June, 2014, Executive Summary, p. xvii.

212. Ibid., Executive Summary, p. xviii.
213. Andrew D. Schmulow, "The four methods of financial system regulation: An international comparative survey", *Journal of Banking and Finance Law and Practice*, Vol. 26, no. 3 (November, 2015), p. 169.
214. A.D. Schmulow, *Twin Peaks: A Theoretical Analysis*, in 'The Centre For International Finance and Regulation (CIFR) Research Working Paper Series', no. 064/2015/ Project No. E018, The Centre For International Finance and Regulation (CIFR), 1 July, 2015, p. 4.
215. Ibid, p. 18; See further: Frederic S. Mishkin, *Over the Cliff: From the Subprime to the Global Financial Crisis*, in 'NBER Working Paper Series', no. 16609, National Bureau of Economic Research, December, 2010; U.S. Securities and Exchange Commission, *SEC Enforcement Actions. Addressing Misconduct that Led To or Arose From the Financial Crisis*, U.S. Securities and Exchange Commission, 26 May, 2015; Steve Denning, "Lest We Forget: Why We Had A Financial Crisis", *Forbes*, (22 November, 2011), published electronically; Ray Martin, "Bank of America's great mortgage give-away", in *CBS News*, series edited by CBS Money Watch, published by CBS Interactive Inc., 9 May, 2012, 10:32 am, accessed: 26 September, 2015; Rick Rothacker, "The deal that cost Bank of America $50 billion—and counting", 'News, Business, Banking', *The Charlotte Observer*, 16 August, 2014; L. Randall Wray, "Setting the Record Straight One More Time: BofA's Rebecca Mairone Fined $1Million; BofA Must Pay $1.3Billion", *New Economic Perspectives*, (2 August, 2014), (accessed: 26 June, 2015), published electronically; Edward Wyatt, "Promises Made, Then Broken, By Firms in S.E.C. Fraud Cases", 'Business Day', *New York Times*, New York ed., 8 November, 2011.
216. Andrew D. Schmulow, *Journal of Banking and Finance Law and Practice*, op cit, p. 165.
217. Ruth Williams, op cit, 2016.
218. Australian Financial Markets Association, *Submission to the Financial Sytem Inquiry*, Australian Financial Markets Association, 31 March, 2014, p. 2.
219. Financial System Inquiry, op cit, November, 2014, p. 239.
220. Pat McConnell, "War on banking's rotten culture must include regulators", 'Business & Economy', *The Conversation*, 4 June, 2015 2.14 pm AEST.
221. The Treasury & Australian Prudential Regulation Authority, *Financial Industry Levies for 2015–16*, The Treasury & Australian Prudential Regulation Authority, 1 July, 2015, p. 2 ff.
222. Australian Securities and Investments Commission, *Penalties for corporate wrongdoing*, Report Number: 387, Australian Securities and Investments Commission, March, 2014, p. 15.
223. Pat McConnell, "ASIC needs a win in 2017, but it's not likely to come from the banks", 'Business & Economy', *The Conversation*, 15 January, 2017 10.47 am AEDT.
224. Anthony Shorrocks, James B. Davies, Rodrigo Lluberas & Antonios Koutsoukis, *Global Wealth Report 2016*, in 'Global Wealth Report', Credit Suisse, November, 2016, p. 40.

References

Statutes

Australian Prudential Regulation Authority Act (Cth), No. 50 of 1998, (Australia).
Australian Securities and Investments Commission Act (Cth), No. 51 of 2001, (Australia).
Banking Act (Cth), No. 6 of 1959, (Australia).
Competition And Consumer Act (Cth), No. 51 of 2010 as amended, (Australia).
Competition And Consumer Act (Cth), Schedule 2, The Australian Consumer Law, No. 51 of 2010, (Australia).
Corporations Act (Cth), No. 50 of 2001, (Australia).
Financial System Legislation Amendment (Financial Claims Scheme and Other Measures) Act (Cth), No. 105 of 2008, (Australia).
Insurance Contracts Act (Cth), No. 80 of 1984 as amended, (Australia).
Life Insurance Act (Cth), No. 4 of 1995 as amended, (Australia).
National Consumer Credit Protection Act (Cth), No. 134 of 2009, (Australia).
National Consumer Credit Protection Regulations (Cth), No. Select Legislative Instrument No. 44 of 2010 as amended, (enacted: 13 June, 2014), (Australia).
Retirement Savings Accounts Act (Cth), No. 61 of 1997 as amended, (Australia).
Superannuation (Resolution of Complaints) Act (Cth), No. 80 of 1993 as amended, (Australia).
Superannuation Industry (Supervision) Act (Cth), No. 78 of 1993 as amended, (Australia).

Regulations

Australian Securities and Investments Commission, "*Approval and oversight of external dispute resolution schemes*", Regulatory Guide 139, published by Australian Securities and Investments Commission, June, 2013, pp 1–58, http://download.asic.gov.au/media/1240742/rg139-published-13-june-2013.pdf.
Australian Securities and Investments Commission, "*Credit licensing: Responsible lending conduct*", Regulatory Guide 209, published by Australian Securities and Investments Commission, November, 2014, pp 1–57, http://download.asic.gov.au/media/2243019/rg209-published-5-november-2014.pdf.
Australian Securities and Investments Commission, "*Licensing: Internal and external dispute resolution*", Regulatory Guide 165, published by Australian Securities and Investments Commission, July, 2015, pp 1–58, http://download.asic.gov.au/media/3285121/rg165-published-2-july-2015.pdf.
Australian Securities and Investments Commission, "*Payday lenders and the new small amount lending provisions*", Report 426, published by Australian Securities and Investments Commission, March, 2015, pp 1–44, http://download.asic.gov.au/media/3038267/rep-426-published-17-march-2015.pdf.

Cases

Blomley v Ryan, HCA, 1956, (99, CLR (28 March, 1956), 362 http://www.austlii.edu.au/au/cases/cth/HCA/1956/81.html.
Commercial Bank of Australia Ltd v Amadio, HCA, 1983, (151, CLR (12 May, 1983), 447 http://www.austlii.edu.au/au/cases/cth/HCA/1983/14.html.

Louth v Diprose, HCA, 1992, (175, CLR (2 December, 1992), 621 http://www.austlii.edu.au/au/cases/cth/HCA/1992/61.html.

Books and Book Chapters

Corones, Stephen & Philip Clarke, *Australian Consumer Law, Commentary and Materials*, 4th ed., published by Thomson Reuters, Pyrmont, NSW, 2011, 1–888 pages, pp 888.

Pearson, Gail, "Failure in corporate governance: financial planning and greed", Chap. 8, in *Handbook on Corporate Governance in Financial Institutions*, edited by Christine A. Mallin, in 'Business', published by Edward Elgar, Cheltenham, UK, 27 May, 2016, pp 185–209.

Journal Articles

Ali, Jasmine & Marcus Banks, "Into the Mainstream: The Australian Payday Loans Industry on the Move", *JASSA, The Finsia Journal of Applied Finance*, no. 3, 2014, pp: 35–42, https://www.finsia.com/docs/default-source/jassa-new/jassa-2014/jassa-2014-issue-3/jassa-3-2014-complete-issue.pdf?sfvrsn=5.

Ali, Paul, Malcolm Anderson, Cosima McRae & Ian Ramsay, "The financial literacy of young Australians: An empirical study and implications for consumer protection and ASIC's National Financial Literacy Strategy", *Company and Securities Law Journal*, Vol. 32, no. 5, 2014, pp: 334–352, http://www.financialliteracy.gov.au/media/558653/research-financialliteracyofyoungaustralianscslj20142pdf0.pdf.

Dao, André, Andrew Godwin & Ian Ramsay, "From enforcement to prevention: international cooperation and financial benchmark reform", *Law and Financial Markets Review*, Vol. 10, no. 2, 1 June, 2016, pp: 83–101, http://dx.doi.org/10.1080/17521440.2016.1211385.

Drummond, Stanley, "Misleading or deceptive conduct in insurance", *Insurance Law Journal*, Vol. 14, no. 1, 2002, pp: 1–16, http://www.lexisnexis.com.ezproxy.library.uwa.edu.au/au/legal/results/tocBrowseNodeClick.do?rand=0.7176164015730689&tocCSI=267871&clickedNode=TABQAABAAB.

Drummond, Stanley, "Unconscionable Conduct in Insurance", *Insurance Law Journal*, Vol. 14, no. 2, 2003, pp: 103–127, http://www.lexisnexis.com.ezproxy.library.uwa.edu.au/au/legal/results/enhPubTreeViewDoc.do?nodeId=TABPAABAAC&backKey=20_T25207463118&refPt=&pubTreeWidth=277.

Field, Chris, "Pay day lending: an exploitative market practice", *Alternative Law Journal*, Vol. 27, no. 1, February, 2002, pp: 36–40, http://www.austlii.edu.au/au/journals/AltLawJl/2002/12.html - fn1.

Rajapakse, Pelma & Jodi Gardner, "The Unconscionable Conduct and Consumer Protection in Subprime Lending in Australia", *Banking & Finance Law Review*, Vol. 29, no. 3, 2014, pp: 485–515, http://search.proquest.com.ezproxy.library.uwa.edu.au/docview/1552113429/64953F695379421BPQ/5?accountid=14681.

Schmulow, Andrew D., "The four methods of financial system regulation: An international comparative survey", *Journal of Banking and Finance Law and Practice*, Vol. 26, no. 3, November, 2015, pp: 151–172, http://www.westlaw.com.au.ezp01.library.qut.edu.au/maf/wlau/app/document?&src=search&docguid=Ifd3c1ffa88f11e584c5a2b5af565fd9&epos=1&snippets=true&fcwh=true&startChunk=1&endChunk=1&nstid=std-anz-highlight&nsds=AU-NZ_SEARCHALL&isTocNav=true&tocDs=AUNZ_AU_JOURNALS_TOC&context=56&extLink=false&searchFromLinkHome=false.

Reports

Arthur, Don, *What counts as welfare spending?*, in *'Parliamentary Library Research Paper'*, no. Research Paper Series, 2015–16, Social Policy Section, Parliament of Australia, published by Parliament of Australia, Canberra, ACT, 21 December 2015, pp 1–6, http://parlinfo.aph.gov.au/parlInfo/download/library/prspub/4262560/upload_binary/4262560.pdf;fileType=application/pdf.

Australian Financial Markets Association, *Submission to the Financial Sytem Inquiry*, Australian Financial Markets Association, published by Australian Financial Markets Association, Sydney, NSW, 31 March 2014, pp 1–133, http://www.afma.com.au/afmawr/_assets/main/lib90058/afmafsisubmission.pdf.

Australian Prudential Regulation Authority, *Monthly banking statistics*, in *'Statistics'*, Banking Statistics, Australian Prudential Regulation Authority, published by Australian Prudential Regulation Authority, Sydney, NSW, October 2016, pp 1–20, http://www.apra.gov.au/adi/Publications/Documents/MBS-October-2016-PDF.pdf.

Australian Prudential Regulation Authority, *Quarterly Superannuation Performance*, in *'Statistics'*, Superannuation Statistics, Australian Prudential Regulation Authority, published by Australian Prudential Regulation Authority, Sydney, NSW, June 2016, pp 1–37, http://www.apra.gov.au/Super/Publications/Documents/2016QSP201606.pdf.

Australian Securities and Investments Commission, *Annual Report 1998/99*, series edited by Australian Securities and Investments Commission, Australian Securities and Investments Commission, published by Australian Securities and Investments Commission, Sydney, NSW, 18 October 1999, pp 1–109, http://download.asic.gov.au/media/1327346/complete_edited200612-1998-99.pdf.

Australian Securities and Investments Commission, *Annual Report 2015–2016*, series edited by Australian Securities and Investments Commission, Australian Securities and Investments Commission, published by Australian Securities and Investments Commission, Sydney, NSW, 14 October 2016, pp 1-220, http://download.asic.gov.au/media/4058626/asic-annual-report-2015-2016-complete.pdf.

Australian Securities and Investments Commission, *Australian Financial Attitudes and Behaviour Tracker: Wave 4: September 2015 – February 2016*, in *'National Financial Literacy Strategy'*, no. ASIC report 481, Australian Securities and Investments Commission, published by Australian Securities and Investments Commission, Sydney, NSW, December 2016, pp 1–68, http://www.financialliteracy.gov.au/media/559536/australian-financial-attitudes-and-behaviour-tracker_wave-4.pdf.

Australian Securities and Investments Commission, *Penalties for corporate wrongdoing*, series edited by Australian Securities and Investments Commission, Report Number: 387, Australian Securities and Investments Commission, published by Australian Securities and Investments Commission, Sydney, NSW, March 2014, pp 1–79, http://download.asic.gov.au/media/1344548/rep387-published-20-March-2014.pdf.

Australian Securities and Investments Commission, *Submission by the Australian Securities and Investments Commission*, series edited by Review of the financial system external dispute resolution framework, Australian Securities and Investments Commission, published by EDR Review, Sydney, NSW, October 2016, pp 1–58, http://www.treasury.gov.au/~/media/Treasury/Consultations and Reviews/Consultations/2016/Review of the financial system external dispute resolution framework/Submissions/PDF/Australian_Securities_and_Investments_Commission.ashx.

Banks, Marcus, Ashton De Silva & Roslyn Russell, *Trends in the Australian small loan market*, in *'Commissioned Paper Series'*, Australian Centre for Financial Studies and School of Economics, Finance and Marketing, RMIT University, published by Australian Centre for Financial Studies, Melbourne, Vic, October 2015, pp 1–52, http://australiancentre.com.au/wp-content/uploads/2015/10/Commissioned-paper-Trends-in-the-Australian-small-loan-market.pdf.

Brailey, Denise, *Australia's 'Banking Cartel Scandal' - The Rise of White-Collar Crime*, in *'Senate Economics Standing Committee, 2016 Inquiry into 'Penalties for White-Collar Crime''*, no. Submission 23, Banking and Finance Consumers Support Association (Inc.), published by Banking and Finance Consumers Support Association (Inc.), Perth, WA, 29 March 2016, pp 1–74, http://webcache.googleusercontent.com/search?q=cache:AEw8ogBITgwJ:www.aph.gov.au/DocumentStore.ashx%3Fid%3Dbe84b97d-5d0a-41d4-acd7-d20fc6cb345b%26subId%3D411906+&cd=1&hl=en&ct=clnk&gl=au&client=safari.

Commonwealth Bank, *Annual Report*, in *'Annual Reports'*, Commonwealth Bank, published by Commonwealth Bank, Sydney, NSW, 2016, pp 1–192, https://www.commbank.com.au/content/dam/commbank/about-us/shareholders/pdfs/annual-reports/2016_Annual_Report_to_Shareholders_15_August_2016.pdf.

Community Law Australia, *Unaffordable and out of reach: the problem of access to the Australian legal system*, National Association of Community Legal Centres, published by National Association of Community Legal Centres, Sydney, NSW, July 2012, pp 1–13, http://www.communitylawaustralia.org.au/wp-content/uploads/2012/07/CLA_Report_Final.pdf.

Davis, Kevin, *Depositor Preference, Bail-in, and Deposit Insurance Pricing and Design*, Department of Finance, University of Melbourne, and Australian Centre of Financial Studies and Monash University, Melbourne, VIC, 14 September 2015, pp 1–24, http://www.kevindavis.com.au/secondpages/workinprogress/2015-09-06-Depositor Preference and Deposit Insurance.pdf.

Department of Social Services, *Income support customers: a statistical overview 2013*, in *'Statistical Paper Series'*, no. Statistical Paper No. 12, Department of Social Services, Department of Social Services, published by Australian Government, Canberra, ACT, January 2015, pp 1–91, https://www.dss.gov.au/sites/default/files/documents/01_2015/sp12_accessible_pdf_final.pdf.

Financial Ombudsman Service, *Financial System Inquiry - Financial Ombudsman Service Submission*, in *'Submissions'*, Financial Ombudsman Service, published by Financial Ombudsman Service, Melbourne, Vic, April 2014, pp 1–28, https://www.fos.org.au/custom/files/docs/fos-submission-to-fsi-inquiry.pdf.

Financial Rights Legal Centre, *Review of the small amount credit contract laws, September 2015*, in *'Submission by the Financial Rights Legal Centre'*, Financial Rights Legal Centre, published by Financial Rights Legal Centre, Sydney, NSW, October 2015, pp 1–32, http://financialrights.org.au/wp-content/uploads/2015/10/Submission-to-SACC-Review-Financial-Rights.pdf.

Financial System Inquiry, *Financial System Inquiry Final Report*, series edited by The Treasury of the Australian Government, The Treasury, Commonwealth Government of Australia, published by The Australian Government, the Treasury, Canberra, ACT, November 2014, pp 1–320, http://fsi.gov.au/files/2014/11/FSI_Final_Report.pdf.

Financial System Inquiry, *Financial System Inquiry Interim Report*, series edited by The Treasury of the Australian Government, The Treasury, Commonwealth Government of Australia, published by The Australian Government, the Treasury, Canberra, ACT, July 2014, pp 1–460, http://fsi.gov.au/files/2014/07/FSI_Report_Final_Reduced20140715.pdf.

Klapper, Leora, Annamaria Lusardi & Peter van Oudheusden, *Insights From The Standard & Poor's Ratings Services Global Financial Literacy Survey*, in *'Financial Literacy Around the World'*, Global Financial Literary Excellence Center (GFLEC), published by Global Financial Literary Excellence Center (GFLEC), Washington, DC, 18 November 2015, pp 1–27, http://gflec.org/wp-content/uploads/2015/11/Finlit_paper_16_F2_singles.pdf.

Law Council of Australia, *Review of the Financial System External Dispute Resolution Framework*, Law Council of Australia, published by Law Council of Australia, Canberra, ACT, 7 October 2016, pp 1–32, https://www.treasury.gov.au/~/media/Treasury/Consultations and Reviews/Consultations/2016/Review of the financial system external dispute resolution framework/Submissions/PDF/Law_Council_of_Australia.ashx.

Mishkin, Frederic S., *Over the Cliff: From the Subprime to the Global Financial Crisis*, series edited by National Bureau of Economic Research, in *'NBER Working Paper Series'*, no. 16609, National Bureau of Economic Research, published by National Bureau of Economic Research, Cambridge, MA, December 2010, pp 1–32, http://www.nber.org/papers/w16609.

Mylenko, Nataliya, Adetola Adenuga, Roziah Baba, Elizabeth Davidson, Ros Grady, Johanna Jaeger & Valentina Saltane, *Global Survey on Consumer Protection and Financial Literacy: Results Brief - Regulatory Practices in 114 Economies*, in *'Publications'*, The Financial Inclusion and Infrastructure Global Practice, The World Bank, published by The World Bank, Washington, DC, 2013, pp 1–25, http://responsiblefinance.worldbank.org/~/media/GIAWB/FL/Documents/Publications/Global-Consumer-Protection-and-Financial-Literacy-results-brief.pdf.

North, Martin & Gill North, *The Stressed Finance Landscape Data Analysis*, series edited by Digital Finance Analytics and Monash University Centre for Commercial Law and Regulatory Studies (CLARS), in *'Digital Finance Analytics, Reports'*, Digital Finance Analytics and the Centre for Commercial Law and Regulatory Studies, Monash University, published by Financial Rights Legal Centre, Melbourne, Vic, October 2015, pp 1–32, http://financialrights.org.au/wp-content/uploads/2015/10/The-Stressed-Financial-Landscape-Data-Analysis-DFA2.pdf.

Professor Rosalind Croucher (President and Commissioner in Charge), Justice Berna Collier (part-time Commissioner) & The Hon Susan Ryan AO, Age Discrimination Commissioner (part-time Commissioner), *Grey Areas—Age Barriers to Work in Commonwealth Laws (DP 78)*, series edited by Australian Law Reform Commission, in *'Publications'*, no. 78, Vol. Chapter 5, 'Social Security', Australian Law Reform Commission, published by Australian Law Reform Commission, Sydney, NSW, 2 October 2012, pp 113–146, SKK Book Chapter2.docx.

Professor Rosalind Croucher (President), The Hon Justice John Middleton, Federal Court of Australia (part-time Commissioner), & The Hon Justice Nye Perram, Federal Court of Australia (part-time Commissioner), *Elder Abuse - Discussion Paper 83*, series edited by Australian Law Reform Commission, in *'Publications'*, no. (DP 83), Australian Law Reform Commission, published by Australian Law Reform Commission, Sydney, NSW, December 2016, pp 1–259, https://www.alrc.gov.au/sites/default/files/pdfs/publications/dp83.pdf.

Ramsay, Ian, Julie Abramson & Alan Kirkland, *Review of the financial system external dispute resolution and complaints framework, Interim Report*, in *'EDR Review'*, Markets Group Financial System Division, The Treasury, Commonwealth Government, published by The Treasury, Canberra, ACT, 6 December 2016, pp 1–201, http://www.treasury.gov.au/~/media/Treasury/Consultations and Reviews/Reviews and Inquiries/2016/Review into EDR/Key Documents/PDF/EDR_interim.ashx.

Ramsay, Ian, Julie Abramson & Alan Kirkland, *Review of the financial system external dispute resolution framework, Issues Paper*, in *'Consultation on the financial system external dispute resolution framework'*, Markets Group Financial System Division, The Treasury, Commonwealth Government, published by The Treasury, Canberra, ACT, 9 September 2016, pp 1–30, https://consult.treasury.gov.au/financial-system-division/dispute-resolution/supporting_documents/EDR_issues_paper.pdf.

Schetzer, Louis, Joanna Mullins & Roberto Buonamano, *Access to Justice & Legal Needs, A project to identify legal needs, pathways and barriers for disadvantaged people in NSW*, in *'Background Paper'*, Law & Justice Foundation of New South Wales, published by Justice Research Centre, Sydney, NSW, August 2002, pp 1–72, http://www.lawfoundation.net.au/ljf/site/articleIDs/012E910236879BAECA257060007D13E0/$file/bkgr1.pdf.

Schmulow, A.D., *Twin Peaks: A Theoretical Analysis*, series edited by The Centre For International Finance and Regulation (CIFR), in *'The Centre For International Finance and Regulation (CIFR) Research Working Paper Series'*, no. 064/2015 / Project No. E018, The Centre For International Finance and Regulation (CIFR), published by The Centre For International Finance and Regulation, Sydney, NSW, 1 July 2015, pp 1–40, http://www.cifr.edu.au/project/Australia_twin_peaks_approach_for_China_and_Asia.aspx.

Senate Economics References Committee, *The Performance of The Australian Securities and Investments Commission*, series edited by Senate Standing Committees on Economics, in *'Executive summary'*, Parliament of Australia, published by Commonwealth of Australia, Canberra, ACT, 26 June 2014, pp xvii-xxii, http://www.aph.gov.au/Parliamentary_Business/Committees/Senate/Economics/ASIC/Final_Report/b02.

Shorrocks, Anthony, James B. Davies, Rodrigo Lluberas & Antonios Koutsoukis, *Global Wealth Report 2016*, in *'Global Wealth Report'*, Research Institute, Credit Suisse, published by Credit Suisse, Zurich, CH, November 2016, pp 1–63, http://publications.credit-suisse.com/tasks/render/file/index.cfm?fileid=AD783798-ED07-E8C2-4405996B5B02A32E.

The Treasury, *Architecture of Australia's tax and transfer system*, The Treasury, Commonwealth Government of Australia, published by Commonwealth Government of Australia Attorney-General's Department, Canberra, ACT, August 2008, pp 1–344, http://taxreview.treasury.gov.au/content/downloads/report/architecture_of_australias_tax_and_transfer_system_revised.pdf.

The Treasury, *Part Two: Detailed analysis*, in *'Australia's future tax system, Report to the Treasurer'*, Vol. 2 of 2, The Treasury, Commonwealth Government of Australia, published by Commonwealth Government of Australia Attorney-General's Department, Canberra, ACT, December 2009, pp 1–783, http://taxreview.treasury.gov.au/content/downloads/final_report_part_2/afts_final_report_part_2_vol_2_consolidated.pdf.

The Treasury & Australian Prudential Regulation Authority, *Financial Industry Levies for 2015–16*, The Treasury & Australian Prudential Regulation Authority, published by The Treasury & Australian Prudential Regulation Authority, Canberra, ACT, 1 July 2015, pp 1-19, http://www.apra.gov.au/CrossIndustry/Documents/Financial-Industry-Levies-current.pdf.

Turner, Grant, *Depositor Protection in Australia*, in *'Bulletin'*, Reserve Bank of Australia, published by Reserve Bank of Australia, Sydney, NSW, December Quarter 2011, pp 45–56, https://www.rba.gov.au/publications/bulletin/2011/dec/pdf/bu-1211-5.pdf.

U.S. Securities and Exchange Commission, *SEC Enforcement Actions. Addressing Misconduct that Led To or Arose From the Financial Crisis*, U.S. Securities and Exchange Commission, published by U.S. Securities and Exchange Commission, Washington, DC, 26 May 2015, http://www.sec.gov/spotlight/enf-actions-fc.shtml.

Vandenbroek, Penny, *Employment by industry statistics: a quick guide*, in *'Parliamentary Library Quick Guide'*, no. Research Paper Series, 2015–16, Statistics and Mapping Section, Parliament of Australia, published by Parliament of Australia, Canberra, ACT, 14 April 2016, pp 1–6, http://parlinfo.aph.gov.au/parlInfo/download/library/prspub/4497908/upload_binary/4497908.pdf;fileType=application/pdf.

Wilkins, Roger, *The Household, Income and Labour Dynamics in Australia Survey: Selected Findings from Waves 1 to 14, The 11th Annual Statistical Report of the HILDA Survey*, series edited by Melbourne Institute of Applied Economic and Social Research, in *'The Household, Income and Labour Dynamics in Australia (HILDA) Survey'*, The University of Melbourne, published by The University of Melbourne Melbourne Institute of Applied Economic and Social Research, Melbourne, Vic, 2016, pp 1–120, https://www.melbourneinstitute.com/downloads/hilda/Stat_Report/statreport_2016.pdf.

Conference Proceedings

Harman, Mr Justice Joe, "From Alternate to Primary Dispute Resolution: The pivotal role of mediation in (and in avoiding) litigation", *Paper presented at the National Mediation Conference*, Melbourne, published by Federal Court of Australia, 2014, pp 1–26, http://www.federalcircuitcourt.gov.au/wps/wcm/connect/fccweb/reports-and-publications/speeches-conference-papers/2014/speech-harman-alternate-to-primary-dispute-resolution.

Press Releases

Australian Securities and Investments Commission, "16–060MR ASIC commences civil penalty proceedings against ANZ for BBSW conduct", published by Australian Securities and Investments Commission, Sydney, NSW, Friday, 4 March, 2016, pp 1, http://asic.gov.au/about-asic/media-centre/find-a-media-release/2016-releases/16-060mr-asic-commences-civil-penalty-proceedings-against-anz-for-bbsw-conduct/.

Electronic Articles

Denning, Steve, "Lest We Forget: Why We Had A Financial Crisis", *Forbes*, (22 November, 2011), published electronically by Forbes.com LLC, Jersey City, NJ, http://www.forbes.com/sites/stevedenning/2011/11/22/5086/.

Jacobson, David, "Life insurance claims handling inquiry", *Bright Law*, (4 April, 2016), (accessed: 16 May, 2016), published electronically by Bright Legal Services Pty Ltd, Brisbane, Qld, http://www.brightlaw.com.au/financial-services/life-insurance-claims-handling-inquiry/.

Legal Services Commission of South Australia, "What credit contracts are regulated by the NCC?", *Law Handbook*, (20 June, 2013), (accessed: 14 December, 2016), published electronically by Legal Services Commission of South Australia, Adelaide, SA, pp. 1–5, http://www.lawhandbook.sa.gov.au/ch10s04s01s02.php.

McConnell, Pat, "ASIC finally pulls the BBSW trigger on ANZ", 'Business & Economy', *The Conversation,* published by The Conversation Media Group, Melbourne, VIC, 4 March, 2016 5.52 pm AEST, https://theconversation.com/asic-finally-pulls-the-bbsw-trigger-on-anz-55766.

McConnell, Pat, "ASIC needs a win in 2017, but it's not likely to come from the banks", 'Business & Economy', *The Conversation,* published by The Conversation Media Group, Melbourne, VIC, 15 January, 2017 10.47 am AEDT, https://theconversation.com/asic-needs-a-win-in-2017-but-its-not-likely-to-come-from-the-banks-70810.

McConnell, Pat, "CommInsure case shows it's time to target reckless misconduct in banking", 'Business & Economy', *The Conversation,* published by The Conversation Media Group, Melbourne, VIC, 8 March, 2016 9.38 am AEDT, https://theconversation.com/comminsure-case-shows-its-time-to-target-reckless-misconduct-in-banking-55748.

McConnell, Pat, "Market manipulation – ASIC better get it right, first time", 'Business & Economy', *The Conversation,* published by The Conversation Media Group, Melbourne, VIC, 9 February, 2016 1.54 pm AEDT, https://theconversation.com/market-manipulation-asic-better-get-it-right-first-time-54388.

McConnell, Pat, "War on banking's rotten culture must include regulators", 'Business & Economy', *The Conversation,* published by The Conversation Media Group, Melbourne, VIC, 4 June, 2015 2.14 pm AEST, http://theconversation.com/war-on-bankings-rotten-culture-must-include-regulators-42767.

Schmulow, Andrew, "Why rigging of the bank bill swap rate hurts everyone", 'Business & Economy', *The Conversation,* published by The Conversation Media Group, Melbourne, VIC, 9 March, 2016 2.29 pm AEDT, https://theconversation.com/why-rigging-of-the-bank-bill-swap-rate-hurts-everyone-55826.

Snyder, Darren, "Senate to investigate life industry", 'News/Insurance, Regulatory', *Financial Standard,* published by Rainmaker Group, Sydney, NSW, Tuesday, 8 March, 2016 12:21 pm, http://www.financialstandard.com.au/news/view/80775108.

Wray, L. Randall, "Setting the Record Straight One More Time: BofA's Rebecca Mairone Fined $1Million; BofA Must Pay $1.3Billion", *New Economic Perspectives*, (2 August, 2014), (accessed: 26 June, 2015), published electronically, http://neweconomicperspectives.org/2014/08/setting-record-straight-one-time-bofas-rebecca-mairone-fined-1million-bofa-must-pay-1–3billion.html.

Wright, Chris, "Regulation: Banking's dark side reaches Australia", *Euromoney*, published by Euromoney Institutional Investor PLC, London, 6 April 2016, http://www.euromoney.com/Article/3543401/Regulation-Bankings-dark-side-reaches-Australia.html.

Press

Ferguson, Adele, "A banking royal commission couldn't make the sector's reputation any worse", 'Business/Banking & Finance/Financial Services/Opinion', *The Australian Financial Review,* AFR Weekend ed., published by Fairfax Media, Sydney, NSW, 11 April, 2016 at 08:46 am, http://www.afr.com/business/banking-and-finance/financial-services/a-banking-royal-commission-couldnt-make-the-sectors-reputation-any-worse-20160410-go2tso.

Ferguson, Adele, "Financial misconduct costs a fortune", 'Business/Comment', *The Sydney Morning Herald,* Business Day ed., published by Fairfax Media, Sydney, NSW, 17 September, 2016, http://www.smh.com.au/business/comment-and-analysis/financial-misconduct-costs-a-fortune-20160916-grhp8g.html.

Ferguson, Adele, "Hearing into ASIC's failure to investigate CBA's Financial Wisdom", 'Business Day', *The Sydney Morning Herald,* published by Fairfax Media, Sydney, NSW, 3 June, 2014, http://www.smh.com.au/business/hearing-into-asics-failure-to-investigate-cbas-financial-wisdom-20140602-39ept.html.

Ferguson, Adele, "Royal commission: not a populist whinge for burned bank customers", 'Comment', *The Sydney Morning Herald,* published by Fairfax Media, Sydney, NSW, 13 August, 2016, http://www.smh.com.au/business/banking-and-finance/royal-commission-not-a-populist-whinge-for-burned-bank-customers-20160812-gqqyll.html.

Ferguson, Adele & Ben Butler, "Commonwealth Bank facing royal commission call after Senate financial planning inquiry", 'Banking and Finance', *The Sydney Morning Herald,* Business Day ed., published by Fairfax Media, Sydney, NSW, 26 June, 2014, http://www.smh.com.au/business/banking-and-finance/commonwealth-bank-facing-royal-commission-call-after-senate-financial-planning-inquiry-20140625-3asy6.html.

Han, Misa, "Big four banks, AMP charged $178 m for no financial advice", 'Business/Banking & Finance', *The Australian Financial Review,* published by Fairfax Media, Sydney, NSW, 27 October, 2016 at 11:37 am, http://www.afr.com/business/banking-and-finance/big-four-banks-amp-charged-178m-for-no-financial-advice-20161026-gsbr5r.

Patrick, A. Odysseus, "Flush and Dominant, Australia's Banks Come Under Pressure", 'Dealbook', *New York Times,* New York ed., published by The New York Times Company, New York, NY, 14 October, 2016, https://www.nytimes.com/2016/10/15/business/dealbook/australia-banks-under-pressure.html?_r=0.

Rothacker, Rick, "The deal that cost Bank of America $50 billion – and counting", 'News, Business, Banking', *The Charlotte Observer,* published by The McClatchy Company, Charlotte, NC, 16 August, 2014, http://www.charlotteobserver.com/news/business/banking/article9151889.html.

Wilkins, Georgia, "Big banks to refund $178 million to financial advice customers", 'Business', *The Sydney Morning Herald,* published by Fairfax Media, Sydney, NSW, 27 October, 2016, http://www.smh.com.au/business/banking-and-finance/big-banks-amp-may-have-to-refund-178-million-to-customers-over-advice-they-never-received-20161026-gsboid.html.

Williams, Ruth, "'Tough cop' ASIC too timid on enforcement: Allan Fels", 'News & Views/Banking', *The Sydney Morning Herald,* published by Fairfax Ltd, Sydney, NSW, 15 April, 2016, http://www.smh.com.au/business/banking-and-finance/tough-cop-asic-too-timid-on-enforcement-fels-20160414-go6jqe.html.

Wyatt, Edward, "Promises Made, Then Broken, By Firms in S.E.C. Fraud Cases", 'Business Day', *New York Times,* New York ed., published by The New York Times Company, New York, NY, 8 November, 2011, http://www.nytimes.com/2011/11/08/business/in-sec-fraud-cases-banks-make-and-break-promises.html?_r=0.

Web Pages and Internet Resources

Anonymous, "Population of Australia 2016", in *Australia2016 Population*, published by Australia2016 Population, 2016, accessed: 5 December 2016, http://australiapopulation2016.com.

Australian Bureau of Statistics, "Key Findings", in *6523.0 - Household Income and Wealth, Australia, 2013–14*, published by Australian Bureau of Statistics, Canberra, ACT, 4 September, 2015, accessed: 5 December 2016, http://www.abs.gov.au/ausstats/abs@.nsf/0/5F4BB49C975C64C9CA256D6B00827ADB?Opendocument.

Australian Bureau of Statistics, "March Key Figures", in *3101.0 - Australian Demographic Statistics, Mar 2016*, published by Australian Bureau of Statistics, Canberra, ACT, 22 September, 2016, accessed: 5 December 2016, http://www.abs.gov.au/AUSSTATS/abs@.nsf/mf/3101.0.

Australian Bureau of Statistics, "Summary", in *3235.0 - Population by Age and Sex, Regions of Australia, 2015*, published by Australian Bureau of Statistics, Canberra, ACT, 18 August, 2016, accessed: 5 December 2016, http://www.abs.gov.au/ausstats/abs@.nsf/mf/3235.0.

Australian Prudential Regulation Authority, "About the Financial Claims Scheme", in *Home*, series edited by Australian Prudential Regulation Authority, published by Australian Prudential Regulation Authority, Sydney, NSW, accessed: 8 January 2017, https://www.fcs.gov.au/about-apra.

Australian Prudential Regulation Authority, "Financial Claims Scheme", in *Cross Industry*, series edited by Australian Prudential Regulation Authority, published by Australian Prudential Regulation Authority, Sydney, NSW, accessed: 9 January 2017, http://www.apra.gov.au/CrossIndustry/FCS/Pages/default.aspx.

Australian Prudential Regulation Authority, "Financial Claims Scheme for banks, building societies and credit unions", in *Cross Industry*, series edited by Australian Prudential Regulation Authority, published by Australian Prudential Regulation Authority, Sydney, NSW, accessed: 9 January 2017, http://www.apra.gov.au/CrossIndustry/FCS/Pages/fcs-adi-html.aspx.

Australian Prudential Regulation Authority, "Insurers Authorised to Conduct New or Renewal Insurance Business in Australia", in *General Insurance*, series edited by Australian Prudential Regulation Authority, published by Australian Prudential Regulation Authority, Sydney, NSW, accessed: 8 December 2016, http://www.apra.gov.au/GI/Pages/new-or-renewal.aspx.

Australian Prudential Regulation Authority, "Registered Life Insurance Companies", in *Life Insurance & Friendly Societies*, series edited by Australian Prudential Regulation Authority, published by Australian Prudential Regulation Authority, Sydney, NSW, accessed: 8 December 2016, http://www.apra.gov.au/lifs/pages/registered-life-insurers.aspx.

Australian Taxation Office, "Super accounts data overview", in *Research and statistics*, published by Australian Taxation Office, Canberra, ACT, 15 August, 2016, accessed: 11 January 2017, https://www.ato.gov.au/About-ATO/Research-and-statistics/In-detail/Super-statistics/Super-accounts-data/Super-accounts-data-overview/.

Christodoulou, Mario, "ASIC: $20 trillion worth of financial products may be affected by BBSW rigging", in *News*, series edited by Australian Broadcasting Corporation, published by Australian Broadcasting Corporation, Sydney, NSW, 29 July 2016, 3:16 pm, accessed: 16 October 2016, http://www.abc.net.au/news/2016-07-29/asic-20-trillion-worth-of-financial-products-bbsw/7673322.

Henderson, Anna & Dan Conifer, "Commonwealth Bank boss Ian Narev says no-one sacked over CommInsure scandals", in *Breaking News*, series edited by Australian Broadcasting Corporation, published by Australian Broadcasting Corporation, Sydney, NSW, 4 October, 2016, 11:17 pm, accessed: 30 January 2017, http://www.abc.net.au/news/2016-10-04/commonwealth-bank-boss-says-no-staff-axed-comminsure-scandals/7901884.

International Monetary Fund, "Financial Soundness Indicators (FSIs): At a Glance", in *Access to Macroeconomic & Financial Data*, published by International Monetary Fund, Washington,

DC, 12 July, 2016, accessed: 9 December 2016, http://data.imf.org/?sk=9F855EAE-C765-405E-9C9A-A9DC2C1FEE47.

Letts, Stephen, "Banks facing $180 million compensation payments for gouging fees without advice", in *Breaking News*, series edited by Australian Broadcasting Corporation, published by Australian Broadcasting Corporation, Sydney, NSW, 27 October, 2016, 1:02 pm, accessed: 30 January 2017, http://www.abc.net.au/news/2016-10-27/banks-facing-180-million-compensation-payments/7971006.

Martin, Ray, "Bank of America's great mortgage give-away", in *CBS News*, series edited by CBS Money Watch, published by CBS Interactive Inc., New York, NY, 9 May, 2012, 10:32 am, accessed: 26 September 2015, http://www.cbsnews.com/news/bank-of-americas-great-mortgage-give-away/.

Members Own Health Funds, "Members Own Health Funds", in *Home*, published by Members Own Health Funds, Geelong, Vic, 2016, accessed: 8 December 2016, https //membersown.com.au.

Reserve Bank of Australia, "Household Debt – Distribution – E7", in *Statistical Tables*, published by Reserve Bank of Australia, Sydney, NSW, 2001-2017, accessed: 10 January 2017, http://www.rba.gov.au/statistics/tables/.

Trading Economics, "1959-2016", in *Australia Household Saving Ratio*, published by Trading Economics, New York, NY, 2016, accessed: 8 December 2016, http://www.tradingeconomics.com/australia/personal-savings.

Trading Economics, "1976–2016 ", in *Australia Consumer Credit*, published by Trading Economics, New York, NY, 2016, accessed: 8 December 2016, http://www.tradingeconomics.com/australia/consumer-credit.

Trading Economics, "1977-2016", in *Australia Households Debt To Gdp*, published by Trading Economics, New York, NY, 2016, accessed: 8 December 2016, http://www.tradingeconomics.com/australia/households-debt-to-gdp.

Audiovisual Materials

Ferguson, Adele & Deb Masters, "Banking Bad", in Four Corners, *Audiovisual Material*, Documentary, Four Corners/Fairfax Publishing, Australian Broadcasting Corporation, Sydney, NSW, 5 May, 2014, http://www.abc.net.au/4corners/stories/2014/05/05/3995954.htm.

Andrew D. Schmulow BA Honours LLB (*Witwatersrand*) PhD (*Melbourne*). He is a Senior Lecturer in Law, The University of Western Australia; an Advocate of the High Court of South Africa; the Founder, Clarity Prudential Regulatory Consulting, Pty Ltd; a Visiting Researcher, Oliver Schreiner School of Law, University of the Witwatersrand, Johannesburg; and a Visiting Researcher, Centre for International Trade, Sungkyunkwan University, Seoul.

James O'Hara is a commercial lawyer at MinterEllison. He holds a Bachelor of Commerce (Corporate Finance) and a Bachelor of Laws with Distinction from the University of Western Australia. James' principal area of practice is in commercial litigation including contractual disputes, construction, property law, insolvency, banking, corporate law, insurance and debt recovery. He has appeared as Counsel in Magistrates Court, District Court, Supreme Court and Federal Court proceedings. Prior to joining the Perth office of MinterEllison, James served as the Associate to the Honourable Justice Hall of the Supreme Court of Western Australia.

Chapter 3
Financial Consumer Protection in Bangladesh

Muhammad Ziaulhaq Mamun

1 About the Study

1.1 Background

A person or entity having a bank account, a loan, investment account, or an insurance policy with a financial institution is a consumer of financial services. As a consumer of a financial service one has certain rights, and the consumer group as a whole should get adequate protection in a financial market. A financial system can protect consumer rights if it can offer transparency and appropriate choices. Consumer protection is designed to ensure the rights of consumers as well as fair trade, competition and accurate information in the marketplace. Consumer protection code for financial institutions also exists in several instances that prescribe how a financial institution deals with consumers. The relevant product information and consumer protection codes are crucial for protecting consumers' rights. These rights are necessary and their effective implementation is a must so that the financial consumers are better aware of their rights and risks, the terms and conditions, the services and the accompanying charges and thereby do not find themselves in unwanted situations with financial complications.

M. Z. Mamun (✉)
University of Dhaka, Dhaka, Bangladesh
e-mail: mzmamun@yahoo.com; mzmamun@ibadu.edu

© Springer Nature Singapore Pte Ltd. 2018

T.-J. Chen (ed.), *An International Comparison of Financial Consumer Protection*,
https://doi.org/10.1007/978-981-10-8441-6_3

Bangladesh is a country with literacy rate of 61.5%. Hence, it has a lot of financial consumers who do not know how to read and write and understand their rights and risks betters. Because of their lack of knowledge in this particular aspects, many financial consumers end up incurring huge losses by getting entangled in an arena that they are not familiar with. What makes the situation worse is, it's not just the illiterate or less educated who face troubles, young entrepreneurs at times find themselves in similar precarious situations because although they may know how to read and write, they sometimes do not know how the rules translate in real life scenarios. They may often find themselves having unexpected interest amount, among many other things. Moreover, there are also some proportion of people who consider the whole process of banking and financial services a complicated arena with a lot of traps and avoid availing the services altogether. As these situations have a negative impact on the lives of consumers and also the country's economy as a whole, Bangladesh Bank (BB hereafter) has come up with initiatives that make the scenario much better and the financial services much reliable.

Financial inclusion drives of the BB have brought remarkable improvements in several socio-economic fronts and the consumer base of banks improved remarkably. Notable changes have taken place in terms of higher access to finance and increased geographical penetrations of the financial services. The changed approach of banking expanded credit flow to agricultural, SME, and environmentally-friendly sectors, and brought a large number of un-banked/under-banked socially disadvantaged people into the ambit of financial services. A considerable number of vulnerable people have opened accounts with the banks, and the central bank has established refinance schemes targeting different underprivileged groups. Inclusive drives of the Bangladesh Bank have also been rightly addressing the issues of financial literacy and consumer protection targeting mainly the vulnerable section.

1.2 The Issue

The population of Bangladesh has been increasing at a high rate since the liberation, despite the fact that the percentage change in population growth has been decreasing in the same time. The economy of Bangladesh is also improving, the GDP of Bangladesh was increasing at 6% (according to data from World Bank) in 2013, which is higher than both India and Pakistan.

Due to the increased population and improving economy, the number of financial consumers of Bangladesh have also improved. The government of Bangladesh is not doing much directly ensure to protection of these consumers, but a lot of indirect measures have been taken by the government as well as private investors. This paper looks into such work and attempts to paint a picture of the protection financial consumers have in Bangladesh.

1.3 Objectives

1.3.1 Broad Objective

To explore the measures taken for financial consumer protection in Bangladesh.

1.3.2 Specific Objectives

(a) Know who financial customers are and analyze their economic conditions
(b) Understand various consumer protection systems
(c) Look at the financial systems in Bangladesh and the current state of financial consumer protection systems
(d) Propose improved ways to protect the financial consumers of Bangladesh
(e) Analyze the market issues and give plausible solutions.

1.4 Methodology

Secondary sources were mostly used for data collection, i.e., Information from the web-pages of Bangladesh Bank, Bangladesh Bureau of Statistics (BBS), etc. Online news portal(s) were also a source of data collection.

1.5 Scope

This report mainly covers the rights that are there in Bangladesh for financial consumers. This report explains why the rights are important, discusses about different financial institutions and financial services and also provides suggestions as to how the risks that the financial consumers may have can be curtailed.

1.6 Limitations

Some of the data that were used in the report are taken from 2015 and older statistical reports as the websites from which the data were collected are not updated.

2 Understanding Financial Consumers

2.1 Who Are Financial Consumers

The term "Financial Consumer" refers to any consumers of financial services. Financial services are the economic services provided by the finance industry, which encompasses a broad range of businesses that manage money, including credit unions, banks (both commercial and investment banking), general banking (loans, current and savings accounts etc.), foreign exchange services, credit-card companies, insurance companies, accountancy companies, consumer-finance companies, stock brokerages, investment funds, assets and fund management and some government-sponsored enterprises. Consumers who receive services from the aforementioned institutions are the financial consumers. In the broad sense, any stakeholder of the financial services industry is considered a financial consumer.

In Bangladesh, a large number of population remains always outside the list of "Financial Consumer" as they are not directly part of this financial sector. However, with growing use of mobile financial services, and Bangladesh Bank's focus on financial inclusion, the number of people with access to financial services is increasing steadily. And with this increased number of financial consumers, the need for increased regulations for their protection has also become more important.

2.2 Economic Situation of Financial Consumers

Bangladesh is one of the most densely populated countries in the world. The population of Bangladesh has been increasing has been increasing at a rapid rate since liberation. The population of Bangladesh is recorded to be 156.6 million in 2013, although if the trend continued it should be considerably more than that now (Fig. 1).

The growth rate of Bangladesh was 1.2% (annual change) in 2013 according to data from World Bank. This is the same as that of India, and lower than that of Pakistan (1.6%). The population growth rate was increasingly high (over 2%) in the early 1960s before starting to gradually decrease from 1970 until recent times (Fig. 2). Despite the decrease Bangladesh is one of the most densely populated countries in the world—being the 8th most populated country in the world in 2011 despite its very small size.

From Fig. 3, we can see that the life expectancy of the people of Bangladesh is not exceedingly high as the proportion of people over 65 is low. A large part of the population of Bangladesh, both male and female, is from 20–50, which means there is a considerable supply of labor force in Bangladesh. A lot of Bangladeshis can contribute to the economic growth of the nation if they are properly utilized.

Bangladesh is a rising economy and there has been a general positive trend in the wealth of the citizens of this nation in the recent years.

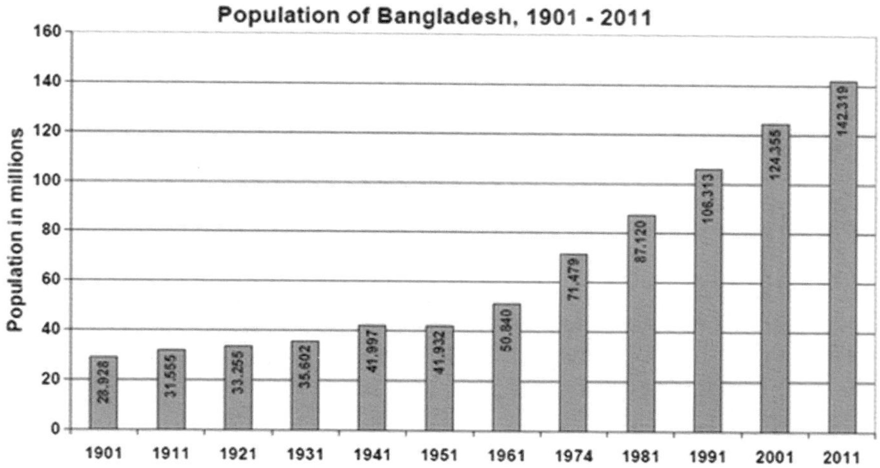

Fig. 1 The population of Bangladesh over time (Source: BBS 2015)

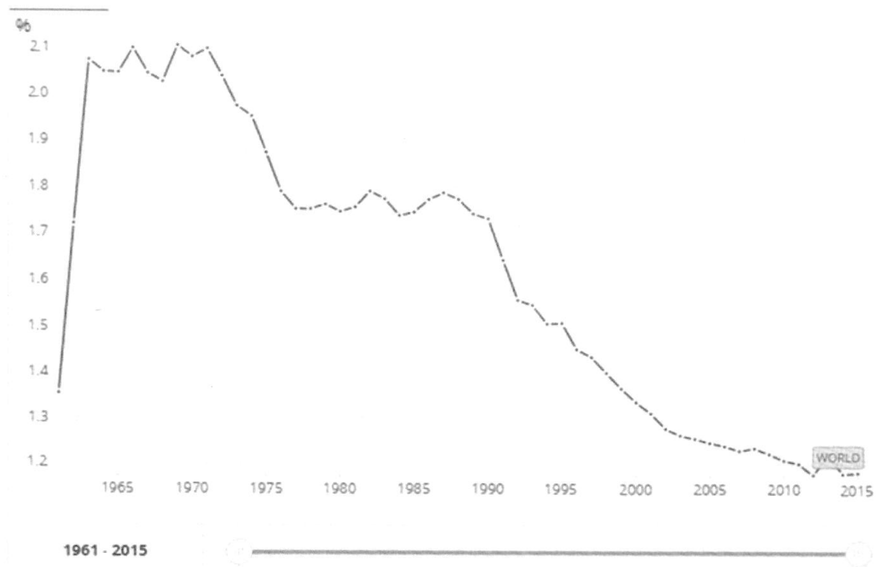

Fig. 2 Population growth rate of Bangladesh (Source: BBS 2015)

We can see from Fig. 4 that the disposable personal income of Bangladesh has been steadily rising from 2008–2012 before taking a huge leap from 2012–2013 and becoming steady once again after that. From the data available in this graph, the disposable personal income was at its peak on 2014 before taking a slight dip from

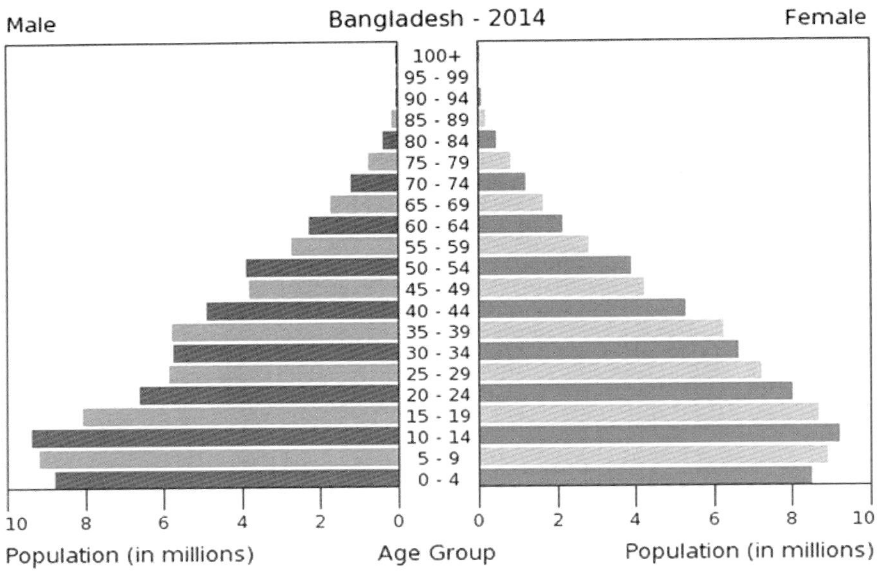

Fig. 3 The age structure of the population of Bangladesh (Source: BBS 2015)

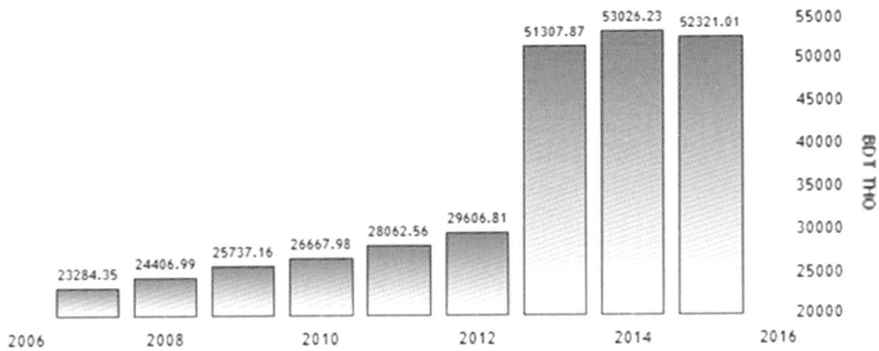

Fig. 4 Bangladesh disposable personal income (Source: BBFSDa 2014)

53026.23 BDT in 2014 to 52321.01 BDT in 2015. The increase in disposable personal income means that the buying power of the people has also increased.

Next, we can look at what percent of GDP is accounted for by the financial system over the years, as we compare and contrast the figures when stacked against other countries. We see that from 1995 to 2014, the Financial System Deposits to GDP has doubled in Bangladesh (from 24–48%) which is a significant growth when compared to other countries (Fig. 5). Although many countries have more voluminous figures, the growth indicates that financial systems are expanding in

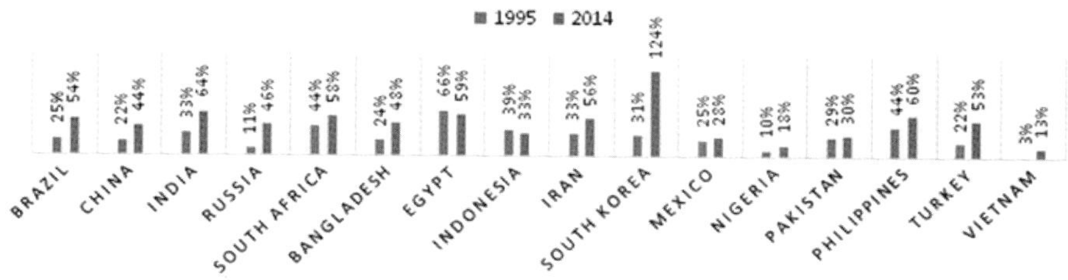

Fig. 5 Financial system deposits to GDP (%) (Source: BBFSDa 2014)

Table 1 Overview of mobile financial market as of March 2012 (Source: BBFSDb 2014, Greg Chen, n.d.)

Banks licensed to offer mobile financial services	Mobile operator partners	Launch date	Registered customers	Agents	Cumulative transactions ($ millions)
Trust Bank	Teletalk	Aug-10	1104	329	0.02
Dutch Bangla Bank	Airtel	May-11	172,020	3181	11.0
	Banglalink				
	Citycell				
	GrameenPhone				
BRAC Bank/ bKash	Banglalink	Jul-11	237,423	5383	14.8
	Robi				
	GrameenPhone				
Mercantile Bank	GrameenPhone	Feb-12	1392	170	12.5
Bank Asia	None	Mar-12	0	30	0.01
			442,289	9093	25.9

operations and thus contributing more to GDP. This means that the financial consumer base is also growing.

Another interesting statistic to look at would be the increase in mobile financial services in Bangladesh over the last few years. In Table 1, we see that as of 2012, many banks have partnered up with telecom operators to smoothen the business transactions offered by banks. It is notable that Dutch Bangla Bank Limited has partnered up with the most mobile companies, while bKash boasts the highest figures in terms of transactions ($14.8 million) and registered customers (237,423). (Greg Chen, n.d.)

The increase in mobile financial services indicates an increase in the demand for easier financial operations. The fact that new MFIs are flourishing means that there is a gradual increase in the financial consumer-base of the country. From the overall discussion, it is evident that the financial consumers are increasing and these consumers need a proper protection system similar to the ones existing in developed countries.

3 Financial Institutions of Bangladesh

3.1 Banking Sector

After the independence in 1971 from Pakistani regime, banking industry in Bangladesh started its journey with 6 nationalized commercialized banks, 2 state-owned specialized banks and 3 foreign banks. Bangladesh Bank (BB) is the central bank since the country's independence. Its prime jobs include issuing of currency, maintaining foreign exchange reserve and providing transaction facilities of all public monetary matters. BB is also responsible for planning the government's monetary policy and implementing it thereby.

Bangladesh has had only 7.8 banks per 10,000 adults in 2012 and this increased slightly to 8.2 banks per 100,000 adults in 2014 (Fig. 6). Whilst there has been an increase, it has been slight and Bangladesh still has much fewer banks per the adult population compared to countries like Brazil, Russia, Iran, Turkey, etc. On the flip side of the coin, Bangladesh has more banks per adult population than China, Nigeria, and Egypt etc. These are countries that are doing well financially.

In 1980s after opening up of the banking sector banking industry achieved significant expansion with the entrance of private banks. Banks in Bangladesh are primarily considered to be scheduled banks.

3.1.1 Scheduled Banks

The scheduled banks get license from Bangladesh Bank to operate under Bank Company Act, 1991 (Amended up to 2013). At present there are 57 scheduled banks in Bangladesh who operate under full control and supervision of Bangladesh Bank which is empowered to do so through Bangladesh Bank Order 1972 and Bank Company Act 1991. Scheduled Banks are classified into following types:

(1) State Owned Commercial Banks (SOCBs): There are 6 SOCBs which are fully or majorly owned by the Government of Bangladesh.
(2) Specialized Banks (SDBs): 2 specialized banks are now operating which were established for specific objectives like agricultural or industrial development. These banks are also fully or majorly owned by the Government of Bangladesh.

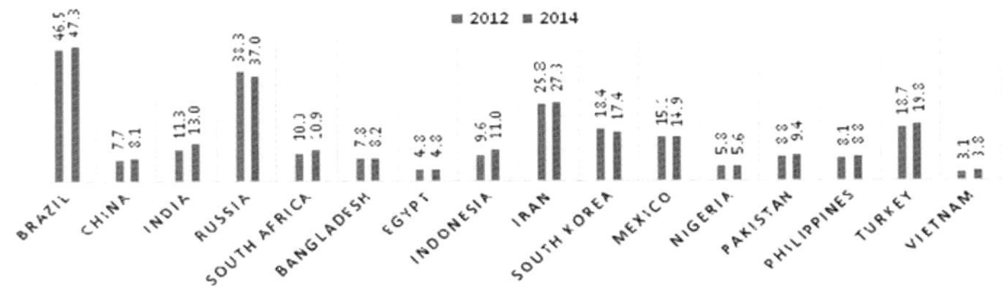

Fig. 6 Bank branches per 100,000 adults (Source: BBFSDb 2014)

(3) Private Commercial Banks (PCBs): There are 40 private commercial banks which are owned by the private entities. PCBs can be categorized into two groups:

   (A) Conventional PCBs: 32 conventional PCBs are now operating in the industry. They perform the banking functions in conventional fashion i.e. interest based operations.
   (B) Islami Shariah based PCBs: There are 8 Islami Shariah based PCBs in Bangladesh and they execute banking activities according to Islami Shariah based principles i.e. Profit-Loss Sharing (PLS) mode.

(4) Foreign Commercial Banks (FCBs): 9 FCBs are operating in Bangladesh as the branches of the banks which are incorporated in abroad. (*Bangladesh Bank 2015*).

The assets and deposits of scheduled banks in Bangladesh are shown below in Table 2. Private commercial banks have the largest percentage of deposits (at 63.9% in 2014). Their total assets increased from the previous year. The State Owned Banks also have a large percentage of deposits (28% in 2014) and their total assets also increased from the previous year. The DFIs are quite low compared to the rest and decreased in percentage amount from 2013 to 2014 and this is something the government could look and try to increase in an attempt to improve the overall economy of Bangladesh.

The national savings of Bangladesh has remained fairly constant over the recent years (Table 3). There has been a slight increase from FY 12 to FY 13 before decreasing slightly more in FY 14 and thereafter remaining more or less constant.

In 2010, 32% of Bangladeshis above the given age have an account in a financial institute as per this data provided, but this went down as only 29% of the same demographic had a bank account in 2014 (Fig. 7).

One of the reasons for the percentage decrease could be due to the increase in population of Bangladesh without the actual number of account holders substantially decreasing. Government could be doing more to raise awareness in this regard, to ensure a larger percentage of the population is aware of the facilities of banks.

3.1.2 Non-scheduled Banks

The banks which are established for special and definite objective and operate under the acts that are enacted for meeting up those objectives, are termed as Non-Scheduled Banks. These banks cannot perform all functions of scheduled banks.

(1) Non-bank Financial Institutions (NBFIs):

Non-Bank Financial Institutions (NBFIs) are those types of financial institutions which are regulated under Financial Institution Act, 1993 and controlled by Bangladesh Bank. Now, 31 FIs are operating in Bangladesh while the maiden one

Table 2 Assets and deposits of Banks in Bangladesh (Bangladesh Bank 2014–15)

Bank types	2013						2014					
	No. of banks	No. of branches	Total assets	% of industry assets	Deposits	% of deposits	No. of banks	No. of branches	Total assets	% of industry assets	Deposits	% of deposits
SCBs	4	3520	2108.5	26.4	1631.2	26	5	3553	2517.1	27.5	1952.1	28
DFIs	4	1494	454.8	5.7	343	5.5	3	1500	333.8	3.7	237.6	3.4
PCBs	39	3602	4948.2	61.8	3939.3	62.8	39	3917	5787.1	63.3	4449.4	63.9
FCBs	9	69	488.7	6.1	359.5	5.7	9	70	505	5.5	326	4.7
Total	56	8685	8000.2	100	6273	100	56	9040	9143	100	6965.1	100

Table 3 Domestics savings and investments in Bangladesh in percentages of GDP (Bangladesh Bank 2014–15)

Particulars	FY12	FY13	FY14	FY15
Public				
Investment	5.8	6.6	6.6	6.9
Domestic savings	1.4	1.5	1.5	1.6
Domestic savings-investment gap	−4.4	−5.1	−5.1	−5.3
Private				
Investment	22.5	21.8	22.0	22.1
Domestic savings	19.9	20.6	20.6	20.7
Domestic savings-investment gap	−2.6	−1.2	−1.4	−1.4
Total				
Investment	28.3	28.4	28.6	29.0
Domestic savings	21.2	22.0	22.1	22.3
Domestic savings-investment gap	−7.1	−6.4	−6.5	−6.7
National savings	29.9	30.5	29.2	29.1

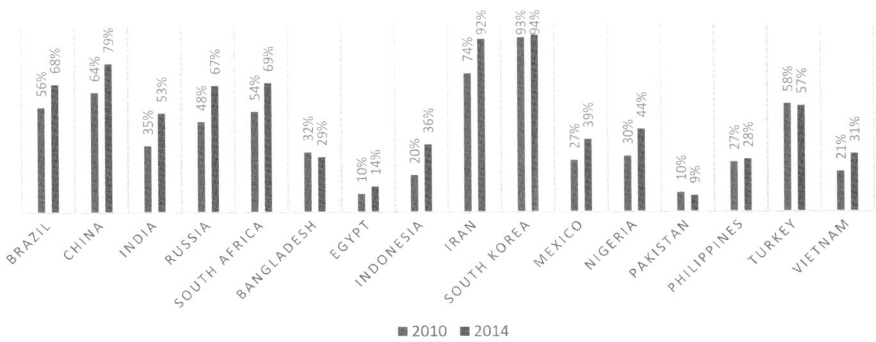

Fig. 7 Percentage of population (age 15+) that have accounts at a formal financial institution (Source: BBFSDa 2014)

was established in 1981. Out of the total, 2 is fully government owned, 1 is the subsidiary of a SOCB, 13 were initiated by private domestic initiative and 15 were initiated by joint venture initiative. Major sources of funds of FIs are Term Deposit (at least six months tenure), Credit Facility from Banks and other FIs, Call Money as well as Bond and Securitization. (*Bangladesh Bank 2015*)

The major difference between banks and FIs are as follows:

- FIs cannot issue checks, pay-orders or demand drafts.
- FIs cannot receive demand deposits,
- FIs cannot be involved in foreign exchange financing,
- FIs can conduct their business operations with diversified financing modes like syndicated financing, bridge financing, lease financing, securitization instruments, private placement of equity etc.

There are now 4 non-scheduled banks in Bangladesh which are:

- Ansar VDP Unnayan Bank,
- Karmashangosthan Bank,
- ProbashiKollyan Bank,
- Jubilee Bank.

3.2 Insurance Companies

Insurance sector in Bangladesh emerged after independence with 2 nationalized insurance companies- 1 Life and 1 General; and 1 foreign insurance company. In mid 80s, private sector insurance companies started to enter in the industry and it got expanded. Now days, 62 companies are operating under Insurance Act 2010. Out of them, 18 are Life Insurance Companies including 1 foreign company and 1 is state-owned company, and 44 General Insurance Companies including 1 state-owned company. Insurance companies in Bangladesh provide following services:

1. Life insurance,
2. General insurance,
3. Reinsurance,
4. Micro-insurance,
5. Takaful or Islamic insurance.

Bangladesh Government has taken decision to modernize the insurance law both Life and Non-Life insurance sector. In this context, on 27th July, 2008 the cabinet approved two ordinances Insurance Regularity Authority (IRA) Ordinance 2008 and insurance Ordinance (IO) 2008. This two Ordinances will promulgate shortly after president's assent. Also Insurance Sector in Bangladesh transferred in Finance Ministry from Commerce Ministry by an executive order of Bangladesh Government.

3.2.1 Capital Requirement for Insurers in Bangladesh

Company Registered in Bangladesh (Non-life)
Aminimum Paid up Capital of BDT 400 million is required to be registered for insurance operation.

Company Registered in Bangladesh (Life)
Private Life insurers must have a minimum Paid up Capital of BDT 300 million/ USD 4.31 million of which the sponsor must pay 60% at the outset and the balance 40% by public subscription within three years.

Company Registered Outside Bangladesh
Private Non-life insurers must have a minimum Paid up Capital of BDT 300 million/ USD 4.31 million which has to be deposited in Bangladesh through remittance.

3.2.2 Legal Provisions for Insurance Operator in Bangladesh

Section 43 of the Insurance Act 2010 as specifies that
Non-life insurers must have assets invested in Bangladesh exceeding their liabilities by at least BDT 1 million or 20% of the net premium income whichever is higher.

Section 22 of Insurance Act 2010 Specifies that
Foreign Investors can hold or purchase shares of a company up to prescribed limit by the Government and it won't be higher than the prescribed limit.

Legal Reserve for Unexpired Risks
100% is required for Marine Hull and Aviation Hull
40% for all other classes. Some insurers carry over 50%.

Compulsory insurances in Bangladesh

- Auto Third Party Liability for bodily injury and property damage (limited cover) is compulsory.
- Aviation liability.
- All Imports must be insured in Bangladesh with state owned SadharanBima Corporation or a private insurer, unless an exemption is obtained.

All the insurance companies in Bangladesh may be classified as follows (see Table 4).

Some of the Insurance Companies that are currently in operation in Bangladesh are:

- American Life Insurance Co.
- Bangladesh Co-operative Insurance Ltd.
- Bangladesh General Insurance Co. Ltd.
- Bangladesh National Insurance Co. Ltd.
- Delta Life Insurance Co. Ltd.
- Eastern Insurance Co. Ltd.
- Federal Insurance Co. Ltd.
- Green Delta Insurance Co. Ltd.

Table 4 Different type of insurance companies in Bangladesh (Source: IDRA 2015)

Ownership	Non-life	Life	Total
Government owned	1	1	2
Private sector	44	29	74
Foreign	0	2	1
Total	45	32	77

- Jiban Bima Corporation.
- Mercantile Insurance Company Ltd.

3.3 *Micro Finance Institutions (MFIs)*

The member-based Microfinance Institutions (MFIs) constitute a rapidly growing segment of the Rural Financial Market (RFM) in Bangladesh. Microcredit programs (MCP) in Bangladesh are implemented by various formal financial institutions (nationalized commercial banks and specialized banks), specialized government organizations and Non-government Organizations (NGOs). The growth in the MFI sector, in terms of the number of MFI as well as total membership, was phenomenal during the 1990s and continues till today. Despite the fact that more than a thousand of institutions are operating microcredit programs, but only 10 large Microcredit Institutions (MFIs) and Grameen Bank represent 87% of total savings of the sector and 81% of total outstanding loan of the sector. Through the financial services of microcredit, the poor people are engaging themselves in various income generating activities and around 30 million poor people are directly benefited from microcredit programs. Credit services of this sector can be categorized into six broad groups:

(1) General microcredit for small-scale self-employment based activities
(2) Microenterprise loans
(3) Loans for ultra-poor
(4) Agricultural loans
(5) Seasonal loans
(6) Loans for disaster management.

Currently, 599 institutions (as of October 10, 2011) have been licensed by MRA to operate Micro Credit Programs. But, Grameen Bank is out of the jurisdiction of MRA as it is operated under a distinct legislation- Grameen Bank Ordinance, 1983 (*Bangladesh Bank 2015*) (Fig. 8).

3.3.1 Services for Financial Consumers

Some of the common Consumer Finance Services products for individuals are:

(1) Personal Loan
(2) Education Loan
(3) Home Loan
(4) Car Loan
(5) Marriage Loan
(6) Medical Loan
(7) Executive Loan
(8) Card Payments
(9) Products for Businesses

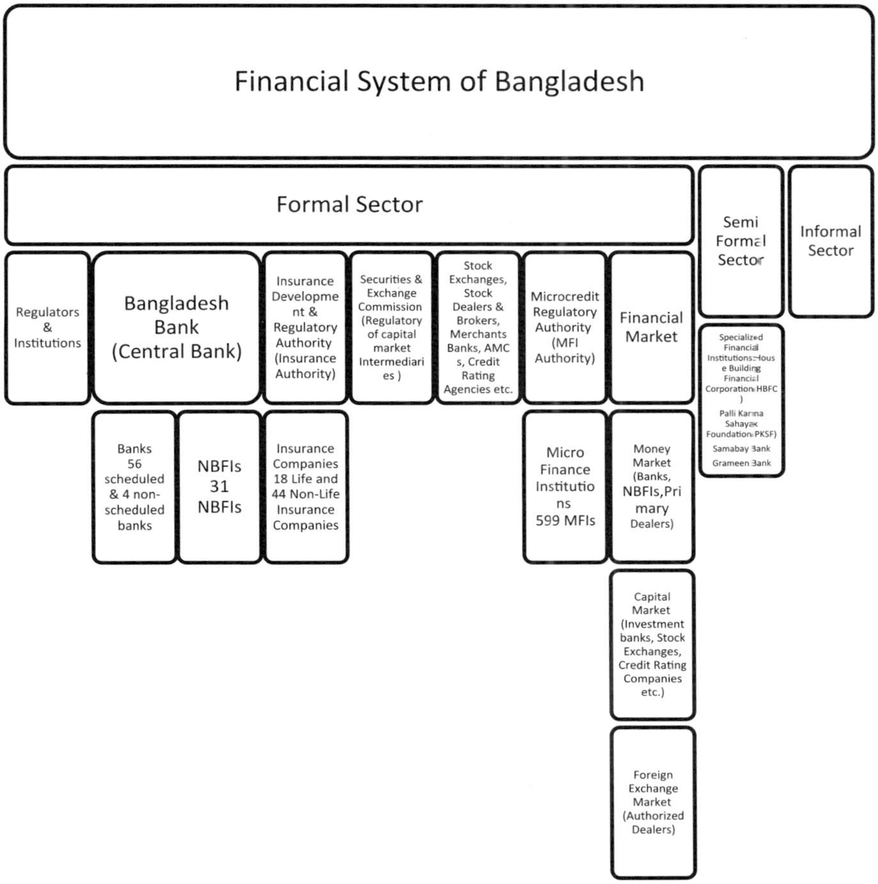

Fig. 8 Overall financial system in Bangladesh (Source: Bangladesh Bank, 2015)

(10) Lease Financing
(11) Working Capital Financing
(12) Term Loan Financing
(13) Project Financing
(14) Private Placement of Equity
(15) Brokerage
(16) Portfolio Management
(17) Investment Banking
(18) SME and MME Loans.

The consumer services growth in Bangladesh is quite promising. Figure 9 shows the growth in recent years.

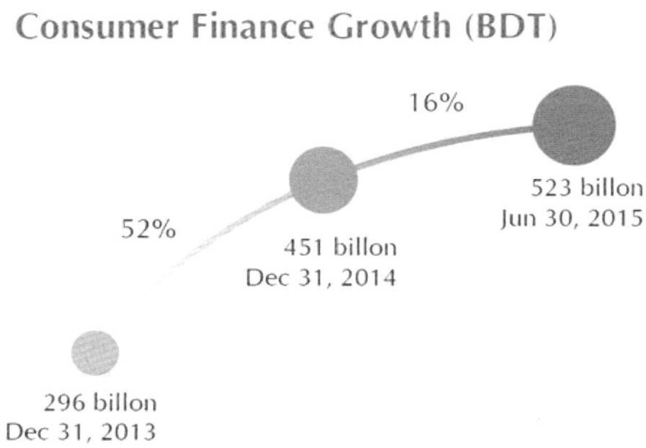

Fig. 9 Consumer finance growth in Bangladesh (Source: Mutual Trust Bank 2015).

3.4 *Who are the Targets as Financial Consumers?*

Islamic banks are focused in selling two specific types of products. Islamic banks are market leaders in Personal loans (against FDR, DPS, PF, MBS, DBS etc.) and Consumer goods products. Private commercial banks are market leader with 43% of the product bundle, Salary loan and loan for Education, Marriage, Treatment, and Travel. Foreign commercial banks are the market challenger in this product bundle with 24% of the pie. It is notable that, Islamic banks have as little as 2.3% market shares in this product bundle. "Other personal loans" is another category of personal loan, in that, IBs hold only 1% of the share while PCBs hold 65% and FCBs hold 10%.

Consumer goods (TV, Freeze, Air Cooler, Computer, Furniture etc.) hold 28.17% of the total consumer finance (BDT 522.6 billion) and second leading product in the market of consumer finance, which is almost BDT 150 billion. IBs have occupied 37% of total consumer goods, followed by PCBs with 30% and FCBs with 9%. Average sizes of account for Consumer goods finances are, BDT 385,440 for IBs, BDT 320,983 for PCBs and BDT 316,338 for FCBs. Credit card is 5% of total retail finance market. 75% of the Credit card market is occupied by private commercial market and 24% by foreign commercial banks.

Islamic banks, market leader in other products hold as little as 1% of the market of Credit card. Foreign commercial banks are major players in two product segments, Loan for Treatment and Travel/Holiday Loan. (Mutual Trust Bank 2015).

Grace Period: Grace period should only be allowed to a new business project or a project of an existing business that will require some time to generate enough cash for repayment. The maximum limit of the grace period should not exceed one year from the date of final disbursement. In case of large industrial projects or syndication financing, grace period may be extended up to another 6 months (Department of Financial Institutions and Markets 2013).

3.5 Marketing

A comparative study done in 2008, focused on the various aspects of marketing, advertising, market positioning, promoting etc., of some selected private commercial banks in Dhaka city. The private commercial banks, operating in Bangladesh, constantly focus on understanding and anticipating customer needs. They already made significant progress within a very short period of their existence. Many of the banks have been graded as top class banks in the country through internationally accepted CAMEL rating.

Public relations for promotional purpose are used in medium extent. Analysis on promotional tools used by banks shows that advertising are widely used method of promotion than personal selling. The ranking on three mediums of promotion are as follows: (1) Advertising, (2) Personal selling, (3) Public relations.

Advertising Media: All banks use newspapers as the promotional campaign and it is used to communicate about the new offer or any new news about the existing product and service of the banks. TV commercials are now widely used communicating vehicle by the banks as the survey showed. Out- door advertising media like bill-board, brochures etc. are being used by the banks in medium extent. Percentage use of three major advertising media are as follows: (1) Newspapers (100%), (2) Outdoor Advertising (BTL and Billboards) (88%), (3) TV Commercials (50%).

Personal Selling: Personal selling in the PCBs is not used in an extensive or structured form. The role of personal selling is taken by the relationship managers but mainly by the officers in branches. Only 25% of the banks use the personal selling strategy to market their products. Visiting corporate clients negotiating with them for the rate, presentation, attending client for both corporate and personal banking etc. are some job done by personal selling (Zahid 2008).

4 Financial Consumer Protection System

Financial customers may run into many sort of problems and can be overcharged or deceived. So there are some rules in Bangladesh that have been made in order to protect the financial consumers.

4.1 Rules for Consumers Rights Protection

Customers' right and protection and better service get due emphasis in the strategies of Bangladesh Bank (BB). As the regulator as well as the supervisor of the banks and financial institutions, Bangladesh Bank has established a full-fledged department known as "**Financial Integrity and Customer Services Department (FICSD)**". FICSD aims to attain the following objectives:

- To protect the interests of the customers related to Banks and Financial Institutions (FI) within the legal and regulatory frame-works.
- To redress the grievances of the customers and to attend the complaints received against Banks/FIs or its any official.
- To improve banker-customer relationship.
- To ensure the standard of customer-services of the Banks/FIs.

To ensure improved customer service, as part of FICSD, a 'Customer Interest Protection Centre' (CIPC) was established in the head office and branch offices of BB in March 2012. Since the establishment of CIPC, complaints are being lodged every working day through phone, fax, email, SMS, website and postal service from all over the country. Electronic complaint form is available in the Bangladesh Bank website to facilitate quick submission of complaints. To make CIPC service available, a hotline number "16236" was launched formally in January, 2012 and a huge awareness program was undertaken to familiarize this number. (The Financial Express 2016).

BB has also strengthened requirements for disclosing standardized, comparable pricing information on financial products. As a result, consumers have the scope to know simplified, adequate, and comparable information about the prices, terms and conditions, and inherent risks of financial products and services. Financial statements of all banks are now prepared in accordance with Bangladesh Accounting Standards (BAS) and Bangladesh Reporting Standards (BFRS). All the time, we are very closely monitoring the true and fair view of annual reports of banks for ensuring availability of proper information for stakeholders. Privacy, confidentiality, data integrity, and data protection of client information is also well regulated and enforced in the banking sctor, including the rapidly growing branchless banking sector.

On top of which, Bangladesh Bank's Department of Financial Institutions and Markets have set guidelines for financial consumer service design policies. Below are some of the points:

4.2 Policy for Financing Limit

The '*single party exposure*' limit as defined in the FI Act, 1993 is applicable for lending facility on any of the products or services. FIs should also consider the product/service concentration risk while making any financing decision. Credit facility to any single product under any of the broader categories shall not exceed 50% of total portfolio of the FI at any point of time. [Note: e.g. in case of term loan; Term loan (for corporate), Term Loan (for SME), Term Loan (for Agriculture), Term Loan (Syndication) shall be treated as different products].

However, this limit may be extended up to 80% only for those FIs which are providing credit solely to one particular specialized area such as SME, housing, agriculture, infrastructure development etc.

Policy on Insurance Coverage: Though not mandatory, but a minimum 100% Insurance coverage against each asset-side product is recommended.

Pricing Strategy: Is will calculate their own Cost of Fund using the Base Rate as per the instruction of BB. While calculating the Risk premium, an FI should consider the level of risks associated with the product/service along with the customer/investor profile. Therefore, Risk premium should be varied depending on the CRG of the loan/investment profile. FIs may determine the price of a liability-side product by considering prevailing market rate, demand-supply for liquidity, competitors' response, lending capability, overall economic trend, seasonal factors etc.

Tenure of Repayment: For the purpose of these guidelines, the tenure of repayment for any asset-side product will be determined depending upon the nature of the product and purpose of the business. For each product, FIs will fix up the maximum tenure.

Grace Period: Grace period should only be allowed to a new business project or a project of an existing business that will require some time to generate enough cash for repayment. The maximum limit of the grace period should not exceed one year from the date of final disbursement. In case of large industrial projects or syndication financing, grace period may be extended up to another 6 months. (Department of Financial Institutions and Markets 2013).

Financial Education Initiative: Consumer consciousness is however of utmost importance to protect their rights. In this perspective, I would like to emphasize on two issues. One is financial literacy and the other is demand driven research. Bangladesh Bank firmly believes that financial knowledge is a key to protect consumers' rights. As a result, a diverse financial education initiative has been undertaken in a rigorous manner by BB across the country. Creation of a dynamic and interactive web portal linked to BB website containing story books, games, videos, a calculator and informative writes up on different financial services; preparation of televisions commercials and radio broadcasting commercials; and awareness creating press layouts are included in this initiative. The recently concluded Banking Fair was one of the most successful Financial Literacy events of the banking sector. Thousands of consumers of financial services flocked into the fair to know about their rights and various aspects of financial products. The interactive session between customers and CEOs of banks was the most fruitful engagement for customer interest protection. Additionally, BB has identified 'strengthening financial education initiatives' as an important core objective in its recently announced strategic plan for 2015–2019. A very specific action plan as well as timeline for reaching this purpose has also been outlined in this document.

Because of the presence of these rules and their effective execution, financial customers can have their rights protected and save themselves from getting deceived through any way. These policies and guidelines have to be upheld in order to make financial customers more confident about their dealings with banks and financial institutions.

5 Special Financial Services and Systems

5.1 For the Elderly Group

For the elderly group, FCP agencies and financial institutions offer extra protections and hold relevant activities to get them aware of financial risks. Taking banking industry as an example, protections are provided in branch offices.

(1) *Service Counters*

Service counters usually offer special services and protections to the elders. The elders are especially taken care of, for they may be optically challenged or they can't express their need clearly. Separate service counters and chairs are set in banks. Sonali Bank for example, has separate stations for elderly consumers.

Lobby managers may check if elders run into telecom frauds because elders are prone to telecom frauds due to their unawareness of popular telecom tricks. In Bangladesh, there was a trick where unsolicited text messages promising huge wins on lotteries were sent around different telecom services. While many consumers were fishy and either ignored the message, or contacted their banks for more information, some fell victim to this scheme. Untold amounts were lost as elderly citizens sent their savings in the hopes winning it big. Thus, lobby managers and tellers have to pay attention to elders that seem flustered.

Being active and intelligent in the face of such occasions will bring about change in the industry. Warm, welcoming and patient lobby managers are important in this endeavor. The aim should be to simplify the services as much as possible for all user of the service.

(2) *Other FCP Activities*

Since the elderly have higher risks, it's necessary to hold more activities for them. Television commercials and shows that dissect the evils of these telecom frauds have helped raise awareness about the issue.

Most of the time, the target for these schemes are people who are uneducated, ignorant or are geographically immobile. Crime shows especially have done a tremendous job in increasing awareness by showcasing in an easily graspable manner, the various ways in which telecom frauds are committed. The audience base are usually the consumers themselves, or other individuals who are connected with the consumer and can spread the message via word of mouth.

5.2 *For the Poor Group*

Microfinance, or inclusive finance, the financial products and services for small business and low- and middle-income citizens. It includes savings, money transfer and insurance.

In Bangladesh and the greater world, the concept of micro finance has been revolutionized Dr. Yunus who worked closely with parties involved to create a model that benefitted the most vulnerable of individuals in the grass roots level. Micro finance has experienced more than ten years of experimentation and demonstration, both micro credits and micro insurance keep on developing and serve more and more people.

(1) *Micro Loans*

Micro loans are loans for low-income citizens and micro-enterprises. Micro loans, which often don't require collaterals and have higher rates, aim at offering financial services to the poor. Micro-credit associations help develop the service capability of micro loans. Microcredit in Bangladesh is still provided by large banking services. It still has not received a lot of popularity in the main banking sector but is increasingly popular with NGOs and other government bodies interested in financially activating the most vulnerable groups in our community. Grameen Bank especially has lead a pioneering role in popularizing and proving the concept of microfinance.

Many grassroots individuals have benefitted from microcredit. Women especially have a lot of microcredits and this was one of the main aims of the Grameen Institute. It introduces and promotes the concept of inclusive finance, maintains close relationship and cooperation with policy and regulatory departments of Bangladesh Bank. It makes efforts to enhance level and capacity of micro finance in Bangladesh by undertaking activities of policy advocacy, self-regulation etc.

(2) *Insurance*

Insurance is also an important part of micro finance. Though it's not as developed and popular as micro loans, it's been developing quickly. Some kinds of micro insurance products are available in the market now, including loan guarantee insurance, trade credit insurance, export credit insurance and so on. Insurance companies provide many different products to the people. Policies and regulation on part of the government have also further catalyzed the speed with which these services were made available to the mass population.

5.3 For the Young

The young people need some financial knowledge to get familiar with finance in their daily life and aware of financial frauds. Therefore there are various activities which can enrich their life and at the same time make them educated in finance.

(1) *Brochures*

Brochures are commonly used materials to help the young learn about finance. In Bangladesh, BB regularly prints a series of brochures for the public. The brochures for the young people has various illustrations to make them easier to understand and have useful topics, such as how the currency comes, what interest is, what insurance is, what mortgage is etc. to help the young people learn about finance, financial products and financial planning. Additionally, the brochures introduce several banking products, including their definition, category, characteristics, prices and samples.

(2) *Activities in School*

Institutions often hold activities inside the school, which can help students learn financial knowledge as well as enrich their life. When the finance education is combined with popular types of activities, students are more willing to join in and thus the learning effect is better.

Many academic syllabuses now have basic principles of money and other financial services as part of the course and this has lead to a general increase in the knowledge about the services available. Banks have also opened saving schemes that are joint accounts, to allow underage individuals to get a head start in life through saving and proper financial planning.

5.4 BKash

Another huge initiative to indirectly protect financial consumers by assisting them in safe and fast money transfer is bKash. The Brac Bank-initiated mobile banking service is at present the country's leading service provider in mobile banking. Dutch-Bangla Bank and Islami Bank Cash are next in line, after bKash, as the service-providers in mobile banking, in terms of volume of transactions, clientele coverage and number of personnel, directly or indirectly, involved in the process of making such services available to the people.

Bkash is a versatile platform that provides a safe, convenient way for unbanked Bangladeshis to transfer money. Since its inception in 2011, bKash has gained massive popularity all over Bangladesh. People use the service to pay from simple mobile bills, basic expenses to huge sums of money for business purposes. Bkash provides greater access to financial services, improves efficiency and generates new opportunities for income generation of low-income population.

5.5 Credit and Debit Cards

The term "Credit Card" generally means a plastic card issued by Scheduled Commercial Banks assigned to a Cardholder, with a credit limit, that can be used to purchase goods and services on credit or obtain cash advances. Debit card refers to a card issued by a bank allowing the holder to transfer money electronically to another bank account when making a purchase.

Standard Chartered Bank is the pioneer issuer of credit card in Bangladesh. In January 1997, the bank launched its local currency based credit cards from both visa and MasterCard. In the first few years, it got a huge response from the consumers because it reduced the risks of carrying cash and fosters expensive buying.

Bangladesh is a late comer in plastic money market. A few banks have introduced cards in early 2000s, but it gained momentum after 2005. Now 52 banks out of 57 in the country have cards as their products. According to Bangladesh Bank, there are nearly 7500 ATMs where around 350,000 transactions take place per day. The amount transacted through ATMs is TK 250 crore daily. Presently, there are 32,000 point of sales/transactions terminals where over 35,000 transactions take place per day. Nearly BDT. 30 crores are transacted through these points of transactions daily. Now more than 20 local private banks are in the cards business.

The following are some rules for the card issuers:

(1) *Protection of Customer Rights*:

1. The Card Issuer shall not reveal any information relating to customers without obtaining specific consent of the Customer.
2. Unsolicited loans or other facilities shall not be offered to the Customers based on the Credit Card.

(2) *Dispute Resolutions*:

1. The Card Issuer shall have an appropriate dispute resolution mechanism and service procedure and shall resolve the same within a minimum period.
2. The Card Issuer shall also have a mechanism to escalate automatically unresolved complaints from a call center to higher authorities and the details of such mechanism should be put in public domain through their website.
3. The name, designation, address and contact number of important executives as well as the dispute resolution officer of the Card Issuer should be displayed on the website. There should be a system of acknowledging customers' complaints for follow up, such as complaint number/docket number, even if the complaints are received on phone.
4. The Card Issuer shall resolve the disputed transaction of the Customer promptly and as per the franchise rules of VISA, Master Card, or any other international Card company/association, taking into account the nature of the transaction, distances, time zone etc.

(3) *Fraud Control*:

1. Card Issuer should set up internal control systems to combat frauds and actively participate in fraud prevention committee's/task forces which formulate laws to prevent frauds and take proactive fraud control and enforcement measures.
2. Card Issuing Banks are authorized to block a lost card immediately on being informed by the Customer and formalities, and inform it immediately to Bangladesh Bank.
3. Banks may consider introducing, at the option of the customers, an insurance cover to take care of the liabilities arising out of lost cards.
4. Employees those are specialized in fraud monitoring and investigation are to be placed in risk management department.

(4) *The right to impose penalty*:

Bangladesh Bank reserves the right to impose any penalty on card issuing Scheduled Banks under the provisions of the Bank Company Act, 1991 (Amended up to 2013) for violation of any clause of these guidelines.

6 Protection of Customers in the Capital Market

There are two stock exchanges in Bangladesh, namely Dhaka Stock Exchange (DSE) and Chittagong Stock Exchange (CSE). All the securities and trading activities of the country is looked after by a body known as **Bangladesh Securities and Exchange Commission (BSEC)**. The Bangladesh Securities and Exchange Commission (BSEC) was established on 8th June, 1993 as the regulator of the country's capital market through enactment of the Securities and Exchange Commission Act 1993. Through an amendment of the Securities and Exchange Commission Act, 1993, on December 10, 2012, its name has been changed as Bangladesh Securities and Exchange Commission from previous Securities and Exchange Commission. The Commission consists of a Chairman and four Commissioners who are appointed for fulltime by the government for a period of four years and their appointment can be renewed only for further one term. The Commission has overall responsibility to formulate securities legislation and to administer as well. The Commission, comprised of 17 separate departments, is a statutory body, and attached to the Ministry of Finance.

BSEC aims to protect the investors of securities, develop and maintain a fair transparent securities market and ensure proper issuance of securities and compliance of laws. This is achieved through the following activities:

- Regulating the business of the Stock Exchanges or any other securities market.
- Registering and regulating the business of stock-brokers, sub-brokers, share transfer agents, merchant bankers and managers of issues, trustee of trust deeds, registrar of an issue, underwriters, portfolio managers, investment advisers and other intermediaries in the securities market.
- Registering, monitoring and regulating of collective investment scheme including all forms of mutual funds.
- Monitoring and regulating all authorized self-regulatory organizations in the securities market.
- Prohibiting fraudulent and unfair trade practices relating to securities trading in any securities market.
- Promoting investors' education and providing training for intermediaries of the securities market.
- Prohibiting insider trading in securities.
- Regulating the substantial acquisition of shares and take-over of companies.
- Undertaking investigation and inspection, inquiries and audit of any issuer or dealer of securities, the Stock Exchanges and intermediaries and any self-regulatory organization in the securities market.
- Conducting research and publishing information.

6.1 Departments Under BSEC

(1) *Administration and Finance (A&F) Department*:

Administration and Finance department deals with human resources, all sorts of logistic activities, to carry out day to day executive functions as well as finance and accounts. As part of Administrative functions, administration officials performed activities regarding correspondence with concerned ministries, recruitment and training of human resources, procurement, motor pool etc. In connection with financial activities, finance and accounts officials prepare budget and financial statement of the Commission, collect revenue and disburse payments, maintain Gratuity/Pension fund, General and Contributory Provident Fund etc.

(2) *Capital Issue Department (Initial Public Offering has been renamed)*:

Capital Issue Department of the Commission accords consent to issue equity and debt securities through initial public offer and also other than public offer. Public and private limited companies are required to take consent of the Commission for raising capital whose capital exceeds Tk. 10 and 100 million respectively. This department also approves the issuance of listed companies' rights share and repeat public offer.

Another department related to capital market is *Capital Market Regulatory Reforms and Compliance (CMRRC) Department*. CMRRC department drafts amendments of securities laws, suggests reforms of the market and provides clarifications.

(3) *Central Depository System (CDS) Department*:

Central Depository System (CDS) department supervises activities of Central Depository Bangladesh Limited (CDBL), activities of depository participants, dematerialization of listed companies' shares under depository system, issue and transfer of securities in dematerialized form, beneficiary owners (BO) accounts, and issue order/notification etc. related to depository system, under the Depository Act, 1999, the Depository Regulation, 2000 and Depository (User) Regulation 2003.

(4) *Chairman's Office*:

Function of the department is to conduct Commission Meeting and Coordination Meeting.

(5) *Corporate Finance Department (CFD)*:

The Corporate Finance Department (CFD) supervises and monitors the listed companies after issuance of primary shares in light of the securities laws. Activities of the department are oversight and reporting on issuers of listed securities related to on time submission of audited financial statements, half yearly financial statements and annual reports/minutes, examination of the aforesaid financial statements and reports/minutes, appointment of statutory auditors in compliance with securities laws, utilization of fund (IPO and Rights), compliance of conditions of notification regarding corporate governance, compliance of other securities laws, supervision and follow-up of the special audits conducted by the Commission, and review of existing securities laws, rules and regulations concerning CFD and proposed amendments thereto.

(6) *Enforcement Department*:

Under the Securities laws, the Enforcement Department takes legal measures including imposition of penalty against those who breach/violate securities laws in consideration of nature of crimes they commit. Prior to taking measures, it follows due process that includes giving the accused an opportunity of being heard. All departments of the Commission send referral to Enforcement Department if they see any violation of securities laws.

(7) *Financial Literacy Department*:

Financial Literacy department deals with training, education and allied matter related to Nationwide Financial Literacy Program of BSEC.

The vision of the Financial Literacy Program is to provide financial education to each and every people of Bangladesh. More precisely, BSEC wants to make individuals understood at their level of needs, the role of money in their lives, the need and use of savings, the advantages of using formal financial sectors, various ways to convert their savings into investments, develop self-protection through understanding risks and a realistic recognition of the attributes of these options.

Financial literacy gives the twin benefit of protecting from financial frauds as well as planning for financially secured future. Financial literacy gives consumers the necessary knowledge and skills required to assess the suitability of various financial products and investment opportunities available in the financial market.

(8) *International Affairs Department*:

International Affairs Department (IAD) is responsible for the following activities;

(a) Maintaining relationship with all the capital market regulators of the world;
(b) Maintaining constant liaison with the International Organization of Securities Commissions (IOSCO), including all its Committees and Working Groups;
(c) All matters related to IOSCO Multilateral Memorandum of Understanding (MMoU).

(9) *Law Department*:

Functions of Legal department are assisting the lawyers engaged by the Commission to conduct the cases filed by or against the Commission in different courts, preparing written objection and statement on cases filed against the Commission, preparing para wise comments on writ petition filed against the Commission, signing case related documents with affidavit before the concerned officer of the court, preparing plaint/requisition for certificate cases, filing certificate cases and conducting those to realize the penalty imposed by the Commission, vetting the letters, orders, directives sent from different departments of the Commission and providing legal opinion on different matters sent from different departments of the Commission.

(10) *Management Information Systems (MIS) Department*:

Functions of MIS department are development of automation for assisting different departments' activities, development of capital market monitoring system based on computerized data analysis, informing all about securities laws and other related matters through its website www.secbd.org, planning, operating, administering and supporting IT infrastructure at SEC and assisting the Commission in related areas.

(11) *Mutual Fund and Special Purpose Vehicle*:

Mutual Fund and Special Purpose Vehicle Department deals with registration of mutual funds and special purpose vehicles, their monitoring, supervision and compliance, and any other function related to them.

(12) *Registration and Licensing Department*:

Registration Department looks after registration and renewal of all stock brokers, stock dealers, merchant bankers, credit rating agencies, depository participants, authorized representatives, asset management companies, trustees, custodians, and permission regarding branch opening of stock brokers. Licensing of intermediaries help the Commission to discharge its oversight functions more effectively.

(13) *Research and Development (R&D) Department*:

Research and Development Department of the Commission conducts investors' education program twice a month for the general investors, organize capital market related presentation/seminar for various government and non-government organizations, deals with the Commission's various publications like annual report (Bangla and English), quarterly report(Bangla and English), quartery Bangla news letter-Parikrama, furnishes various reports and information to the government and other institutions including Ministry of Finance and different regulatory authorities.

(14) *Supervision and Regulation of Markets and Issuer Companies (SRMIC)*:

SRMIC Department supervises stock exchanges and deals with complaints lodged against issuer companies as per securities laws. The functions include monitoring of declaration about sale/purchase/transfer of securities by the sponsor/director of the listed companies, monitoring of monthly shareholding position of sponsors/directors, monitoring of disclosure of price sensitive information of listed companies, approval of transfer of shares of listed companies outside the stock exchange, monitoring all activities of stock exchanges (except securities transactions), taking effective measure to address complaints against issuer, monitoring of AGMs/EGMs and dividend payments for all listed companies.

(15) *Supervision and Regulation of Intermediaries (SRI) Department*:

Function of SRI Department is supervision of performing activities of merchant bankers, stock dealers/stock brokers, depository participants, security custodian banks, merchant bankers, security lenders and borrowers and other market intermediaries.

(16) *Surveillance Department*:

Surveillance Department keeps vigil on securities transactions in Bangladesh. To identify unlawful trading activities, surveillance department watch and analyze the trading in both the stock exchanges through on-line and off-line surveillance system and prepare daily, weekly and monthly trade reports at the end of trading by pointing market condition and observation of surveillance officials. In order to ensure proper compliance of securities related laws, surveillance department conducts investigation and enquiry against involving parties regarding market manipulation, insider trading and other malpractices, if any. The main purpose of the said activities is to ensure fair-trading and build-up confidence of investors in the securities market.

6.2 ADB Project: Improvement of Capital Market Governance

The project is a loan project financed by Asian Development Bank under the Improvement of Capital Market and Insurance Governance Project ADB TA Loan-2232 BAN. Main objective of the project is development of the capital market in Bangladesh.

7 Addressing Market Issues

7.1 How to Enhance Simplicity of Products?

Financial markets of Bangladesh have changed over the years. Many new products and services are being introduced every year. The face of the market now is vastly different from the rudimentary times when it was just conceived. Finance innovation shows up in form of new financial products. However, with more complex financial products and investment portfolios, systematic risk has become a more serious problem that could ruin the finance world in just a few days.

Entirely new financial products have the problem of inexperience. Rules and regulations, even with the best of intentions, may fall short of their objectives because the financial product in question is relatively new. It takes time for financial services to mature and the full extent of their influence is known.

The 2008 financial crisis is exactly an example illustrating the disadvantage of various financial products which are too complicated. Therefore, how to enhance simplicity of products in the market is an important issue for consumer protection.

Financial products are unique and every product has its own unique forms of treatment. However, there are common elements to all financial products as listed in the following.

(1) *Issuer*

Each financial product must be sold by its issuer. Bond is issued by the debtor, stock is issued by the enterprises. Issuers make income through selling financial products to others. At the same time the issuer will assume the obligations that come with the financial income. In order to ensure the performance of these obligations, the majority of financial products must meet certain conditions and accept supervision from the government and investors after the issuance.

(2) *Buyer*

Investors do not have the freedom to indiscriminately buy the financial services that are available in the market. Some markets (such as interbank lending markets) are only open to a small proportion of financial institutions. Therefore, investors should in advance know whether they have the right to buy a certain financial products. Business should also know the possible buyers before issuing a financial product so as to estimate the potential funding.

(3) *Duration*

Financial products have maturity, which varies from a relatively short term to a very long term. The duration of financial products can be classified into limited and unlimited terms. Most of the bonds and all money market products are limited in a period of time, but the stock has no time limit. Both of the issuers and the investors should choose the appropriate period of financial products according to their own needs. Additionally, they must consider the fluctuations of interest rates in the future.

(4) *Price and Yield*

Price is the core element of a financial product because the investor's investment is equal to the price of the product. Yield is another core element of a financial product, which indicates the revenue of the product to its owners. Financial products have two main revenue streams: one is interest income, and another is capital gain.

(5) *Risk*

Risk is generally regarded as a possibility of loss. The investment risk of financial products usually result from future uncertainty. Investment opportunities in the market are a combination of risks and benefits. To obtain a high income, investors must bear high risk because high income is usually accompanied with high risk.

According to the five characteristics of financial products indicated in the above, product simplicity enhancements should aim to make the aforementioned attributes more effective. Greater concern should be placed on the transactions involving financial services. Special terminology make it tough for consumers to understand financial services. A lucrative product can be misunderstood simply because consumers do not understand the technical jargon related to the industry.

7.2 How to Reduce Price Dispersion While Upholding Price-Quality Competition?

The financial market of Bangladesh is a booming one. The market itself is relatively young and is venturing into new territories of services that are deemed necessary. The commerce ministry and Bangladesh Bank together have brought revolutionary changes in the market to help it diversify its product portfolio in a controlled and safe manner.

History has shown us that runaway commerce can be devastating. Unfettered speculation can lead to inflated prices and absurd nominal portfolios with little real assets. In the end, it leads to dead investments that are poured into bloated stocks with high uncertainty. In 2006 Bangladesh faced a similar disaster where rampant speculation and failed DSE safeguards lead to thousands of investors losing value on their investments.

The current financial industry is countering competition. Lots of new but similar products are being issued by different financial institutions. In order to occupy the market, these companies try to attract investors by means of price reduction. We need to understand the structural problems and institutional deficiencies in this competitive state, and find the corresponding treatment methods. If this problem is not solved, it is bound to affect the healthy development of Bangladesh's economy.

In fact, reasons for this vicious competition in the Bangladesh financial sector are very simple.

Firstly, Bangladeshi finance is not only affected by the bad habits of the international financial community, but also due to a structural imbalance. Bangladeshi financial products lack a more effective and safe product innovation. Secondly, the performance incentive mechanism is unique and irreplaceable.

Firms compete in a zero sum environment and fight to take control of the consumer base. Consumers also lack the technical and academic dispositions required to effectively appraise the value of similar competing financial services. Institutions are used to robbing other agencies of clients on account of directivity and effectiveness. The "index economy" with Bangladeshi characteristics is also an important reason for Bangladesh's GDP index to go up in last 10 years. To better protect the rights of the financial consumers, actions must be taken by the financial authorities.

First of all, if people here can change the "xenophile" habit of thinking, then we can reduce the pressure of private banks. Many domestic banks have one or two foreign banks as their strategic partners. In fact, the contribution of these private banks to Bangladesh is significant.

Investments made from foreign sources and funding for entrepreneurial and industrial ventures have seen an increasingly large share of private funds being mobilised. They also perform better in performance indexes, namely debt retrieval and other such performance metrics. Foreign banks make the use of Bangladesh banks to improve its fame and market share in Bangladesh. In view of this, the Bangladesh banks can learn more technical skills and management methods from foreign banks and benefit from each other. Instead of focusing attention on domestic market and competition, Bangladesh bank is supposed to put more emphasis on international market.

The Bank heist of nearly a 100 million BDT last year was especially reminiscent of how far the country lag behind the rest of the world in terms of banking security. Technology is constantly evolving to make banking more secure and financial services more reliable all the time. Associating with foreign banks that use these technological revolutions in their operations can have a learning effect. Eventually, the aim is to have Bangladesh Bank use the same technology and achieve an unparalleled security in banking.

Next, instead of chasing high income by means of cutting price, financial institutions are advised to emphasize on risk management. It is common sense that high profit is always accompanied by high risks. Based on systematic risk management, it would be obvious to discover that risk management could improve the quality of asset and consequently enhance competitive power. In the long term, giving up purely chasing turnover is a more rational transformation for most of the financial institutions in Bangladesh.

Plagiarism is another well-known problem over the Bangladesh financial markets. It is important and effective if the government could stipulate specific laws with regards to plagiarizing. For example, to launch more regulations on new thriving products, as indicated in IDRA 2010.

References

Bangladesh Bank Financial Stability Department, BBFSDa. (2014, March). *Financial Stability Report.* Retrieved from Bangladesh Bank, Central Bank of Bangladesh: www.bb.org.bd

Bangladesh Bank Financial Stability Department, BBFSDb. (2014, March). *Scheduled Bank Statistics.* Retrieved from Bangladesh Bank, Central Bank of Bangladesh: www.bb.org.bd

Bangladesh Bureau of Statistics, BBS. (2014, March). *Rural Credit Survey.* Retrieved from Bangladesh Bureau of Statistics, Government of the People's Republic of Bangladesh: http://www.bbs.gov.bd/

Bangladesh Bureau of Statistics, BBS. (2015, March). *Bangladesh Vitality Reports.* Retrieved from Bangladesh Bureau of Statistics, Government of the People's Republic of Bangladesh: http://www.bbs.gov.bd/

BSEC, (2017). Bangladesh Securities and Exchange Commission, Notice, Additional Supplement, Bangladesh Gazette, June 2017, Government of Bangladesh.

IDRA. (2010, March). *Draft Regulations.* Retrieved from Insurance Development & Regulatory Authority Bangladesh: http://www.idra.org.bd/

IDRA. (2015, March). *IDRA Profile.* Retrieved from Insurance Development & Regulatory Authority Bangladesh: http://www.idra.org.bd/

Greg Chen. (n.d.). *The Growth of Mobile Financial Services in Bangladesh.* Retrieved from CGAP: http://www.cgap.org/blog/growth-mobile-financial-services-bangladesh

Mutual Trust Bank, MTB. (2015, October). Mutual Trust Monthly Business Review. *MTBiz.*

The Financial Express. (2016, January 4). Ensuring consumer protection in banking.

Muhammad Ziaulhaq Mamun is a professor at the Institute of Business Administration (IBA), University of Dhaka, Bangladesh. He did his Bachelor in Civil Engineering, Master of Business Administration (MBA) in Management Science, MBA in general Management, and Ph.D. in Urban Development Management. He is a Post-doctoral Fellow of Urban Environmental Management Program of the Asian Institute of Technology, Bangkok. With more than 30 years teaching and research experience, he has specialization in the areas of risk, disaster, quality, and operations management. He has authored four books, edited one book and contributed in nine book sections. Dr. Mamun has over 145 publications (72 journal articles and 73 conference proceedings) in planning and management related areas. Dr. Mamun is awarded the most prestigious "UGC (University Grants Commission, Bangladesh) Award 2013" for his academic excellence in the area of Economics and Business Studies. He is two times winner of the most prestigious University of Dhaka Ibrahim Memorial Gold medal for his outstanding academic and research work.

Chapter 4
Financial Consumer Protection in Canada: Triumphs and Tribulations

Robert R. Kerton and Idris Ademuyiwa

> *The imbalance of power between consumers and providers is particularly marked in financial markets. In part, this is due to the complex nature of financial products and services which often have a deferred expected pay-off to the consumer and, in many cases, are purchased only rarely.*
>
> World Bank, 2012.

1 Financial Consumers in Canada

Financial consumers are individuals or economic agents who purchase or use financial products and services with the intention of improving their well-being. Historically, services were supplied by trusted informal sources (e.g.: family, religious group or informal co-operatives). Over the last century financial consumers have made most purchases from formal intermediaries in the Canadian financial services sector. More recently, financial consumers have engaged in opportunities not under state regulation including direct digital transactions like crowdsourcing and consumer-to-consumer exchanges.

Four factors are key to understanding financial consumers protection in Canada:

(i) Compared to most countries, Canada was relatively early in establishing a specific agency to protect financial consumers. The Financial Consumer Agency of Canada (FCAC) was created in 2001[1] in time to address the worldwide crisis of 2007–08. This type of agency is exceptionally important whenever consumers are not protected by the vigorous rivalry assumed by perfect competition. The FCAC, like most of Canada's financial regulators has provided more triumph than tribulation.

R. R. Kerton (✉)
University of Waterloo, Waterloo, Canada
e-mail: kerton@uwaterloo.ca

I. Ademuyiwa
Centre for International Governance Innovation (CIGI), Waterloo, Canada

© Springer Nature Singapore Pte Ltd. 2018

T.-J. Chen (ed.), *An International Comparison of Financial Consumer Protection*,
https://doi.org/10.1007/978-981-10-8441-6_4

(ii) Secondly, the historical development of legislation to protect financial consumers is based on four financial sectors regulated under the *Bank Act*,[2] *Cooperative Credit Associations Act*,[3] *Insurance Companies Act*,[4] *Trust and Loan Companies Act*,[5] *The Investment Canada Act*,[6] and under other rules providing incentives and boundaries for financial institutions in Canada. These include accounting regulations, rules to limit self-dealing, to require diversification, to protect national security etc.

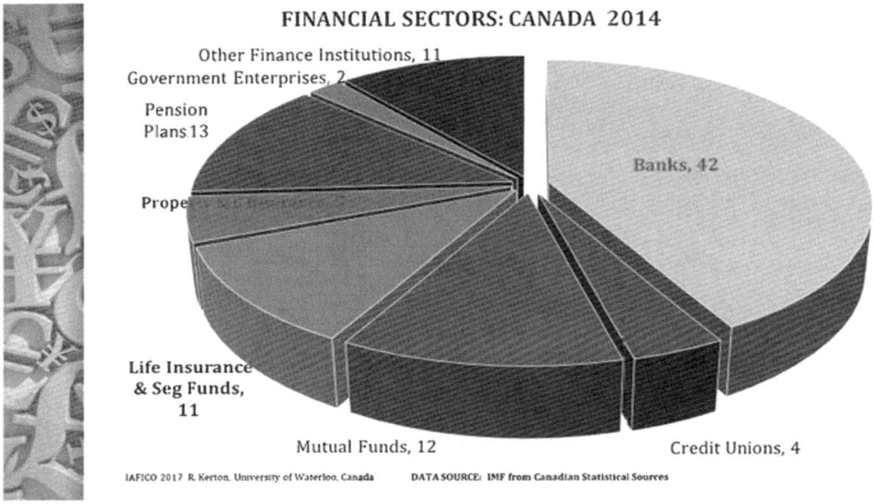

This legislative focus on suppliers was called the "four pillars" of finance in Canada. To consumers, the term "four pastures" seemed more apt because the firms, like cows in each fenced-off sector, chomped contentedly on the grass in its protected area without challenging any of the fences.[7] From the 1950s to the 1980s, the grass behind each fence looked especially green. By the 1990s, deregulation eliminated fences—a policy aimed at increasing competition. Instead, a wave of mergers and takeovers led to big banks dominating the trust pasture and the investment field. The result is now six giant bank-based financial conglomerates. Concentration also took place *within* banking: those six now handle more than 93% of transactions of the banking sector.

(iii) Thirdly, Canada has ten provinces and a financial firm can be incorporated under federal laws or under alternative *provincial* legislation. As a result, Canada has at least fourteen agencies regulating financial services. Efforts to harmonize financial regulations have long been underway, but progress has been made at a glacial pace. One result of this complex web of rules is high compliance costs for firms. Less noticed are equally devastating effects on (a) consumers, and (b) on market efficiency. For redress, disappointed consumers need to know where to obtain justice—a very difficult task. This is illustrated nicely by the experience of Margaret Stanstead, a local volunteer for the Consumer's Association of Canada (Manitoba) in the city of Winnipeg in the 1970s—prime time of the consumer movement. She single-handedly answered 5,385 phone calls for consumer assistance before apologizing that she "never had the strength to be active." She went on to handle more than 35,000 calls. The bulk of her work related to helping consumers overcome the complexity of Canada's redress systems by directing them to the correct agency. Decades later, consumers still face a system assessed by the Competition Bureau in 2017 as "complex, prescriptive and fragmented".[8] High search costs make it more difficult to assess choices, switch suppliers, *and* to seek redress.[9] Canada's complicated and uneven financial regulation is unmistakably a source of tribulation.

(iv) Fourthly, the federal *Competition Act*[10] contains *Canada-wide* regulations for truthful marketing (market conduct rules), plus measures to counter monopoly. Competition regulation is national in scope and applies to practices of both traditional services and to digital offerings. The key issue for the financial services sector—and the basis for regulation—is quality.[11] There is a reason why market conduct rules provide the key to the success of FinTech: quality is the vital component of innovation and fintech. If consumers can detect quality, they move to the sellers with the best offerings. When the financial market rewards *the right innovations*, it improves the lives of consumers at all income levels.

1.1 Economic Situation of Financial Consumers in Canada

Canada's financial sector is especially important to the economy: by 2015, it accounted for 7.0% of GDP, one of the highest proportions in the G7. The sector provides over 791,000 jobs, which constitutes 4.4% of all jobs in Canada.[12] The number will still be impressive even if adjusted downward to correct for Canada's slow movement to share technology in selling real estate,[13] and Canada's lack of transparency about hidden fees in selling mutual funds.

The demographic dimension of Canadian consumers provides an understanding of the scope for consumer protection. Table 1 shows the dynamics of the Canadian population over time. One striking feature is the continuous decline in the proportion of young people and the increase in the fraction of older consumers. This trend is particularly evident with the seniors whose share of the population has increased from about 9% in 1980 to about 16.5% by 2016. It is projected to increase to between 23 and 25% by 2036. The working population is stable at over 65% and is projected to remain around this figure. It is expected that there will be an increase in financial services designed for seniors: life and health insurance, retirement savings plans, and wealth management. Vulnerability of seniors may require a

Table 1 Demographic composition of canadians (1980–2016)

	1980	1990	2000	2010	2016
Total population	24,515,667	27,691,138	30,685,730	34,005,274	36,286,425
Children (0–14) %	22.7	20.7	19.2	16.5	16.1
Teenagers (15–19) %	9.9	7.0	6.8	6.6	5.7
Young adults (20–39) %	33.7	34.4	29.6	27.2	27.5
Middle adults (40–64) %	24.3	26.6	31.8	35.5	34.2
Seniors (65 and above) %	9.2	11.0	12.1	14.1	16.5

Source Statistic Canada, CANSIM Table 051-0001

specific consumer protection mechanism like the extended 'cooling off' period recommended by the OECD.[14] Recent immigrants, persons in isolated areas and other vulnerable consumers may need additional consumer protection.

In terms of income structure, Table 2 shows the aggregate income structure for Canadian tax filers and their dependents. A majority (over 72%) derives income from employment earnings and a similar proportion enjoys some income from at least one form of government transfer. Investment income is also a source of income to over 30% of tax filers while other forms of incomes account for less. The table also shows that majority of Canadians increasingly earn more than the low-income cutoff (LICO), which was about $24,300 for one person in the more urbanized areas of the country in 2014. Furthermore, the median income has been increasing and is significantly higher than the LICO.

The demographic structure shows a steady increase in the fraction of seniors. That fact demonstrates a need for effective and efficient consumer decisions by the senior age cohort. This would be easier to realize if financial services providers operated in a competitive market. The evidence on the degree of competition in various sectors is compelling: Statistics Canada recently concluded a longer term view of profitability in Canada with "The companies that manage Canadians'

Table 2 Income structure (2010–2014)

	2010	2011	2012	2013	2014
Total income ($ million)	25.22	25.60	25.80	26.17	26.62
Total employment income ($ million)	18.41	18.77	18.94	19.13	19.38
Investment income ($ million)	7.67	7.75	7.74	7.83	7.86
Total government transfers ($ million)	18.75	18.76	17.75	18.01	18.51
Private pensions ($ million)	3.66	3.76	3.87	3.98	4.10
Registered retirement savings plan (RRSP)	0.39	0.39	0.40	0.40	0.41
Other income ($ million)	5.25	5.05	5.06	5.14	5.17
Percent with $25,000 or more	55.9	57.0	58.5	59.1	60.0
Median income ($)	29,250	30,180	31,320	32,020	32,790

Source Statistic Canada, CANSIM Table 111-0007 and Table 111-0008

money made up the industry with the highest profit margins."[15] Competition is determined by: (a) **enabling measures** like transparency of documents, ready access to redress, consumer education and fair rules for market conduct; (b) overall **competition policy** as well as **sector-specific protection policies** like licensing and restrictive charter rules, deposit insurance, risk ratings of consumers and of financial institutions, including prudential policies affecting down payments, lending limits, capital ratios, and reserves. Next, we examine the structure and performance of the major industries in the Canadian financial service sector.

2 Dimensions of Financial Services Sector in Canada

2.1 The Banking Industry

Chartered Banks dominate the Canadian financial services sector and are crucial to the growth of the economy. The largest banks operate under the exclusive jurisdiction of the federal government. Federal regulation covers prudential security under the *Bank Act*[16] through the Office of the Superintendent of Financial Institutions (OSFI). They belong to one of the following three groups: Schedule I banks [30 chartered domestic banks]; Schedule II banks [24 foreign bank subsidiaries under the control of their eligible foreign institutions but regulated by the *Bank Act]; and* Schedule III banks [28 foreign bank branches which are restricted to working with deposits above $150,000; and 3 foreign bank branches whose activities are restricted to lending]. Both Schedule I and II banks receive deposits and engage in private and commercial lending while Schedule III banks are for sophisticated participants who need less supervisory protection.

2.2 Measuring Soundness and Stability

Canada's banking industry remains distinctively sound. *The World Economic Forum's Global Competitiveness Report of 2015 ranked Canadian banks as the soundest in the world for the eighth consecutive year.* Table 3 shows the recent impressive performance of the six major banks (which hold about 93% total bank assets in Canada). The evidence reveals that between 2014 and 2015, average consolidated revenue of the "Big Six" rose by 4.3% from about C$20.5 billion to about C$21.4 billion. Meanwhile, their average net income increased from about C$5.5 billion to about C$5.8 billion representing an increase of about 4.8%. Their average efficiency rate stood at about 58.4%, and average non-interest expense or operating cost increased from about C$11.6–C$12.4 billion in the same period. This rise in operating cost partly explains the modest but continuous reduction in return on equity from about 17.1% in 2012 to 15.6% in 2015.[17] This return on equity is

Table 3 Selected performance indicators of the "Big Six" Canadian Banks

Banks	Years	Market capitalization ($ billions)	Net income ($ millions)	Consolidated revenue ($ millions)	Total non-intérêt expansés ($ millions)	Efficiency rate (%)
BMO	2014	53.00	4,333	16,718	10,921	65.3
	2015	48.90	4,405	18,135	12,182	64.2
BNS	2014	84.00	7,298	23,604	12,601	52.6
	2015	74.00	7,213	24,049	13,041	53.4
CIBC	2014	40.80	3,215	13,376	8,525	63.7
	2015	39.80	3,590	13,856	8,861	63.9
NBC	2014	17.30	1,538	5,464	3,423	58.6
	2015	14.60	1,619	5,746	3,665	58.6
RBC	2014	117.40	9,004	34,108	17,661	51.8
	2015	107.90	10,026	35,321	18,638	52.8
TD	2014	102.40	7,883	29,961	16,496	55.1
	2015	99.60	8,024	31,426	18,073	57.5
"Big Six" Average	2014	69.15	5,545.17	20,538.5	11,604.5	57.85
	2015	64.13	5,812.83	21,422.17	12,410.0	58.40
Average return of equity (all six in %)		**2012** 17.1	**2013** 16.2	**2014** 16.6	**2015** 15.6	

Source PWC Perspectives on the Canadian Banking Industry (2014 and 2016 Edition). The "Big Six" banks include The Bank of Montreal (BMO), The Bank of Nova Scotia (BNS), Canadian Imperial Bank of Commerce (CIBC), National Bank of Canada (NBC), Royal Bank of Canada (RBC) and Toronto-Dominion Bank (TD)

twice the level of international peer banks.[18] Long term profits of 15% or more are higher than a competitive level, a factor that normally attracts new entrants.

Perhaps the strongest measure of the soundness of Canada's banks is their performance during the worldwide financial meltdown in 2007–08. Not one of Canada's banks needed to be rescued. Another measure is the regularity of dividend payments. The CIBC, for example, has not missed a regular dividend since 1868.[19] This is a remarkable achievement. Yet given that in the years since 2008, return on equity of Canadian banks has been at or above 15% compared to eight or 9% for international peer banks,[20] consumers may well ask if *too much* attention is paid by regulators to 'safety and soundness' and not enough to competition, especially to higher prices paid by Canadian consumers—and by firms that are too small to use disintermediation by raising funds directly. Canadian banks make significant contributions to the economy in terms of output, employment and tax revenue. That said, the industry accounts for close to 4% of the Gross Domestic Product (over $65 billion in 2015) and employs over 280 thousand Canadians. The top six banks operate in more than 65 countries and have more than 3700 branches outside

Canada.[21] These same banks paid an annual average of about $7.8 billion in taxes per year between 2012 and 2015.

The structure of the Canadian banking industry is important. The *Big Six* behave like an unorganized collusive oligopoly—though firms frequently act more like they are under monopolistic competition—where banks offer differentiated products.[22] Eggert[23] finds that although banks strategize toward product differentiation, their products and services remain largely similar. The *Big Six* took advantage of amendments to the *Bank Act* (made in the 1980s and 1990s) to increase their size relative to all other financial institutions. As noted, amendments removed regulatory "fences" and allowed banks to enter the securities and trust businesses leading to the acquisition of the major trust and brokerage firms, some of which were weak or failing.

Of importance to regulators and policymakers, is whether the structure of the industry leads to soundness and efficiency or promotes competitiveness in the industry over time. Canadian banks, as noted, are widely adjudged to be sound, lessening worries about sudden failure. It is evident that those regulators who are obliged to focus on soundness are not concerned by "unorganized collusive" behavior if it aids soundness and safety. Consumers' priorities extend beyond soundness whenever reliability is achieved, in part, through high fees and interest charges. Further, firms using financial services point out forcefully that their competitiveness is compromised by oligopolistic bank prices[24] … and knock on effects ultimately harm consumers.

A study conducted by Bain and Companies Inc. for Power Financial Corporation in 2003 found that the leverage enjoyed by the bigger banks resulted in higher prices for consumers relative to the 1980s.[25] Interest rate spreads were higher and bank charges and other fees were increasing. It is instructive to note that the *Big Six* have more dominance now than in the early 2000s when the Bain study was conducted. A more recent study—conducted in 2014 by the Financial Consumer Agency of Canada—found that bank price increases on normal monthly chequing plans have been moderate, whereas the charges associated with variable fees have increased significantly.[26]

Many agencies have claimed credit for the stability of the Canadian sector relative to the 2007–08 when other countries suffered from a collapse of major financial institutions. Reasons include monetary policy, interest rate policy, differences in supervision, and, in the case of the U.S., a large shadow financial sector —largely unregulated. Much of that is true, though possibly overemphasized by analysts in close contact with their own part of the grand financial elephant. Underemphasized is the key role in the crisis was played by a *malevolent innovation*, making the point that it is naïve to believe every innovation is good. The business model of some innovative firms was to slice and dice packages of low quality mortgages, have them graded incorrectly, then sell the packages to sophisticated buyers as valued assets. The remarkably low quality of mortgage-backed securities and asset-backed commercial paper was certainly not transparent: quality was not detected by financial sector experts.

The measurement of price changes from 2000 on is fraught with difficulty. Some consumer advocates objected to new or increased bank fees, and FCAC research supports that.[27] If market competition has not been providing consumer protection from price increases, the recent proliferation of financial technology firms (FinTechs) holds special promise for Canadian financial consumers.

2.3 The Insurance Industry

For constitutional reasons, health insurance is mostly handled by public plans managed by each province. Total health spending in 2016 was C$228 billion or C$6,300. per person.[28] The USA spends nearly twice as much per person. Canada's spending on health is like the Netherlands, France and Australia based on expenditure per person of about 11% of GDP.

The private insurance industry employs about 150,000 workers and consists of two parts: the life and health insurance component and property and casualty insurance section. The life and health sector paid C$ 84 billion in benefits in 2015 and held C$ 760 billion in assets.[29] Payouts for the property and casualty sector amounted to C$32 billion in 2015 and invested assets were about C$115 billion. Canadian firms selling life and health policies operate in more than 20 countries serving more than 45 million consumers. Three firms, Sun Life Financial, Manulife Financial and Great-West Life are among the largest 15 such firms in the world. If foreign sales are used as a metric, Canada's life and health firms have earned more competitive success abroad than other Canadian financial institutions. Income from foreign insurance sales accounts for 42% of all firms' worldwide insurance revenue compared to 29% for all Canadian banks.[30]

Provincial and federal governments share jurisdiction over private insurance companies. The federal government's Office of the Superintendent of Financial Institutions (OSFI) regulates the *solvency* and financial soundness of domestic insurers—and the solvency of authorized branches of foreign insurers. The *provinces* regulate insurers' operations and several aspects of market conduct. In the unlikely event of insolvency of an insurer, two industry-financed organizations provide recovery of reasonable level of claims of policy holders in both the life and properties insurance components. They are *Assuris* and the Property and Casualty Insurance Compensation Corporation (PACICC). Most of their activity is at the provincial level.

The Property and Casualty Insurance industry (P&C) is somewhat competitive in sub-sectors covering automobile, homes and personal property, personal liability and commercial property. Three provinces have publicly operated auto insurance plans (British Columbia, Saskatchewan and Manitoba). Seven other provinces use private firms. In 2015 more than 207 private P&C companies did business in Canada and more than two-thirds of them were federally regulated.[31]

The market for auto insurance has unusually broad price dispersion. Most consumers are unable to detect quality when they buy because it is so often learned later—from reimbursement practices. Firms range from excellent through average with a few firms providing poor service. With no indicators for quality information, the poorest sellers remain in business instead of losing customers to the best firms. If Canada had public statistics on firm-level satisfaction like the American Customer Satisfaction Index,[32] the best firms would be rewarded as informed consumers moved from lower quality suppliers. The industry is characterized by a relatively high level of foreign presence with nearly half of the industry being foreign owned. These features reflect the ease of entry into the industry and consequent level of competition. This competition includes a cacophony of information that is confusing to most consumers. Overall, the industry continues to have respectable earnings. Table 4 shows some of the basic indices of performance.

The data on net written premium in Table 4 reflects the growth in the industry in recent times. Premium revenue received by private P&C insurers, adjusted for ceded premiums (reinsurance) increased by about 10% between 2011 and 2015. There is an increase in the level of concentration in the industry: the top five companies now account for around 40% of net written premium income. The P&C insurance industry paid a total of about $8 billion in taxes to both provincial and federal government (about the same as the banks in 2014) and employed over 120 thousand workers in 2015. Both tax paid and employment have been increasing over time. For soundness, insurers are required to invest in less risky government and corporate bonds. The return on investment is often more than double underwriting earnings (Table 4).

The Canadian Life and Health Insurance industry is the second part of the insurance industry and it is as important as the P&C component. The industry serves more than 28 million Canadians—over 75% of the population—with individual and group life insurance, annuities and supplementary health benefits. The industry is competitive having about 150 life and health insurers out of which 41 are foreign-owned as at 2015. Table 5 shows the performance of the industry and some of its contributions to the Canadian economy in recent years.

Table 4 Performance of P&C insurance industry

	2011	2012	2013	2014	2015
Net written premium (in $ billions)	42.8	43.7	45.0	46.6	47.0
Proportion of top 5 firms (%)	40.2	41.9	41.8	–	43.3
Net claims incurred (in $ billions)	28.6	27.8	30.1	30.3	29.4
Total taxes paid (in $ billions)	7.4	7.5	6.7	8.2	–
Investment (in $ billions)	98.4	104.2	106.6	–	114.6
Return on investment (in $ billions)	4.0	3.9	3.3	4.4	–
Underwriting earning (in $ billions)	0.9	2.1	0.6	1.4	–
Employment	115, 400	118,600	118,800	–	122,500

Source Different editions (2013–2016) of the Insurance Bureau of Canada (IBC) Fact

Table 5 Canadian life and health insurance industry performance

	2013	2014	2015
Benefit payments ($ billions)	76.2	84.2	83.5
Premium revenue	92.2	99.4	103.0
Investment assets	646.0	721.2	760.0
Long-term investment	570.0	630.0	690.0
Total tax paid	5.5	5.6	6.6
Employment	150,100	155,000	148,600

Source Different editions (2014–2016) of the Canadian life and health insurance association (CLHIA) Fact Book

Apart from banks and insurance companies, other industries in the Canadian financial services sector are the co-operative and retail associations which are predominantly regulated by provincial governments, trust and loan companies whose regulations could be federal or provincial, and the different provincial securities market which are regulated by the provincial/territorial securities commissions and harmonized by Canadian Securities Administrators (CSA).

3 Financial Consumer Protection Systems

The Canadian consumer protection system encompasses measures taken by the selling institutions, by rules and regulations established to guide these institutions, and by government institutions in charge of making the rules, supervising and monitoring their implementation. In banking, some observers who are not convinced the system is adequate have concerns about the overall level of consumer debt in Canada (total consumer debt is at a record level in 2017). This concern is not related to imprudent lending practices of major institutions—where the loan to value ratios are respectable- but to potential impact on consumers. First: have consumers taken account of the impact of a possible upward change in interest rates or are consumers victims of the well-established 'present bias'?

Second, have consumers made prudent loans and investments—or are they naïve … or have they been tricked by lenders or low rates? This concern may be exaggerated somewhat because, while the ratio of debt to disposable income has steadily increased since 2000, the ratio of debt to assets has not changed significantly. New mortgages have high loan-to-income ratios. Starting in 2016, new rules have modified incentives: larger down payments are required for the portion of a price greater than C$500,000 Secondly, buyers must take out insurance on mortgages with low down payments. Thirdly, amortization periods have generally been restricted to 25 years for payment calculations. The first two shift the onus to appropriate decision-makers while the third removes an option that can be based on informed choices of lenders and borrowers.

3.1 *Financial Consumer Protection Regulations and Direction*

Responsibility for regulation is shared between the provincial or territorial governments and the federal government. All provinces have responsibilities for some provincial consumer protection regulations, though the biggest financial institutions are under federal laws. In general, provinces protect customers of co-operative associations (reasonably well), pay-day loan companies[33] (not so well) and other credit institutions.

Prior to the creation of the Financial consumer Agency of Canada in 2001, regulation was not much concerned with consumer protection: the focus was mainly on prudential matters and 'stability' of financial institutions. Some protections are in the weaker form of a 'voluntary code of conduct', a technique which works reasonably well for highly ethical firms and less well for others. In the securities market, investors are protected by certain provisions in the federal *Criminal Codes* against unhealthy insider trading and frauds—though the criminal process is costly for smaller investors. Too, *a measure of confusion exists because there are so many provincial securities commissions responsible for enforcing relevant sections of various Securities Acts.*[34] Provinces are reluctant to concede regulatory powers and some sellers have opposed change. A little harmonization is visible but movement to a nation-wide system has been unconscionably slow.

The financial consumer protection framework in Canada needs to be geared towards having a comprehensive financial consumer code which adopts basic principles such as commitment to consumers' interests; facilitating access to financial services; ensuring significant levels of transparency; responsible business conduct; and practices by financial institutions and providing efficient avenues for redress. The FCAC has negotiated at least five voluntary codes of conduct. The major consumer NGOs in Canada, PIAC, Option consommateurs, Union des consommateurs and the Consumer Council of Canada,[35] have argued for a code of conduct—but one that is enforceable with binding directives. The high-level principles developed by the OECD constitute an appropriate model.[36]

A long-time problem of perverse incentive systems had sellers of financial services, especially sellers of mutual funds, rewarded for fees that were hidden from consumers. Ever since the 1950s, this resulted in decisions that were lucrative for sellers collecting the hidden rewards and bad for consumers.

4 Ex-Ante Financial Consumer Protection

Among other things, protecting consumers involves putting in place measures to prevent and or minimize unfair, deceptive and abusive practices. For an outright prevention of consumer exploitation, measures must be in place prior to transactions. We examine a few in the following paragraphs.

4.1 Protection on Prudential Issues: The Office of the Superintendent of Financial Institutions

In 1987 two major agencies were transformed into a new national agency to look after prudential matters. "The Office of the Superintendent of Financial Institutions (OSFI) is an independent federal government agency that regulates and supervises more than 400 federally regulated financial institutions and 1200 pension plans to determine whether they are in sound financial condition. Federally regulated financial institutions include all banks in Canada, and all federally incorporated or registered trust and loan companies, insurance companies, cooperative credit associations, fraternal benefit societies and private pension plans."[37] OSFI concentrates its attention on prudential matters, including (a) risk assessment in all sectors, and (b) national and international standard-setting, including capital ratios.

Canada uses a Financial Institutions Supervisory Committee to ensure cohesion among regulators in the financial services sector: OSFI, the Department of Finance, the Bank of Canada, the Canada Deposit Insurance Corporation and the Financial Consumer Agency of Canada (FCAC). This five-Agency Committee is not highly visible to the public, but it is important. It deserves some credit for Canada's relative success dealing with the worldwide financial crisis of 2007. OSFI has its focus on prudential practices and solvency. Consumer protection is included in policy-making through the other agencies, especially the FCAC and the Ministry of Finance. The IMF pays close attention to OSFI and prudential matters but, regrettably, it does not even assess the FCAC or consumer empowerment.[38]

OSFI has a strong record of achievement. It earned a share of praise for Canada's ability to withstand the worldwide crisis in 2007. The IMF gave credit to three factors: to supervisory care; to Canada's "widely held rule" restricting ownership by any one financial group to 20% of all voting shares; and "… to a decision in 1999 to prevent two sets of giant banks from merging and creating internationally vulnerable institutions."[39] Little notice has been given by the IMF to the financial cushion provided to Canadian banks by profits routinely greater than 15% of equity (compared to 9% or less for banks in comparable countries). One way to look at this is to say that Canadians, through higher bank fees, paid an insurance-like premium to provide a financial cushion to protect Canadian banks against collapse.[40]

Prudential caution is important, but it is not enough by itself to ensure the financial market serves its customers. As Elizabeth Warren famously said: "It is impossible to buy a toaster that has a one-in-five chance of bursting into flames and burning down your house. But it is possible to refinance your home with a mortgage that has the same one-in-five chance of putting your family out on the street—and the mortgage would not even carry a disclosure of that fact."[41] Ex ante consumer protection requires independent scrutiny of harmful low-quality financial innovations being introduced into the marketplace—often accompanied by selling malpractices. Negative innovations reduce dynamic efficiency as well as fairness. As Akerlof and Shiller demonstrate, the damage from financial lemons can be system-wide.[42]

Recent IMF reviews of OSFI's supervision of the financial services sector rated Canada as a poster child for financial preparedness.[43] The IMF assesses the 700 employees of OSFI as "…well trained in the expertise needed", though the same is not said for all provincial regulatory agencies.[44] The country scores well on stress tests and it has met the Basel 3 targets for 2019 more than 3 years ahead of time.

4.2 *Payments Canada*

Systems operated by Payments Canada clear and settle more than 7.4 billion payments each business day.[45] It is undertaking a multi-year effort to modernize Canada's clearance system by 2020. The United Kingdom has already moved to same-day cheque clearance, and Australia is close behind. Delays in processing payments have frustrated Canadian consumers for decades. Canadian law now requires that banks immediately make available the first $100 of the cheque amount. Banks under federal regulation must now clear cheques for up to $1500 in 5 business days from the date they make a deposit with an employee at a bank (not at an ATM). Amounts greater than $1500 deposited with an employee during banking hours must be cleared in 7 days, not including the day of deposit.[46] This is probably the slackest standard extant. It has been easy for institutions to meet Canada's unconscionably weak standard for customer service.

Online arrangements have not delivered expected benefits, partly because "closed systems" controlled by some institutions are not interoperable with an open worldwide system. That system is based mainly on standards—particularly ISO 20022 which Payments Canada is trying to implement. A second major payments shortcoming is described as follows: "Canadian banks' customers are frustrated by the fact that they have to visit a branch to conduct certain key banking tasks, such as opening an account or getting a loan."[47] Further, electrons must move slowly in Canada: a consumer making an online transfer from one big bank to another is warned that a 'clearance delay' may occur.

From 1997 on, one exception was ING Direct Canada, an upstart telephone/computer bank that proved service could be better. It grew quickly as an online bank without bricks-and-mortar branches. In 2012, ING Canada (with 1.8 million customers) was purchased by Scotiabank and renamed Tangerine. Arguably, this purchase removed an independent firm that might have grown to be a vigorous competitor challenging the Bix Six banks.

In 2015, Payments Canada, working with Finance Canada and the Bank of Canada, undertook a long-awaited bold move toward the digital age in clearing payments. The process looked promising and most analysts expected a move to real-time clearances. In 2017, to the surprise of many, the trial run of Distributed Leger Technology (DLT) demonstrated, to the Bank of Canada and Payments Canada, that use of DLT using current Blockchain technology, would decrease the resilience of Canadian banking.[48] It could not be shown that either of the two systems examined could deliver proof of finality for transactions. Further, DLT needs to provide more centralization and requires better protection of privacy before it is implemented. Efficiency gains were indeed validated by the trial, cross-border benefits were clear, and additional uses were uncovered.[49] After decades of service that is slower than clearing practice elsewhere, and a long policy lag, further delay is disappointing.[50]

Some improvement in clearance procedures are promised for September of 2018. Consumer protection would soon improve in two crucial ways. A 2017 consultation paper proposes to require every payment service provider to have in place a process for dispute resolution. Secondly, consumers will no longer be liable for losses from payment exchange failures unless the consumer is responsible for causing the loss.

4.3 Addressing Imbalance: Simpler Documents, Public Interest Research

Enhanced access to information facilitates better informed decision making by consumers and improves efficiency. One major challenge for consumers in all financial sectors is informational vulnerability. A typical (often amateur) financial consumer faces a plethora of differentiated and complex products[51] but the consumer lacks adequate resources needed to see through the informational overload to detect information needed for a good decision. As the World Bank points out: "*The imbalance of power between consumers and providers is particularly marked in financial markets. In part, this is due to the complex nature of financial products and services which often have a deferred expected pay-off to the consumer and, in many cases, are purchased only rarely.*"[52] The consumer's search problem is worsened whenever there is misleading information or when there are "lemons" in the market.[53]

The ongoing imbalance between the informational challenge to a consumer and the consumer's capability underscores the need for consumer financial literacy and education, especially its provision as a public good. Too often, analysis suggests there is some target level of financial literacy that will meet consumer needs. That is unhelpful because, so many new services arrive weekly. The difficulty of a financial decision D, depends on the size of the challenge, C, relative to the consumer's set of skills, K. If C is the complexity of the financial product, K might be financial literacy.[54]

$$D = \frac{C}{K}$$

It is important to recognize that both C and K are changing. Rapid changes in financial literacy are unlikely, while C is affected by the ongoing burst of new financial services, including digital innovations. It would be a mistake to be too certain that financial literacy is the only—or the very best—policy that can be implemented in a market with so many complex services to assess.[55] The worldwide scandal with 'mortgage-backed securities' in 2008 provides convincing evidence that highly sophisticated experts could not make sound choices. Between 2000 and 2005 the Financial Consumer Agency of Canada made impressive progress by getting financial institutions to *simplify* complex documents. A research survey conducted after the first FCAC transparency initiative, found that fully 73% of the institutions being regulated had made changes to policies and procedures *because of* the FCAC's actions and decisions.[56]

Consumer action groups, who are not as well funded as similar groups in other countries, seek a wider range of policies. The most prominent consumer NGOs are: Option consommateurs, the Public Interest Advocacy Centre (PIAC), Union des consommateurs, and the Consumers Council of Canada. These groups face the notorious "public goods problem": they lack the ability to earn supporting income from researching and advocating policies in the public interest. In the early 1970s, a public consumer research organization, the national Canadian Consumer Council, was created. Despite the public need for better balance in consumer policy, the independent Council was very quickly eliminated in a budget cut.

The arrival of e-commerce brought new, and often different, issues to market transactions and created a parallel challenge to traditional forms of consumer protection. Canada increased funding for financial literacy to good effect but did not do the same for consumer protection. Many consumer protection agencies were keenly aware of a need for research. In 2013, a 4-year research initiative was funded by the Social Sciences and Humanities Research Council of Canada. The Partnership connected interdisciplinary research at universities to consumer policy-makers. The ongoing project is known as the Partnership for Public Policy Oriented Consumer Interest Research (PPOCIR). The initiative is a broad partnership of academics, policy-makers and consumer NGOs. Participants include four consumer NGOs, four consumer protection agencies (including the Financial Consumer Agency of Canada), the Canadian Standards Association, plus the University of Waterloo, Université Laval, McGill University, Ryerson University, Guelph University and the University of Alberta.

The Partnership for PPOCIR has a guaranteed focus on consumer policy. Research is proposed by consumer protection agencies, consumer NGOs, or universities, and conducted by experienced graduate students with supervision by academics, NGOs and/or by protection agencies. A network of some 50 academic researchers in at least nine different disciplines has been created. Workshop Summaries and three superb interdisciplinary surveys are available online.[57] Recent topics include peer to peer lending, a search for consumer-oriented standards, international networks, and a behavioral tool for encouraging savings.[58] There is a case for linking such a Canadian initiative with IAFICO.

The federal Ministry of Innovation Science and Economic Development Canada,[59] has a modest Office of Consumer Affairs (OCA) to create policy tools and to coordinate consumer policies among federal and provincial agencies, consumer groups and businesses. The OCA operates within the Ministry of Innovation, Science, and Economic Development. It is not staffed with expertise to ensure that innovations are welfare-increasing. Without better support, Canada has no agency focused on detecting harmful versus helpful innovations.

The OCA operates a small but highly significant program to allow the consumer voice to be heard on some issues. A recent review of the program found the program brought better balance and broader evidence-based views to public discussions and "…there is a strong rationale for public investment in supporting consumer groups to do policy research…."[60] In 2016, seven consumer groups were awarded thirteen grants ranging from C$ 49,000 to C$ 93,000 on very specific topics like online privacy, the sharing economy, chargebacks in distant transactions, and practices of financial recovery companies. OCA provides the grants on a competitive basis.[61] The program to help consumer NGOs conduct evidence-based research has had a visible impact on consumer protection.[62] Michael Geist points to examples of policy success from that seed financing. One example is PIAC's Pilot Project on a Canadian Code of Practice for Consumer Protection in Electronic Commerce. This is an initiative to develop verifiable codes, rather than law, to provide effective consumer protection online."[63]

4.4 Financial Literacy

One of the FCAC's primary mandates is to strengthen financial literacy in Canada. Recent amendments to the *FCAC Act* established the office of a Financial Literacy Leader to coordinate the Agency's activities for this objective. In 2014 Jane Rooney was appointed Canada's first Financial Literacy Leader. The FCAC offers educational and search resources in the form of more than 60 online publications as well as a detailed Canadian Financial Literacy Database.[64]

In Canada, the Constitution gives responsibility for education to provinces—a reality that makes a national Canada-wide strategy is difficult (costly) to implement. Financial institutions are required to provide a certain level of information to their customers to help make informed decisions about products and services. Industry associations (e.g. Canadian Bankers Association) provide additional information about services of their own members.

The FCAC has an ongoing relationship with a non-profit organization: the Canadian Foundation for Economic Education (CFEE).[65] CFEE has a remarkable record of success with schools in all provinces and in some U.S. states. The program helps students learn fundamental principles like budgeting, substitution, opportunity cost, setting financial goals, banking, etc. The key to this success is helping the student achieve the feeling of 'control'.[66] Behavioral research since the work of Rotter (dating from 1954) has verified the key role of perceived control.[67] Individuals who see themselves as having some control over outcomes are active in pursuing financial strategies. Those who feel (rightly or wrongly) that outcomes are beyond their control, do not deploy active tactics. A more specific test has been developed to assess *consumers* for the control they believe they have—or do not have. Perceived control explains search behavior.[68] The line of research supports ***empowerment*** as a key policy for consumer protection.

4.5 Measuring Canada's Success with Financial Literacy

The FCAC coordinates a National Strategy for Financial Literacy by collaborating with other regulators, ombudsmen, not-for-profits and financial institutions to increase awareness about its activities and resources. All available data provides evidence of commendable level of financial literacy in Canada, though there are vulnerable sub-groups. The Canadian Financial Capability Survey conducted by Statistics Canada in 2014 found that out of a 14-question quiz on financial matters,

Table 6 Performance of the industry and some of its contributions to the Canadian economy in recent years

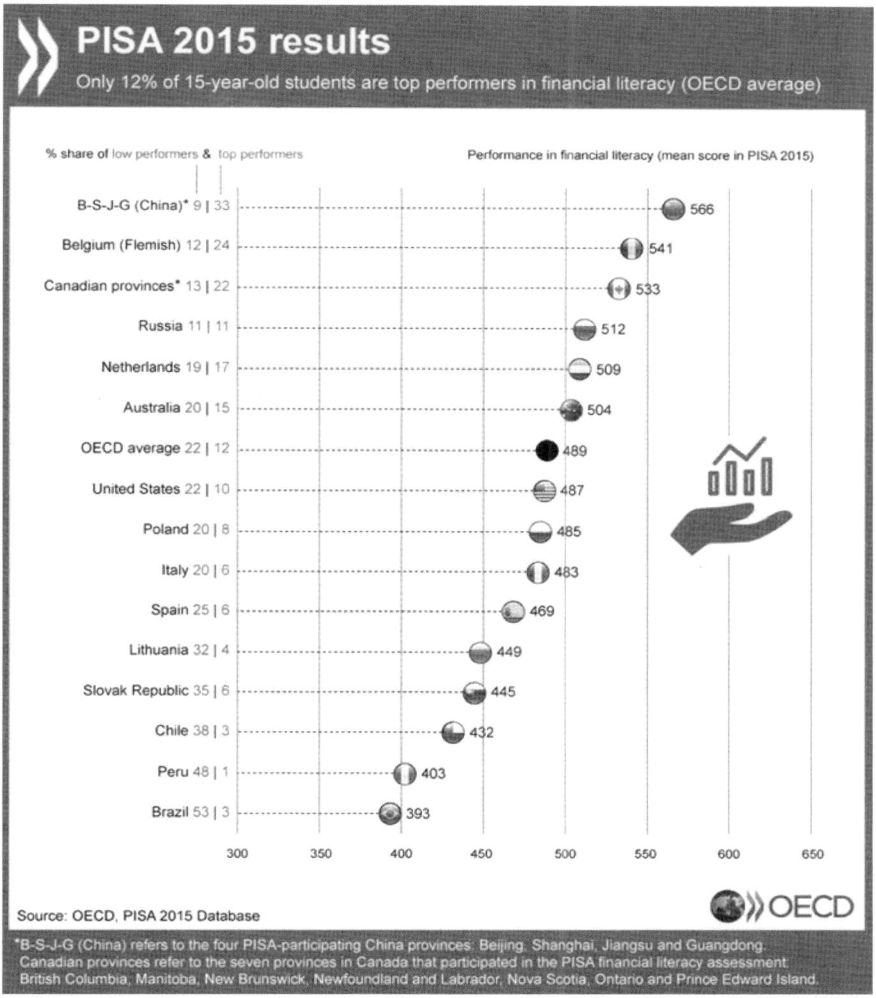

30% answered 8 or 9 questions correctly, 26% answered 10 or 11 questions correctly and 20% answered at least 12 questions correctly.[69] Further evidence of Canada's success is provided by a completely different set of surveys: the international OECD survey of 15-year old students from 15 countries and economies around the world.[70] See Table 6. The OECD study found that 87% of Canadian students achieved its baseline level of understanding. Canada is second on that score among 15 jurisdictions tested. Overall, Canada does very well on financial literacy relative to comparable countries.

4.6 Empowering Consumers for Self-protection

The simplification of complex documents and enhancing consumer literacy are but two of a broader set of policies to empower consumers in the financial marketplace. Canada now does better on the transparency of documents and on financial literacy but not on other components of empowerment: consumer engagement, funded consumer research, evidence-based advocacy, readily available quality benchmarks, service testing, rules to reduce 'noise' and easy redress. Leadership on those matters rests in Europe, the US and Australia.

The European Commission conducted extensive research on empowering consumers.[71] It collected statistical evidence from 56,471 consumers in 29 countries (27 EU countries plus Iceland and Norway). The research identified Norway as the clear leader having best practices in all major components of consumer empowerment: consumer skills, level of information on rights and prices and 'consumer engagement' (complaint behaviour including experience with frauds).

The finding is not surprising: Norway has consumer education in schools, a national consumer ombud for redress, and a national consumer research centre (SIFO) ever since 1939. SIFO provides studies for evidence-based consumer policy. In 2017, SIFO's expertise included 30 researchers.[72] The EU study of 31 countries found that shoppers in Norway outperform consumers elsewhere, even among less educated and low-income sectors. The favourable performance of Norway is surely based on the full range of policies implemented, though the EU report highlights: "The reason probably lies in the Norwegian welfare system that trains low-medium educated citizens to look for their rights (both legal rights and rights as consumers)."[73]

Sound evidence for identifying successes and failures are found in careful benchmarks of consumer satisfaction. Benchmarking is an evidence-based method for improving quality: it is effective and 'light-handed' regulation. Alas, consumer satisfaction evidence *is not now publicly available* in Canada. The National Quality Institute (NQI)[74] was created in 1992 with pathbreaking support from Industry Canada (now Innovation Canada), aided by the University of Waterloo's Institute for Improvement in Quality and Productivity, and connections with Claes Fornell, founder of major initiatives in Sweden and the US. In 1995 and 1997 the NQI conducted large-sample surveys of consumer experience, providing Canadians with evidence. Included were financial services: banking, insurance, and credit unions. After those two reports, the "public goods" support ended and the funding model of the NQI changed to one where services are sold to firms and agencies seeking expertise on how to improve quality.

In 2011, the NQI transformed into Excellence Canada. It now provides useful signals to *sellers,* but reports are not available to consumers. This loss matters because publicly available results on quality could improve the rate at which the market functions. Data can reveal—to consumers and to firms—the best services and the worst choices. The market can then provide shifts that accelerate quality improvements. As it is, firms can make important adjustments to problem areas where quality problems reside: service defects, hidden fees, consumer behavioral eccentricities in decision-making, misuse of financial services, practical shortcomings arising from the power imbalance, exclusions, inadequate redress practices, fraud from fake web sites or e-sellers, and competitors offering financial lemons driving out superior services. For consumers, a more effective model is provided by *firm-specific* benchmarks provided by the American Customer Satisfaction Index (ASCI).[75] Recently, more than a dozen countries have adopted the ASCI model, first, to improve quality for domestic consumers and second, as part of a strategy to increase exports.

Canada has no English language testing agency to present test results on the financial sector. *Consumer Reports*, published in the U.S. sells well in Canada and includes some specific Canadian information. However, it does not cover Canada's financial services. *Protégez-vous*, an independent not-for-profit publication published in French, has an active web site, and provides useful information on Canadian financial services, and it also provides advocacy to protect consumers.[76] The world's very best agency for testing financial services is *Finanztest*,[77] published specifically on the financial services sector in Germany since 1991. It has influenced many financial practices to benefit consumers. Indeed, it is a national policy for improving quality to achieve success with exports by German financial institutions.

4.7 Price and Quality Regulations; Market Conduct

Price controls are virtually non-existent in the Canadian financial services sector. The main political parties have long agreed that competition is the best way to ensure fair prices are charged.[78] In this approach, Canada's Competition Bureau has an important role in assessing mergers (notably in the highly concentrated banking sector), plus a crucial role supervising market conduct. For example, it has introduced provisions to restrict 'astroturfing' which is the planting of false recommendations online to cripple the digital economy. Astroturfing is designed to degrade the signals from authentic ratings of products and services.[79]

Financial markets regulators ensure that the products and services provided by financial institutions in the industries conform to the consumer provisions in federal or provincial legislation. The FCAC plays a role, particularly with federally regulated institutions. For example, FCAC is mandated to ensure that bank products and services conform to the consumer provisions in the Bank Act. In addition, FCAC has a mandate to ensure that financial institutions act in line with their codes of conduct and commitments to deliver quality products and services.

In general, competitive pricing, entry barriers and market conduct are addressed by the national Competition Bureau. Specific market practices are handled by federal and provincial licensing regulations. Financial literacy is supervised by the Financial Consumer Agency of Canada. Financial quality is addressed by all three agencies.

4.8 Salesperson Licensing and Qualification Controls

Financial services and products are becoming increasingly complex and diversified. Therefore, it is important that salespersons or representatives of financial institutions are well trained, knowledgeable and appropriately motivated. This not only allows them to deliver their services efficiently to consumers but also ensures that they follow all consumer protection regulations and minimize the incidence of misrepresentation of facts and fraudulent practices. Hence the licensing, regulations and supervision of financial institutions to ensure staff members attain a minimum level of proficiency, and that they are motivated to take full account of the consumer's interest, not their own. Currently, measures are being improved to protect consumers against unknown or unanticipated investment fees.

In Canada, there are no specified requirements for staffing the major financial institutions like banks and insurance companies. For example, neither the *Bank Act* nor the *Insurance Companies Act* contains provisions stipulating the qualifications for different roles. Rather, these institutions have autonomous internal recruitment rules intended to ensure that only well trained and qualified individuals serve consumers. In general, an effective standard has been sustained over time. This is by no means perfect: major banks have recently pressured tellers to meet sales targets in ways that harmed some tellers and pushed consumers into unwanted services bearing extra fees.[80] The publicity ended the practices, not regulatory action.

In principle, the wealth management, investment and securities industries have strict regulations accrediting salespersons giving investment advice, or soliciting investment funds, or managing customers' portfolios. This is intended to guarantee a level of quality in sellers who deal directly with customers. The Mutual Fund Dealers Association (MFDA)—a self-regulatory organization for mutual funds firms in Canada—by its *MFDA Rule 1.2* requires members to ensure that potential salespersons complete training on specific topics and, further, to ensure that new sellers are supervised for a specified period before they are licensed. Similarly, the Investment Industry Regulatory Organization (IIROC)—a self-regulatory organization for investment and trading activities on debt and equity market places in Canada—has Rule 2900 which is designed to ensure that approved agents in the marketplace have attained a level of education and proficiency.[81] These measures are thoughtful … but inadequate.

One major problem has existed for decades: concealed incentives. Financial consumers were not aware that an advisor might be choosing investments that gave a hidden payment to the advisor for directing business to that seller. This was most apparent in the purchase of mutual funds and investments with ongoing 'trailer fees'. For more than six decades, most consumers paid high fees for mediocre, non-optimal, advice. No penalty was enforced, and no redress provided to consumers for hundreds of million dollars of harm. The lesson—for Canada and for any jurisdiction—is that industry-based self-regulation will be inadequate in protecting consumers whenever the sum of economic incentives favors consumer abuse.[82]

In 2016 a CRM2 standard improved the general level of transparency. Yet the consumer's search cost is still too high because some advisors "… have been left behind, either by choice or by circumstance."[83] One solution being proposed—and being resisted—is a statutory "best interest standard" with penalties for advice which is not best interest of the investor. The 'best interest standard' seemed promising in 2012 but, 5 years later it still does not have solid support from provincial regulatory agencies, so malpractices will continue as financial tribulation. An effective policy would be to move the onus back to those who design the incentive system by legislating explicit penalties for any concealed payment that provides incentives that may harm consumers.

4.9 Information Disclosure Controls and Consumer-Focused Transparency

A solution to the information problem requires enough transparency to motivate all sellers to reveal every fee and the quality of every significant component of service. As consumer losses from harmful incentives became evident over the decade to 2017, many consumers moved away from managed accounts to exchange-based investments. Prior to about 2003 many financial documents were unnecessarily complex, legalistic and far beyond the reading level of most financial consumers.

> Excessive product differentiation, difficult language, long and complicated contracts, terms that are one-sided, contain a high noise to signal ratio, and create information overload all increase the consumer's search cost. Financial services are especially problematic. Analysis of 131 Canadian contracts in 1998 for 16 financial services revealed major challenges. For example, the average credit card application in Canada, measured on the Flesch-Kinkaid score, required a consumer to have grade 16 understanding in the English version (N = 7), while the French contract (N = 5) required grade 19.[84]

As noted, the creation of the Financial Consumer Agency of Canada in 2001 made a sharp improvement in the readability of financial contracts. By 2004 a stunning revision of documents had been achieved. For example, mortgage contracts which formerly required readers to understand at the grade 16 level were rephrased to be understandable by consumers at the grade 11 level. Significantly, the *larger* institutions made changes in the first 4 years of FCAC's operation. Most institutions being regulated reported that they had made changes to policies and procedures *because of* the FCAC's actions and decisions.[85]

It is important to recognize how much more effective this policy of plain language is—compared to trying to make the same progress through training to increase financial literacy. The financial literacy policy to get consumers to be able to understand documents written at a grade 16 level would be prohibitively costly and could only succeed with a fraction of consumers. Public policy on document complexity and information overload is essential because, as noted above, economic research shows that higher profits result from "noise" in any market. Noise is accidentally or deliberately created to confuse those consumers with little experience.[86] For example, the FCAC has identified no fewer than 150 different versions of credit cards in Canada. To help consumers deal with the noise, the FCAC has created a 'selector tool'.[87]

The value of brevity and clarity in Canadian financial documents is demonstrated by an FCAC survey of consumer experience with credit card agreements. FCAC research on alternative information tactics was conducted in French and English and published in 2017.[88] "*Among all the types of documents tested, the information boxes are the most read and referenced when looking for specific information about their credit cards.*"[89] Consumers prefer the information box over all other methods of communication—so long as the box does not defeat itself by including long passages of text. Progress was made by the FCAC in getting financial firms to use the information box. However, some of this gain in transparency has been lost as firms move to digital methods. Screen after screen of terms and conditions can present cognitive overload and legal imbalance. Documents that permit consumers to succeed use well-known tactics for clarity: a table of contents, numbered points, brevity, bigger fonts, layout simplicity, and the highlighting of important elements like interest rates, penalties, grace periods, etc.

'Disclosure' is a problematic concept. Transparency is a consumer-oriented concept while "disclosure" is a legal term defined from a seller's perspective. In a 'disclosure' regime, a regulation can be completely satisfied by deploying legalese —too often confounded by information overload. *Transparency* is an enabling policy based on the consumer's understanding. In general, when products and services are transacted between financial institution and consumers, industry legislation (such as *Bank Acts, Insurance Companies Act*, etc.) makes it compulsory to give a summary document to the consumer. As stipulated in the *Bank Act*, when an account is opened, the statement should explicitly state the terms and conditions agreed upon, disclose all the fees, charges and interest applicable and if changes are made, the bank is to disclose the changes to the rates before they occur.

The FCAC can act when a financial institution does not live up to a regulation. A recent decision illustrates how much work this is for the regulator to gain action that seems much weaker than what other countries achieve by way of motivation. In 2017, the Commissioner upheld six charges against a financial institution that did not live up to disclosure regulations. The fine was $365,000, but in line with FCAC policy, the financial institution was not named.[90]

Despite that, as PIAC and Option Consommateurs have shown, a debilitating weakness in Canada's disclosure regime rests in the ability of financial institutions to include words to:

(a) unilaterally end a contract without notice,
(b) unilaterally change terms effective immediately,
(c) exclude liability even when the institution is negligent,
(d) restrict the period to dispute transactions, and
(e) permit a bank to charge undisclosed fees.[91]
The 2017 Electronic Access Agreement of RBC includes the bank's notice that it can:
(f) "change any feature of the [online] services without giving you notice" and, it can
(g) shift the risk of software failure from the bank or its expert supplier to the consumer.

In addition, consumers have been injured by incentives placed on agents to tempt them to make decisions contrary to the consumer interest. As noted, bank tellers were given targets that resulted in fees for unwanted services, and, for decades investment advisors included a concealed fee that added expenses to consumers for mutual funds that were not of the quality level a fully informed consumer would choose. **While the country earns well deserved international recognition for leadership in prudential matters, Canada exhibits a major weakness in consumer protection with poor rules for market conduct**.

Canada puts high-quality resources into prudential regulation, as assessed by the IMF, yet the country is sadly lacking in regulatory capability that could bring selling practices up to the level available in other countries. The portion of FCAC dealing with research and fair selling practices urgently needs mandate change and additional resourcing.[92] It is equally vital to strengthen the Office of Consumer Affairs to assess negative innovations and the Competition Bureau's departments addressing market conduct.

In the best of circumstances, disclosure can advance to transparency, especially when an information box is provided. A functional document (either physical or electronic) must contain the seller's contacts for complaints, the dispute resolution procedure, and the exact contact of an industry regulator or ombudsman. It is now expected that such documents must be written clearly, and in language easy enough for an average consumer to comprehend. Usually, industry regulators decide the amount and type of information to be disclosed in such documents and institutions are required to make this summary document available *before or during* the transaction. Improved readability has led to modest improvements in onus and in incentive-based responsibility, but *balance* in any contract needs major attention from agencies responsible for consumer protection.[93]

In 2001 Canada's FCAC had an international head start in consumer protection, one that turned out to be highly useful when the global financial crisis arrived in 2007–08. However, the original scope of the FCAC was limited and after 2008 the lead in consumer protection passed to the UK and Australia, and, in 2011, to the US when it finally created its Financial Consumer Protection Bureau. Canada's consumer NGOs have increasingly sought a broader mandate for the FCAC. In 2016, two of the largest consumer groups, Option consommateurs and PIAC, argued that the FCAC "…was given very limited powers when it was created in 2001, which have not been significantly increased over the past 15 years. Let us only say that it pales in comparison with bodies such as the United States' Consumer Financial Protection Bureau."[94] The US Bureau has 1623 employees while the FCAC operated in 2017 with 85.[95]

In 2014, the Public Interest Advocacy Centre (PIAC), strongly urged that Canada adopt an enforceable code of conduct based on rules from the *G20 High Level Principles on Financial Consumer Protection*[96] and, secondly, on the *Good Practices for Financial Consumer Protection* as assessed internationally by the World Bank Group.[97] Either one would be a big improvement.

The G20 report of the OECD distinguishes between *financial literacy programs* (where Canada performs well) and the complementary *role of oversight bodies* (where Canada now lags best practice). PIAC places emphasis on the need for a *comprehensive* consumer financial code that *has the force of law*.[98] PIAC points out that the wording used to describe the FCAC's mandate: "supervise," "promote" and "monitor", fails to specify "enforce".[99] Union des consommateurs argues that the time for mild incentives has passed and serious sanctions and additional powers must be added to the FCAC mandate.[100] The Consumer Council of Canada (CCC) describes the imbalance in power between a consumer and a huge financial institution. The CCC has taken pains to illustrate that it is naïve to believe the volunteer model can finance redress. In 2014 the Council urged substantial strengthening of the FCAC to enable the agency to seek redress with "full enforcement authority behind it, including criminal and civil sanctions…".[101]

Imbalance can be measured another way. Jacques St. Amant points out the challenge facing an FCAC with (then) 75 employees tasked with supervising consumer practices of more than 400 financial institutions. It is time, he argues, to rethink the FCAC and to develop more effective mechanisms for stakeholder participation.[102] James Callon, former Deputy Commissioner of the Financial Consumer Agency of Canada, maintains that while Canada was once a leader in consumer protection, "The new standards of consumer protection mandates being discussed and implemented in the major economies represents a wave of change with respect to how market conduct regulators will regulate sellers of financial products and services."[103] With its weak mandate, FCAC was still able to claim that "…in calendar year 2016, financial institutions reimbursed customers more than $15 million as a result of our supervisory work."[104] In the US, the CFPB average return to cheated consumers is about US$2 billion per year.[105]

Callon recommends a more prospective, principles-based FCAC, one able to issue binding directions and binding rules with monetary penalties for contravention. FCAC needs to be mandated to act as a public advocate and given sufficient budget to conduct the research needed for more active roles in consumer protection.[106]

4.10 Anti-trust/Competition Laws

The major anti-trust law in Canada is the *Competition Act*. This legislation is enforced and administered by the Competition Bureau whose primary responsibility is to enhance competition in the market place and thus ensure Canadians enjoy competitive prices, product choices and quality services. In the liberalized Canadian financial sector with no direct price controls, Canadians depend heavily on the Competition Bureau to make sure the market remains competitive and non-collusive tendencies and exploitations are minimized. Therefore, the Competition Bureau, in collaboration with other financial sector regulators, has been active in periodic assessment of the market place to optimize competition. It examines proposed mergers and addresses issues of misleading information and unfair market practices. This has been important for consumers, but the reach of the Competition Bureau is limited by regulations inhibiting foreign banks from entering Canada, a factor that helps explain the persistence of supernormal profits, as noted above.

It is not surprising that the Competition Bureau and the Department of Finance have prevented mergers between big banks in the interest of competition and consumer welfare. Prominent examples include the rejection of the proposed merger between the Royal Bank of Canada (RBC) and Bank of Montreal (BMO), and a proposed merger between Toronto-Dominion Bank (TD) and Canadian Imperial Bank of Commerce (CIBC), both in 1998.

5 Ex-Post Financial Consumer Protection

5.1 Complaints and Dispute Settlement

Over many decades, the “redress” approach to protection in purchasing financial services in Canada has been a slow move to regulation *to ensure that a system for redress is in place* for consumers. The Ombudsman for Banking Services and Investments (OBSI) was created by the banks in 1996 and expanded to include investment dealers in 2002. NGOs concerned with consumer protection are not happy about the fact that of financial institutions in Canada can select a redress system: they can choose to have unresolved complaints go to OBSI or to a private sector firm selling Alternate Dispute Resolution. Research is needed to see which method best manages consumer protection based on fairness and promptness. Perhaps neither is strong enough to provide the incentives needed.

An independent review of OBSI was conducted in 2016 by Nikki Pender and Deborah Battell, formerly the banking ombudsman in New Zealand. The assessment placed "… a focus on the extent to which OBSI meets international definitions and expectations of an ombudsman."[107] The Report concluded that OBSI did follow its mandate, *yet it fails at the fundamental responsibility of an ombudsman*:

> "OBSI is unlike other comparable international financial sector ombudsmen in that it does not have the authority to bind firms to observe its compensation recommendations (binding authority). This drives its operating model and prevents it from fulfilling the fundamental role of an ombudsman, securing redress for all consumers who have been wronged…"
>
> Further, "The real mischief, however, is not that some consumers receive less, but that OBSI's current mandate allows this to happen. It, in effect, tilts the playing field in favour of firms. The fact this is happening in a complex industry that has a significant impact on people's well-being…" … "OBSI has an operating model that makes it unable to prevent future complaints from arising, improve the investment industry, [or] lift consumer confidence in the investment market."[108]

OBSI is not a regulatory agency but "…an industry-funded dispute resolution service, and it is hard to conceive of one with less teeth."[109] OBSI agrees with consumers about a quarter of the time, yet both consumers and financial firms are unhappy with opaque decisions.[110]

A complementary policy would help: widely publicized satisfaction ratings based on sound methodology. A significant problem in Canada is the plethora of 'service-specific' acts passed into law. That, plus frequent misunderstandings about federal versus provincial responsibility. have resulted in confusion about exactly where a consumer needs to go to seek redress. The consumer's search cost is dauntingly high. From about 1950 to about 1990, national and provincial consumers associations, staffed by volunteers, worked to help consumers find the correct path toward redress. These same non-governmental organizations (NGOs) played an important role in advocating better legislation for consumers of financial services.[111]

In the 1990s, research into difficulties faced by Canadian consumers of financial services was conducted as part of a major national inquiry, the MacKay Task Force on the Future of the Canadian Financial Services Sector.[112] One policy outcome of the Task Force was the creation of the Financial Consumer Agency of Canada in 2001. Among other duties, the FCAC now provides important advice on where to seek redress. Consumer NGOs would like the FCAC to be better resourced and more proactive.[113] Even so, the FCAC can be counted as a Canadian triumph because it was established early—in 2001 and well prior to the worldwide financial crisis of 2007–08 where the consumer protection was one useful policy. Other countries have copied the FCAC model of consumer protection. Particularly interesting is the example of Ireland because it pointedly copied components of Canada's FCAC after the 2007 crisis. Subsequently, Ireland passed the FCAC in protecting consumers by improving its mandate over time.[114]

Complaints and complaint resolution are normal features of markets. The extent and pace at which problems are redressed affects customers' loyalty to financial institutions and influences the general level of confidence in the financial sector.

5.2 *Defensive Marketing*

Research has confirmed that private firms often have a strong incentive to look after complaints of their customers.[115] Importantly, this private incentive—defensive marketing—can be strong enough to satisfy consumer problems. Defensive marketing is reliable whenever the cost of retaining a disappointed customer is less than the cost of obtaining a new customer. More specifically, redress is justified by marginal revenue being greater than marginal cost. Evidence has established that private complaint resolution is most successful in markets that are highly competitive.[116]

Redress is a key provision for consumers and a highly important source of information for sellers. The information gathered by "defensive marketing" allows sellers to improve the product or service, with innovations important to their customers. Unhappily, innovation and consumer success in Canada are both seriously hampered by widespread lethargy in redress practices. This impedes consumer triumph and, importantly, reduces success by Canadian firms trying to sell abroad. In 2014, a special joint study was published by Statistics Canada, *the Survey of Innovation and Business Strategy, 2012*, with the distressing finding that only 40% of firms in the survey had explicit redress policies (See Table 7). Finance and

Table 7 Enterprises with systematic problem resolution practices for the production of goods or delivery of services, selected sectors, all surveyed industries. Statistics Canada; 2012

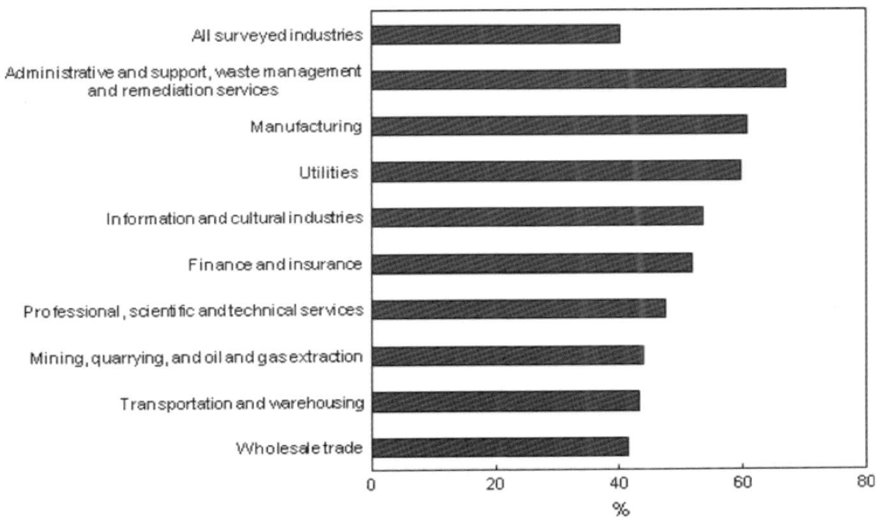

Insurance is in the middle of the pack, 5th out of 9 sectors.[117] If a sector hopes to succeed internationally, it should score better than a median. The category 'Finance and Insurance' is too broad: as indicated above, the Insurance sector succeeds well with exports, so it probably is at the top of the Finance and Insurance group in resolving consumer problems.

As noted, defensive marketing is most reliable in markets that are highly competitive. When the cost of switching firms is high, or when 'noise' makes it costly to discover superior sellers, additional policies for consumer protection are needed. These two issues are especially important in the financial services sector. For example, the Canadian consumer may see more than a hundred firms selling auto insurance. Web-based search engines regularly fail because they do not tell consumers when their search engine looks only among firms belonging to a related holding firm. Further, the focus of a search is only on one feature: price. *Quality* is revealed only to the small fraction of car owners experiencing a claim. Unhappily, this information is available much too late: after an accident.

When defensive marketing works, it is a thing of beauty requiring no explicit public policy beyond fair competition. When it fails, the best consumer protection policy would be a widely available public benchmarking system identifying precise offerings of superior quality. More than a dozen countries have recently moved to a system like the American Customer Satisfaction Index. That system removes the noise and empowers consumers to reward sellers offering high quality.

5.3 Financial Consumer Protection Institutions

Step one of the dispute resolution process starts with the financial institution. Federal financial sector laws (e.g. *Bank Act, Insurance Companies Act,* etc.) in Canada contain clauses requiring financial firms to provide procedures for complaint management and dispute resolution, whether their supervision is federal or provincial.

For grievances that are not resolved by the banks themselves, complaints can be brought to the Ombudsman for Banking Services and Investments (OBSI). Recently, the TD Bank and the Royal Bank of Canada, two of the largest banking institutions, left the general Banking Ombud system (OBSI) to provide expertise from a private firm. ADR Chambers which now supplies Alternate Dispute Resolution (ADR) for the two banks. The office is called ADR Chambers Banking Ombuds Office (informally: ADRBO). So far, no convincing independent test has assessed—from the consumer's perspective—the effectiveness of ARDBO compared to the ombud used by other institutions (promptness, accessibility, fairness, and satisfaction).

Since 2001, the Financial Consumer Agency of Canada (FCAC) is responsible for ensuring that federal financial institutions comply with sectoral legislation on internal dispute resolution mechanisms. Importantly, financial institutions are required to communicate detailed information about industry ombuds to their customers when a new agreement or transaction is initiated (e.g. on opening an account, securing an insurance policy or entering an investment plan) or when a complaint is received. If the internal resolution mechanism fails, consumers can further seek redress with the industry ombudsman. There are three major ombudsmen serving the four pillars of financial services in Canada, namely the Ombudsman for Banking Services and Investments (OBSI; for banks; trust and loan companies; mutual funds and investment dealers), the General Insurance Ombud Service (for property and casualty insurance companies), and the Canadian Life and Health Insurance Ombudsman (for life and health insurance companies). Further, the Investment Industry Regulatory Organization of Canada (IIROC) and the Mutual Fund Dealers Association of Canada (MFDA), are self-regulatory organizations which serve as ombudsmen for investment dealers and mutual funds respectively.

After proper evaluation of the specific cases, the ombudsmen provide non-binding recommendations to financial institutions including restitution and compensations. Financial institutions often comply with these recommendations. Otherwise, ombudsmen can publicly report instances where their recommendations are not fully implemented. IIROC and MFDA, can impose strict disciplinary actions on members ranging from fines to suspension, termination of membership and permanent barring of salespersons from employment by members. If a consumer is not satisfied with the ombudsman's recommendation, recourse can be sought through arbitration or the legal system, but this is rarely pursued, perhaps due to the expense.

As noted above, there have been ongoing concerns about the complaint and dispute resolution system in Canada. These includes the level of consumers' accessibility and awareness about the ombudsmen, the length of time taken for restitution thereby inducing consumers to become tired of the process, and the independence of the ombuds since they are mostly funded by the financial institutions. In 2006, the system was judged by a Senate examination to be efficient—with independent ombudsmen whose boards are not dominated by the institutions.[118] The opposite conclusion was reached in an official 2016 study by the former Ombud of New Zealand who found Canada's OBSI fails at "… the fundamental role of an ombudsman, securing redress for all consumers who have been wronged."[119]

The big financial institutions in Canada comply with financial transparency provisions. An objective way to ascertain this is to examine the proportion of consumer complaints related to clarity and readability. The 2015 report of the Ombudsman for Banking Services and Investments (OBSI) reveals that disclosure problems rank low among the complaints received from customers. Three major sources of complaints are credit card terms, mortgage penalties, and costly or unexplained exchange rates used for international transactions.[120]

5.4 Deposit Insurance and Customer Compensation Schemes

All industries of the Canadian financial services sector have some form of guarantee as protection for their customers in the event of the failure or distress of financial institutions. These measures are intended to instill confidence in the financial system by providing an orderly process of dealing with failures. Most of the savings in Canada are covered by institutions holding federal charters. Large banks (equity more than C$ 5 billion) must be widely owned: no Canadian or foreign investor may own more than 20% of voting shares. Key documents must be stored in Canada. Ownership restrictions are advanced as measures for assuring prudential goals. These goals have been well served but Canada's focus on prudential success has inhibited entry. This has led to giant institutions with oligopolistic behavior that poorly serves consumers and small firms (high fees, remarkably slow responses to market signals for interest rate reductions, and barriers to innovation.)[121] The economic model that seems most appropriate is 'unorganized collusive oligopoly' where firms behave somewhat like a dominant firm. A key component of the 'noisy monopolist' model is present because consumers have great difficulty making optimal choices among the flood of barely-differentiated services.[122]

For banks and other institutions taking consumer deposits, Canada has a national deposit insurance scheme coordinated by the Canadian Deposit Insurance Corporation (CDIC). The CDIC Act, covers deposits up to C$100,000 per depositor per insured category in banks, federally regulated trust and loan companies and many deposit-taking co-operative credit associations. Not covered are mutual funds, guaranteed investment certificates with a term longer than 5 years, foreign currency deposits, stocks and bonds. In 2017, the protected savings covered amounted to about C$ 750 billion.[123]

As noted above, the World Economic Forum has, for 9 years in a row, rated Canada as having one of the soundest banking systems in the world. No Canadian bank was in solvency danger in the dotcom bubble of 1997–2001 nor the world-wide financial crisis of 2007–08. The most recent bank failure in Canada was more than two decades ago in 1996. As of the year ended March 2016, there were 78-member institutions ranging from the giant financial institutions that began as banks, to operations of foreign institutions with Canadian charters, to a few financial technology firms holding federal charters.[124] The CDIC collected about C$ 361 million in premiums in 2016 and made provision for insurance losses amounting to C$ 1.3 billion. Given the high international ranking of the soundness of Canadian banking and deposit institutions, and given the size of CDIC assets, customers appear to be adequately protected in the unlikely event of a failure.

5.5 *Insurance*

Insurance policyholders are also protected from failure or distress of their insurance companies. The institutions responsible are *Assuris* (formerly the Canadian Life and Health Insurance Corporation) and Property and Casualty Insurance Compensation Corporation (PCICC). *Assuris* guarantees 85% of insurance benefits promised by members to policyholders and guarantees deposits of policyholders at 100% up to a limit of C$100,000. The same holds for tax-free savings account holders. PCICC guarantees repayment of outstanding claims: auto and commercial insurance claims of up to C$250,000 and home insurance claims of up to C$300,000. The plan is funded through fees paid by member firms. Both Assuris and PCICC can transfer policyholders from a failing insurance company to a solvent member. This is rarely needed but has been achieved with little stress to customers of the failing insurance companies.

Quality among automobile (P&C) insurers is difficult to discern, so consumers are not easily able to move from inferior sellers to those with the best offerings. Consumer protection on insurance disputes (not related to price) is handled tolerably well by provincial regulatory agencies though adjudication delays can be problem. Recent technology, by measuring actual driving behavior, offers improved risk identification and lower premiums for safer driving.

5.6 *Securities Dealers and Exchanges*

The large securities dealers are owned by the big banks which account for two thirds of the value of all securities issued (excluding a tiny portion of new funds provided to start-ups by angel financiers). "The Investment Industry Regulatory Organization of Canada regulates 177 investment dealers and several exchanges."[125] Compensation schemes also extend to customers of investment dealers and mutual fund administrators. However, regulators believe consumers "know" these investments are risky, so protection is restricted to specific risks due to *insolvency* of the investment firm. Insolvency payments for failed securities firms are handled by the Canadian Investor Protection Fund (CIPF), while the Mutual Fund Dealers Association is backed by the Investor Protection Corporation (IPC). Both institutions have coverage limits of C$1 million for systemic risks to all general accounts. Protection is based on *number* of shares held so any decline in a share's value is not compensated. Investor losses that do not result in official insolvency of the seller are not compensated. This puts a remarkably shortsighted focus on prudential matters and shows complete disregard for the importance of market malpractices. The independent group defending investor rights in Canada is the Canadian Foundation for Advancement of Investor Rights (C-FAIR).[126] It has found firms that do not belong to either compensation plan. C-Fair has been seeking a rule requiring all investment firms to be members of an industry organization with an insolvency plan that protects clients. Quebec's regulation is superior: complaints can be directed to Autorité des Marches Financière for disputes *on fraud or selling tactics* related to insurance, financial planning, mutual funds and claims adjustment.[127]

6 Current Issues: The Consumer Interest in Innovation in Financial Services

Evidence on Canada's experience shows several triumphs with *prudential regulation* and many tribulations with complementary policies for *market conduct.* There are two very powerful reasons for intelligent efforts to bring consumer protection against malevolent selling practices up to the level of prudential care. This is a rare time in the history of consumer protection in financial services when disruptive technology gives two system-changing challenges *and* opportunities. Both will determine the success or failure of the future of the sector.

The first is the fact that digital technology has provided a leap in the capability of those who would deceive. As Joseph Stiglitz has observed, "Much of recent innovation has led to products that make cheating the public easier. The implications are complex and profound."[128] From the point of view of consumer protection, fintech is a sword with two very sharp edges. Fintech offers web-based search methods that can efficiently offer information never available before: information on truly new financial offerings, on prices, and, importantly, on experience-based quality. It offers gains from cost reduction in the creation and distribution of financial services. Yet there is a second edge that can cut painfully. Fake products, fake ratings and fake identities are sure to be huge problems. Why? The Willy Sutton principle. Asked Why do you rob banks? Willy famously said, "Because that's where the money is." The most aggressive abuses of technology will be deployed in the financial services sector for the same reason. Cyber risks will be higher than expected. It is generally correct to say that first mover advantage goes to those deploying deception … and policy is obliged to *respond* to problems rather than anticipating them. Sound policies for consumer protection will give rewards to firms with the best offerings, not to scam artists. Quality is front and centre, including "… a redress system which is up to best international practice to give consumers and institutions an edge with superior financial products."[129] Regulatory paralysis is one enemy. A solution incorporates innovative security through the application of digital technology—including big data, pattern recognition, and artificial intelligence.

In Canada, the Ministry of Finance has a working group on Fintech which has a broad base of representation.[130] This breadth may alleviate the expected difficulty identified by the Competition Bureau as the "unintentional entrenchment of incumbent firms".[131] It is natural for existing firms to exaggerate the prudential risk from any innovation that disturbs the status quo. On the opposite side, too many experts wear rose-coloured glasses that see all innovation as positive. Neither of these positions is helpful. What is needed is evidence-based regulation that *reduces rewards for harmful innovations* and makes it easier for positive innovations to enter the financial market—and soon. This will help consumers (and every firm using financial services) while it will, at the same time, reward precisely those firms with superior offerings. Success will facilitate exports of financial services, improving wellbeing elsewhere.

The second problem is rooted in the reality that digital financial services are international, while traditional consumer protection has been national or sub-national. In the digital era, financial consumer protection absolutely must be trans-national, hence the urgency of evidence-based decision-making with an international perspective. This explains the importance of an International Academy of Financial Consumers IAFICO) connecting international research to consumer protection policy.[132]

Cooperative liaisons among national agencies for consumer protection are direct and useful responses to the new digital reality. Major consumer protection networks include: Consumers International www.consumersinternational.org; BEUC: the European Consumer Organization http://www.beuc.eu/; the American Council of Consumer Interests www.consumerinterests.org; the OECD Committee on Consumer Policy www.oecd.org/sti/consumer; ISO—COPOLCO www.iso.org/iso/copolco; and the International Consumer Protection Enforcement Network www.icpen.org. Of special promise is the International Financial Consumer Protection Organization (FinCoNet), founded in 2013 by national financial consumer protection agencies, has 24 full member countries. www.finconet.org. FinCoNet can accelerate policy-sharing, including best practices. It is currently led by Lucie Tedesco Commissioner of Canada's FCAC. Thus far, FinCoNet has facilitated vital input from final users, particularly on mis-selling.[133]

In any country with limited competition in its financial sector there is great promise in disruption from new sources of financial services. The arrival of potential competition in Canada has motivated small improvements in customer satisfaction. New entrants offering financial technology (fintech firms) can be a breath of fresh air. Markets with oligopolistic behaviour—and high switching costs—do not provide incentives to move consumers to superior sellers. An extra policy is essential: *publicly available satisfaction measures*. Financial firms now make private use of customer satisfaction benchmarks, a sharp change from two decades ago.[134] However, this is confidential information collected for the financial institution by one of a half dozen private survey firms. *Consumers* do not get statistically reliable broad-based information on quality. Information shared on web sites is notoriously easy to degrade[135] so reliable sources are crucial. With optimal regulation, the market will offer better prices, fewer financial lemons, and positive new services. The goal is to provide appropriate incentives for prudential decisions, but only when that facilitates policies to enhance consumer success.

In general, there is solid evidence showing triumph with *prudential* regulation in Canada's financial services sector. *Market conduct* regulation is a source of tribulation. The lag is especially challenging if real progress is to be made with innovative (positively disruptive) financial services.

Notes

1. A financial consumer is one covered by the consumer provisions of the *Financial Consumer Agency of Canada Act* of 2001 (henceforth referred to as *FCAC Act*) as defined in Secttion 2, paragraph (a) to paragraph (e) of the *Act*. The FCAC glossary does not define a consumer, nor does it define a financial consumer.
2. An Act to provide "a legislative framework that enables banks to compete effectively and be resilient in a rapidly evolving marketplace, considering the rights and interests of depositors and other consumers of banking services, contributes to stability and public confidence in the financial system and is important to the strength and security of the national economy." Bank Act S.C. 1991, c. 46. Act current to 2017-05-23 and last amended on 2017-04-01. http://lois.justice.gc.ca/eng/acts/B-1.01/FullText.html.
3. An Act to revise and amend the law governing cooperative credit associations Cooperative Credit Associations Act (S.C. 1991, c. 48). Act current to 2017-05-23 and last amended on 2017-01-15. http://lois.justice.gc.ca/eng/acts/C-41.01/index.html.
4. An Act respecting insurance companies and fraternal benefit societies. Insurance Companies Act (S.C. 1991, c. 47). Act current to 2017-05-23 and last amended on 2017-01-15. http://lois.justice.gc.ca/eng/acts/I-11.8/index.html.
5. An Act to revise and amend the law governing federal trust and loan companies. Trust and Loan Companies Act (S.C. 1991, c. 45). Act current to 2017-05-23 and last amended on 2017-01-15. http://lois.justice.gc.ca/eng/acts/T-19.8/index.html.
6. Investment Canada Act. An Act "...to provide for the review of significant investments in Canada by non-Canadians in a manner that encourages investment, economic growth and employment opportunities in Canada and to provide for the review of investments in Canada by non-Canadians that could be injurious to national security'. Act current to 2017-05-23 and last amended on 2015-04-24.
7. Robert R. Kerton, 1995. "A Consumer Test for Financial Regulation in Canada," *Policy Options/ Options Politiques*, Institute for Research on Public Policy, 16 (5), June.
8. Canada, Competition Bureau, 2017. *Competition Bureau of Canada FinTech Market Study—Update*; p. 10. file:///C:/Users/Robert/AppData/Local/Microsoft/Windows/INetCache/Content.Outlook/RQN6RD5P/EN%20Presentation%20Competition%20Bureau%20Market%20Study%20-%2025%20July%202017%20(002).pdf Ottawa.
9. Jurisdictional complexity explains the special need for the Financial Consumer Agency of Canada. The FCAC helps financial consumers by reducing search difficulties (simplifying language in contracts, for example) and by directing web-using consumers to the correct redress agencies.
10. Competition Act (R.S.C. 1985, c C-34). Act current to 2017-05-23 and last amended on 2015-03-09. http://lois.justice.gc.ca/eng/acts/C-34/page-1.

html#h-1 One of the key purposes of the Act is "… to provide consumers with competitive prices and product choices."

11. Financial quality is central to the mission of the International Academy of Financial Consumers (IAFICO); "Financial development, in fact, is more associated with quality improvement than with quantity growth in financial services." Hongjoo Jung, 2017. *International Review of Financial Consumers*; Vol. 2; p.i. file:///C:/Users/Robert/AppData/Local/Microsoft/Windows/INetCache/Content.Outlook/RQN6RD5P/IRFC%20Vol.2%20No.1.
12. Conference Board in Canada, 2016. *An Engine for Growth. 2016 Report Card on Canada and Toronto's Financial Services Sector.* http://www.tfsa.ca/storage/reports/EngineforGrowthFinancialServicesStateoftheSector2016.PDF. "Toronto is one of the largest financial centres in North America and ranks 10th on the Global Financial Centres Index, while Montréal and Vancouver rank in the top 25. Canada, Department of Finance, 2016. *Supporting a Strong and Growing Economy*: Ottawa; p. 9. https://www.fin.gc.ca/activty/consult/ssge-sefc-eng.pdf.
13. The Toronto Real Estate Board, with nearly 40,000 agents is a case study with more sellers than would be needed with open information on listings. "Competition Bureau Sues Canada's Largest Real Estate Board for denying services over the Internet". http://www.competitionbureau.gc.ca/eic/site/cb-bc.nsf/eng/03781.html.
14. OECD, 2014. *Update Report on the Work to Support the Implementation of the G20 High Level Principles on Financial Consumer Protection*; G20/OECD Task Force on Financial Consumer Protection Principles; P.6 and principles 4, 6 and 9). OECD http://www.oecd.org/daf/fin/financial-education/G20EffectiveApproachesFCP.pdf.
15. Statistics Canada, Canada Yearbook 2011; Business performance and ownership; Ottawa. https://www.fin.gc.ca/activty/consult/ssge-sefc-eng.pdf. The insurance sector has the best record of success in meeting international competition with exports.
16. The Bank Act was first passed in 1871, amended to allow federal credit unions in 1991, and is now reviewed every five years. The 2017 Bank Act (S.C. 1991, c. 46).is at http://lois.justice.gc.ca/eng/acts/B-1.01/FullText.html.
17. PWC, 2016. *Embracing the Fintech movement; Perspectives on the Canadian Banking Industry*; pp. 32–33. https://www.pwc.com/ca/en/banking-capital-markets/publications/5056-01-canadian-banks-2016.pdf.
18. Canada, Department of Finance, 2016. *Supporting a Strong and Growing Economy*: Ottawa; p. 11. https://www.fin.gc.ca/activty/consult/ssge-sefc-eng.pdf.
19. CIBC site at https://www.cibc.com/en/about-cibc/investor-relations/share-information/common-share-information/common-dividends.html.
20. Canada, Ministry of Finance, 2016. *Supporting a Strong and Growing Economy: Positioning Canada's Financial Sector for the Future*; A Consultation Document for the Review of the Federal Financial Services Sector; April 26, 2016, p. 11.

21. Export Development Corporation (EDC) 2017. Exportwise; http://exportwise.ca/how-canadas-financial-institutions-pave-way-global-export-success/.
22. Charles Gibney, Sami Bibi and Bruno Lévesque, 2014. *Banking fees in Canada*; FCAC, Ottawa; June. https://www.canada.ca/content/dam/canada/financial-consumer-agency/migration/eng/resources/researchsurveys/documents/bankingfees-fraisbancaires-eng.pdf Their research follows research by J. Allen, & Walter Engert, 2007. "Efficiency and Competition in Canadian Banking". *Bank of Canada Review*, 33–45.
23. Claudio Eggert, 2012. A Strategy Analysis of the "Big Five" Canadian Banks. http://dtpr.lib.athabascau.ca/action/download.php?filename=mba-12/open/eggertclaudioProject.pdf.
24. Canadian Federation for Independent Business, 2016. "Smallest businesses face biggest barriers getting bank financing"; Toronto, October 4. http://www.cfib-fcei.ca/english/article/8761-smallest-businesses-face-biggest-barriers-getting-bank-financing.html The Canadian Federation of Independent Business has regularly sought policies that will provide increased competition and lower bank charges. http://www.cfib-fcei.ca/english/article/8761-smallest-businesses-face-biggest-barriers-getting-bank-financing.html.
25. Power Financial Corporation, 2003. Submission to Minister of Finance Future Structure of The Canadian Financial Services Industry. Submission in Response to Finance Canada's Large Bank Mergers in Canada. http://www.fin.gc.ca/consultresp/mergersrespns_16-eng.asp.
26. Charles Gibney, Sami Bibi and Bruno Lévesque, 2014. *Banking fees in Canada*; FCAC, Ottawa; June. https://www.canada.ca/content/dam/canada/financial-consumer-agency/migration/eng/resources/researchsurveys/documents/bankingfees-fraisbancaires-eng.pdf.
27. Evidence on price changes must be collected on a difficult fee-by-fee basis, then compared to fees elsewhere. The study by the FCAC by Charles Gibney, Sami Bibi and Bruno Lévesque, found that bank fee increases on chequing plans have been moderate, whereas the charges associated with variable fees have increased significantly.
28. Canadian Institute for Health Information 2016. National Health Expenditure Trends, 1975–2016; Ottawa https://secure.cihi.ca/free_products/NHEX-Trends-Narrative-Report_2016_EN.pdf.
29. CLHIA Submission to the House of Commons Committee on Finance on the 2018 Federal Budget; n.d. https://www.clhia.ca/domino/html/clhia/clhia_lp4w_lnd_webstation.nsf/page/7D336251224 5CD2985258172004B085B/$file/2018%20Federal%20Budget%20Submission%20August%204%202017.pdf.
30. Export Development Corporation (EDC) 2017. Exportwise; http://exportwise.ca/industry-without-borders-canada-fintech-companies-need-export-ready/.
31. See IBC FACT, 2016 and the OSFI website.
32. American Customer Satisfaction Index, 2017. http://www.theacsi.org/index.php?option=com_content&view=article&id=149&catid=&Itemid=214&i=Property+and+Casualty+Insurance.

33. Bank of Canada 2016. Financial System Review; Ottawa http://www.bankofcanada.ca/wp-content/uploads/2016/06/fsr-june2016.pdf p. 11.
34. The FCAC website lowers the consumer's search cost by providing information on specific sections, on codes of conduct and on public commitments by most of these types of institutions (see http://www.fcac-acfc.gc.ca/Eng/forIndustry/regulatedEntities/Pages/home-accueil.aspx).
35. Union des consommateurs, 2014. «Observations d'Union des consommateurs sur le document de consultation: Cadre de protection des consommateurs de produits et services financiers du Canada» https://www.fin.gc.ca/consultresp/fcpf-cpcpsf/116-fcpf-cpcpsf.pdf. Consumers Council of Canada, 2014. Submission to Finance Canada re: Canada's Financial Consumer Protection Framework. https://www.fin.gc.ca/consultresp/fcpf-cpcpsf/082-fcpf-cpcpsf.pdf.
36. OECD, 2014. *Update Report on the Work to Support the Implementation of the G20 High Level Principles on Financial Consumer Protection*; G20/OECD Task Force on Financial Consumer Protection Principles. Especially principles 4, 6 and 9). OECD http://www.oecd.org/daf/fin/financial-education/G20EffectiveApproachesFCP.pdf.
37. Canada, Office of the Superintendent of Financial Institutions, 2017. http://www.osfi-bsif.gc.ca/Eng/osfi-bsif/Pages/default.aspx.
38. This is no surprise because "OSFI's mandate is focused exclusively on protecting the savings of depositors and policyholders…." International Monetary Fund 2014. IMF Country Report 14/29 Canada, Financial Sector Stability Assessment; https://www.imf.org/external/pubs/ft/scr/2014/cr1429.pdf; p. 24. Lack of attention to consumer empowerment reduces consumer success and directly lowers the efficiency of financial markets. "According to the survey by the World Economic Forum, Canada has the world's best banking system." *The Best Banking Systems in the World*; finweb.com https://www.finweb.com/banking-credit/the-bestbanking-systems-in-the-world.html. The word "best" clearly applies to prudential matters, not necessarily to overall consumer protection.
39. Ibid; p. 24. The central players in preventing merger were the Minister of Finance and the Competition Bureau.
40. For example, a report on 2009 profits of RBC noted a contribution from Canadian customers: "……the bank's overall profits would have risen from 2008 were it not for a $1 billion goodwill impairment that stems from the declining value of the bank's US business. *The Globe and Mail*, Feb 9, 2010 Report on Business; p. B9.
41. Elizabeth Warren, 2008. "Product Safety Regulation as a Model for Financial Services Regulation," *Journal of Consumer Affairs*; 42:3; pp. 452–60.
42. George A. Akerlof and Robert J. Shiller, 2015. *Phishing for Phools: The Economics of Manipulation and Deception*; Princeton University Press.
43. https://www.imf.org/external/pubs/ft/scr/2014/cr1429.pdf. Benchmarks of the resilience of the financial system for comparable countries shift over time but from 2005 to 2017, market perceptions of banking system resilience reveal Canada at the top when compared with the measures for the U.S., the Euro area, Australia or the U.K. Cameron MacDonald, Maarten R.C. van Oordt,

2017. *Financial System Review*; Bank of Canada; p. 33. http://www.bankofcanada.ca/wp-content/uploads/2017/06/fsr-june2017.pdf.
44. "There are some large credit unions regulated at the provincial level that require the provincial supervisors to have the capacity, on a standalone basis, to effectively supervise them and for the respective provinces to have the fiscal resources to backstop depositors and resolve any nonviable ones in an orderly fashion. Because of the wide dispersion of supervisory talent across the provinces, however, it can be challenging for all provincial supervisors, on a standalone basis, to acquire the breadth, depth of experience, and supervisory capacity needed for the task." International Monetary Fund, 2014. IMF Country Report 14/29 Canada, Financial Sector Stability Assessment; p. 24. http://www.osfi-bsif.gc.ca/Eng/Docs/ar-ra/1516/eng/p2-eng.html.
45. Payments Canada, 2017 and https://en.wikipedia.org/wiki/Payments_Canada
46. Financial Consumer Agency of Canada, 2017. "Cheque hold periods and access to funds." https://www.canada.ca/en/financial-consumer-agency/services/rights-responsibilities/rights-banking/cheque-hold-access-funds.html#toc0. Payments Canada has had, since 2001, expert user representation via a formal 20-person Advisory Council but that has not tipped the balance toward system efficiency or consumer protection. https://www.payments.ca/about-us/how-we-collaborate/stakeholder-advisory-council.
47. pwc Canada, 2017. *Canadian Banks 2017# Bankovation;* "Pain Points for 2017" B McFarland and D.A. Kazarian at https://www.pwc.com/ca/en/industries/banking-capital-markets/canadian-banks-2017.html.
48. Payments Canada. Bank of Canada and R3, 2017. Distributed Ledger Technology for Domestic Interbank Payments Settlement https://www.payments.ca/sites/default/files/29-Sep-17/jasper_report_eng.pdf.
49. Ibid.
50. Maureen Gillis and Alexandru Trusca, 2017. "Not There Yet": Bank of Canada Experiments with Blockchain Wholesale Payment System; Cyberlex; June 19. http://www.canadiancybersecuritylaw.com/2017/06/not-there-yet-bank-of-canada-experiments-with-blockchain-wholesale-payment-system/.
51. Complexity may simply be an inevitable part of financial products and this may seriously reduce the promise that "financial literacy" can solve the search problem. OECD research identified 14 different components of a mortgage application. OECD, 2009. *Financial Literacy and Consumer Protection: Overlooked Aspects of the Crisis*, *OECD* Recommendation on Good Practices on Financial Education and Awareness Relating to Credit; June; p. 18. Andrew Kormylo conducted research where he asked Canadian bank customers to identify the components of banking service. Francophone banking service consumers in Quebec offered, (unprompted) 20 different characteristics from their own experience. The result of prompting by the interviewer (based on different services suggested by other consumers in the sample) led to respondents identifying 32 different components. A. Kormylo, MA, "Consumer Satisfaction with Banking: The Concept of Quality in the Service Sector," University of Waterloo, 1991.

52. World Bank, 2012. *Good Practices for Financial Consumer Protection*; p. 89.
53. Robert R. Kerton and Richard Bodell, 1995. "The Marketing of Lemons: Quality, Choice and the Economics of Concealment," *Journal of Consumer Affairs*, 29(1), pp. 1–28.
54. Financial literacy can be increased by investing in individual 'search capital' like numeracy. Individual capital has a payoff that is amplified by 'collective search capital' like FCAC enforcement of plain language documents, or competition policy, for a second example, by enforcing rules against 'astro-turfing' or the planting of fake online assessments of financial services. The denominator needs to account for the combination of private and public search capital. Robert R. Kerton, 1980. "Consumer Search Capital, delineating a concept and applying it to developing countries"; *Journal of Consumer Policy*, Vol. 4; pp. 293–305.
55. The *Journal of Consumer* Affairs devoted a whole issue to these topics. The evidence is convincing that a 'key facts panel' (reducing C rather than increasing K) offers the highest short run payoff. John Kozup and Jeanne Hogarth, 2008, "Financial literacy, public policy, and consumers' self-protection–more questions, fewer answers," *Journal of Consumer Affairs* 42 (2).
56. Decima Research, 2007. *FCAC Stakeholder and Partner Research (Final Report)*, Financial Consumer Agency of Canada; pages 12 and 19. http://www.fcac-acfc.gc.ca/eng/Publications/SurveyStudy/Misc/PDFs/2007SurSPR-eng.pdf.
57. Canadian Partnership for Public Policy Oriented Consumer Interest Research (PPOCIR) http://ppocir.uwaterloo.ca/ppocir-knowledge-centre/.
58. 2016 Workshop of the PPOCIR http://ppocir.uwaterloo.ca/wp-content/uploads/2017/04/2016-PPOCIR-SUMMARY-Workshop-English.pdf.
59. https://www.ic.gc.ca/eic/site/oca-bc.nsf/eng/h_ca02207.html See also https://www.ic.gc.ca/eic/site/oca-bc.nsf/eng/ca02559.html.
60. Office of Consumer Affairs, 2017. *Contributions Program for Non-Profit Consumer and Voluntary Organizations: 20 Years Later*. Summary of Workshop with 11 Consumer Groups held on March 31, 2017; p. 6.
61. 2016–17 Project Summaries: Contributions Program for Non-profit Consumer and Voluntary Organizations, Office of Consumer Affairs; https://www.ic.gc.ca/eic/site/oca-bc.nsf/eng/ca02942.html.
62. Canada's 'Contributions Program for Non-Profit Consumer and Voluntary Organizations' is a research program for consumer NGOs funded based on competitive proposals from consumer NGOs.
63. Lawson, Philippa, Nathalie St-Pierre, Marcel Boucher, David Cuming, 2003. "Pilot Project: Canadian Code of Practice for Consumer Protection in Electronic Commerce"; Public Interest Advocacy Centre\; Ottawa), online: http://www.ic.gc.ca/app/oca/crd/dcmnt.do?id=1602&lang=eng. The code was endorsed by federal, provincial and territorial consumer ministers in 2004.

64. Financial Consumer Agency of Canada, 2017. Canadian Financial Literacy Database http://itools-ioutils.fcac-acfc.gc.ca/RDCV-BRVC/sear-rech-eng.aspx?f0=2&f5=14&WT.mc_id=CFLD-TA-YoungAdults. See also https://en.wikipedia.org/wiki/Financial_Consumer_Agency_of_Canada.
65. Canadian Foundation for Economic Education http://cfee.org/resources/.
66. One successful CFEE strategy to empower young people has students compete with presentations explaining solutions to financial problems they, themselves, identify and research. The success of this program demonstrates that young people can gain the control needed to make deliberate decisions.
67. Rotter, J.B. 1954. *Social learning and clinical psychology*. NY: Prentice-Hall. Rotter, J.B. 1966. "Generalized expectancies of internal versus external control of reinforcements". *Psychological Monographs*. 80(609); pp. 1–28.
68. Michael A. Busseri, Herbert M. Lefcourt, Robert R. Kerton, Locus of Control for Consumer Outcomes: Predicting Consumer Behavior1, *Journal of Applied Social Psychology*, 1998, **28**, 12, 1067–1087. http://onlinelibrary.wiley.com/doi/10.1111/j.1559-1816.1998.tb01668.x/full. In 2016 the FCAC published a summary of a commissioned study that identified a distinct role for financial confidence interacting with financial knowledge in consumer decision-making. Boris Palameta, Cam Nguyen, Taylor Shek-wai Hui and David Gyarmati, The Social Research and Demonstration Corporation. https://www.canada.ca/content/dam/canada/financial-consumer-agency/migration/eng/resources/researchsurveys/documents/link-confidence-outcomes.pdf.
69. Statistics Canada, 2014. *New facts about financial literacy in Canada*; Ottawa. http://www.statcan.gc.ca/daily-quotidien/160323/dq160323b-eng.htm.
70. OECD, 2017. Students' Financial Literacy: PISA Results (Volume IV) May 24; Paris. http://www.oecd.org/finance/financial-education/pisa-2015-results-volume-iv-9789264270282-en.htm. The sample size is about 48,000 students and the dispersion among scores ***within*** every country is remarkably high. Surveys were conducted in 2015.
71. European Commission, 2011. The Consumer Empowerment Index; JRC Scientific and Technical Reports; Michela Nardo, Massimo Loi, Rossana Rosati, Anna Manca; EUR 24791 EN; p. 52.
72. Norway's National Institute for Consumer Research (SIFO) was founded in 1939 and had a staff of 50 in 2000. http://www.nanoplat.org/?q=node/23. This type of online research capability would bring Canada forward considerably. Prior to the internet era, Canada did have long run capability with a national Consumer Research Council in the early and mid-1970s.
73. European Commission, 2011. The Consumer Empowerment Index; JRC Scientific and Technical Reports; Michela Nardo, Massimo Loi, Rossana Rosati, Anna Manca; EUR 24791 EN; p. 52. http://ec.europa.eu/consumers/consumer_empowerment/docs/JRC_report_consumer_empowerment_en.pdf.
74. The NQI is at http://www.nqi.ca/en/about-us/ and Excellence Canada at http://excellence.ca/en/about-us/

75. The American Customer Satisfaction Index is at http://www.theacsi.org/.
76. https://www.protegez-vous.ca/partenaires/autorite-des-marches-financiers/Ce-que-vous-devez-savoir-sur-l-assurance-vie.
77. https://www.test.de/shop/finanztest-hefte/.
78. Charles Gibney, Sami Bibi and Bruno Lévesque, 2014. *Banking fees in Canada*; FCAC, Ottawa; June.
79. Competition Bureau, 2017. "Competition Bureau focuses on fake online reviews during fifth annual '2 Good 2 B True Day'. March 9, 2017; Ottawa. https://www.canada.ca/en/competition-bureau/news/2017/03/fake_online_reviewstoogoodtobetrue.html?=undefined&wbdisable=true.
80. CBCnews Business, 2017. GO PUBLIC, "'We are all doing it': Employees at Canada's 5 big banks speak out about pressure to dupe customers", March 15 http://www.cbc.ca/news/business/banks-upselling-go-public-1.4023575.
81. See MFDA and IIROC websites for details on *MFDA Rule 1.2* and *IIROC Rule 2900.*
82. This is an example of Akerlof's market for lemons. Consumers lose, and so do sellers with superior offerings, some of whom will feel obliged to offer concealed rewards to get brokers to handle their offerings. George A. Akerlof, 1970. "The Market for "Lemons": Quality Uncertainty and the Market Mechanism" *The Quarterly Journal of Economics*, . http://links.jstor.org/sici?sici=0033-5533%28197008%2984%3A3%3C488%3ATMF%22QU%3E2.0.CO%3B2-6. Overall economic incentives depend on many factors, mainly on the effectiveness of "noise" or regulatory devices to guarantee the concealment of information, the size of any penalty—administered by a court or by the market through reputational loss, the probability of being apprehended and the economic payoff from the practice. 1995 Robert R. Kerton and Richard W. Bodell, "The Marketing of Lemons: Quality, Choice and the Economics of Concealment" The Journal of Consumer Affairs, 29(1), pp. 1–28.
83. Andrew Marsh, 2017. "The four pillars of financial advisor trustworthiness"; *Globe Investor 13/6/2017*. https://www.theglobeandmail.com/globe-investor/globe-wealth/the-four-pillars-of-adviser-trustworthiness/article35292479/.
84. Research by Paul Beam, Helene Carty and Judith Colbert, in Robert R. Kerton, 1998, *in Consumers in the Financial Services Sector*, Volume 1: *Principles, Practice and Policy—the Canadian Experience*, pp. 31–205; ISBN 0-662-27146-7; tables IV.2 AND IV.3: pp. 198–99; Research Papers for the Task Force on the Future of the Canadian Financial Services Sector. Ottawa. ISBN 0-662-27146-7.
85. Decima Research, 2007. *FCAC Stakeholder and Partner Research (Final Report)*, Financial Consumer Agency of Canada; pages 12 and 19. http://www.fcac-acfc.gc.ca/eng/Publications/SurveyStudy/Misc/PDFs/2007SurSPR-eng.pdf. A Decima Research survey of stakeholders and partners found that while only 41% of respondents rated the agency 'excellent' or 'good' (out of four choices) on market conduct and consumer protection, fully 73% of the institutions being regulated reported that they had made changes to policies and procedures because of the FCAC's actions and decisions.

86. Profit from the price discrimination deployed under this strategy is explained in Stephen Salop, 1977; "The Noisy Monopolist: Imperfect Information, Price Dispersion and Price Discrimination, *Review of Economic Studies*, 44 (3) pp. 393–406.
87. http://itools-ioutils.fcac-acfc.gc.ca/stcv-osvc/ccst-oscc-eng.aspx.
88. Financial Consumer Agency of Canada, 2017. Testing of Credit Card Disclosure Statements and Accompanying Card Holder Agreement -Final Report prepared by: ACNielsen company of Canada prepared for: Financial Consumer Agency of Canada. http://epe.lac-bac.gc.ca/100/200/301/pwgsc-tpsgc/por-ef/financial_consumer_agency/2017/029-16-e/report.pdf.
89. Ibid, p. 14.
90. In 2016 the FCAC notified an unspecified bank of seven charges related to a failure to inform borrowers of fees—in advance—as required by Canada's Cost of Borrowing Regulations and Electronic Documents regulations. In the end, the Commissioner upheld 6 of 7 alleged violations and assessed a fine of $365,000. The charges are provided, the defence, and the final decision are provided on a section of the FCAC web site that is not very easy to locate. At no point is the offending financial institution identified. Government of Canada, 2017. *Decision 128 from Financial Consumer Agency of Canada*. https://www.canada.ca/en/financial-consumer-agency/services/industry/commissioner-decisions/decision-128.html
91. The references to specific bank documents are in Public Interest Advocacy Centre and Option consommateurs, 2016. Positioning Canada's financial sector for consumers: Comments on a consultation document for the review of the Federal financial sector framework; p. 38. https://www.fin.gc.ca/consultresp/pdf-ssge-sefc/ssge-sefc-50.pdf.
92. The FCAC has promised that, in 2017–18, the Agency will conduct an industry review into bank sales practices to assess the impact such practices have on consumers. "As well, the Agency will continue to respond to the evolving nature of market conduct oversight by ensuring its structure and resources are up to the challenge." Lucie Tedesco, 2017. *Financial Consumer Agency of Canada: 2017–18 Business Plan;* Commissioner's Message: Looking to the Future; https://www.canada.ca/content/dam/fcac-acfc/documents/corporate/planning/business-plan-2017-18.pdf. The level of resourcing will be key.
93. Some banks use contracts for use of Automated Teller Machines (ATMs) that include terms stating the bank "…is in no way responsible for malfunctioning ATMs, even if they are located on bank-owned property."
94. Jacques St. Amant, the Public Interest Advocacy Centre and Option consommateurs, 2016. Positioning Canada's financial sector for consumers: Comments on a consultation document for the review of the Federal financial sector framework); p. 36. https://www.fin.gc.ca/consultresp/pdf-ssge-sefc/ssge-sefc-50.pdf.
95. Financial Consumer Agency of Canada Annual Report 2016–17 https://www.canada.ca/content/dam/fcac-acfc/documents/corporate/planning/annual-reports/FCAC-annual-report-2016-17.pdf.

96. Organisation for Economic Co-operation and Development, "G20 High-Level Principles on Financial Consumer Protection" (October 2011). Online: http://www.oecd.org/dataoecd/58/26/48892010.pdf. The recommendations include a duty for sellers to reveal conflicts of interest, protection not generally provided in Canada.
97. World Bank, "Good Practices for Financial Consumer Protection" (June 2012). http://siteresources.worldbank.org/EXTFINANCIALSECTOR/Resources/Good_Practices_for_Financial_CP.pdf.
98. PIAC observes that much of Canada's lag in supervisory practice could be overcome by making use of codes already in place in Australia and Ireland. Public Interest Advocacy Centre (PIAC), 2014. Comments of the Public Interest Advocacy Centre on the Ministry of Finance Consultation Paper: *Canada's Financial Consumer Protection Framework;* pp. 8–9 https://www.fin.gc.ca/consultresp/fcpf-cpcpsf/096-fcpf-cpcpsf.pdf.
99. Ibid.; p. 28.
100. Union des consommateurs, 2014. «Observations d'Union des consommateurs sur le document de consultation: Cadre de protection des consommateurs de produits et services financiers du Canada»; p. 10, 18. https://www.fin.gc.ca/consultresp/fcpf-cpcpsf/116-fcpf-cpcpsf.pdf.
101. Consumers Council of Canada, 2014. Submission to Finance Canada re: Canada's Financial Consumer Protection Framework. https://www.fin.gc.ca/consultresp/fcpf-cpcpsf/082-fcpf-cpcpsf.pdf.
102. Jacques St Amant, 2014. «Consultation du ministère des Finances relative au cadre de protection des consommateurs de services financiers» https://www.fin.gc.ca/consultresp/fcpf-cpcpsf/121-fcpf-cpcpsf.pdf.
103. James Callon, 2014. Submission on *Canada's Financial Consumer Protection Framework Consultation;* p. 12.
104. Lucie Tedesco, 2017. *Communication, Collaboration and Consultation—Requirements for a strong consumer protection framework*; Speech to the Annual Consumer Session, Ottawa; March 30, 2017; p. 2.
105. In the 6 years from its start in July 2011, the CFPB has required the return of about US$12 billion to 29 million consumers who had been cheated. Remarks of CFPB Director Richard Cordray at the People and Places Conference, Arlington; 31 May 2017. https://www.consumerfinance.gov/about-us/newsroom/prepared-remarks-cfpb-director-richard-cordray-people-and-places-conference/.
106. Op cit. James Callon; pp. 17–21.
107. Deborah Battell and Nikki Pender, 2016. *Independent Evaluation of the Canadian Ombudsman for Banking Services and Investments' (OBSI) Investment Mandate*; OSBI; p. 5.
108. Ibid, p. 1.
109. Rita Trichur, 2017. "The Weakest Link; The Globe and Mail Report on Business Magazine; Nov. 2017; p. 18.
110. Battell and Pender, p. 49.

111. Robert R. Kerton et al., "Developments in the Canadian Financial System." Submission to the Senate Standing Committee on Banking, Trade and Commerce for the Consumer's Association of Canada (CAC), March 21, 1995. In August 1995, an invited presentation of research was given by the Consumers Association of Canada as testimony on *Bill C-100 to Amend, Enact and Repeal Laws Relating to Financial Institutions*; for the House of Commons Committee on Finance, Trade and Economic Affairs (Peterson Committee). The CAC and other consumer groups testified before the same Committee and before the Senate of Canada Committee on Banking (Kirby Committee) on Oct. 2, 1996.
112. Kerton, Robert R, 1998. Consumers in the Financial Services Sector, Volume 1: *Principles, Practice and Policy—the Canadian Experience*, (author/ editor) pp. 267. The consumer situation in seven comparable countries was examined in Volume 2 (R. Kerton, Editor*): Consumers in the Financial Services Sector: International Experience*, Research Papers for the Task Force on the Future of the Canadian Financial Services Sector. Ottawa. ISBN 0-662-27146-7 and ISBN 0-662-27147—http://publications.gc.ca/collections/Collection/F21-6-1998-8-1E.pdf. Les consommateurs et le secteur des services financiers; disponible à http://finservtaskforce.fin.gc.ca/research/recherch.htm.
113. In early 2017 the FCAC was accused of being effete or late responding to egregious selling practices of major banks who quietly changed the teller-consumer interface by providing tellers with incentives to sell extra fee-earning services that consumers did not need nor understand. Go Public, CBC Television. See also "'*We are all doing it': Employees at Canada's 5 big banks speak out about pressure to dupe customers"*; March 15, 2017. http://www.cbc.ca/news/business/banks-upselling-go-public-1.4023575. On June 5, 2017 the FCAC told a parliamentary Committee it had reviewed research into sales targets and bank selling practices in at least three other countries in 2016 and further, that after the CBC Go Public program the FCAC increased its focus on express consent and disclosure of fees. http://www.cbc.ca/news/politics/banks-finance-mps-hearings-1.4146800.
114. Central Bank of Ireland, Consumer Protection Code, 2012, pp. 5–6. Last accessed February 19, 2014 at http://www.centralbank.ie/regulation/processes/consumer-protectioncode/documents/consumer%20protection%20code%202012.pdf.
115. A. Andreason and A. Best, 1977. "Consumer Complains—Does Business Respond?" *Harvard Business Review*.
116. Fornell, Claes, (2007), *The Satisfied Customer: Winners and Losers in the Battle for Buyer Preference*. N.Y.: Palgrave Macmillan. Fornell, Claes, David Van Amburg, Forrest Morgeson & Barbara Bryant, (2005). *The American Customer Satisfaction Index at 10 Years*. Ann Arbor: The Stephen M. Ross School of Business.
117. Canada, 2014. *Survey of Innovation and Business Strategy*, Statistics Canada; *The Daily*, March 28, 2014. http://www.statcan.gc.ca/daily-quotidien/140328/dq140328a-eng.htm. The survey covered 2010–2012 and the sample included

7818 enterprises in Canada with at least 20 employees and revenues of $250,000 or more. Included were 14 sectors but three of the four largest (by number of enterprises) had samples too small to be reported separately in the table: the retail, construction and wholesale trades.

118. See the 2006 Standing Senate Committee on Banking, Trade and Commerce Report title "Consumer Protection in the Financial Service Sector". http://publications.gc.ca/collections/collection_2007/sen/YC11-391-1-02E.pdf.
119. Deborah Battell and Nikki Pender, 2016. *Independent Evaluation of the Canadian Ombudsman for Banking Services and Investments' (OBSI) Investment Mandate*; OSBI; p. 1.
120. One example notes that "Amex didn't inform card users about the commission, let alone tell them the rate. The company simply converted the charge on credit cards to Canadian dollars using an exchange rate that it unilaterally chose." Sue Montgomery, Canwest News Service, 2009. "Quebec court orders banks to pay back credit card fees: Charges accrued on purchases made in foreign currency." Friday, June 12. http://www2.canada.com/topics/news/story.html?id=1688464. The Quebec Superior Court ordered restitution of approximately US$ 180 million.
121. Canadian Federation for Independent Business, 2016. "Smallest businesses face biggest barriers getting bank financing"; Toronto, October 4. http://www.cfib-fcei.ca/english/article/8761-smallest-businesses-face-biggest-barriers-getting-bank-financing.html.
122. Stephen Salop, 1977; "The Noisy Monopolist: Imperfect Information, Price Dispersion and Price Discrimination, *Review of Economic Studies*, 44 (3) pp. 393–406.
123. Canada Deposit Insurance Corporation 2017. http://www.cdic.ca/en/newsroom/newsreleases/Pages/further-steps-on-bail-in-regime-will-strengthen-cdic-power-to-resolve-large-banks-in-failure.aspx.
124. Canada Deposit Insurance Corporation Annual Report, 2016.
125. "Examples include the Toronto Stock Exchange (TSX), the TSX Venture Exchange, the Montréal Exchange, the Canadian Securities Exchange, the Aequitas NEO Exchange, the Natural Gas Exchange, ICE Futures Canada and 12 alternative trading systems." Canada, Department of Finance, 2016. *Supporting a Strong and Growing Economy*: Ottawa; p. 18. https://www.fin.gc.ca/activty/consult/ssge-sefc-eng.pdf.
126. Founded in 2008. See https://faircanada.ca/about-us/ FAIR has strongly supported a best interest standard. https://faircanada.ca/submissions/fair-canada-comments-on-proposed-best-interest-standard-and-proposed-targeted-reforms/.
127. In cases of embezzlement or deceptive selling practices, the Autorité can make restitution up to C$ 200,000 from an industry-financed fund. https://lautorite.qc.ca/en/general-public/assistance-complaint-and-compensation/file-a-complaint/.
128. Joseph E. Stiglitz, Nobel Laureate in Economics in his forward to George Akerlof and Robert Shiller, 2015. Phishing *for Phools: The Economics of Manipulation and Deception*; Princeton.

129. Robert R. Kerton, 1990. "Financial Quality and the Consumer Interest," *Canadian Banker* 97 (4); pp. 6–13. "La qualité des services financières et l'intérêt du consommateur," *Le Banquier*, Juillet/Août, pp. 24–31.
130. Finance Canada Payments Consultative Committee (FINPAY).
131. Competition Bureau Canada, 2017. *Fintech Market Study—Update*; Ottawa; p. 14. file:///C:/Users/Robert/AppData/Local/Microsoft/Windows/INetCache/Content.Outlook/RQN6RD5P/EN%20Presentation%20Competition%20Bureau%20Market%20Study%20-%2025%20July%202017.p.
132. The Academy links international research to policy. Its goals: "IAFICO aims to serve as a global platform for sharing information, knowledge on "Financial" products and services, regulations and supervision, institutions and culture, education and training in order to reasonably serve financial consumers' interests and well-being as well as to facilitate long-term financial development from an impartial perspective." https://www.iafico.org/about.
133. A report to FinCoNet from Consumers International contains several useful regulatory steps that are key to inspiring a firm to change the incentive structure to make it more profitable to offer effective services rather than to rely on mis-selling. Consumers International, 2017. "Public Consultation: Impact of Sales Incentives on the Sale of Consumer Credit Products," FinCoNet. http://www.finconet.org/Consumers_International_Response_PC.pdf An additional rule not yet in the CI recommendations, would require that consumers be reimbursed for the harm done to them from mis-selling. This rule encourages firms to report 'mis-selling risk' to their boards.
134. Robert R. Kerton,1990 "Financial Quality and the Consumer Interest," Canadian Banker 97 (4); pp. 6–13. "La qualité des services financières et l'intérêt du consommateur," Le Banquier, Juillet/Août, pp. 24–31.
135. Competition Bureau, 2017. "Competition Bureau focuses on fake online reviews during fifth annual '2 Good 2 B True Day'. March 9, 2017; Ottawa. https://www.canada.ca/en/competition-bureau/news/2017/03/fake_online_reviewstoogoodtobetrue.html?=undefined&wbdisable=true.

Acknowledgements This research was supported by a Partnership Development Grant from the Social Sciences and Humanities Research Council of Canada, and a grant from the Faculty of Arts at the University of Waterloo.

Robert Kerton served as Chair, Economics, and Dean of Arts at the University of Waterloo, Canada. He earned: B.Com (Toronto), M.A. (Carleton) and Ph.D. (Duke). Bob's research is on consumer protection. In 1990, he wrote "Financial Quality and the Consumer Interest," and in 1995, "A Consumer Test for Financial Regulation in Canada." Bob administered consumer research for a national enquiry on Canada's financial services sector. Published in 1998, the research immediately influenced policy. Bob was President of the American Council on Consumer Interests in 2004–05. From 2014–2018 he helped lead an interdisciplinary research/policy project including several universities, consumer NGOs and consumer protection agencies.

Idris Ademuyiwa holds an M.Sc. in Economics from the University of Ibadan, Nigeria, an M.A. in Economics from the University of Waterloo, Canada and his published research is on trade and macroeconomics. Idris is currently Research Associate at the Centre for International Governance Innovation (CIGI) in Waterloo, Ontario.

Chapter 5
Financial Consumer Protection in China

Xian Xu

1 Financial Consumer

1.1 Official Definition of Financial Consumer

When the traditional concept of consumer is applied to the financial sector, sometimes its meaning is ambiguous, and the existing legislation for consumer protection in financial industry is insufficient, of the lack which makes setting definition of financial consumer in China a real necessity. Fan (2012) said, from the reality of China, the more feasible approach is to make a clear definition of financial consumer, so that it covers the entire financial services, and in the consumer protection system is to follow the minimum coordination principle, only to make the provisions of the industry by the regulatory authorities based on industry characteristics and the regulatory organizations need to implement the details.

China, at present, has no specialized and comprehensive law concentrated on protecting rights of financial consumers. Therefore, there is no legal meaning of "financial consumer" in China.

However, a more general law, Law of the People's Republic of China on Protection of Consumer Rights and Interests, initially and systematically provides articles concerning the protection of consumers' rights in any industry (From Official Government Website 2013). It was first put into effective use in January 1st, 1993 and recently got revised on October 25th, 2003. In this law, Article 2 claims that the rights and interests of consumers in purchasing and using commodities or receiving services for daily consumption shall be under the protection of the present Law, or under the protection of other relevant laws and regulations in absence of stipulations in this Law. More specifically, Article 7 emphasizes that consumers

X. Xu (✉)
Fudan University, Shanghai, China
e-mail: xianxu@fudan.edu.cn

© Springer Nature Singapore Pte Ltd. 2018

T.-J. Chen (ed.), *An International Comparison of Financial Consumer Protection*,
https://doi.org/10.1007/978-981-10-8441-6_5

shall, in their purchasing and using commodities or receiving services, enjoy the right of the inviolability of their personal and property safety. Consumers shall have the right to demand business operators to supply commodities and services up to the requirements of personal and property safety.

In conclusion, although Law of the People's Republic of China on Protection of Consumer Rights and Interests protects the rights and interests of consumers, it does not provide a definition of consumer. Given that there is still no specific law specifically about the protection of financial consumers' rights, legal meaning of financial consumer is not defined in China as well.

1.2 Economic Situation of Financial Consumer

First, let us have a look at population, age structure and income situation in China (Fig. 1).

Although the population of China remains increasing, it is still kept under 1.4 billion with its growth rate around 0.5%. Next, age structure is pictured below (Fig. 2).

Explicitly, the age structure remains extremely steady. In recent years, the population under age 14 decreased, while the population over age 65 increased, which makes a sustainable supply of labor force a problem for China in the future.

In addition, per capita disposable income is introduced here (Fig. 3).

As we can see, per capita disposable income keeps increasing from 2007 to 2014, which potentially means the ability of purchase correspondingly increases. The average growth rate is around 16%. Given the growth rate, per capital disposable income could reach 70,275 in 2020.

As for social security system, China has basically formed its social security system through tremendous reformation over the last 30 years. On the one hand, in urban cities, social security system is composed of endowment insurance, medical

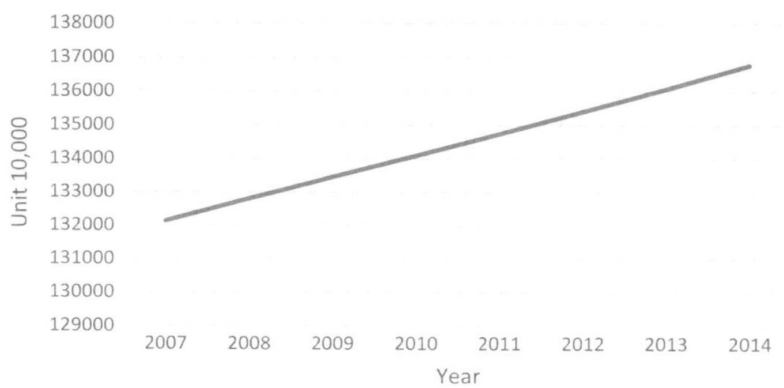

Fig. 1 Population of China (2007–2014). *Source* Official website of National Bureau of Statistics of the People's Republic of China: http://www.stats.gov.cn/

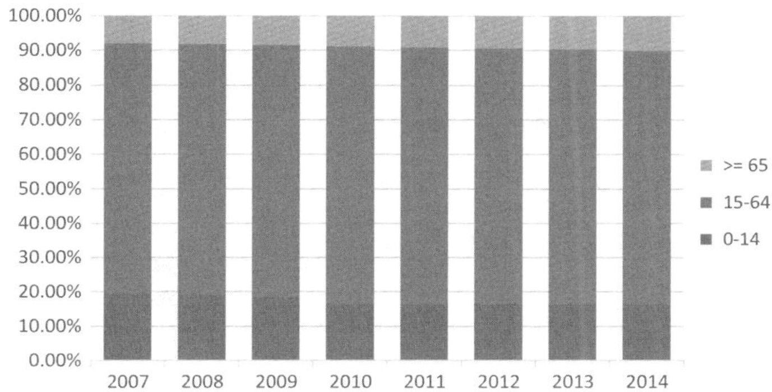

Fig. 2 Age structure. *Source* Official website of National Bureau of Statistics of the People's Republic of China: http://www.stats.gov.cn/

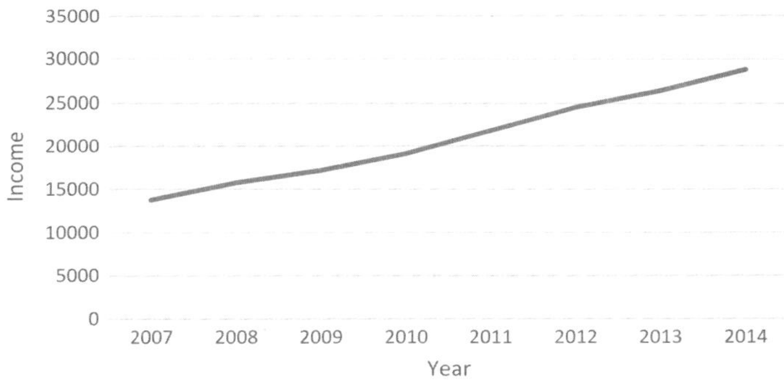

Fig. 3 Per capita disposable income. *Source* Official website of National Bureau of Statistics of the People's Republic of China: http://www.stats.gov.cn/

insurance, unemployment insurance, employment injury insurance, and maternity insurance. In addition, the social security system has successfully guaranteed the lowest allowance for people in those areas. On the other hand, in rural areas, China keeps on trying to fulfill a basic allowance system and accelerate reforming the health care system.

The following Table 1 illustrates that the participants of social security system steadily increases in China (Fig. 4).

Overall, the number of participants has increased from 2009 to 2014. Comparing the situation among these five insurances, medical insurance shows the most rapid increase. From absolute number of participants, medical insurance also ranks the first and maternity insurance the last in terms of number of participants.

Social security system plays an important role in the Chinese society. Premium collected by the system is managed by separate funds of different social insurance. The following figures show the trend of the fund value of different kind of social insurance in China (Figs. 5 and 6).

Table 1 Participants of social security system (2009–2014) (Unit 10,000)

	2009	2010	2011	2012	2013	2014
Medical insurance	40,147	44652.5	47343.2	53641.3	57072.6	59746.9
Endowment insurance	23549.9	25707.3	28391.3	30426.8	32218.4	34124.4
Unemployment insurance	12715.5	13375.6	14317.2	15224.7	16416.8	17042.6
Employment injury insurance	14895.5	16160.7	17695.9	19010.1	19917.2	20639.2
Maternity insurance	10875.7	12335.9	13892	15428.7	16392	17038.7

Referred from http://data.stats.gov.cn/

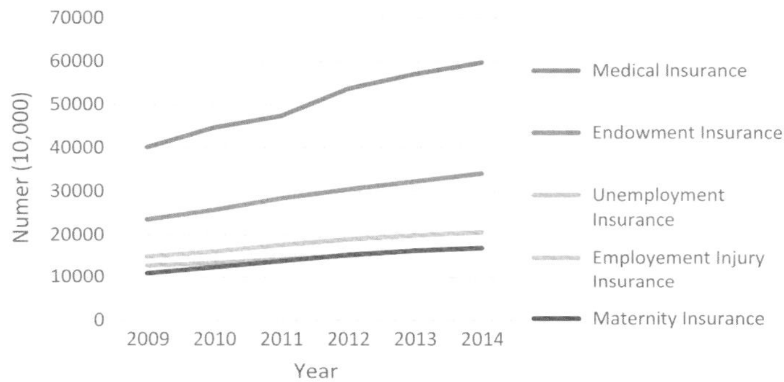

Fig. 4 Participants of social security system. *Source* Official website of National Bureau of Statistics of the People's Republic of China: http://www.stats.gov.cn/

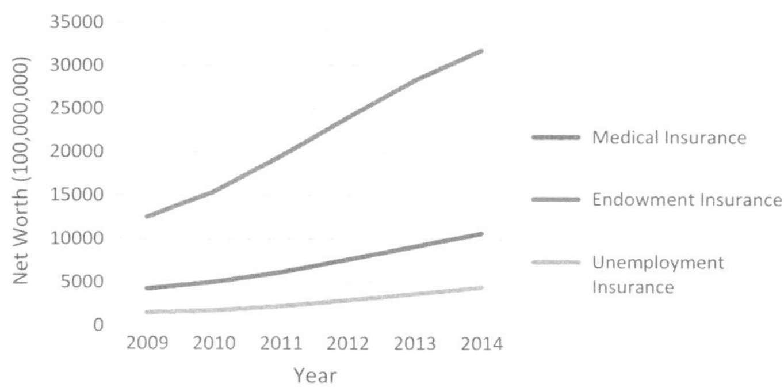

Fig. 5 Fund net worth. *Source* Official website of National Bureau of Statistics of the People's Republic of China: http://www.stats.gov.cn/

As we can see, from 2009 to 2014, the fund net worth keeps positive, which means fund of these five insurances remain relatively maintainable. From the perspective of absolute number, fund of endowment insurance has the largest surplus and maternity insurance owns the least net worth.

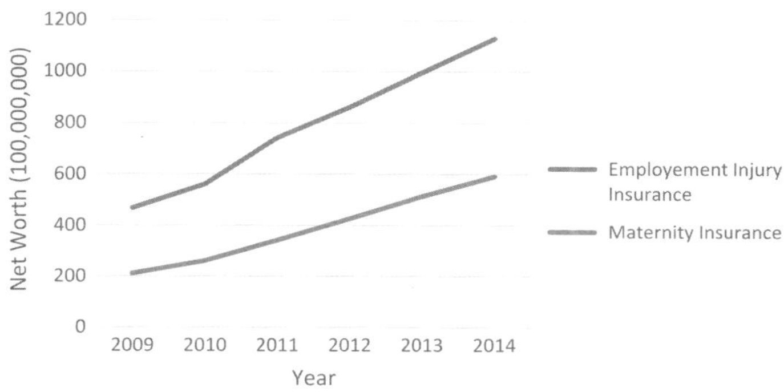

Fig. 6 Found net worth. *Source* Official website of National Bureau of Statistics of the People's Republic of China: http://www.stats.gov.cn/

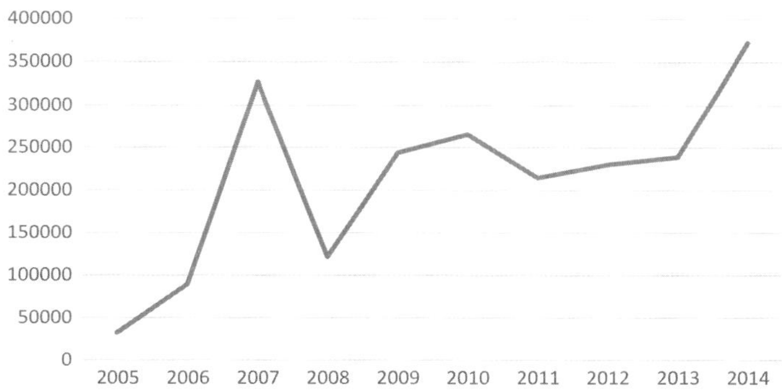

Fig. 7 Security capitalization (100,000,000). *Source* From official website of China Security Regulatory Commission http://www.csrc.gov.cn/pub/newsite/sjtj/

In final part, basic situation of security and insurance industries are further introduced (Fig. 7).

As is shown above, although security capitalization seems a little bit volatile, the absolute quantity shows a tendency to increase. From less than 5 trillion in 2005, the security capitalization has grown up to nearly 40 trillion in 2014, almost 8 times the quantity in 2005 in the past 10 years. Therefore, the development of security market in China is still prospective in next few years (Fig. 8).

Different from security capitalization, insurance premium keeps on increasing for the past 10 years. Premium in 2014 is almost 4 times that in 2005 (Fig. 9).

The number of insurance organizations has almost doubled in the past ten years. Its continuous increase shows that more and more investors are interested in the insurance industry (Fig. 10).

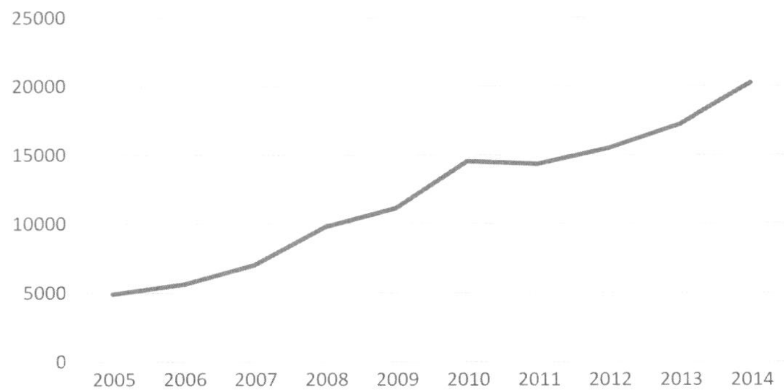

Fig. 8 Insurance Premium (100,000,000). *Source* From official website of China Insurance Regulatory Commission http://www.circ.gov.cn/web/site0/tab5179/

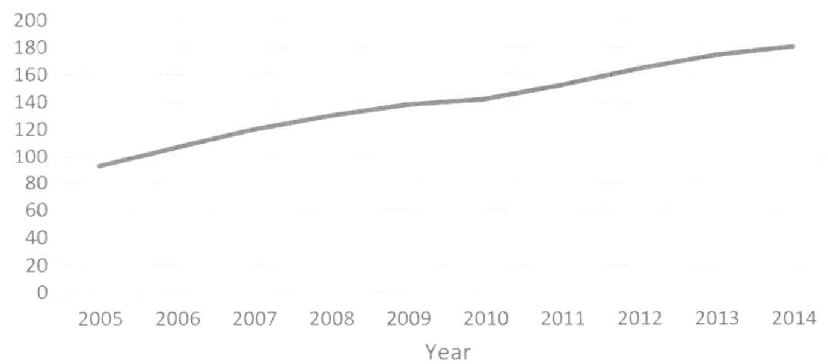

Fig. 9 Number of insurance companies and organizations. *Source* From official website of China Insurance Regulatory Commission http://www.circ.gov.cn/web/site0/tab5179/

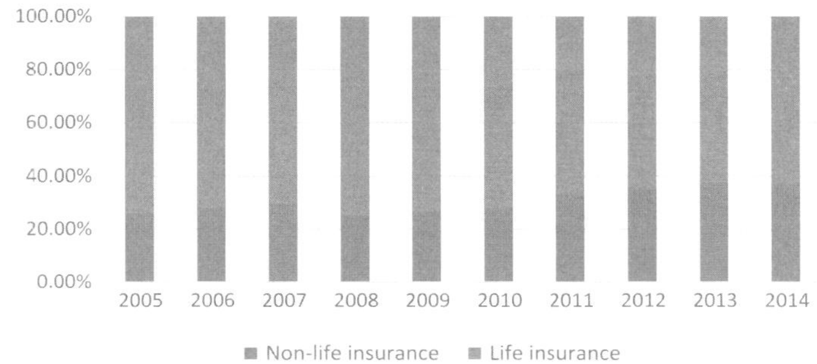

Fig. 10 Percentage of life and non-life insurance premium. *Source* From official website of China Insurance Regulatory Commission http://www.circ.gov.cn/web/site0/tab5179/

The percentage of non-life insurance increases from 25 to 38% in past ten years, probably due to the development of obligatory car insurance, the increasing awareness of insurance, and the development of Chinese economy, among many other factors.

2 Financial Consumer Protection System (Software)

2.1 Relevant Laws and Rules

Basically, people could find the basement of the financial consumer protection from the Constitution. However, when it comes to details, these two law catalogues may provide more specified regulation: Economic Laws, which contain the Law of the People's Republic of China on the Protection of Consumer Rights and Interests, Law of the People's Republic of China on Commercial Banks, Law of the People's Republic of China on the People's Bank of China, Law of the People's Republic of China on Funds for Investment in Securities, Law of the People's Republic of China on Regulation of and Supervision over the Banking Industry, etc. and the Civil and Commercial Laws, which contains the Insurance Law of the People's Republic of China, Law of the People's Republic of China on Securities, Contract Law of the People's Republic of China, etc. In all, almost all the relevant laws about Chinese financial consumer protection system could be found in these above mentioned two catalogues of Chinese law system.

Besides the laws, the administrative rules and regulations also play an important part in the legal framework. There are several parts of administrative regulations. First, there are the regulations released by the State Council, such as the Regulations of the People's Republic of China on Administration of Foreign-funded Financial Institutions and the Regulations of the People's Republic of China on Administration of Foreign-funded Insurance Companies. Also, some government authorities of the State Council will release some important national rules and regulations as well. These institutions are the People's Bank of China, China Insurance Regulatory Commission, China Banking Regulatory Commission and China Securities Regulatory Commission. As all of these national institutions are simultaneously the regulatory institutions of Chinese financial market, their rules and regulations, especially those coming from the regulatory institutions, are updated frequently, in order to catch up with the development of the financial market. Last but not the least, if it comes to the range of province, the regulations which are drawn up from the provincial regulatory institutions should not be missed, either. Additionally, all these laws, rules and regulations are publicly available and easily accessible by online.

2.2 Rationale and Direction of Financial Consumer Protection System

Apart from the law, the Chinese financial consumer protection system has a quite close relationship with the financial regulatory institutions. In other words, one of the most important responsibilities of all the regulatory institutions is the consumer protection. For instance, the main responsibilities of the China Securities Regulatory Commission are:

- to maintain a transparent, fair and equitable market;
- to strengthen the protection of investors, small investors in particular;
- to facilitate the sound development of the capital market.

All these regulatory institutions take the consumer-protecting duty not only in the form of applying the rules and regulations, but also in the way that almost every regulatory institution has a direct connection with common consumers. For example, if an insurance consumer wants to make complaints on his insurance contract, he or she could visit the website of the China Insurance Regulatory Commission and send his complaints online, or he could call the hotline to make a complaint, or he could write a letter to the China Insurance Regulatory Commission. No matter how he makes the complaint, once the institution receives the information, it will consider the complaint and treat it based on the Regulation of Insurance Consumer Complaints Management and help the consumer to deal with the problem. Thus, when people talk about Chinese financial consumer protection system, mostly, it means the financial regulatory system.

Nowadays, the financial regulatory system is often called "One Bank and Three Commissions" system. "One Bank" means the People's Bank of China, which is also the central bank of China, "Three Commissions" refer to China Insurance Regulatory Commission, China Banking Regulatory Commission and China Securities Regulatory Commission. All of these institutions work together to protect the legitimate rights and interests of the financial consumers. However, recently, the trend goes strongly that the financial industry starts to mix their service, which brings a big challenge to the "One Bank and Three Commissions" system. Xia (2005) shows that financial holding companies represent the development trend of mixed business model. How to construct an effective financial supervision organization system which is suitable for the current financial mixed trend is a common concern in the theoretical and practical circles. Based on the analysis of the game model, this paper analyzes the financial innovation of the commercial holding bank of the financial holding company, and the mixed supervision mode can not only lead the self-restraint of the financial holding company, but also promote the financial innovation The China should establish a mixed mode of supervision to maintain the overall stability and efficiency of the financial system, which is conducive to the realization of information sharing among all regulatory principals, strengthening cooperation and enhancing the consistency of action. The supervision behavior may need the cooperation among all the regulatory institutions, since the financial product may be a mixture, or the financial company may do its business in different fields at the same time. For example, Ping'an is one of the enterprises in China's financial market that have get the permission to run the insurance companies, banks, fund companies, security companies simultaneously. Then it will be a great challenge to do the regulation with this group company because it is hard to completely separate its business into different fields. Thus, the cooperation among the commissions is undoubtedly necessary. However, it is still in a discussion that how to make the cooperation more efficient but the attempt has already been on the way.

2.3 *Ex-ante Protection*

Usually, all the consumers' protecting actions are divided into two types: ex-ante protection and ex-post protection.

2.3.1 Consumer Literacy and Education

Basically, all of the "One Bank and Three Commissions" system institutions will conduct the consumer education work and treat it as an important part of consumer protection work. For instance, the China Securities Regulatory Commission lists the work of investor education as the sub-work of investor protection. The investor education project is divided into two parts:

- tips of risk and protection
- knowledge of securities.

In the first part about the tips of risk and protection, people could find a lot of free documents and e-books of failure investing cases, typical fraud cases, the instruction of complaints and also the tips of bringing a lawsuit. In the second part about the knowledge of securities, there are a lot of free documents to help investors and consumers to understand the security market and the recent regulations. In particular, there is a buildup of 13 national education centers for securities and futures investors in May of 2016 to give a better literacy throughout the country. Besides, the People's Bank of China, as the central bank of China, also treats the work of consumer education as an important work. People could easily find the introduction of finance on its website, and there are a lot of free e-books and documents of the financial knowledge, of the security tips of online finance, of the national debt, etc. In a word, financial consumer could easily learn a lot of knowledge about finance itself, the law and rules of finance and the risks of financial behavior from the website of the regulatory institutions. And there are also a lot of literacy activities offline, especially around March 15th every year, which is the day of the National Consumer Rights Protection Day.

2.3.2 Product and Price Regulation

The product and price regulation is also an important part of the consumer protection system. Often, these regulations are deep into the details of the product designing process. Let's take China's insurance market as an example. The China Insurance Regulatory Commission is the main regulatory institution of China's insurance market. On August 10th, 2015, it published the Interim Rule of Preferential Personal Tax Type of Health Insurance. It sets a lot of restrictions of this new type insurance product, for example, the insured amount of medical insurance should not be less than 200,000 yuan; the deductibles should not be set in the medical insurance; insurance company should not charge initial fees and other administrative costs from individual accounts, etc. In this instance, the regulation of this new type of health insurance product is carefully set in detail. And this is not the only case, the China Banking Regulatory Commission also pay high attention to the details of banks' loan business. On February 2nd, 2016, it published the regulations to restrict the first payment ratio of commercial individual housing loans with 25% in principle, floating down around 5 percentage points. In China's consumer protection system, the product or price regulation is one of the most common methods, as it could affect the market directly, also rapidly. Also, as these rules are often provided in details, it could be changed very often, following with corresponding laws, thus people should pay more attention to the updates of the information.

2.3.3 Salesperson Qualification Control, Legal/Contractual Authority of Salesperson

As mentioned above, the product or price regulation method has direct effect on the market, whereas the control of salesperson's qualification and legal/contractual authority of salesperson is an indirect way to protect financial consumers. It is easy to find a man to buy a life insurance for himself from an insurance broker who knows nothing about the insurance product? As a result, there must be some rules to protect the consumers' rights and interests from the low-qualified salesmen, and China has built up the relevant regulations in every financial field. Take insurance industry again as an instance, the Provisions on the Supervision and Administration of Insurance Brokerage Institutions (2015 Amendment) stipulates that an insurance brokerage institution shall provide its practitioners with training on insurance law and insurance business and education on professional ethics. And the pre-job training received by an insurance brokerage practitioner shall not be less than 80 h, and an insurance brokerage practitioner shall receive on-the-job training and education every year for not less than 36 h accumulatively, including not less than 12 h of training on legal knowledge and education on professional ethics.

Similarly those qualifications are asked also for the other financial field including banking or security industry in the form of rules or regulations. These provisions and rules protect the consumers indirectly, being certainly an indispensable part of China's financial consumer protection system.

2.4 *Ex-post Protection*

2.4.1 Information Disclosure Control

Information disclosure control is one of the most important jobs of all the regulatory institutions, while every institution has some other rules for their own field. As such, the information disclosure rule in insurance industry is made by the China Insurance Regulatory Commission, while one for security industry is made by the China Securities Regulatory Commission, etc. Usually, these rules will make the provision about which activity of the company should be public, how and what should be public in its annual report, etc. And each year, every commission itself will give out a collective annual report of all the companies in its own field, which contains almost every detail that should be public in that year.

Take the banking industry as an example. Banks are required to make their financial reports, status of risk management, directors and senior managerial personnel changes and other significant matters known to the public. Minghui (2004) shows that disclosure of internal control of commercial bank is helpful to improve the internal control of the bank, and it can provide additional useful information to users.

In China, however, the internal control disclosing practice of listed commercial bank is so poor that its relevant information may be sometimes omitted or concealed. The paper suggests revising relevant rules to rule the internal control reporting behavior of bank. Besides, the China Banking Regulatory Commission will announce the collective annual report of the whole industry, which will contain the details about assets and liabilities, risk index, efficiency indicators, etc. The Banking Regulatory Commission take the responsibility to supervise reports of all the commercial banks and if any banks did not disclose in accordance with the provisions, they would get punished by being ordered to stop the business, to correct to provisions, or to revoke the business license, etc. In sum, a financial company shall set up a management and information disclosure system under the instruction of the regulatory authority under the State Council.

2.4.2 Appropriateness Principle, Good Faith and Fair Treatment Rule

One of the main responsibilities of the China Securities Regulatory Commission is to maintain a transparent, fair and equitable market. Actually, the good faith and fair treatment rules are constructed in the whole financial market, no matter whether it is the market of banking, securities, insurance, etc. Moreover, the good faith and fair treatment rule should be obeyed during the whole process of not only business but also the regulatory work itself. For instance, it is written clearly in the Insurance Law of the People's Republic of China:

– Article 11: An insurance contract shall be concluded by agreement upon negotiation, and the rights and obligations of both parties shall be determined according to the principle of fairness. An insurance contract shall be concluded

out of free will, unless the insurance is mandated by laws or administrative regulations;
- Article 114: Insurance companies shall, in accordance with the provisions of the insurance regulatory authority under the State Council, fairly and reasonably determine the insurance clauses and premium rates, and shall not damage the legitimate rights and interests of policy holders, the insured and beneficiaries. Insurance companies shall perform their obligation of paying indemnity or insurance benefits in a timely manner in accordance with insurance contracts and this Law;
- Article 134: An insurance regulatory authority shall, in accordance with the principles of legality, openness and fairness, supervise and administer the insurance industry according to its duties prescribed by this Law and the State Council, to maintain the order of the insurance market and protect the legitimate rights and interests of policy holders, insured and beneficiaries;
- Article 157: The staff of an insurance regulatory authority shall be devoted to their duties, handle affairs in accordance with the law and be fair and uncorrupt, and shall neither seek illegitimate benefits by taking advantage of their positions nor disclose commercial secrets of the relevant entities or individuals which they have access to.

It is easy to see that the fairness is asked throughout the whole system, including the regulatory work as well. Generally speaking, the good faith and fair treatment rule is the one of the basements of financial industry, thus it is highlighted in every aspect, and is almost announced in every statement related to financial activities. Furthermore, for all commercial activities, there is the Law of the People's Republic of China Against Unfair Competition, which details takes actions to protect fair-market environment. Thus, the financial market is, of course, under the regulation of this law and every business and regulatory work shall follow the instruction of this law.

2.4.3 Anti-trust Competition Laws

Also, anti-trust competition is an important work of regulatory institutions too. It is written in the law to protect the fair competition in the financial industry. For example, the insurance sector, according to the Insurance Law of the People's Republic of China, announced that the establishment of an insurance company shall be subject to the approval of the insurance regulatory authority under the State Council. When examining an application for the establishment of an insurance company, the insurance regulatory authority under the State Council shall take into consideration the development of the insurance industry and the need for fair competition. Insurance companies shall follow the principle of fair competition in their business operations, and shall not engage in unfair competition; Stated in the Law of the People's Republic of China on Regulation of Supervision over the Banking Industry that the banking industry shall be regulated and supervised in such a way as to protect fair competition in the industry and increase the competitiveness of the industry, etc. Apart from these laws, the Anti-Monopoly Law of the People's Republic of China, which in details work for preventing and restraining monopolistic conducts, protecting fair competition in the market, enhancing economic efficiency, safeguarding the interests of consumers and social public interest, promoting the healthy development of the socialist market economy. There is also a special commission called the Anti-Monopoly Commission, which is established by the State Council and is in charge of organizing, coordinating, guiding the national anti-monopoly work of all industries. Thus, all the financial industries are certainly under the supervision of this Anti-Monopoly Commission and shall obey the anti-monopoly law as well.

2.4.4 Emergency Prohibition of Problematic Products

Basically, it is rare to see problematic products in China's financial market. But once it happened, it would affect the market immediately and might cause chaos. Thus it is very important for the regulatory institutions to make plans in case of the emergent situation. In China, all financial regulatory institutions have prepared for the emergency case. They care not only about what these commissions themselves should do, but also about what the financial company should do when facing an emergence. Again, take the insurance regulating institution as an example. Although in this case the product did not cause chaos to the market: In 2013, a number of commercial train-ticket-selling websites were found that they tried to tying the compulsory traffic accident insurance in their ticket sales. Once it was exposed, the China Insurance Regulatory Commission immediately took actions to regulate this commercial behavior. It made a notice to all the insurance companies, to ask them to stop the risky behavior and to strengthen their sales behavior management. The commission also sent its sub-institution a notice to strengthen the supervision. Almost on the first day after the notice, this tying-selling behavior promptly disappeared. The reaction of the commission is so fast and efficient. Basically, once the problematic products or the wrong business behavior are found by the regulation commission, the related supervising commission would stop the business as soon as possible, and tried their best to repair the market order. Further, if the situation was very serious, the responsible person of the financial company would be asked to take the responsibility according to relevant laws and regulations.

2.4.5 Complaints and Dispute Settlement

Practically, any complaining customers will try to contact the financial company first. Then, if the communication with the financial company could not satisfy the customer, they could visit the website of the corresponding supervising commission to leave a message or write an e-mail to make complaints. He could also call the hotline of the relevant department. All the regulatory commissions promise that every message and mail will be replied and they will help the customer with further communication with the relevant company. In addition, all complaints will be tracked by the supervision to make sure the complaints are handled properly.

Further, the complaints are not only about the business company but about the regulatory institution itself as well. First, people could make complaints at the corresponding website, if the request is reasonable and legitimate, the commission itself will solve it rapidly. Or, if the customer is still not satisfied with it, he could make his complaints to the higher office. If nothing helps, he could bring an administrative lawsuit, too. Last but not least, all the complaints, no matter what it is about, will be treated based on the rules and regulations.

2.4.6 Deposit Insurance Scheme

There are also some other special systems to protect consumers. For instance, the Deposit Insurance Regulation, was adopted at the 67th executive meeting of the State Council on October 29, 2014, and came into force on May 1, 2015. By this regulation, a system was established that could create and regulate the deposit insurance business, protect the lawful rights and interests of depositors according to the law, timely prevent and eliminate financial risks, and maintain financial stability. In short, banks pay the premium for insurance to protect depositors. Once an individual bank faces insolvency, the deposit insurance would pay the deposit to the depositors for banks, thus maintaining the uninterrupted service of banking system, and improving the credit level of the banking industry.

2.4.7 China Insurance Security Fund

The China Insurance Security Fund (CISF) is an industrial risk bailout fund derived from contributions made in accordance with the Insurance Law of the People's Republic of China and the Measures for Administration of the Insurance Security Fund.

On December, 30th, 2004, the China Insurance Regulatory Commission (CIRC) issued the Measures for Administration of the Insurance Security Fund, which specifies that the security fund is classified into two parts: security fund of property insurance companies and that of life insurance companies. The document also specifies that the CIRC is responsible for the concentrated management and coordinated use of the fund, while the Security Fund Council shall supervise the management and use of it. In March 2005, CIRC released the Notice on Issues Concerning the Payment of Insurance Security Fund, specifying that insurance companies should put the insurance security funds they had withdrawn by the end of 2004 into the special security fund account opened by CIRC within 2005, which is the initiation of concentrated management of the insurance security fund. In February 2006, the Security Fund Council was established, which members include related ministries, commissions and insurance companies, granting the mission to supervise the management and use of CISF.

Due to the rapid development of the insurance industry in China during the past decade, there are stricter requirements for the management and operation of the security fund. In 2007, the CIRC suggested establishing a company and implementing professional operation of the CISF in a market-oriented manner, which was approved by the State Council. In September 2008, CIRC, the Ministry of Finance and the People's Bank of China jointly issued the new Measures for Administration of the Insurance Security Fund, and established the China Insurance Security Fund Co., Ltd., instead of the Security Fund Council. It is now responsible for collecting, managing and employing the CISF.

So far, it is the CISFC that works as a shelter for Chinese insurance industry. It has 6 scopes of its duty to build a solid foundation to further cement the risk barrier of the insurance industry, and safeguard policy interests of insurance consumers:

- Engage in the collection, management and employment of CISF;
- Monitor risks in the insurance industry, and advances regulatory resolution suggestions to CIRC when targeting at any material risk within the operation and management of insurance companies, which may endanger policyholders and the whole industry;
- Provide bailout for policyholders, policy transferee companies, other individuals and institutions, or participates in risk resolution of the insurance industry;
- Participate in the liquidation of an insurance company when it is dissolved or declared bankruptcy according to the law;
- Take over and disposes of liquidation assets;
- Run other businesses approved by the State Council.

3 FCP Institution

3.1 *Financial Regulation Institution*

There are three agencies which regulate banking, securities and insurance respectively. They're all authorized by the State Council and located in Beijing.

3.1.1 People's Bank of China (PBC)

People's Bank of China is the central bank of China, which was established in December 1948. In the earlier time, it has the functions of CBRC, CIRC and CSRC until these three commissions were established. PBC has 26 departments, and among them is one for financial consumer protection.

Financial Consumer Protection (FCP) Bureau is the bureau for research of FCP issues, drafting relevant regulation policies, monitoring risks of financial products and for financial consumer protection. It has 5 departments, which are the General Office, Department of Inspection, Department of Financial Consumer Education; Department of Complaint Investigation, and Department of System Research.

By the way, PBC plays a very important role in deposit insurance fund. Deposit Insurance Regulation is firstly issued in 2015 (From Official website of China government 2015). It is aimed at protecting the interest of depositors. It is clear from the legal system that the depositor has the right to claim the insured deposit, which is very important to the interests of the depositors and is a matter of great concern to the depositors. To this end, the regulations clearly stipulate that the depositor has the right to require the deposit insurance fund management institution to use the deposit insurance fund to pay the insured deposit situation: First, the deposit insurance fund management organization as the insurance organization to take over the organization; Second, the deposit insurance fund management institutions Third of the people's court ruled that the bankruptcy applications to the insured institutions; four other conditions approved by the State Council. In order to protect the timely payment of the depositors, the regulations also clearly stipulate that the deposit insurance fund management agencies should be in the above situation occurred within 7 working days in full payment of deposits.

PBC is involved in deposit insurance fund because this fund is legally managed by PBC. In order to ensure the safety of the deposit insurance fund, the regulations restrict the use of the deposit insurance fund and stipulate that the use of the deposit insurance fund shall be governed by the principles of safe, mobile and value-added, limited to the People's Bank of China, the government bonds, the central bank bills, Higher financial bonds and other high-grade bonds, as well as other forms of funds approved by the State Council. Given to that most of consumers in China invest their treasure in deposit in big bank, PBC plays a paramount role in protecting the interest of financial consumers.

3.1.2 China Banking Regulatory Commission (CBRC)

China Banking Regulatory Commission (CBRC) is the regulation institution of banking in China. Before the establishment of CBRC in April 2003, the banking industry was regulated by the People's Bank of China, the central bank in China. Then the functions are transferred to CBRC.

(1) *Main functions*

The main functions of CBRC are listed as follows:

- Formulate supervisory rules and regulations governing the banking institutions;
- Authorize the establishment, changes, termination and business scope of the banking institutions;

- Accounting Department
- International Department (Office of Hong Kong and Macau SARs and Taiwan Affairs)
- Staff Compliance and Disciplinary Bureau
- Human Resources Department
- Publicity Department
- CBRC Headquarters CPC Committee
- Party School
- CBRC Staff Union
- CBRC Youth League Committee
- CBRC Service Center.

The chairman of CBRC was Liu Mingkang from 2003 to 2011, and is Shang Fulin from 2011.

3.1.3 China Insurance Regulatory Commission (CIRC)

China Insurance Regulatory Commission (CIRC) is the regulation institution of insurance products and services. Insurance industry was also regulated by People's Bank of China earlier, and in 1995, the release of the Insurance Law made the People's Bank of China have some adjustments and set up the Insurance Bureau for regulation. Then in November 1998, CIRC was founded.

(1) *Main functions of CIRC*

CIRC is the main institution that supervises and regulates the Insurance industry in China, and its responsibilities are listed as follows:

- set up policies and guidelines for industry development as well as laws and regulations for supervision and regulation;
- verify and approve insurance companies, insurance groups, insurance intermediaries etc. and their mergence, split and settlement etc.;
- qualify the senior managers and to set up standards for insurance practitioners;
- verify and approve certain kinds of insurance products that concerns public interest and some compulsory insurance products, and file the policy clauses and premium rates of other products;
- inspect and punish illegal behavior and non-insurance institutions that have insurance business;
- supervise and regulate the insurance institutions overseas established by domestic institutions;
- set up information standards and systems of evaluation, warning and monitoring for insurance risk as well as insurance market status, and compile and release data and reports;
- undertake other transactions from the State Council.

(2) *Basic structure and professionals*

CIRC has 16 internal departments apart from training center and service center, which are as follows:

- The general office
- Department of development and reform
- Department of policy research
- Department of financial accounting and solvency
- The insurance FCP bureau
- Supervision department of property insurance and reinsurance
- Supervision department of life insurance
- Supervision department of insurance intermediaries
- Supervision department of insurance funds management
- The international office
- Department of legal affairs
- Department of statistics
- Department of disciplinary inspection
- Department of Human resource
- The supervision bureau
- Department of party committee propaganda.

Apart from the office in Beijing, CIRC has 35 local offices in different provinces and cities. The chairman of CIRC was Ma Yongwei from November 1998 to October 2002, then was Wu Dingfu from October 2002 to October 2011, and is Xiang Junbo from October 2011.

3.1.4 China Securities Regulatory Commission (CSRC)

China Securities Regulatory Commission (CSRC) is the regulation institution of securities. CSRC was founded in October 1992.

From the 1980s, the securities market emerged in China, and was regulated by People's Bank of China. In 1990, Shanghai Stock Exchange and Shenzhen Stock Exchange were founded, then CSRC was established as the executive agency of the State Council Securities Commission in October 1992. It was not till April 1998 that CSRC became the ministerial institution under the State Council to regulate and supervise the securities industry.

(1) *Main functions of CSRC*

The functions of CSRC are as follows:

Study and formulate policies and development plans for the securities and futures markets; draft the relevant laws and regulations on the securities and futures markets as well as put forward suggestions for formulation or modification of the said laws and regulations; and work out the relevant rules, regulations and measures for the securities and futures markets; Exercise a vertical administration over the domestic securities and futures regulatory institutions and conduct a unified supervision over the securities and futures markets; and perform a regulatory supervision over the managements and the managerial officials of the relevant securities companies; Supervise the issuance, listing, trading, custody and settlement of stocks, convertible bonds, bonds of securities companies, and bonds and other securities under the charge of CSRC as assigned by the State Council; Supervise the securities investment bonds; approve the listing of corporate bonds; and supervise the trading of the listed treasury bonds and corporate bonds.

Supervise the securities market behaviors of the listed companies and their shareholders who shall fulfill the relevant obligations according to the relevant laws and regulations; Supervise the listing, trading and settlement of domestic contract-based futures; and monitor the overseas futures businesses of the domestic institutions in accordance with the relevant regulations; Supervise the securities and futures exchanges as well as their senior managerial personnel in accordance with the relevant regulations; and supervise the securities and futures associations in the capacity of a competent authority; Supervise the securities and futures business institutions, securities investment fund management companies, securities depository and clearing corporations, futures clearing institutions, securities and futures investment consulting institutions, and securities credit rating institutions; Examine and approve the qualifications of fund custodian institutions, and supervise their fund custody businesses; Formulate and implement measures on the qualifications of senior management for the relevant institutions; and guide the Securities Association of China and the Futures Associations of China in the administration of the qualifications of the personnel engaged in securities and futures businesses; Supervise the direct or indirect issuance and listing of shares overseas by domestic enterprises as well as the listing of convertible bonds by the companies listed overseas; supervise the establishment of securities and futures institutions overseas by domestic securities and futures business institutions; and supervise the establishment of securities and futures institutions in China by overseas institutions for securities and futures businesses; Supervise the communication of the securities and futures information; and take charge of the management of the statistics and information resources for the securities and futures markets; Work with the relevant authorities in the examination and approval of the qualifications of the accounting firms, the asset evaluation institutions and their personnel for securities and futures intermediary businesses; and supervise the law firms, the lawyers and the eligible accounting firms, the asset appraisal institutions and their personnel in their securities and futures business activities; Investigate and penalize the activities in violation of the relevant securities and futures laws and regulations; Administer the foreign exchanges and international cooperation affairs of the securities and futures sector in the capacity of a competent authority; Perform other duties as assigned by the State Council.

(2) *Basic structure and professionals*

CSRC has 25 departments, which are listed below:

- General Office
- Department of Public Offering Supervision
- Department of Unlisted Public Company Supervision
- Department of Market Supervision
- Department of Fund and Intermediary Supervision
- Department of Listed Company Supervision
- Department of Futures Supervision
- Enforcement Bureau (Office of Chief Enforcement Officer)
- Department of Legal Affairs (Office of Chief Counsel)
- Office of Administrative Sanction Committee
- Department of Accounting (Office of Chief Accountant)
- Department of International Affairs
- Investor Protection Bureau
- Department of Corporate Bond Supervision
- Department of Innovative Business Supervision
- Department of Private Fund Supervision
- Anti-Market Misconduct Bureau (Office of Standardization of Regional Trading Platforms)
- Department of Personnel and Education
- Department of Publicity, CPC Committee
- Disciplinary Bureau
- CPC Committee of CSRC Headquarters
- Enforcement Task Force
- Research Center
- IT Service Center
- Administrative Service Center.

Also SCRC has 35 local offices in other provinces and cities other than in Beijing. Since February 2016, Liu Shiyu is the chairman of SCRC. There were 7 former chairmen of SCRC, among which is Zhou Xiaochuan, who is the chairman of People's Bank of China now.

3.2 Deposit Insurance Institution

Deposit insurance is the insurance for bank depositors against the risk of losing deposits when banks are not able to pay the debts, and thus promotes the stability of the financial system. It promotes financial stability serving as a component of financial safety net. In US, a national deposit insurance scheme was established in 1930s. Until now, there are more than 110 countries that have instituted deposit insurance scheme.

3.2.1 The Deposit Insurance in China

In China, the discussion of implementing deposit-insurance system started in 2007. Before it is discussed in business field, many experts and specialists have already issued lots of papers with regards to DIS (Deposit Insurance System) in China. Haibo (2004) insists that it is important for China to absorb DIS's advantages and lessons which will also be beneficial to deepening China's financial reform, preventing and mitigating systemic financial risks and maintaining economic development. XiangCong (2006) concludes legislation research on subrogation priority for Deposit Insurance Institutions. Hongbo (2008) shows that deposit insurance is helpful to the financial stability but it may also cause moral hazard in banks. The People's Bank of China released a report of financial stability in July 2012, mentioning that it is the time to prepare for the deposit insurance. Then in the report of financial stability in 2013, it says the deposit-insurance system is about to be introduced.

In November 2014, the regulation on deposit insurance (draft for discussion) was released, and then officially published in March 2015. The system was launched in May 2015. This is the article according to which the deposit-insurance system can be established. The People's Bank of China is responsible for running the fund for deposit insurance.

In this article several details are revealed. For each depositor, the bank they use offers the deposit insurance with a coverage limit of 500,000 CNY. The insurance applies to commercial banks, rural cooperative banks and rural credit cooperatives, but doesn't apply to foreign bank branches and Chinese bank branches overseas. Also, the deputy director of financial stability bureau had an interview after the release of the regulation article in which he explained some more ideas behind this article.

Generally, the deposit insurance covers 2–5 times of the GDP per capita, while the 500,000 CNY limit is 12 times of the GDP per capita in 2012, which also means a 100% coverage for more than 99.5% depositors. And the premium is collected from the banking institutions with a low premium rate, so that it won't affect the financial condition much.

3.2.2 Deposit Insurance Institution

Financial Stability Bureau is one of the departments under People's Bank of China, and it has several departments, among which Department of deposit insurance is specified for deposit insurance affairs.

The financial stability bureau is for analyzing and evaluating systemic risks, offering policy suggestions, evaluating effects of major financial activities (M&A etc.), setting up standards for regulating financial holding companies and mixed financial activities as well as supervising them, demonstration and management of the reconstruction, settlement of some financial risk-relating assets and relevant institutions, and inspecting the use of funds of central bank for managing financial risks.

The financial stability bureau has 10 departments, namely:

- the General Office;
- Department of financial system reform;
- Department of financial stability evaluation;
- Secretariat of Financial Sector Assessment Program;
- Department of risk monitoring and evaluation of banking industry;
- Department of risk monitoring and evaluation of securities industry;
- Department of risk monitoring and evaluation of insurance industry;
- Department of risk monitoring and evaluation of financial holding companies;
- Department of central bank assets;
- Department of deposit insurance.

3.3 Dispute Settlement Organization

3.3.1 Financial Arbitration Institution

For dispute settlement, there are local arbitration institutions, which also serve for financial disputes. Those arbitration institutions have experts in finance, laws and economics etc., which ensures their professionalism in financial arbitration. For cities, the arbitration system not only helps protect financial consumers, but may also attract more overseas foreign financial firms, as the arbitration results are recognized by foreign countries.

Here we take Shanghai Court of Financial Arbitration as an example. Shanghai Court of Financial Arbitration is an affiliate of Shanghai Arbitration Commission. It was founded in 2007, located in Lujiazui business district. When founded, Shanghai Court of Financial Arbitration had 78 legal experts as arbitrator, including 14 experts from the U.S., Germany, Canada, Japan, France, South Korea, Singapore and Hong Kong. It accepts disputes in deposits and loans, securities and funds, insurance products etc., and has accepted to handle more than 200 disputes every year.

3.3.2 Financial Consumption Mediation Center

Also there are mediation centers for financial consumers. Shanghai got its Financial Consumption Dispute Mediation Center in December 2014. The Mediation Center has 48 experienced mediators, and in 2015, they answered 21,278 phone calls, among which 14,273 are about complaints, and 7005 are for consulting. The Mediation Center started mediation in May 2015, and has resolved more than 80 disputes. In May 2016, the Mediation Center signed memorandums with banking institutions in Shanghai, aiming at a faster settlement mechanism for disputes under 5000 CNY. Till April 2016, the Mediation Center has resolved more than 130 disputes.

4 Special FCP Systems

4.1 For the Elderly Group

For the elderly group, FCP institutions as well as financial institutions offer extra protections and hold relevant activities to get them aware of financial risks. Take banking industry as an example, protections are provided in branches as well as in the elders' communities.

4.1.1 Service Counters

Service counters offer special services and protections to the elders. Lobby managers ask customers the service they need, and then give suggestions; elders are especially taken care of, for they may be optically challenged or they can't express their need clearly. Separate service counters and chairs are set in some bank branches, China Construction Bank in Shanghai, for example, set 10 elder-serving demonstration branches in 2015, offering well-designed services for elders.

In additional, lobby managers check if elders run into telecom frauds. Elders are prone to telecom frauds due to their unawareness of popular telecom tricks. Elders often are asked to make a transfer to the frauds' account after the frauds get their trust, and lobby managers and tellers are described to be not reliable or nosy. Victims tend to make a transfer to a stranger's account and refuse to tell the reason for the transfer. It makes it more difficult when the frauds now often tell victims that the transfer must be made on an ATM to avoid attentions from the tellers. Thus lobby managers and tellers have to pay attention to elders that seems flustered or too alert. Under that condition, if they are convinced that customers encounter telecom frauds, they will use various way to prevent losses: checking the "emergency" with victims, calling the police, trying to calm them down, showing anti-fraud brochures, or even refusing to serve.

Sometimes unusual operations also help. In June 2016, an elder in Hunan province tried to make a transfer to a fraud account and didn't listen to the tellers. Before he succeeded in making the transfer, the lobby manager chose to shut down the ATM saying it was broken and called the police, and successfully stopped the fraud.

4.1.2 Other FCP Activities

Apart from protections on service counters, FCP institutions hold kinds of activities for protecting elders against financial risks.

Banking institutions put a lot of efforts to prevent customers from various kinds of frauds. Since the elderly have higher risks, it's necessary to hold more activities for them. Take China Construction Bank in Shanghai for example, they visit community elderly universities and nursing homes from time to time, holding various activities such as social gatherings, lectures as well as setting up publicity centers to help elders get familiar with ordinary financial products and get aware of popular financial frauds.

Some special kinds of FCP activities for the elders are held sometimes. In June 2015, a non-commercial FCP drama called "the Secret of Xiao Ka" was on show. In the drama, Xiao Ka is a young girl trying to promote a so-called pension investment project to the elders in their community, while an undergraduate volunteer there investigates it and tries to find the truth. This non-commercial FCP drama is part of a plan from CBRC, aiming at spreading basic financial and anti-fraud knowledge among the elders. The drama is free to watch and will also be on show in several communities in Beijing.

4.2 For the Poor Group

Microfinance, or inclusive finance, the financial products and services for small business and low- and middle-income citizens. According China Association of Microfinance, it includes savings, money transfer and insurance by referring to the international microfinance development and rule.

In China, the concept of micro finance has been written in the resolution of the third plenary session of 18th Central Committee of CPC, and is the focus of the State Council in the field of financial reform. Micro finance has experienced more than ten years of experimentation and demonstration, both micro credits and micro insurance keep on developing and serve more and more people.

4.2.1 Micro Loans

Micro loans are loans for low-income citizens and micro-enterprises. Micro loans often don't require collaterals and have higher rates, and aim at offering financial services to the poor to help them improve their lives. After years of development, micro loans become common and are known by micro entrepreneurs. According to a report from People's Bank of China, there are 8810 micro loan companies and the loan balance is 936.4 billion Yuan in 2015.

Micro-credit associations help develop the service capability of micro loans. China Association of Microfinance is the first national member-based association in microfinance sector in China, which has about 2000 formal members covering 29 provinces and cities. It introduces and promotes the concept of inclusive finance, maintains close relationship and cooperation with policy and regulatory departments such as CBRC and People's Bank of China. It makes efforts to enhance level and capacity of micro finance in China by undertaking activities of policy advocacy, self-regulation etc.

What's more, with the help of IT technology, micro loans are also provided online. The Alibaba Group which is famous for e-commerce and third-party payment, has set up financial services companies to develop micro finance products using its advanced technology for both enterprises and individuals. IT companies have advantages in risk evaluation, business process optimization etc., thus make micro loans more accessible.

In 2014, The CBRC specified a notice to undermine risks on microloan for both borrowers and lenders. On one hand, in order to protect the borrowers, which are mainly micro-enterprises, the CBRC asks lenders, most of which are banks, to determine a reasonable determination of loan period. The loan itself should be designed based on small micro-enterprises' production and management characteristics, sizes, risk conditions and other factors, in order to meet the borrower's needs of operation. Also, more micro-enterprise loan products are asked to be enriched. The CBRC encourages banks to create more liquidity products which may reasonably use circular loans, the annual trial loans, etc. to reduce the repayment pressure of small business. Moreover, for those small companies which still have financing needs after the expiry of working capital, the bank could satisfy new loan requirements conditionally. On the other hand, to protect the lenders and control system risk, the CBRC asks banks to classify loan risk based on the classification standards of the five-level classification of loans, by taking full consideration of borrowers' repayment ability, normal operating income and credit rating etc. The lenders are also asked to develop their management system, business operation process, customer access and business authorization standards. They should also reasonably design and improve their loan contracts, guarantee contracts and other supporting documents, as well as their information technology systems. The CBRC also asks banking financial institutions to take objective and accurate judgments about small business and identify those micro enterprises' risk situation by paying dynamic attention to the borrowers' management situation, cash flows and other risk-early warnings.

4.2.2 Micro Insurance

Micro insurance is also an important part of micro finance. Insurance helps manage risk and promotes economic growth as well. Though it's not as developed and popular as micro loan, it's been developing quickly, and there have already been some kinds of micro insurance available in the market. Micro insurance products in the market are loan guarantee insurance, trade credit insurance, export credit insurance and so on. Insurance companies like China Export and Credit Insurance Corporation have been providing many kinds of products which are attractive to micro enterprises, not to mention that the government provides extra preferential policies.

According to the chairman of CIRC, Xiang Junbo, in the first half of 2015, micro loan credit insurance has been available in 25 provinces in China with a total premium of 6.7 billion Yuan and an insured amount of 180.5 billion Yuan. The number of micro enterprises which get benefit from micro insurance is 0.3 million with a YOY growth of 56%. Besides, the insurance industry has made over 3 billion Yuan of equity investment on micro enterprises using methods like private equity funds and venture capital funds.

Similar to micro loans, more kinds of micro insurance are developing with the help of modern IT technology. Take mutual plans as an example, they are mutual insurance associations and platforms for health risks such as cancer, which try to offer protection with a lower cost with the help of IT technology, and now there are more than 10 operating platforms and hundreds of thousand members. Those newly-developed insurance products are exploring their market position, offering more choices to customers.

The CIRC also makes notices to support micro Insurance and control risks. It asks insurance companies to innovate their insurance products, perfect their operating process, and improve their use of insurance funds in order to expand the insurance service for small and micro enterprises. To improve the service of micro insurance, the CIRC asks insurance companies to optimize the insurance operation process with the support of cloud computing, large data, mobile Internet and other new technologies and speed up the claim process to reduce the urgent funding pressure of small enterprises. Apart from insurance products themselves, the CIRC also encourage insurers to broaden their value-added services, such as professional advisory services to provide market analysis for micro business with insurance companies' professionally accumulation and integration of risk data. Last but not least, Both the CIRC and the CRBC want to promote the cooperation between banks and insurance companies, which could help improve the bancassurance information system and support the construction of both sides. It will also do benefit to strengthen both banks and insurers in the information disclosure, post-loan management, business training and other aspects of cooperation, to prevent false trade financing and fraud credit fraud risk in the whole system.

4.3 For the Young

For the young generation, it's necessary to offer them some financial knowledge to get familiar with finance in daily life and normal financial frauds. In addition, for the young, there are more kinds of activities which enrich their life as well as get them educated in finance.

4.3.1 FCP Brochures

FCP brochures are useful materials to help the young learn about finance. Take banking industry as an example, SBRC regularly prints a series of brochures for the public. In September 2014, SBRC released brochures of basic knowledge of finance (banking industry) for kids and for youths.

The brochure for kids has various illustrations to make it easier to understand and has 12 useful topics for kids, such as how the currency comes, what interest is, what insurance is, what mortgage is etc., to help kids learn about finance, financial products and financial planning. Meanwhile, the brochure for youth contains more details. It introduces banking products, including their definition, category, characteristics, prices and samples as well as some more professional and innovative ideas such as structured financial products, wechat bank and third-party payments.

4.3.2 FCP Activities in School

FCP institutions often choose to hold activities inside the school. Various activities can help student learn financial knowledge as well as enrich their life, and it's easier to hold large-scale activities with the help of the schools. Besides, combined with popular types of activities, students are willing to take part in and thus get a better result.

CBRC's Banking Consumer Protection Department and Shanghai Office has led a series of activities in primary and senior high schools in Shanghai every year since 2013, including financial knowledge contests and financial speech contests. 85 schools and 8000 students in 2014 and 106 schools and 10,000 students in 2015 took part in the activities.

4.3.3 Protection Against Certain Risks

Apart from regular protection methods, FCP institutions take care of certain risks that threaten the financial condition of the young. Online lending or P2P lending became more and more popular in recent years; it provides loans to undergraduates with a rather high lending rate since the undergraduates don't have steady income. According to some documents from CBRC, it's not allowed for lending institutions to issue credit cards to the young without the permission of their parents, but those online lending agencies approve loans only by asking for student ID cards. On the other hand, undergraduates are often not able to manage their financial conditions well and are prone to buy more than they could afford, the risk level is higher than normal personal loans. What makes it worse is that some illegal methods may be used by those lending agencies and thus put extra pressure on the borrowers and their families. Even some committed suicide due to the insolvency.

FCP institutions did investigations as well as issued some documents to regulate the market and protect the undergraduates. In Chongqing, local CBRC Office as well as two relevant departments issued a document in August 2016 containing a negative list, forbidding some risky operations, including approving loans using student IDs; they also conducted investigations and made more efforts on enhancing public awareness.

5 Market Issues

5.1 How to Enhance Simplicity of Products?

Recently, finance innovation has hit Chinese market hundreds of times. In reality, finance innovation shows up in form of new financial products. However, with more complex financial products and investment portfolios, systematic risk has become a more serious problem that could ruin the finance world in just a few days. The 2008 financial crisis is exactly an example illustrating the disadvantage of various finance products. Therefore, it is essential to discuss how to enhance simplicity of products in current market.

Firstly, let us have a look at the dispensable element of financial products. Financial product is a series of stipulation and trades. Although different finance products may follow their own rules and regulations, every finance product normally is armed with following component:

5.1.1 Issuer

Each finance product must be sold by its issuer. The issuer of the bond is the debtor, and bond without debtor is hard to imagine. Stock is the same. There must be a specific issue of enterprises. The company is the common property of the stock subscription. Issuer obtain income through selling financial products to others, but not any individual or enterprise can issue financial products to the community. Corresponding to such financial income, the issuer shall also assume taking the obligations.

In order to ensure the performance of these obligations, the majority of financial products issued by the issuer ought to meet certain conditions, and accept supervision from the government and investors after the issuance.

5.1.2 Buyer

Not all investors can buy any financial products he wants from the financial markets. Some markets (such as interbank lending markets) are only open to a small proportion of financial institutions. Therefore, investors before the subscription of a financial product, should in advance know whether they have the right to buy the products. Enterprises should also know the possible investors of this product in order to estimate the potential sources of funding before issuing a financial product.

5.1.3 Duration

Financial products have maturity. In general, the money market is relatively short term, but the product in capital market is relatively long.

The duration of financial products can be divided into limited and unlimited. Most of the bonds and all money market products are limited in a period of time. As for the stock, in theory, there is no time limit.

Issuers should choose the appropriate period of financial products according to their own needs. For investors, as well, the duration of financial products should be based on the scale of its funds, too short or too long, respectively, to take the risk of falling interest rates or rising.

5.1.4 Price and Yield

Price is the core element of financial products. Because the purpose of financing the sale of financial products is to get the equivalent of the income of the product price, the investor's investment amount is equal to the price of his purchase of financial products.

Yield is another core element of financial products, which indicates that the product has a ratio of revenue to its owners. Financial products revenue includes two kinds: one is the securities referred to as interest income, income or regular income, and the second is capital gain or loss. Interest income is the interest income earned during the holding period of the financial products, such as the income of the bond on time to pay the interest income or the income of the stock to pay the dividend on time. Capital gain or profit or loss is the appreciation or depreciation of the capital that is brought about by the fluctuation of the stock price.

5.1.5 Risk

Risk is generally regarded as a hazard, or as a possibility of loss or failure. It can be considered that the investment risk of financial products is due to the uncertainty of the future. There are four kinds of investment opportunities in the market, which are the combination of risks and benefits:

- high risk and low income.
- low risk and high income.
- high risk and high income.
- low risk and low return.

- Conduct fit-and-proper tests on the senior managerial personnel of the banking institutions;
- Formulate the rules of prudent operation for banking institutions;
- Conduct off-site surveillance of the banking institutions, set up the IT system to analyze and evaluate the risk level of banking institutions;
- Conduct on-site examination of the banking institutions, and take enforcement actions against rule-breaking behaviors;
- Conduct consolidated supervision of the banking institutions;
- Provide proposals on the resolution of problem deposit-taking institutions in consultation with relevant regulatory authorities;
- Compile and publish statistics and reports of the overall banking industry in accordance with relevant regulations;
- Initiate activities for international exchange and cooperation;
- Conduct take-over or help restructuring of banking institutions which may have severe credit risk and impair the interest of the depositors;
- Revoke banking institutions which have conditions of illegal or faulty operations;
- Check the account balance of banking institutions and personnel that involves in illegality, and apply for freezing accounts that involves in money laundering;
- Revoke banking institutions and ban banking activities that are unauthorized;
- Responsible for the administration of the supervisory boards of the major State-owned banking institutions;
- Other functions delegated by the State Council.

(2) *Basic structure and professionals*

Currently CBRC has 28 departments, which are listed as follows:

- General Administration Department
- Policy Research Bureau
- Prudential Regulation Bureau
- On-site Examination Bureau
- Legal Department
- Financial Inclusion Affairs Department
- Banking Information Technology Supervision Department
- Banking Innovation Supervision Department
- Banking Consumer Protection Department
- Policy Banks Supervision Department
- Large Commercial Banks Supervision Department
- National Shareholding Banks Supervision Department
- City Commercial Banks Supervision Department
- Rural Financial Institutions Supervision Department
- Foreign Banks Supervision Department
- Trust Companies Supervision Department
- Non-bank Financial Institutions Supervision Department
- Anti-illegal Fund Raising Office (Banking Safety and Security Bureau)

For investors, to obtain a high income, it must bear the high risk, high income must be accompanied by a high risk. But in turn, if investors bear a high risk, but not necessarily be able to ensure high returns, because the meaning of high risk itself is uncertain. High risk results may be high yields, but also may be low yields, and may even be high loss. Income is clearly at risk as a price.

To sum, the characteristics of finance products can be summarized as above. Enhancement of simplicity of finance products should be put in how to strengthen these five characteristics. More specifically, who issued the product? Who is qualified to buy it? When is the maturity of it? What is the risk and yield embedded in it? How much is it? As long as these five elements are satisfied, the product could be judged as meeting basic conditions of financial products. Others like special terminology, which is strange to ordinary consumers, could sometimes makes it tough for consumers to understand. Though descriptions of the product could be wonderful, they hardly leave an impression on consumers. Salesman would need to be better in translating these arcane terminologies in simple words.

5.2 *How to Reduce Price Dispersion While Upholding Price-Quality Competition?*

Recently, the current finance industry is countering "cruel" competition. Lots of new but similar products issued by different finance institutions. In order to occupy the market, these companies try to attract investors by means of reducing price. It exactly reflects the current situation of the vicious competition in China's financial sector. We need to understand the structural problems and institutional deficiencies in this competitive state, and find the corresponding treatment methods. If this problem is not solved, it is bound to affect the healthy development of China's economy.

In fact, reasons for this vicious competition in the Chinese financial sector are very simple. Firstly, Chinese finance is not only affected by the bad habits of the international financial community, but also due to a structural imbalance, Chinese financial products lack a more effective and safe product innovation. Secondly, the system performance incentive mechanism is unique, single and irreplaceable. Institutions are used to robbing other agencies of clients on account of directivity and effectiveness. The "index economy" with Chinese characteristics is also an important reason for China's GDP index to go up in last 30 years. To better protect the rights of the financial consumers, actions must be taken by the financial authorities.

First of all, if we can solve the "xenophile" habit of thinking, we can reduce the pressure of foreign banks. Many domestic banks have one or two foreign banks as their strategic partners. In fact, the contribution of these foreign banks to China is very limited, but foreign banks make the use of China banks to improve its fame and market share in china. In view of this, the China banks can learn more technical skills and management methods from foreign banks and benefit from each other. Instead of focusing attention on domestic market and competition, China bank is supposed to put more emphasis on international market.

Next, instead of chasing high income by means of selling product at lower price, finance institutions are suggested emphasizing on risk management due to common sense that high profit is always accompanied by high risks. Based on systematic risk management, it would be obvious to discover the fact that risk management could improve the quality of asset and correspondingly enhance competitive power. In view of long term, giving up purely chasing turnover, more or less, is a more rational transformation for most of finance institutions in China.

Finally, plagiarism is well-known over China market. Therefore, it is effective if government could stipulate specific laws with regards to plagiarizing. For example, launching more regulations on new thriving products.

References

From official government website: http://www.npc.gov.cn/npc/xinwen/2013-10/26/content_1811773.htm

From Official website of China government: http://www.gov.cn/zhengce/content/2015-03/31/content_9562.htm

Haibo Y. The Problems and Measures of China's DIS Establishment [J]. Journal of Finance, 2004, 11: 003.

Hongbo T. Deposit Insurance System and Bank Corporate Governance [J]. Journal of Financial Research, 2008, 7: 020.

Liao Fan. The concept and definition of financial consumers: From the aspect of comparative method [J]. Global Law Review, 2012, 4: 95–104.

Li Minghui. On Internal Control Disclosure of Listed Commercial Bank [J]. Journal of Finance, 2004, 5: 007.

Liu Xia. Research on effective financial supervision under mixed business model [J]. Journal of Financial Research, 2005 (9): 96–104.

XiangCong C. Legislation Research on Subrogation Priority for De-posit Insurance Institutions [J]. Studies of International Finance, 2006, 7: 011.

Xian Xu is the Director of China Insurance and Social Security Research Center, Fudan University and the Managing Associate Director of Fudan-UC Center on Contemporary China, based on University of California San Diego. He serves also as executive council member of the Insurance Society of China and senior member of Accounting Society of China. He is also a research associate at Centre for European Economic Research in Germany. He obtained his Ph.D. in economics from Karlsruhe Institute of Technology. His research focuses on insurance, disaster economics, and risk management.

Chapter 6
French Financial Market and the French Financial Consumer

Jean-Paul A. Louisot

French citizens tend to have relatively high levels of savings; however this does not contribute to strong individuals' support to the financial market. Traditionally in developed market, the financial assets of most citizens are constituted by their pension funds managed on the basis of the constitution of an individual account, process known as capitalisation whereby each individual owns a set of financial assets, generally through a fund management company. On the contrary, in France, the pensions, for the most part, are based on repartition whereby the workers pay on an ongoing basis the pensions of those retired. The system will be explained further later in this chapter. The result is that financial assets are owned by a limited fringe of the population.

The other channel for individual to participate in the financial markets is the purchase of life insurance and the country lags the other developed country in this matter in spite of tax incentives as there linger in the collective memory what happened to those who subscribed life insurance in Gold-Franc on the eve of World War I and where paid back in Franc totally devalued on the Eve of World War II. Since then, insurance companies have worked hard to restore the citizens' trust and confidence in the product offered.

The French Government is currently considering a serious overhaul of the French retirement systems that may modify the life insurance market and might take place as early as 2020 but there is no way at this early stage to project the size or side of the impact.

J.-P. A. Louisot (✉)
Institut Catholique de Lille, Lille, France
e-mail: jplouisot@aol.com

© Springer Nature Singapore Pte Ltd. 2018
T.-J. Chen (ed.), *An International Comparison of Financial Consumer Protection*,
https://doi.org/10.1007/978-981-10-8441-6_6

1 Financial Consumer

1.1 Legal Definition of Financial Consumer

A consumer is defined by the French legislation as an individual (physical persona who acts for aims that do not pertain) to any commercial, industrial, craft or service providing activity. The financial consumer is not defined as such but can be inferred from the preceding definition as the individual who engages in a transaction to purchase a financial product or service.

Legally, the consumer must be distinguished from the professional: they are not protected by the same legal regime when they purchase goods or services, the consumer is especially protected.

1.2 Economic Situation of Financial Consumer

1.2.1 Total Population, Age Structure, Income Structure (Nominal, Real)

As is reflected in Exhibit 1 here below the median age in France is 40 years, the age at which the number of women exceeds the number of men but close to equality. The pyramid is less inversed than in the rest of Europe thanks to a fertility rate of 2.08 which ranks 110 in the world but first in the EU, the only country above 2.

French demography is one of the most dynamic in Europe and it has specific demographic indicators: the number of birth is in constant increase since 1994 (770,900 in 2001) but decreased slightly in 2002 (762,000). However, with the

Exhibit 1 French population on Jan 1, 2017—*Source* INSEE

Age	Men	Women	Total	% of total
0/9	4,143,408	3,959,928	8,103,135	12.10%
10/19	4,252,317	4,055,139	8,307,456	12.40%
20/29	3,848,128	3,851,685	7,699,813	11.40%
30/39	4,060,940	4,219,566	8,280,506	12.30%
40/49	4,387,994	4,471,847	8,859,841	13.20%
50/59	4,308,162	4,513,788	8,821,950	13.10%
60/69	3,814,743	4,211,194	8,027,935	12.00%
70/79	2,233,964	2,694,919	4,928,983	7.35%
80/89	119,704	1,978,139	3,174,843	4.70%
90/99	206,584	563,246	769,830	1.15%
100 & over	3015	15,617	18,632	0.30%
Total	32,455,859	34,534,967	66,990,826	100.00%
%	48.45%	51.55%	100%	

Republic of Ireland it remained at the highest level of fertility in Europe and the fertility index is now at 2.08, as stated above. However, the age of first pregnancy has increased to 29.4 years.

Infertility is in the range of 12/14% whereas in Germany, the Netherlands and the UK it is in excess of 20%. Mortality is one of the lowest rate and life expectancy one of the highest with 72.3 years for men and 83.0 for women (European average is 81.2).

Immigration plays an important role in the demographic dynamic in France; even though it is lower than in other European countries with an average of 50,000 foreigners welcomed in France every year.

Other indicators make de difference too:

- A decline in out of wedlock's birth since 2000, whereas the were increasing;
- An increase in marriage rate;
- A lesser aging of the population, as young people under 20 represent over 25% of the overall population the 20/64 three fifths and one fifth for over 65 (see Exhibit 1);
- Higher age for maternity: 1.85 child at 30 and 2.04 at 40 (total 2.08).

As far as wealth is concerned the Exhibit 2 gives an idea of the total wealth in non financial assets.

Year after year, French citizens remain, just behind the Germans, the thriftiest among members of the EU. At the end of the third quarter of 2015 the savings rate reached 15.5% of disposable income. Although this is not a record breaking level as it was over 16% between 2010 and 2011 but it shows steady increase. Over the total year in 2015 the average rate was 14.5% (196 billion €) of which financial assets represented 5.5% (74.6 billion €) and housing 8.6% (116.7 billion €).

Over the long run (1950–2015), financial assets have always represented a smaller share than housing. Real estate remains the preferred investment vehicle for French citizens and they have invested between 8 and 10% of their disposable income towards housing in the period 2001–2015.

Exhibit 2 National wealth by institutional sector of non financial assets in 2016—France

Total assets	Household (including ISBLSM)	Non financial companies	Financial institutions	Public administrations	National economy
Non financial assets (NFA)	7507	4459	270	1951	14,187
Of which					
Housing	3580	680	41	61	4362
Other buildings and public works	167	784	63	935	1949
Machinery and equipments	44	518	15	33	611
Land	3546	1468	105	760	5879

Sources Bank of France; Insee—National Account—base 2010

Salary Distribution In 2013, median net salary in France was €1730, and any worker earning more than €3500 is in the top 10% salary.

High Income A recent study by Insee on high income is based on consumption unit rather that real income per head does not provide information on its sources but it still provides an interesting insight on the 1% wealthiest segment, i.e. with more than €84,469 per consumption unit. As a reminder, the concept of consumption unit makes possible a comparison of the standard of living of the households of different sizes. The household income is divided by the number of members of the household: 1 for the first adult, 0.5 for any member above the age of 14, and 0.3 for members under the age of 14. Thus to be in the fist 10%, a household income must be:

- €35,677 for a single person;
- €53,515 for a couple;
- €85,625 for a couple with 3 young children.

This concept allows for comparing households and their capacity of savings but it does not provide a real picture of the dispersion of total income. Therefore, it would be interesting to contrast both indexes.

Te total revenue index that the 3000 wealthiest household have revenues around €3 million.

It is also interesting to note that income taxes are only high for very wealthy households. However, the «well off» pay comparatively more income taxes than the wealthiest. This is due to taxes loopholes, and among the 3000 wealthiest

- 25% pay their fait contribution;
- 20% enjoy some loopholes that reduce their taxes;
- 55% benefit hugely from the system, of whom 25% scandalously.

Income distribution in France in 2010

Group	Adult population (millions)	Yearly income per adult	Monthly income per adult	Share of total income (%)
Total population	50	33 000 €	2 800 €	100
Working class: 50% ^poorest	25	18 000 €	1 600 €	27
Middle class: 40% in the middle	20	35 000 €	3 000 €	42
Upper class: 10% wealthiest	5	103 000 €	8 600 €	31
Of which upper–upper: 1% wealthiest	0.5	363 000 €	30 300 €	11
Of which upper middle: 9% remaining	4.5	73 000 €	6 100 €	20

Assets distribution in France in 2010			
Group	Adult population (millions)	Total asset per adult	Share of total income (%)
Total population	50	182 000 €	100
Working class: 50%^poorest	25	14 000 €	4
Middle class: 40% in the middle	20	154 000 €	34
Upper class: 10% wealthiest	5	1 128 000 €	62
Of which upper–upper: 1% wealthiest	0.5	4 368 000 €	24
Of which upper middle: 9% remaining	4.5	768 000 €	38

Furthermore, the income is not age related as common sense would dictate. There are a number of young people among the wealthy. Contrary to the USA, the number of "wealthiest" is not exploding. And only 0.01% of the wealthiest (6000 persons) have seen their wealth increase at the expense of all the others.

1.2.2 Social Security System (Basic Structure, Participants, Benefits and Expenses)

French Social security has three main components: health insurance, family benefits, and pension insurance. In France, unemployment and dependency benefits are not managed within the Social Security system.

Health Insurance Heath insurance funds are in charge of illness; maternity, disability, death, ordinary accident, workers comp (accident and occupational illnesses).

Family Benefits Since Jan 1, 2006, it is in charge of 14 benefits, as follows:

- Benefits without resource requirements
  - family benefits,
  - family support benefits,
  - Education benefits for handicapped children,
  - child minder benefits,
  - parents presence benefits, and
  - daily allowance of paternity when covered by Health Insurance.
- Benefits depending of level of resources
  - Young children's early days benefit (PAJE),
  - Family supplement benefits,
  - Single parent benefits,
  - Back to school benefits,
  - Handicapped Adults Benefits,
  - Family Housing benefits,

- Relocation Benefits, and
- Minimum Insertion Income financed by local authorities (department) and paid out by the Family Benefits funds.

Pension Insurance Since January 1, 2004 the fund manages the following nine benefits

- Contributory benefits
  - Old age pension,
  - Survivorship pension,
  - Old age pension of surviving spouse.
- Non-contributory benefits
  - Old workers allowance and lifelong support,
  - Mothers Allowance,
  - Additional allowance of the national fund of solidarity,
  - Increase of pension, and
  - Special allowance.

Other Risks of Social Protection As mentioned here above, joblessness and dependency are not part of the 2006 system. The National Solidarity Fund is in charge of managing the special allowance for handicapped adult (L. 2004-626 & D. 2004-1384).

1.2.3 Additional Social Protection

There are two types of additional social protection the compulsory national systems and other that are freely negotiated in each firm.

Complementary Social Protection The first level of compulsory national schemes comprises:

- The complementary pension regimes (Agirc et Arrco) are contributory pension schemes for all salaried personnel,
- Joblessness compensation (UNEDIC).

Both have paritarian management where trade union and employers' organisations share equally the responsibilities. Both systems comply with all the criteria that European jurisprudence has defined for Social Security schemes: premium are independent of risk, they are proportional to income, not for profit management, compulsory affiliation, exemption from contribution under given circumstances (disability, joblessness).

The schemes are within the scope or the coordination of schemes for migrating European workers within the EU.

The UNEDIC manages also the solidarity allowance granted by the state.

Negotiated at the Branch Level or at the Enterprise Level These schemes result from collective conventions, inter-professional agreements, group or enterprises. They can only cover death, healthcare, maternity, disability, joblessness and pension funds contributions. The issue of end of work life indemnity is open to self insurance.

Individual Social Protection Individuals can opt to add to the schemes mentioned above their own covers that they can purchase from insurance companies or from mutual companies.

1.2.4 Pension Systems—The Three Pillars

During International conferences, speakers often refer to the three pillars defined originally by Swiss Insurers:

- First Pillar: National Compulsory Schemes;
- Second Pillar: Social Protection negotiated at the branch, group or company level;
- Third Pillar: All protection and pension contracts entered into by the individuals.

1.2.5 Bank Deposit Holders, Total Number of Bank Accounts, No. of Employees, Financial Statements

Although, there is no formal published statistics only 500,000 French citizens did not have a bank account in 2016. With a population of close to 67 million and taking into account the fact that some have several account it would not be surprising if private accounts were over 200 millions.

The structure of the banking industry in France is much diversified with over 200 institutions of very different sizes and activities. Some are local and cooperative, some have a national network, and some are International players. There are also some investment banks.

In spite of the improvement in the economic environment and the excellent level of credit activity, French banks are still engaged in costs reduction plans. In 2016, the level of staff in constant contraction since 2011 has declined by 0.3%.

With 370,300 staff, banks remain a major private employer in France. They have recruited 41,000 persons in 2016, but the number of hiring did not compensate the number of retirees, as is the case since the economic crisis of 2007–2008. However, the sector continues to propose durable and qualified jobs and still two thirds of the recruitments are for "undetermined duration". The academic level of young recruits continues to rise with 44% holding a post-graduate degree. Financial institutions are strengthening their compliance and IT teams. A new trend has come to light in the banking industry with an upsurge of resignation, and this seems to come mostly from the newly hired.

France has a concentrated market with four banks among the 28 major players in the world banking system according to balance sheet size and known as G20 systemic banks:

- CREDIT AGRICOLE with €2008 billion is number 5
- BNP-Paribas with €1907 billion is number 7
- SOCIETE GENERAL with €1251 billion is number 19
- BPCE with €1148 billion is number 21
- CIC CREDIT MUTUEL with €605 billion is number 41
- ALL OTHER BANKS in France total €1157 billion.

Thus France is at par with China but ahead of Germany who has the largest bank in the world, number 1, but none other among the 28. As a matter of fact the large SME's that exports a lot find financing with 1500 local banks contrary to the much more concentrated field in France. The sector is heavily concentrated; as the numbers here above show the 2 first banks represent 50% of the market and the first 5 86%. This situation leads to a cartelisation at the expense of consumers.

Terminons par une analyse de la structure de nos banques: On constate le poids très important des activités de marché—sauf pour le crédit Mutuel-CIC qui arrive semble-t-il fort bien à servir 30 millions de clients sans avoir besoin de produits dérivés….

Banking Online French are more and more to open account online and Boursorama Banque has reached the 1 million clients threshold and is nearing the historical leader ING Direct. Online offer are growing to include credit and insurance, thus the players are becoming real competition for traditional banks.

French Bank Strategy The interest rate margin is even narrower and the banks are trying to compensate through the development of activities that bring in commissions such as insurance and other bank services. The cost of risk seems under control in 2016, thanks to a more favourable economic environment, and French banks benefit from it.

Top even Banks in France in Terms of Balance-Sheet

- **BNP Paribas**: Slight increase of the net banking product of 1.1% to €43.411 billion. The bank remains the number 1 in France and its net profit reached €7.702 billion.
- **Groupe Crédit Agricole**: Consolidate regional branches, the holding CASA and its subsidiaries including LCL. The group suffered a decrease in its net banking product at €30.427 billion. The activity is stable after retreatment of specific elements. The margin is slightly down to €4.825 billion, due in part to depreciation for an acquisition gap on LCL. The bank remains the number 2 in France.

- **Société Générale**: The net banking product is down 1.3% to €25.298 billion. Retail banking has suffered from low interest rate in spite of a sustained commercial activity. The net result of Socgen was €3.874 billion.
- **Groupe BPCE**: The group result from the merger of Banque Populaire, Caisses d'Epargne, Natixis and all the subsidiaries. The banking product in 2016 is €24.158 billion, an increase of 2% benefiting from a higher outstanding credits amounts and higher savings. This increase allows the bank to retina its 4th rank. The consolidated result is higher at €3.988 billion.
- **Groupe CM11-CIC**: The group comprises 11 federations of Crédit Mutuel, Crédit Industriel and Commercial (CIC) and its subsidiaries. The mutualist group has experienced an increase in its net banking product at **€13.302 billion** (+1.8%). IN a low interest context, the activities bringing in commissions help the bank result set at €2.410 billion.
- **La Banque Postale**: The group La Banque Postale has seen its NBP decrease to **€5.602 billion**, as its performance was impacted by lower revenues on interest rates. The profitability has declined to €694 millions. En 2018 La Banque Postale will launch its 100% digital bank to better fulfil the bank's clients expectations.
- **Crédit Mutuel Arkéa**: The group comprises de 3 regional branches (Bretagne, Sud-Ouest, and Massif Central) and numerous subsidiaries (online bank, lease, factoring, insurance…).The Briton group has a NBP of **€1.852 billion**, an increase of 4.1%, and a profitability of €336 millions. The performance is carried by insurance and asset management. The year has been enriched by several partnerships with start-up and fin techs.

Ranking in Terms of Ratio

The ratio measures the banks performance, the lower the ratio, the more efficient the bank. It is computed by dividing the general expenses by the net bank product.

1. Caisses Régionales of CA à 61.3%
2. Groupe CM 11—CIC 61.7%
3. Société Générale 65.6%
4. BNP Paribas 67.7%
5. Groupe BPCE 69.0%
6. CM ARKEA 69.2%
7. La Banque Postale 82.4%.

Ranking by Number of Staff

1. BNP Paribas—192,092 staff
2. Société Générale—145,700 staff
3. Groupe Crédit Agricole—138,000 staff
4. Groupe BPCE—108,000 staff
5. Groupe CM 11 CIC—69,514 staffs

6. CM ARKEA—6176 staff
7. La Banque Postale—4222 staff.

Ranking in Number of Clients
Difficult to draw conclusions of these numbers as the clients' categories and sizes are not taken into account.

1. Groupe Crédit Agricole 52 millions de clients
2. BNP Paribas P 32 millions de clients
3. Groupe BPCE 31,2 millions de clients
4. Société Générale 31 millions de clients
5. Groupe CM 11—CIC 23,8 millions de clients
6. La Banque Postale 10.7 millions de clients
7. CM ARKEA 3,9 millions de clients.

1.2.6 Total Security Market Capitalization, Security Market Structure

Financial markets offer a place where buyers and sellers of capital can negotiate through financial securities like shares, bonds, treasury notes. Thus companies can find new means to finance their growth, without resorting to bank credit. The companies contact investors on the capital markets through the issuance of quoted securities.

Capital markets are now nearly completely dematerialised and electronic. The Stock Exchange buildings have lost their function of physical confrontation with negotiators yelling their orders around the floor. Modern financial markets are computer networks treating the transactions between financial institutions.

In France, there are two types of market and overall market capitalisation is in excess of €5 billion:

Regulated Markets These are traditional stock exchanges. In France it is the principal list of NYSE Euronext Paris, formerly called Bourse de Paris. Issuers listed on regulated markets must comply with strict rules and supervision, including regarding information to be given to the investors. The market operations and those involved are subjected to strict rules by regulation authorities. Furthermore, the stock exchange and futures markets offer a central counterpart for transactions between sellers and buyers. Sellers do not have to worry about the financial and administrative regulation of their transactions.

"Not-regulated" Market They are none the less controlled, and among them are the others lists of the NYSE Euronext, and the multi-lateral systems of negotiation.[1] Over the counter (OTC) transactions are not subject to the same regulations. Therefore, they are riskier for investors, notably for private individual investors.

NYSE Euronext Paris the historical security market organisation, offers three lists of quotation among which French companies are assigned depending on their market capitalisation:

- **Eurolist**: Regulated market split in several groups (A, B, & C). It contains the most important companies by the size of market capitalisation.
- **Free Market (Marché Libre)**: Not regulated, this market lists the companies that are too young or too small to gain access to the regulated compartments.
- **Alternext**: It is not regulated; this market was created to offer SME's an access to quotation.

1.2.7 Total Number of Insurance Policyholders, Insurance Market Structure (No. of Companies, Not-for-Profit Companies)

In 2015 Europe (including the UK) is the first insurance market in the world, ahead of North America and Asia. Within the E.U., France is number 2 behind the UK but ahead of Germany.

The total premium income in 2015 was €1200 billion, an increase of 1.3% over 2014. Life insurance share is 61%, i.e. a total of €730 billion, a yearly increase of 1.2%. Non-Life insurance with €343 billion represented 29% of the market an increase of 1.1% over the preceding year. The last branch, health insurance, has experienced an increase of 1.5% to reach €127 billion.

Life insurance policies can take the form of individual or group contracts, and they can be "pure insurance" products, savings products or a combination of both. In total, European life insurance premiums rose to €730 billion in 2015, a 1.2% increase on 2014.

In 2014 (the latest year for which a breakdown is available), premiums from individual contracts grew by 12.0% and accounted for 76.7% of all life premiums, compared to 75.5% in 2013. Premiums collected through group contracts grew at a slower pace than individual contracts (4.7%). In 2014, they accounted for 23.3% of all life insurance premiums, compared to 24.5% the year before.

Traditional life contracts 1 grew by 8.9% in 2014, representing 81.3% of all individual life premiums. Unit-linked contracts, which provide both, risk cover and an investment element, grew at a faster pace than traditional contracts (14.1%). As a result, their share of total life premiums increased by 3.8% compared to the year before to 18.7%.

In 2015, life insurance penetration decreased slightly to 4.5 from 4.6% in 2014, but ranged from 0.2% in Iceland, Latvia and Turkey to 9.3% in Finland. An average of €1223 per capita was spent on life insurance in Europe in 2015, compared to €1 214 in 2014. Life insurance density varied in 2015 from less than €20 per capita in Turkey and Romania to more than €3500 in Finland, Switzerland and Liechtenstein.

Life benefits paid increased by 1.7% to €649 bn in 2015, or €1088 per capita.

Non-life insurance, whose two main business lines are motor and property, includes a wide range of cover for individuals, property, vehicles and businesses. Non-life premiums grew by 1.1% in 2015 to total €343 bn. Motor was the largest non-life business line in 2015, accounting for 38% of premiums. Motor premiums grew 1.0% in 2015 to €132 bn. The property market grew 1.6% to €93 bn, accounting for 27% of 2015 non-life premiums. Meanwhile accident premiums increased by 1.2% to €34.2 bn and general liability premiums remained stable at €33.8 bn.

In 2015, non-life insurance penetration decreased slightly from 2.17 to 2.13%, ranging from 0.6% in Latvia to 2.7% in France. An average of €574 per capita was spent on non-life insurance in Europe in 2015, compared to €570 in 2014.

Non-life insurers paid out €222 bn in claims in 2015, an increase of 2.3% on the year before. Motor claims paid increased 1.9% to €101 bn and property claims grew 0.7% to €53 bn. Accident claims paid rose 8.6% to €21.2 bn, while general liability claims remained stable at €20.9 bn.

Property insurance provides protection against risks to property such as fire, theft and some weather damage. The business line includes specialised forms of insurance, such as fire, flood, earthquake or home insurance.

In 2015, property insurance premiums increased 1.6% to reach €93 bn in Europe. This is equivalent to an average of €155 paid in property premiums per inhabitant, which is €2 more than in 2014.

Property claims paid increased by 0.7% to €53 billion in 2015 or €90 per capita.

Health insurance provides individuals or groups with cover for the medical costs of illness or accidents. Health insurers also offer other products, such as critical illness, disability or long-term care insurance. Total European health premiums grew by 1.5% to €124 bn in 2015.

In 2015, health insurance penetration remained stable at 0.8%, but varied from 0.01% in Greece and Romania to 6.1% in the Netherlands. An average of €207 per capita was spent on health insurance in Europe in 2015, compared to €205 in 2014. Health insurance density varied in 2015 from less than €3 per capita in Greece and Romania to more than €1000 in Switzerland and the Netherlands. The Dutch and the Swiss healthcare systems require individuals to purchase private health insurance, which is why they are top performers in terms of health premiums per capita.

Health insurance claims paid grew 4.3% in 2015 to reach €101 bn. The average claim paid per capita amounted to €176, compared to €169 in 2014.

In France, insurers are increasingly supporting French enterprises actively financing French productive and competitive industry. At the end of 2016, the insurers had invested 1386 billion to finance enterprises as of the end of 2016.

The net collection of premium in life insurance has reached €300 million in May 2017, of which €56.4 by insurance companies (it was 59.5 at the same period in 2016). The payments to unit and index linked contracts were at €15.2 billion, i.e. 27% of premium.

As far as, private companies' pension funds are concerned, En 2016, premium collected are up 6% and reach €2.4 billion, of which €163 millions represent voluntary remittance (+11%).

Exhibit 3 AGIRA 1–2005 ACT

Requests to AGIRA		Death of 2016—requests to AFIRA			
		To be settled		Settled in 2016 (for 2016 identifications)	
Requests received in 2016 for confirmed death	Requests received in 2016 that allowed to confirm death	Amount in € (total of technical provisions)	Number of contracts	Amount in € (total of technical provisions)	Number of contracts
34,457	7436	373,408,019	8783	258,847,751	5881

Exhibit 4 AGIRA 2–2007 ACT

Consultations of the AGIRA-RNIPP file of deceased		For deaths identified in 2016 thanks to consultation of the file			
		To settle		Settled in 2016 (for identification in 2016)	
Number of deceased identified thanks in 2016 to the AGIRA-RNIPP files	Number of contracts signed by the identified deceased	Total amount in € (technical provisions)	Number of contracts	Total amount in € (technical provisions)	Number of contracts
49,446	58,884	1,120,135,192	56,337	644,710,156	26,526

Personal protection contracts linked to the Loi Madelin, a specific legislation with tax provisions for self employed and artisan are marketed since 1994 and premium collection as up 3%. Since 2006, persons who believe they might be beneficiaries of life insurance signed by a deceased family member can ask for information at the Association for information management in insurance (AGIRA) for a confirmation. It will help beneficiaries collect when they have no proof of the contact.

The table here above provides global figures on the activity (Exhibits 3 and 4).

1.2.8 Distribution Structure and No. of Insurance Salespersons[2,3]

Insurers sell their products either directly or through a variety of other distribution channels, of which the most familiar are brokers, agents and banc-assurance.

The diversity of distribution channels benefits consumers, whose cultures, needs and preferences vary between markets. It ensures that consumers have better access to insurance products and stimulates competition between providers and distributors on the price and quality of products.

Banc-assurance is the main life distribution channel in many European countries today. Agents and brokers also play an important role, particularly in the distribution of life policies. However, direct sales through employees or distance-selling are less developed in life than in non-life insurance. The distribution of non-life policies in Europe is mainly through intermediaries (agents and, to a lesser extent, brokers) and direct sales by employees and distance-selling.

In France, strict mutual companies[4] sell directly with sales staff in their shops and by their won regulation they receive a salary and no commission. They represent more than half of automobile insurance and homeowners' contracts.

Other companies, for profit and other mutual use three channels of distribution

- ***Agents*** *(Agents Généraux d'Assurance)* who have a contract with a company and, in principle, work exclusively for that company and have the exclusivity of the company's product in a given territory. They operate as a liberal profession and the contract that attaches them to the company is called a nomination treaty. They are compensated with commissions on the contract they bring in and when they retire or resign they receive a compensatory indemnity based on the commissions' amount in the agency. The client base (portfolio) belongs to the company as they act on behalf of the company. There are around 14,000 agents' outlets in France with a total number of employees in excess of 25,000.
- ***Brokers*** *(courtier d'assurance)* are traders who are agent of their customers and the clientele belong to them. They engage in trading with all insurance companies, at least a large number and act as a multi card sales representative. They are compensated by commission paid by the insurer as a percentage of premium income they bring in. When they retire or want to stop their trade, they can sell their client base (portfolio) to a third party. There are 22,000 brokers in France of which 60% are a one person business. However, the ten major mega brokers hold most of the market, of which the top three with millions of commissions are Gras Savoye (Willis-Towers-Watson), Marsh & McLennan Companies France and Verspieren. They handle most of large companies account and make inroads in medium size and SME's.
- ***Salaried sales person*** *(producteurs salariés)*: Some companies sell directly to consumers with a sales force of salaried representative compensated through wages based on a commission on premium brought in. This channel is mostly used for life insurance. No figure is available for their exact number at the industry level, but the total of financial services sales representatives is estimated at 250,000.

2 Financial Consumer Protection—Goal and Legal Environment

As soon as the conditions imposed by the legal definition of consumer[5] are met, the qualification of «consumer» provides the individual with the protecting provisions of the Consumption code (*Code de la consommation*). The protection is applicable in a number of areas: withdrawal period, guarantee of conformity, unfair contract terms, and doorstep selling.

For financial services, traditional as well as e-distributed, consumers are protected in similar fashion, i.e. obligation of information, legal withdrawal rights. These protections have been adapted to the specificity of financial contracts meaning that it concerns (art. I.8, 18° CDE)

- bank services,
- insurance,
- credit granting,
- individual pension,
- investments, and
- payments.

On the specificity of financial services is that the service is defined by conditions: duration, rate of return, insured risk define the financial service. Therefore it is of the utmost importance that precise information is provided.

Information Obligation
Before being bound by an offer, the consumer must be clearly informed on:

- the financial service provider;
- the characteristics and price of the financial service;
- the possibility or not to benefit a withdrawal right;
- the possible ways of extrajudicial appeals.

In the case of a phone call, it is admissible to provide more limited information, so far as the consumer's consent to it expressly.

In any situation, consumer must receive in writing or any other durable medium, the essential information and all contractual conditions. This information must be remitted before the consumer can acquiesce to the offer ***(art. VI.55 to 57 CDE).***

Withdrawal Right
The consumer has a 14 calendar days' withdrawal right after the contract is signed. For life insurance contract the renunciation delay is 30 calendar days, due to the duration of such contracts. The period starts when the consumer receives in writing or any other durable medium, the essential information and all contractual conditions.

However, the withdrawal right does not apply when purchasing financial services the price of which depends on market fluctuations on which the provider has no influence. For example, when purchasing shares, there is no withdrawal right, as it could be used as a mean of speculating allowing the consumer to be guaranteed full repayment no matter what. On the other hand when dealing with a mortgage loan there is a specific protection. The consumer may agree to an early execution but it must be done without the shadow of a doubt and after proper information (***art. VI.58 & 59 CDE***).

Burden of Proof
In case of dispute, it falls on the financial services provider to bring the proof that all the following elements have been fulfilled:

- information obligation,
- compliance with deadlines,
- consumer's authorisation for the conclusion of the contract,
- if necessary, his authorisation for an early execution (before the end of the withdrawal period).

2.1 Relevant Laws and Regulations

The act to create the consumers' protection code abrogated 26 acts or part of acts and it soon appeared that the work of codification was substantial. And if the code does not contain all the texts to protect consumers, it does not only contain dispositions to protect the consumer.

However consumers' protection is not all in the code and other codes are important, significantly in the context of financial services:

- **Insurance contracts**: Most provisions to protect consumers are to be found in the insurance code with partial repeat from the consumers' code. Such is the case for distance purchase of insurance services integrated in the code of insurance, adapted repeat from it.
  Provisions are also found in the Code of mutuality and the Code of Social Security. As a matter of fact, companies selling or distributing insurance products may fall within the scope of different codes. Provident societies are to comply with the SS code whereas other mutual companies fall within the Mutuality Code. If, for the most part, the provisions are identical in the different codes, some rules may differ depending on the organisation the consumer contract with.
  Some provisions were to be found here and there in other codes, like the sport code for the obligation of sports club to offer each member an accident insurance. To summarize the protection of consumers buying insurance stems from several separate codes and in the end very little from the code of consumption.
- **Banks and other financial services**: Whereas Consumer credit and the property loan are governed by the consumption code, other bank/client relations and means of payment are governed by the Financial and monetary code.[6]

2.2 Rationale and Direction of FCP

If government let the market forces to play freely though the relaxation of regulation to give access to the financial markets to many more players, consumers might fall victim to the negative consequences of financial inclusion. The damages suffered may include debt distress linked to excessively high interest rates, to undue grating of loans, the loss of savings or assets pawned in the hands of unscrupulous players who enter the market seeking short term profits. It can be acceptable that high interest rate are charged in difficult to serve markets, with high risks, but in the absence of control and oversight some financial institutions would be inclined to overbill for services.

When buyers and sellers conclude a transaction, information is a key element in establishing a relationship of powers. Consumers, especially if they are new to financial markets, lack knowledge of financial transactions and more generally the inner works of financial markets. On the other hand, service providers legitimately try to obtain as much information as they can to evaluate the risk a client may pose to them.

Market transparency encourages institutions to compete on the basis of best products and services offered at lower prices. The development of high quality financial services will attract new consumers and, ultimately, expand the market.

Promoting rights, prosperity and well being of consumers are essential Values of the EU and are intertwined in all its legislative effort. Belonging to the EU offers a better protection to consumers. There are 10 principles[7] on which the Union legislation rests in order to protect consumers wherever they happen to be.

2.3 *Ex-ante Protection*

2.3.1 Consumer Literacy and Education

During the last ten years, European governments became aware of the importance of consumers' financial culture as a necessary condition for the stability of Financial Markets. At a time when capital markets become more and more sophisticated and when households bear more responsibilities and risks when they make financial decisions, financial education is a necessity for individuals, not only for their own personal financial wellbeing, but also to enhance the effective functioning of capital markets and the economy.

In the context of post-financial crisis, one domain for which improving consumers' financial culture has become strategic for all countries and raising financial issues awareness is credit. Innovations and increasing complexity of credit markets transfer more financial risk on the consumers who have difficulties in discerning the contractual conditions in credit products and selecting the best offer for them. Several surveys conducted in OECD members states have concluded that the consumers have scant financial knowledge and often overestimate their competencies, their knowledge, and their sensitivity concerning credit offerings. Making ill informed decisions in this area could have disastrous consequences, especially when it comes to mortgage which is probably the most important financial decision an individual or a household may make.

If financial culture is a necessary condition for efficient capital markets, it is however only one component of the authorities' effective answers to the issue of consumers' accountability in financial markets. It is not a substitute for market regulation and consumer protection as mentioned in paragraph 2.1 here above. The financial crisis of 2007–2008 has illustrated the necessity to monitor the "market behaviour"; this proved that ill informed consumers can become easy prey to unfair sales practices and be old credit products clearly not appropriate for their condition.

In the current context, financial education for credit issues should allow individuals to:

- develop the knowledge, the understanding, the competencies, and the confidence needed to assess carefully and understand their rights and duties as borrowers and the various credit solutions they are offered;
- know where to find the important information, objective advice and help, if needed;
- make informed decisions on the best solutions to protect their interest and their relatives', to engage in a pro-active behaviour and be responsible regarding loans and credit lines;
- acquire elementary skills of financial planning regarding their loans taking into account future income and the potential changes in their life cycle;
- understand the consequences of their choices, decisions, and behaviour regarding credit.

2.3.2 Product andj Price Regulation—Information Disclosure Control

As mentioned in paragraph 3, both AMF, for banks and other financial institutions, and ACAM, for insurance organisations, have broad and significant investigative powers but they products and services offered do not need their stamp of approval prior to being marketed, neither at the wording level nor at the pricing level.

The control is a posterior control with strong emphasis on transparent and truthful information so that consumers can make informed financial decisions.

2.3.3 Salesperson Qualification Control, Legal/Contractual Authority of Salesperson

Marketing financial products leads most of the time the provider to supply one or more investment services such as receiving and transmitting order for the account of third parties or servicing not-guaranteed investments. This commercialisation is carried out directly or through other service providers such as:

- agents associated acting on behalf of an investment service provider,
- Financial investments Advisors,
- Direct bank, financial, or insurance sellers.

All the persons selling financial and insurance products are requested to hold a professional qualification that is aimed at assuring the consumers that the persons that propose such products are qualified and have their best interest in mind. Both can work with a certificate of professional *qualification (Certificat de Qualification Professionnelle —CQP)* that is a diploma created within a given branch by representatives of both employers and employees and is recognised by the Collective Convention of the branch that set it up. It certifies the ability to hold a job in the concerned profession.

Holder of university bachelor and master degrees in appropriate fields can access the different positions without being requested to pass the CQP. More and more staff is hired with Engineering degree, Master in Law, Economy, Finance, Marketing, and even MBA.

Actuaries are hired for their specific competencies both by Banks and Insurance/Reinsurance companies.

However when it comes to financial services, the AMF and the ACAM have a mission to ensure that the persons selling financial services to consumers have the proper competencies:

- **BANK and Other financial institutions**—The general regulation of the AMF request that investment service providers working for them in some position in relation with the public have minimum knowledge in 12 domains pertaining to regulations, deontology, and financial techniques. The validation may result from internally organised examinations or external controls certified by the AMF. External exams must be delivered by certified organization that files a written application with the AMF and follow the rules published by it. The exam consists in a 100 questions objective examination (multi-choice) that cover the 12 domain defined with proper weight. The AMF High Council for certification must approve the exam submitted.
  Both channels have very different consequences for the licensee:
  - When holding a certified qualification, the employee does not need a new validation when changing employer;
  - When holding an internal qualification, the employee needs to pass the validation process organized by his/her new employer when he/she changes.
- **Insurance**—Brokers were the pilots of the curriculum leading to the delivery of a professional certification in Insurance (CQP). The graduate of the CQP—Insurance is recognised by the profession and thus can access responsible positions within insurance organisation thanks to the assurance the employers have. When holding a secondary education certificate (Baccaluréat) or higher, the candidate can further attend a one year program leading to 4 different positions, i.e. contract administration, claims manager, underwriter, sales representatives or adviser.
  The parity national commission for insurance professional education *(commission paritaire nationale de la formation professionnelle et de l'emploi—CPNE)* and the French federation of Insurers of Insurance companies (FFSA)[8] confers the qualification.

2.3.4 Appropriateness Principle, Good Faith and Fair Treatment Rule

The rapid development of international litigation concerning investments has given rise to constant refinement of the law relevant to economic operations. Therefore French courts have been inclined to adopt legal principles, sometimes imported from the Anglo-Saxon Common Law.

Arbitral jurisprudence has devoted more and more room to the principle of just and equitable treatment which is part of the protection of legitimate investors' expectations. It is the underlying principle when the authorities insist on fair and transparent information for the investing consumer.

Good faith is the fact that a person act thinking really that his/her facts and acts comply with the law and do not infringe on third party rights and in French law it is assumed as article 2274 of the French Civil Code reads as follows: "Good faith is always assumed, and it falls on the party arguing bad faith to prove it."

Good faith is a legal standard by which a judge can assess litigants' behavior. In contractual law since the 2016 reform good faith is requested to contract as stated in the new article 1104. This requirement is part of the cardinal requests like freedom to contract (Article 1102) or the binding effects of contracts (Article 1103).

However, good faith is continuously questioned by jurisprudence when it comes to protecting consumers against professionals. That means that courts consider generally that the professional sales person (of financial services) is aware of the defects in the products or services he/she has sold.

In the case of insurance contract, there are sanctions if the insured has misrepresented the risk, reduction of compensation if the misrepresentation was involuntary, contract nullity if the misrepresentation was voluntary. However, in both cases the insurer must prove the reality of the misrepresentation and further that the misrepresentation had an impact on the choice to underwrite or not, and/or the level of the premium.

Note that good faith in France differs from the utmost good faith in the UK contracts where relevancy to the conditions of the insurance policy does not have to be proven by the insurer. Some modifications have occurred since the enactment of the new British insurance Act[9] (August 12, 2016).

Pertinence is the link that the judge must find between the evidence a party offers to enter and the subject of the dispute. If the offer is deemed not pertinent the judge does not admit it. When examining the element the judge must ask himself/herself whether if accepted the evidence would present an interest in the resolution of the dispute *(see NCPC article 143 and following, 222 and followings).*

Just and equitable treatment is a conventional regulation technique; it would constitute a minimum standard specific to international investment. It has contributed to the advance of good governance through arbitration sentencing.

2.3.5 Abuse of Dominance and Monopoly

It is a firm's ability to raise its prices is usually constrained by competitors and the possibility that its customers can switch to alternative sources of supply.

When these constraints are weak, a firm is said to have market power and if the market power is great enough, to be in a position of dominance or monopoly (the precise terminology differs according to the jurisdiction). While mere possession of monopoly power does not in itself constitute violation of competition laws, the abuse of such power—particularly if it is used to weaken competition further by excluding rivals—calls for intervention from competition authorities. It is prohibited by article L. 420-2 of the Commerce Code.

Article L. 464-2 of the Commerce commissions the Competition Authority *(Autorité de la concurrence)* to potentially decide on injunctions and penalties for the authors of incriminated practices. When several providers are involved each will receive a justified penalty and will need to be motivated. The maximum fine can be 10% of the worldwide turnover of the highest result in the years since the implementation of non-compliant practices.

Abuse of dominance can be sentenced in civil courts following a legal action on unfair competition. Article L. 420-6 of the Commerce Code, a charge could be filed in criminal court that could sentence any physical person having taken an individual part in the development, the organisation, or the implementation of practices pertaining to article L. 420-2.

2.4 *Ex-post Protection*

2.4.1 Sanction and Role of the APCR

The Prudential Control and resolution Authority (*Autorité de Contrôle prudentielle et de résolution—ACPR*) is the branch of the AMF in charge of sanction should a financial service provider fail to comply with al laws and regulations. The authority clarifies the rights of the member at the control stage, prior to the disciplinary stage. Controllers are held by a duty of loyalty in their search for evidence, so that the defense rights are preserved for the disciplinary stage. The commission makes sure that no irreparable infringement to these rights has been committed prior to the disciplinary stage. The Monetary and financial Code does not condition the opening of the disciplinary stage by the failure of an ACPR recommendation or, even, by the lack of cooperation of the financial institution.

The pursuing authority must establish the evidence of the breaches in front of the Sanction Commission. When there are elements of prima facie evidence resulting from control operations, the defendant must offer contrary evidence. Failing that the probable breach will be considered as proven, even in case of unjustified protests. This is an improvement over the article 9 of the civil procedure code.

As a reminder, the authority reminds all interested parties that the proceedings benefit from no prescription as the Financial and Monetary Code has no explicit provision to this effect. This is considered in compliance with the French Constitution. Any breach, whenever it was committed can lead to prosecution. Proportionality of sanctions (essentially fines) will allow taking into account the fact that breaches may have been committed a long time ago. However, the absence of prescription in a context of rapidly evolving legal environment for bank and insurance practices bears heavily on the activities of final institutions.

The commission does not believe a prejudicial question should be transmitted to the European Court of Justice to the extent that the French State Council (*Conseil d'Etat*) has full authority to assess its decisions. Several cases are currently pending in the French State Council, which has refused in January 2015 to transmit to the Constitutional Council—French Supreme Court in constitutional matters (*Conseil Constitutionnel*) the "priority question of constitutionality" as it deems the sanctions of the Sanction commission of the ACPR to comply with the Constitution.

The rules for the proceedings in the Sanction Commission are gaining in quality through experience with a better respect for defense rights. Dematerialized so far, the proceedings should take place in a new court room. However, there remains the issue of publicity for the commission audition agenda to ensure the public nature of the proceedings in accordance with article 22 of the Civil Proceedings Code.

Improving commercial practices remains a high priority for the ACPR as the duty of advice rests on intermediaries in insurance as well as in the marketing of credit products.

2.4.2 Complaints and Dispute Settlement

As mentioned here below (***paragraph 3.4***) the financial institutions have complied with the injunction of EU authorities and set up mediating agencies. Most insurers have adopted the Insurance mediator whereas banks are slowly moving in that direction while most major players still have their internal independent solution.

2.4.3 Consumers' Protection Scheme

The legal insurance schemes to cover the consequences of acts of terrorism and of natural catastrophes are not developed here.

There are two schemes under which a victim can be compensated, one for bank deposit and one for traffic accident:

Bank Deposit Balance The deposit guarantee and resolution fund *(Fonds de garantie des dépôts et de résolution—FGDR)* allows the depositors (individuals, enterprises, associations, trade associations), in case of the bank failure to be covered for up to €100,000 for the sums deposited on their checking account, savings account, and term deposits. The limit is for a given person in a given institution.

Note that the fund will not compensate for legal savings book—Livret A—Sustainable Development books, and Popular Savings Book). For these savings books, the government grants a direct guarantee up to €100,000.

Traffic Accident The Guarantee fund for compulsory damage insurances (*Fonds de garantie des assurances obligatoires de dommages—FGAO*) compensate victims of a traffic accident when the person responsible is not identified, is not insured or when his insurer is unsolvable. Under all other cases, the insurance company will indemnify.

The FGAO get involved only under certain cumulative conditions:

- Site of the accident: the accident occurred in France or within the European Economic Area (EEA).
- Circumstances: the traffic accident must occur in France or within the EEA, and not on private premises.
- Who can seize the fund? The victim of his/her claimants, when the person responsible for the accident is unknown or uninsured.
  However some individuals will not be compensated the driver if responsible for the accident, the car robber(s) or his accomplices, foreigners not residing in France of the EEA.
- What damages can be covered?
  - Bodily injury without monetary limit

    if the person responsible for the accident (or the animal owner) is unknown,
    if the person responsible for the accident (or the animal owner) is not insured,
    the accident has been caused by a wild animal.
  - Property damages: if the person responsible for the accident is unknown or uninsured **and** the victim has also suffered bodily injury or if the person responsible for the accident is identified but not insured. For property damages the compensation total limit is €1,220,000.

3 Financial Consumers Protection—Regulation Agencies

3.1 Financial Supervision Organizations

There are two major supervisory authorities in France. However, the Commission Bancaire cooperate with France's insurance industry supervisor, the Autorité de Contrôle des Assurances and des Mutuelles—ACAM in all common issues as both aim at protecting consumers and making sure the financial markets operate smoothly.

Autorité des marchés financiers—AMF The Financial Markets Authority is the organisation responsible for the supervision of financial markets in France. This public authority has legal personality and was created in 2003 as a result of the merger of the Financial Markets Council *(Conseil des marchés financiers—CMF)*, of the stock exchange commission (Commission des opérations de Bourse—COB), and the Discipline and Financial Management Council *(Conseil de discipline et de gestion financière—CDGF)*. Part of the Financial Security Act *(Loi de sécurité financière—LSF)* promulgated on August 1, 2003, this merger aimed at setting up a central regulatory body to enhance its efficiency on the wake of a number of financial scandals (WorldCom, Enron, Altran, Vivendi Universal) often linked with the Internet Financial Bubble at the end of the Twenty-first Century (1999–2000).

The Financial Markets Authority ensures the proper functioning of the markets, the truthful information of the investors, and the protection of their savings. As an illustration, asset management companies must seek the AMF's authorisation prior to marketing such products as Unit trust or Mutual funds. The AMF's stamp of approval is also requested for some operations concerning listed companies such as capital increases, takeover bid, initial public offerings, etc. All these decisions are made by a panel of sixteen members of which one half is renewed every thirty months. The chair is appointed by a presidential decree.

The Financial Markets Authority has final say in the decision to impose fine upon offenders that breach financial markets rules, be they individuals, listed companies, or asset management companies. A penalty committee, consisting of members all non-members of the accreditation panel, is in charge of making decisions on the penalties. In 2011 for instance, the Financial Markets Authority has published 20 sanction decisions within its mandate, half concerning service providers' commercial practices. The remaining sanctions were related to failure to comply with the information obligations of listed companies, cases of insiders' trading or of share prices manipulation (actions aiming at artificially influencing share prices).

The AMF was created as a fusion of two previous supervisory authority and all the missions were transferred to the new agency:

- ***Commission des opérations en bourse (COB)***: Created in 1967, the COB, or stock exchange commission, was a specialised public establishment aiming at sound operations of the financial markets. Since an act (August 2, 1989) it was made more in dependent from the authorities. It was in charge of handling citizens' complaints, investigate abnormal movements in share prices, insiders' trading; it controls also the information provided by listed companies and the companies raising public capitals; it was also supervising management funds.
- ***Conseil des Marchés financiers (CMF)***: Created by the act of 1996 aiming at the modernization of financial activities, the CMF was in charge of the general principle of the operating rules for financial markets in.

Autorité de Contrôle des Assurances and des Mutuelles—ACAM Thus, ACAM is the authority in charge of prudential supervision of insurance and reinsurance companies, Mutuality, and welfare institutions. Prudential control means making sure that insurance organisations are not threatened with bankruptcy. To deliver the ACAM lakes sure that the organisations have a proper assessment of their commitments towards insured or members. ACAM controls also the financial health and the diversity of the investments (shares, bonds, real estate) proposed to the public.

Further, the ACAM monitors closely all insurance products (life, home-owners, motor insurance, etc.) sold by all insurance organizations. Among others, ACAM can verify that the insurer provides appropriate information to the customer when it comes to complex products in units of account or to ensure that the exchange rate of the Euro is not too high. Insurance supervisors (*commissaire-contrôleur*) have comprehensive investigating powers. They can visit the insurers' offices to complete their verifications. The control may extend to all aspects of the insurer's activity and last up to 3–4 months.

3.2 Asymmetric Information

Asymmetric information is a situation where all the participants in the market do not have the same information. It constitutes an imperfection for the market that may result in adverse selection and moral hazard. Economic agents, sometimes with the help of specific laws and regulations, develop strategies to counteract this asymmetry.

Adverse Selection To counteract the asymmetric information, sellers may offer deliberately low prices if they are aware that the product or services they propose if they are aware of their hidden defects. Thus, sellers of sound product or services cannot remain on the market and only defective products are left on the market. Thus, asymmetric information leads to an inefficient market. An illustration in the financial market would be the toxic loans offering very low rates to local authorities but also to individuals that could not understand how the exchange rates could impact heavily the principal.

Moral Hazard Asymmetric information is most common in the insurance market. The insurers grant covers but they do not have much information on insured behaviours. The term moral hazard has been coined to refer to situations where the insureds take more risks or change their behaviour as they know they will be compensated should the risk materialise. Such would be the case of an insured taking more risks with his/her health knowing they have a full coverage of medical expenses and potential resulting disability.

Illustration—Toxic Loans In a commercial brochure to promote its new product in March 2008, a leading bank clearly misrepresented the risk involved even to its own sales force with no subtleties: "The best solution in the market", "Reduced savings effort for the client". This presentation of a real estate loan insisted on the stability of the exchange rate Swiss Franc to the Euro, at the time between 1.4/1.6 SF to 1 Euro and did not project what the impact of a change in the rate could be; except that since then it has increased to nearly 1 to 1 thus increasing the principal and the real rate.

3.2.1 Government Interference

The French government has enacted legislation concerning consumers' protection and an Insurance Code for the specificity of the insurances contracts.[10] However, it is important to keep in mind that all countries member of the European Union must transpose in local legislation all the European directives and several are linked to consumers' protection and the management of financial markets, notably the Insurance with the Solvency 2 directive, and the new directive on the protection of personal data.[11]

3.2.2 Terms of the Contract

One way to limit the impact of asymmetric information is to include in the contracts that limit one signatory's action if the other has withheld information or behaved inappropriately. This is the case for insurance contract in case of misreprensation of a risk to be insured (issue of good faith).

3.2.3 Information Search

In some situations, the terms and conditions of a contact rest on the production by one party of sufficient information for the other party to gorge an enlightened opinion that balances the situations and makes that the information becomes symmetric. This is the case for a bank that request information to extend a credit to ensure that the borrower will be in capacity to pay back the loan. This is the case of the questionnaire that a candidate for a life insurance must fill out, including medical tests in some cases. For casualty insurance, it is the declarations by the insured and possible visit of the premises by the insurers' representative.

3.3 Dispute Settlement Organization (Ombudsman Bureau) —Mediator

The creation of the office of mediator in France is relatively new (September 1, 2015) and followed a recommendation of the EU authorities to all branches.

- **Insurers' Ombudsman**: It was established to provide insured with a prompt and cheap way to force a resolution of a litigious situation with an insurer, thus avoiding the delays and cost of a court action.
  The French insurance mediator has received close to 15,000 requests from insured in 2016, the figure represent an increase of 53% over the previous year. In 56% of the appeals, most of the files were resolved with the help of the

mediation and before a formal opinion was written. On the average 28% of the opinion conclude in favour of the insured.
56% of the appeals were concerned with property insurance, and 44% with personal insurance. In this second segment, files concerned automobile insurance (37%) and borrower (24%).
The mediator's action impact was to limit the number of judiciary action. Part of this is due to a high level of acceptance of the mediator's opinion by the insurers (99%) and only two claimants had to go to court after his opinion was delivered.
To avoid conflicts, the mediator has requested the insurers to ask potential clients to answer a questionnaire so that false declaration could be proved if it happened; but also to use pedagogy to educate on the subtleties of insurances like the consequences of driving under the influence or the proper way to cancel a contract.
On the other hand, life insurance subscribers are encouraged to be weary of the beneficiary provision, so that the avoid the situation of escheat, which is the case of a contract the capital of which cannot be paid out due to the fact that beneficiaries cannot be identified (see AGIRA 1 & 2 in paragraph 1.2.7 here above)

- **Banks' Ombudsman**: The French federation of banks (FBF) noted that there is a significant increase in the number of clients entering a petition with the mediator before even trying to settle their conflict with their bank.
  The mediator with the FBF has received 5593 mails in 2016 a 34% increase over the previous year. The increase seems to be linked to a very early appeal. "Early appeals have risen from 626 in 2015 to 1837 in 2016. These letters are sent by angry customers who go straight to the mediator without even trying first to settle the situation with their bank.
  However, this creates a problem as the mediator is not to analyse this type of file as long as the consumer has not entered first a discussion with his/her bank. It is important also to note that the mediator is not competent for intervening in matters concerning the commercial policy of the banks such as the level of fees charged or the refusal of a loan. In such a case, the mediator can only encourage the consumers who have deteriorated relations with their branch to try and settle the issue directly with the customers' relations service of the bank, before entering a claim with the FBF mediator.
  Nevertheless, the issue is whether the dialogue is possible. A survey by the service academy published in 2016 concludes that 71% of bank employees in contact with customers are regularly victims of verbal aggression.
  As far as the files that fall within the missions of the FBF mediator, they have slightly increased from 2368 in 2015 to 2567 in 2016 (+8.4%). For 898 of them a solution was found, of which 408 required an in depth analysis by the mediator's legal team. This evolution is an illustration of the growing acceptance of mediation as a recourse mechanism of bank customers when they have difficulties with their provider. As a consequence, 15 new banks have joined the

service of the mediator of the FBF (as a reminder, a number of large banks have chosen to have their own internal mediator).

The issues submitted to the mediator include the operation and the closing process for a bank account, the mean of payment and fraudulent use of a credit card, renegotiating credit terms and early reimbursement. Of the files analysed by the mediator, 1183 were not quantified, in the absence of financial compensation requested by the customer of because it was not possible to quantify it. In 545 files, the conflict indemnity was estimated to an amount between €500 and 1500, and in 418 between €100 and 500.

Of the written opinion, the mediator concluded in favour of the bank in 77% of the cases. This outcome may seem reasonable to the extent that the conflict was examined twice before: at the level of the branch, and then at the central clients' relations department, and then a third time when the mediation gets involved.

4 Financial Consumers' Protection for the Weakest Groups

The act n° 72-1137 of December 22, 1972, introduced in the French legal system the offence of abuse of weakness which represented an important step in consumers' protection against door step selling and hard sale. These provisions were later modifies to comply with EU legislation, notably the n° 25-577/CEE of December 20, 1985.

The main protection mechanism resulting from this directive and the consumption code consist in a right to repentance for the benefit of consumers. This right is set out in article L. 121-25 of the consumption code; it is a discretionary right that benefits any consumer; they have 7 days to unilaterally withdraw from a contract without motivation. Whereas this delay is a strong protection for most consumers, it might prove a little short for the elderly.

Too often they are in a state of weakness when confronted with doorstep selling and are not really protected by the provisions of the consumption code to the extent that courts seems to have a restricted reading of the provision and do not accept the victim's age as the sole evidence for weakness in the criminal law.

This the reason why legislators have deem reasonable to extend the withdrawal delay for elderly so that they have enough time to talk the matter over with next in kin and also send a certified mail with acknowledgement of receipt mentioning their intention to withdraw. Thus, the legislators proposed to extend the delay to 30 days for consumer above the age of 70. The issue fond another solution in a law enacted in 2011 and regarding financial contrast the following applies:

- for insurance contracts the delay is extended to
  - 30 days for life insurance
  - 14 days for property and casualty insurance.

- For most consumers' credit 14 days.
- For purchase of real estate 10 days.

5 Current Issues in the Financial Product Market

The Financial crisis that the developed world experienced in 2007/2008 has triggered a breach of trust in consumers confronted with complex financial products, the risks of which are not clearly understood and for duration that are often beyond their planning horizon.

Protecting individuals' savings is a crucial component of economic health. The role played by banks and insurance companies ha considerably changed over the last decade as a result of multiple drivers: the arrival of new competitors on the markets, financing channels lacking in regulation, new emerging risks, increasing complexity of financial products, and digitisation not always compatible with current regulations.

The context is rendered even more difficult in view of the present conjuncture where social security and pension funding financial disarray require the authority to take drastic actions that will impact both current workers and retirees, governments have to find ways back to budget balance, public has a growing aversion to risks.

Although these issues might seem technical, they have an immediate impact on public perception of financial markets operations when there is already mistrust as mentioned above. Individual savers have difficulties discerning the right financial decisions for them. In such a context, financial regulation can play a crucial role.

This is the reason why, in addition to strengthening prudential control over banks and insurance companies, public authorities in France as in other E.U. countries have set up, through the transposition of European Directives, new regulations for the marketing of financial products, i.e. securities, security investment shares (*organisme de placements collectif en valeurs mobilières*—***OPCVM***) and life insurance contact.

Within this scope, the Prudential Control Authority (ACP), in charge of both insurance and banks, has created a common pole (ACPR) with the AMF to ensure the marketing of financial products by all players in the field is compliant. As a reminder, the act on bank an insurance regulation (October 22, 2010) has unified the provisions for financial intermediation.

Within the current environment, and in spite of the improvement already enacted, three issues remained to be addressed:

- Are current market structures, designed to receive these activity flows, capable of accommodating this evolution?
- Are current regulations strong enough to protect savers?
- How to face the new challenges stemming from disintermediation and competition?

Complexity is not forbidden in finance but it must be carefully regulated when it reaches a given level. When a financial product is too complex, it should be reserved for professionals. This principle must be applied with an objective assessment of complexity. Is complexity inherent in the products used to manufacture the financial products marketed? The AMF position is that complexity must be evaluated from the point of view of the investor, in other terms is the investor in a position to have a good understanding of the binomial risk/return.

It is essential that consumers do not take risk and complexity as synonyms. Investors, even individuals, must take risks as a condition for optimal financial performance for their own savings and as a finance fuel for the economy. But the decision to take risk must be informed and accepted: excessive complexity may create a veil that prevents the consumer to fully appreciate the situation.

Therefore, the definition of non-complex products, those that can be executed and received through simple orders must be refined. The AMF position is that complexity should be assessed with simple criteria and ideally uniformly applied to the whole range of financial products marketed to non-professionals.

The definition of complex and non-complex financial products according to the MiFID[12] directive will have to be revised to limit the field of "non-complex" to make sure that consumers really understand. As far "too complex" products are concerned it is essential that all agencies involved find a common definition to restore the public's trust.

The ensuing request for complete and transparent information and the complexity of applicable regulations has led to a flurry of communication; all the more that national and international regulations overlap. However, it is not easy to reduce the information produced as each piece of information is related to a specific expectation of the reader and the requirements of normative agencies and regulators. However, the quality might be improved s that each bit of information is drafted so that it makes clear financial meaning. There are four calls for action to improve the legal and regulatory context for the development and marketing of financial products:

- Review all laws and regulations at the National level, and in the European Union authorities,
- Insure real time updating of the information provided,
- Develop a summarized strategic vision, and
- Strive for simplification and transparency.

6 Final Comments

Some of the areas that are problematic in Europe have also been vexing US bank supervisors: inadequate corporate governance and risk management processes and procedures, particularly as they relate to integrating a risk-appetite framework into a bank's strategic planning and operations, and inadequately involved boards of directors with limited understanding of their risk management responsibilities. Coming from very different starting points, it seems the regions are eventually converging toward common principles.

Although bank profitability slightly improved in 2015 and capital positions have further strengthened, European banks continue to struggle with diminished profitability in the ultra-low (or even negative) interest-rate environment. This is forcing banks to transform their business models as they search for alternative sources of income and re-base their cost structures.

Banks need to demonstrate that they can promptly adapt their strategy to material changes in the macroeconomic and competitive environment. To achieve this, the annual strategic-planning and budgeting process will need to become more dynamic. The coherence and consistency of the scenarios (baseline and stressed) used for strategic planning and budgeting must be continually tested and a new iteration needs to be triggered whenever such scenarios do not hold.

As far as financial services for individuals are concerned, there is still no integrated European market as harmonisation is extremely difficult to undertake as national realities still prevailing. A recent report stresses the specificity of the French market which makes it different to the other European markets. Specifically, the French model of universal banking offering a wide range of products based on a long term relationship differs widely from the English model where customers purchase financial markets like in a supermarket.

Also the education level of financial agents in France is higher than the European average. The operation of a bank account represents 57% of household revenues. It is above the European average when coupled with the cost of credit cards, but interest rates, especially for financing housing (mortgage), remain the lowest in Europe in spite of a recent trend upward since the end of the second quarter of 2017.

The channel of distribution are becoming more and more complex with an increasing number of players that makes it hard to control all the commercial documents issued, especially as the ACPR has a limited budget and recently a control official[13] mentioned: "*We will make sure that the existing regulations are fully complied with in terms of the duties of advice, information and warning. We are also keeping a constant watch on all advertising practices and on the introduction of new products, while keeping abreast with an ever changing and growing regulation.*"

Notes

1. "systèmes multilatéraux de négociation"—SMN.
2. Source European Insurance—Key Facts—August 2016.
3. For more information go to https://www.aviva-partenaires.com/Document/fonctionnalites/MEMENTO_JURIDIQUE_ET_FISCAL/ppriv.f.02.03.htm.
4. Also called Mutual without intermediary or MSI.
5. The French Consumption code also defines:

- ***Non-professional***: all legal person acting for purposes that are not in the scope of commercial, industrial, craft, liberal, or agricultural activity;
- ***Professional:*** any physical or legal person, private or public, acting for purposes within the scope of commercial, industrial, craft, liberal, or agricultural activities, even when he/she is acting on behalf of another professional.

6. See July 1, 2017consolidted version—https://www.legifrance.gouv.fr/affichCode.do?cidTexte=LEGITEXT000006072026.
7. See further: Consumer protection in the EU http://www.europarl.europa.eu/RegData/etudes/IDAN/2015/565904/EPRS_IDA(2015)565904_EN.pdf.
8. The GEMA representing the Mutual Insurers has now merged with the FFSA.
9. http://www.legislation.gov.uk/ukpga/2015/4/contents/enacted.
10. Code des Assurances et Code de la consommation.
11. On 4 May 2016, the official texts of the Regulation and the Directive have been published in the EU Official Journal in all the official languages. While the Regulation will enter into force on 24 May 2016, it shall apply from **25 May 2018**. The Directive enters into force on 5 May 2016 and EU Member States have to transpose it into their national law by **6 May 2018**.
12. MiFID—Investment services and regulated markets—Markets in financial instruments directive—is the EU laws aimed at making financial markets more efficient, resilient and transparent, and at strengthening the protection of investors.
13. Fabrice Pesin then Deputy Secretary-General of the ACPR at Patrimonia 2014; he is now National Credit Mediator.
14. 1 Euro = 655 CFA.
15. CIMA—Conférence Interafricaine des Marchés d'Assurance.
16. Conférence Internationale des Contrôles d'Assurances.
17. Benin, Burkina-Faso, Cameroon, Center-African Republic, Congo - Brazzaville, Ivory Coast, Gabon, Mali, Niger, Senegal, Chad, Togo, Madagascar and France.
18. BENIN, BURKINA, CAMEROON, CENTER-AFRICAN REPUBLIC, COMORES, CONGO, IVORY COAST, GABON, EQUATORIAL GUNIEA, MALI, NIGER, SENEGAL, TCHAD, TOGO.

Attachment 1—The Cima Markets

The French Inspired Protection System for Insurance in Africa

This chapter is devoted to the situation in France, with elements drawn for the European Union as although the markets remain national, the road to a unified financial consumers' protection system is well underway. However, as through a convention in which France still plays a role, the French speaking African Insurance Consumers enjoy a protection derived from the French and European system. Furthermore, the existence of two monetary zones using the CFA, a monetary unit directly linked to the Euro with a fix parity,[14] it makes sense to make a mention of the system as an appendix to the French chapter.

There is an additional rationale for this appendix as several of the major European Insurers, including Groupe AXA and Allianz as well as Intermediaries, like Gras Savoye are major players in Africa that they view as growth areas.

As a matter of fact, if African country are far behind in terms of Insurance penetration, they are offering a significant opportunity for development, including micro-insurance. One of the challenges to be overcome is the independence of local insurance supervisors who are traditionally nested within the ministry of finance and take their orders from the elected officials. The CIMA agreement aimed at providing a supra-national answer lto this challenge

Penetration rates in CIMA countries (ration of premium over GDP), is extremely low between 0.34 and 1.89% of GDP; as an element of comparison it is around 6% in Europe. The market is still growing at a rate that, although much higher than developed countries, will not allow it to reach their level before decades!

Most national insurance codes in the French speaking African country are inspired by the French code, as most of their civil legal context. However, in view of the difficulty to form independent solvency control opinion a supra-national consortium for insurance control was formed: CIMA.[15]

The history stems from the creation in 1962 of the CICA[16] whose main mission was to ensure efficient operations for insurance companies and agencies operating in former French Colonies in West Africa and Madagascar. The convention signed on July 27, 1962 gathered 12[17] countries.

The main objectives set where:

- Harmonisation of the national legal and regulatory context;
- Coordination of insurance companies control processes;
- Coordination of the education of African Insurance managers.

As more and more African Insurance leaders were educated, and that national leaders realized the importance of the insurance sector for the development of national economies, they initiated different moves to ensure that insurance premium are invested in the countries, rather than sent to other continents, especially through reinsurance contracts.

To further their goals the African States ratified on July 10, 1992 in Yaoundé (Cameroon) a Convention gathering 14[18] African countries.

All the authority usually attributed to a national supervision agency (authorisation, solvency assessment, injunction and sanction powers, authorisation withdrawal, etc.) have been transferred to the CIMA. The only mission left at the national level for national supervisors are the issues relating to insurance intermediaries and technical experts. As a local relay point, the national supervisors are expected to implement the decisions made at the CIMA level.

The institutions of the CIMA are structured around three organs: the council of Ministers, regrouping the minsters of finance of the 14 countries, the Regional commission for insurance control (*régionale de contrôle des assurances—CRCA*), and the General Secretariat.

The CRCA is the regulation organ and it performs the specific competencies relating to the insurance companies' control. It has the power to sanction. It holds at least two ordinary sessions every year. In practice, it holds a quarterly meeting to rule over the specific situation of the companies that have been controlled.

The CRCA consists in the following members:

- one lawyer with experience in Insurance law;
- two personalities with a solid experience in the African insurance market, one of whom is acting as technical advisor to a country not member of the CIMA, or an international organisation;
- six representatives of the national control agencies;
- the CEO of CICA-RE and a personality qualified in financial markets, appointed jointly by the governors of both central banks of the zone;

The major innovation of the CIMA agreement was to create of body of insurance control commissioners responsible for the permanent control of the insurance organisations in all member countries. They are not only in charge of both a desk and in situ audit, but they conduct also all relevant research for the insurance markets. They are recruited in all member states through a competitive exam process where only merit and competencies are considered.

The installation of the CIMA with its single regulation and supervision scheme has been a signal for a new development of the insurance industry in the member states. Even though adjustments and improvements are still to be made over the years, the CIMA gains have been clearly identified since 1995 when the treaty came into force. Thanks to its clear legal framework, strong management standards, and consistent organisation, the CIMA has generated healthy insurance practices. As a result the market has gained in efficiencies and effectiveness.

Furthermore, some adjustments have been made to modify and strengthen the legal context to improve the environment in which the insurance industry can develop, improve its retention capacity and ensure consumers' protection, especially when they suffer a loss and are entitles to compensation. The following points are achievements of the CIMA agreement:

- Development of community coinsurance to strengthen and consolidate cooperation between member state, so that the native companies are jointly capable of offering covers and limits for major industrial risks what would exceed each individual capacity and thus increase the premium retention at the regional level;
- Adoption of new governance rules that forced insurance companies to develop internal rules framing the roles and the functions of the administration and management bodies and implement internal control and an efficient asset-liability management for their level of activity;

- Development of prudential norms to assess the financial health of insurance companies, and group: consolidation rules, reporting and statistical reports;
- Implementation of rules to curb fixed and administrative costs, including technical assistance;
- Reinforcement of control over intermediaries: adoption of models for slips and statements sot that supervisors can have a better view of the intermediary activity, elaborate a guide for the control of intermediaries;
- Reinforcement of the rules concerning insured and beneficiaries of life insurance contracts;
- Establishment of new experience data tables to improve pricing and reserving in line with the risks underwritten;
- Development of new rules for access to the capacity to make sure of the competencies for the insurance statutory auditors;
- Writing new rules specific for micro insurance so that covers can be extended to insurable populations with lower income;
- Development of a new sanction regime that provide the regulation agency with powers to act swiftly and autonomously sot avoid court proceedings;
- Reform of the bodily injuries compensation resulting from car accidents to avoid litigious situations that could end up in courts; reduce the victims' compensation delays, and accelerate claim settlements process;
- Interdiction of insurance covers delivery without prior payment of a premium to fix one of the worst issue of the CIMA zone, i.e. the very high level of premium backlogs appearing on the insurance companies' balance sheet;
- Taking actions to speed up the compensation process for claims through improved cash situation and solvency;
- Reinforcement of the reporting system thanks to new statements with more frequency.

Thanks to all these consolidation measures, the players in the markets have been encouraged to adjust this structure and organization. New group are born, old ones are expanding and new branches of insurance will be offered thus expanding further the insurance turnover. The African market of insurance has experienced a number of mergers that have given birth to some native international groups of a reasonable size to compete with the International leaders from Europe or North America. The results in terms of premium are starting to show. One area where national insurers are keen to gain expertise and financial capacity is the insurance of larger industrial groups so that the premium can be kept on the continent to help its development.

Jean-Paul A. Louisot ARM, FIRM, holds Ph.D. in Management Sciences (Université PARIS 1 Panthéon Sorbonne—2014), a mining engineer degree, a Master in Economics and an MBA from the Kellogg School of Management. He has worked in risk management for over forty years, as a broker, an underwriter and a risk-manager. Since 1993, his activity is focused on teaching and coaching post graduate students and risk management professionals, while still acting as a part-time risk manager. As curriculum director for CARM_Institute, Ltd, he supervises the ERMP

(Enterprise-wide Risk Management Practitioner) and EFARM (European Fellow in Applied Risk Management) programs. After nine years at Paris 1 Panthéon Sorbonne University, he now teaches postgraduate courses in Risk Management at the Institut Catholique de Lille. He is a frequent speaker in professional conferences in Europe, in Australia, and in the USA. He has published a number of articles and studies on risk management and developed the ERM course at The Institutes in 2009 and in 2014 "ERM: Issues and cases" (Wiley).

Chapter 7
Financial Consumer Protection in Indonesia: Towards Fair Treatment for All

Rofikoh Rokhim, Wardatul Adawiyah and Ida Ayu Agung Faradynawati

The Indonesian financial system has a long story. Financial system hardly existed before 1966 that is when the commercial banks faced the emergence time. After 1966 under Soeharto governance, central banking and banking sector regulation as the basis of the current financial system in Indonesia was introduced and implemented. After 17 years later, financial structure of Indonesia had the first reformation. In total, there are five phases in Indonesian financial system development between 1966 and the present time (Hamada 2003). The first phase, called as formative period, started from 1966 until 1972. The second phase, started from 1973 until 1982, is the period of policy-based finance under soaring oil prices. The third phase, started from 1983 until 1991, is financial-reform period. The fourth phase, started from 1992 until 1997, is the period of financial system's expansion. The last phase, started from 1998 until present, is the period of financial restructuring, which is in this period the government more concern about consumer protection in financial industry. Financial consumer protection is necessary to increase access and usage of financial services. It can build trust between consumer and financial system, hence in encouraging financial inclusion.

1 Characteristics of Indonesian Financial Industry

The Financial service sector in Indonesia is one of the primary determinants of economic dynamics. It can be divided into three main subsectors, namely banking industry, capital market and the nonbank financial industry. Banking intermediation dominated the financial system compare to other subsectors, e.g. capital market and

R. Rokhim (✉) · W. Adawiyah · I. A. A. Faradynawati
Universitas Indonesia, Jakarta, Indonesia
e-mail: rofikoh.rokhim@ui.ac.id

© Springer Nature Singapore Pte Ltd. 2018

T.-J. Chen (ed.), *An International Comparison of Financial Consumer Protection*,
https://doi.org/10.1007/978-981-10-8441-6_7

nonbank financial industry. The volume of the Indonesian capital market continues to be very small, carrying around 539 listed companies.

1.1 Recent Demographic Trends in Indonesia

Indonesia is one of populous country in the world and become the fourth largest country. It has the multitude of ethnic, cultural and linguistic varieties that can be found within the boundaries of a nation state that is the world's largest archipelago. This section will discuss about a number of important aspects regarding Indonesia's demographic composition include the recent demographic trends in Indonesia.

1.1.1 Total Population

The total populations of Indonesia increased to 258.32 million people in 2016 from 255.46 million people in 2015. This number represents 40% of the ASEAN countries' total population (Graph 1) and 3.51% of the world's total population. The total population of Indonesia continually increases every year and The United Nation (UN) was estimated that the total population of Indonesia will reach exceed 270 million people by 2025, exceed 285 million people by 2035 and exceed 290 million people by 2045. But UN estimated that this number would start decline after 2050.

The annual population growth rate of Indonesia stood at an average of 1.51% for the last 10 years, reaching an all time high of 2.66% in 2008 and record low of 1.27% in 2016 (Graph 2).

Based on data from Indonesia Central Bureau of Statistic, Indonesia faces the demographic transition towards a lower fertility rate and a lower mortality rate.

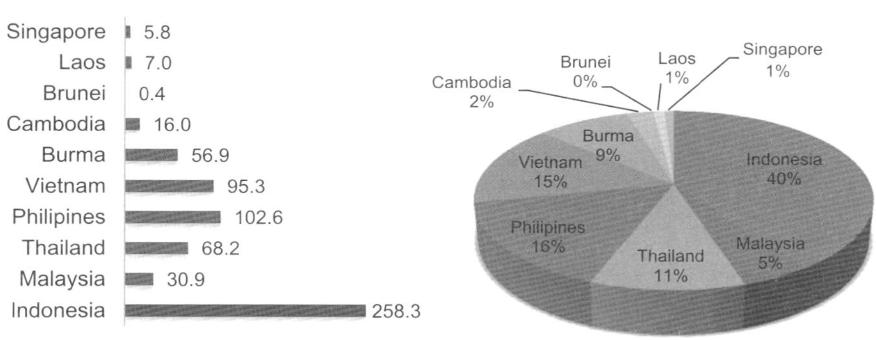

Graph 1 ASEAN countries population in 2016. *Note* Data in million people. *Source* tradingeconomics

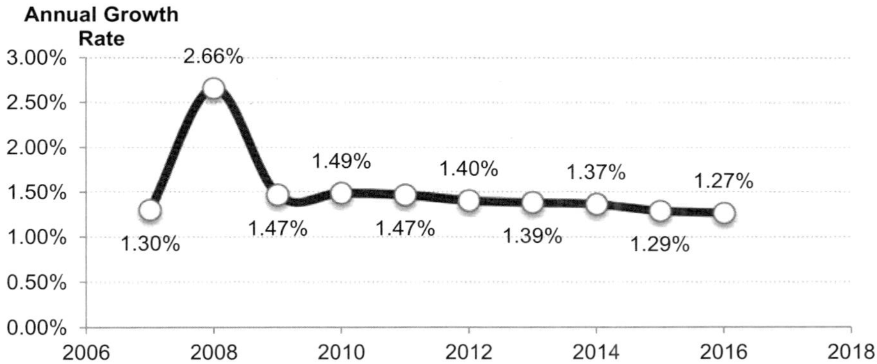

Graph 2 Annual population growth of Indonesia in 2006–2016. *Source* Indonesia Central Bureau of Statistic

Indonesians are now living longer, as indicated by a rise in life expectancy at birth from 70.8 in 2010, 72.7 in 2016 and expected to reach 73.3 in 2025.

1.1.2 Age Structure

A young population dominates the Indonesia's demographic composition. This condition can be one of the strength for Indonesia, because this young population implies a potentially large workforce. Indonesia's total median age is estimated 29.9 years. This indicates that one half of the population is older than 29.9 years, while the other half is younger than this figure. When divided in sexes the female median age is one year older (30.5 years) as compared to the male counterpart (29.3 years). Table 1 indicates the percentage shares of the Indonesian people categorized in five age groups and the corresponding division in sexes (in absolute numbers).

Moreover, the age and sex structure from Table 1 is illustrated as the population pyramid as the following picture (Fig. 1).

Table 1 Indonesian population by sex and age group in 2016

Category	% Of total population	Male (absolute)	Female (absolute)
0–14 years	25.42	33,435,020	32,224,706
15–24 years	17.03	22,397,086	21,604,985
25–54 years	42.35	55,857,415	53,543,682
55–64 years	8.40	9,918,897	11,790,016
65 years and over	6.79	7,630,251	9,913,993

Source CIA World Factbook

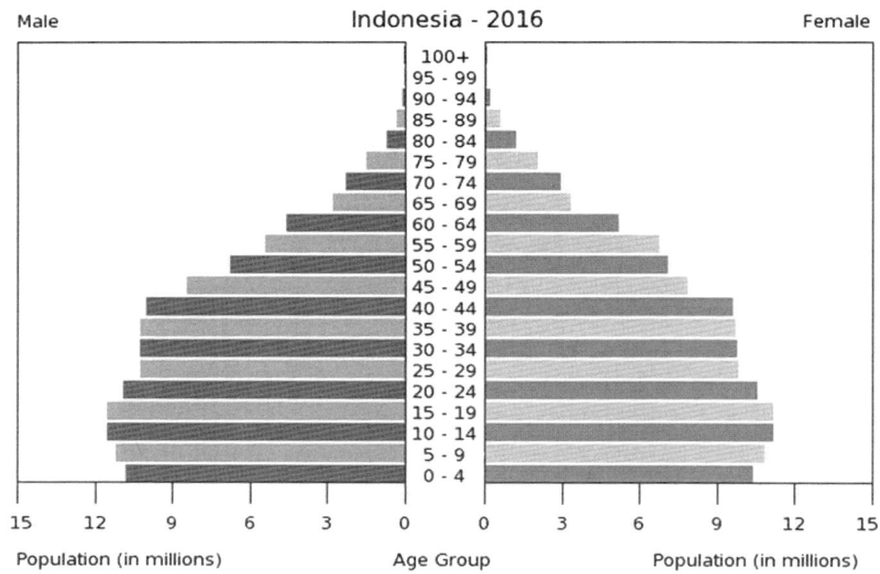

Fig. 1 Population pyramid of Indonesia in 2016. *Source* CIA World Factbook

Figure 1 shows that in 2016, Indonesian population was relatively young with a dominant proportion of economically productive population aged between 15 and 64, whereas the old-age population was small in proportion.

1.2 Characteristics of Indonesian Banking Industry

Banking industry in Indonesia is classified into commercial and rural banks. Classifications of commercial and rural bank are in the payment system and restriction in operational area. Rural bank cannot provide payment transaction services, accept deposits in the form of demand deposits or conduct business in foreign exchange, and commercial banks can do all. Based on statistic data from Otoritas Jasa Keuangan (2016a), there are 118 commercial banks and 1632 rural banks in November 2016 (Figs. 2 and 3).

Since 2012, commercial banks were classified based on core capital and stipulates permitted activities for each classification, known as BUKU (Commercial Bank Based on Business Activities). Based on this classification, banks are classified into four classes, explained in the Table 2.

The assets of commercial and rural banks as of August 2016 at IDR 6165.89 and IDR 111.32 trillion respectively. In banking industry, there is a concentration with the top 5 banks accounting for just fewer than 50% of the sector's assets.

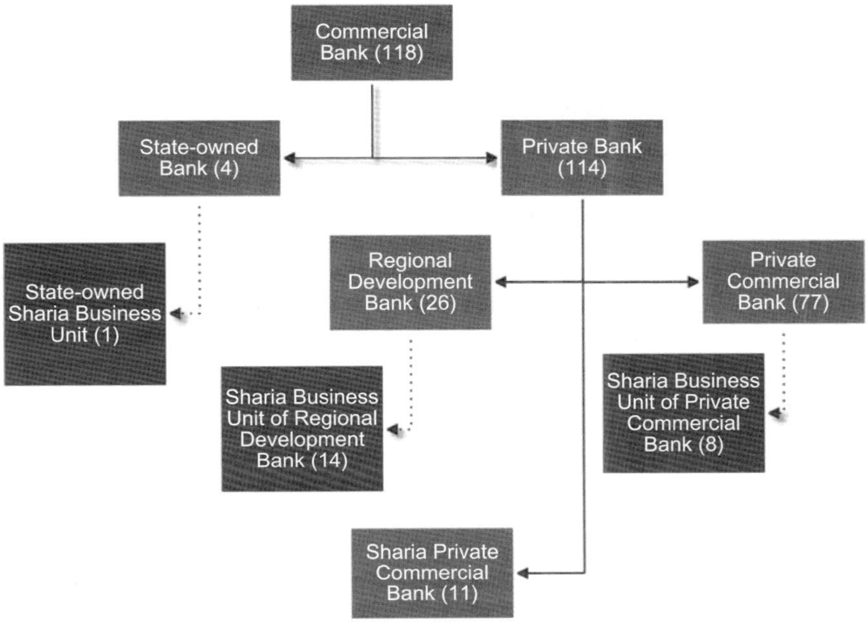

Fig. 2 Numbers and classification of commercial bank. *Source* Otoritas Jasa Keuangan (2016a)

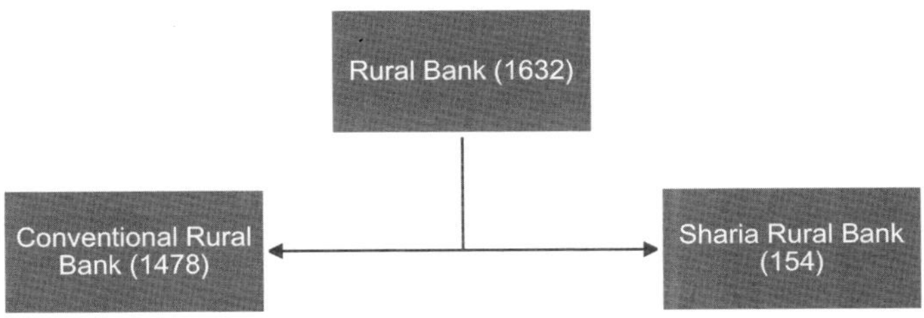

Fig. 3 Number and classification of rural bank. *Source* Otoritas Jasa Keuangan (2016a)

Table 2 Bank grouping by Tier-1 Capital

Category	Tier-1 capital requirement
Class 1	IDR100 billion–1 trillion
Class 2	IDR1 trillion–5 trillion
Class 3	IDR5 trillion–30 trillion
Class 4	> IDR30 trillion

Source Otoritas Jasa Keuangan (2016a)

1.3 Characteristics of Indonesian Non-bank Financial Institutions

Even though financial sector of Indonesia is dominated by banking, but the growth of non-bank financial institutions are also attractive. Non-banking financial institutions are composed of multiple categories of institutions regulated and supervised by OJK (Otoritas Jasa Keuangan/Indonesia Financial Services Authority). Based on statistic data from OJK, there are 136 insurance companies, 252 pension funds, 269 finance companies, 26 special finance service companies, 236 non-banking supporting service companies and 89 microfinance companies (Graph 3).

1.3.1 Insurance

Indonesia, as the largest population among the ASEAN countries, is a big market for insurance companies (Global Business Guide Indonesia 2012). Insurance companies in Indonesia are divided into five types, namely general insurance, life insurance, reinsurance, social insurance and mandatory insurance. The form of insurance companies in Indonesia must be a limited liability company, co-operative or an existing mutual business (this form only applies to AJB Bumiputera 1912) (Table 3).

In 2016, insurance premium reached 340.7 trillion rupiah.

1.3.2 Microfinance Institution

Microfinance institutions provide financial intermediation for small-scale borrower in Indonesia. Microfinance services in Indonesia have been provided not only from

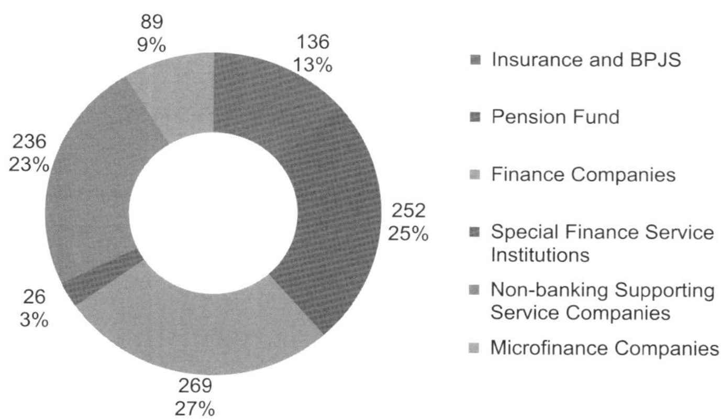

Graph 3 Composition of non-banking institution as of September 2016. *Source* Otoritas Jasa Keuangan 2016b

Table 3 Number of insurance companies in 2016

No.	Types of insurance companies	Number of company
1	Life Insurance	
	a. State-Owned	1
	b. Private National	27
	c. Joint Venture	22
	Sub total	50
2	General Insurance	
	a. State-Owned	3
	b. Private National	58
	c. Joint Venture	15
	Sub total	76
3	Reinsurance	5
4	BPJS (Social Insurance)	2
5	Mandatory Insurance	3
	Total	136

Source Otoritas Jasa Keuangan 2016b

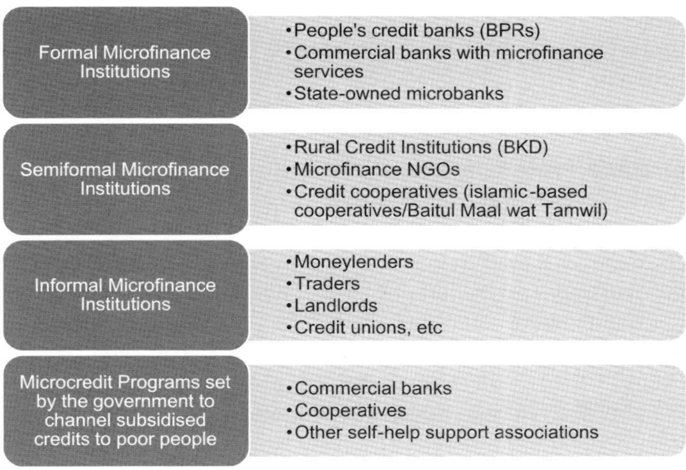

Fig. 4 Types of microfinance institutions in Indonesia. *Source* Otoritas Jasa Keuangan 2016b

one company but several institutions that can be divided into four types. Those types are formal, semiformal, informal and microcredit programs (Fig. 4; Table 4).

There are 89 operating licensed-microfinance institutions with total assets of 283.84 billion rupiah.

Table 4 Types of microfinance institution based on business entity

No	Type of business entity	Number of company
1.	Conventional	76
	Cooperatives	59
	Limited liability company	17
2.	Sharia	13
	Cooperatives	13
	Limited liability company	0
	Total	**89**

Source Otoritas Jasa Keuangan 2016b

2 Soft Infrastructure of Indonesian Financial Consumer Protection System

2.1 Law and Regulation on Financial Consumer Protection

The authority to supervise the implementation of the consumer protection mechanism by all financial services business players in Indonesia is hold by The Indonesia FSA, called as Otoritas Jasa Keuangan (Otoritas Jasa Keuangan 2016c). OJK will request the information and/or data related to the implementation of the consumer protection mechanism at any time from the financial services business player concerned.

2.1.1 Consumer Protection Law

OJK as the supervisor and regulator in the financial services sector define the financial consumer as parties that put their funds and/or utilize the services available at the Financial Services Institutions. The financial consumers include banking customers, capital market investors, insurance policyholders, and Pension Fund participants, based on the laws and regulations in financial services sector.

On 6 August 2013, OJK issued regulation No. 1/POJK.07/2013 concerning Consumer Protection in the Financial Services Sector. This regulation is an implementing regulation for article 31 of law No. 21/2011 regarding on protecting of the public and consumer. It applies to all financial services business players, e.g. commercial banks, securities companies, insurance companies, and other financial institutions. The regulation describes definition and obligations of financial services business players in consumer protection, how to attend complaints and settlement mechanism, as well as the supervisory role of OJK in consumer protection.

Beside that, Central Bank of Indonesia has also issued regulation about consumer protection in the payment services system, namely the Governor of Indonesian Bank's Regulation Number 16/1/PBI/2014.

2.1.2 Product and Price Regulation

The participation of government in competition is protecting public interest. Thus, the government needs to implant a full-fledged the public understanding about the fair competition in business. The Law Prohibiting Monopolistic Practice and Unfair Competition introduced in the beginning of 1998 and sponsored by the IMF. Law of the Republic of Indonesia No. 5/1999 concerning the Anti Monopoly Law was issued in March 1999. This law used to correct monopolistic abuses by private family-controlled conglomerates that rose during the new order (1966–1998) (Maarif 2001).

The entity in developing and applying the Law No. 5/1999 is The Business Competition Supervisory Commission, known as KPPU (Komisi Pengawas Persaingan Usaha). KPPU has an authority to issue guidelines on the application of specific article in the law.

Law No. 5/1999 article 5 defines some prohibited agreement and one of them is pricing agreement, i.e. price-fixing agreement and other pricing practices between competing business players. Price-fixing may exempt if the price within the framework of a joint venture or mandated by law. Also, competing business players are prohibited to set prices below the market price or impose a predatory price (KPPU guideline No. 6/2011) as if it causes unfair business competition or monopolistic practices. Minimum resale price maintenance is also prohibited if it caused unfair competition (KPPU guideline No. 8/2011).

2.1.3 Anti-trust Competition Laws

Indonesia's principal competition law No. 5/1999 concerning Prohibition of Monopolistic Practices and Unfair Business Competition has proposed to be amended by parliamentary in June 2016. Antitrust enforcement has targeted domestic cartels and transactions. Competing business players are not allowed to establish a cartel to regulate the production and/or marketing of product or a trust if it may cause unfair competition and/or monopolistic practices. According to KPPU guideline on cartel No. 04/2010, there are several indicators may lead a cartel:

(a) Small number of business actors and high concentration market
(b) Comparable size of those business actors
(c) Homogeneous products
(d) Multiple contacts between competitors
(e) Overstock/oversupply of products
(f) Affiliation between competitors
(g) High entry barriers
(h) Stable and inelastic demand
(i) Buyers have no counter-vailing power
(j) There is regular information exchange between competitors
(k) There is a regulated price or contract.

2.2 *Policies on Financial Consumer Protection*

2.2.1 Customer Account Management

Financial service institutions need to provide their customer about their consumer's account but as permission of their customer. Banks currently do not have an obligation to issue or provide a monthly statement for customer unless they give an authorization to the bank. Financial Services Authority regulation No. 1/POJK.07/2013 concerning consumer protection in financial sector article 27 stated that the financial service providers have to send reports to the consumers regarding the balance position and deposit movements, funds, assets, or liabilities of the Consumers accurately, on timely basis and in the manners or means according to the agreement with the Consumers.

2.2.2 Disclosure and Sales Practices

There are no specific items of information that should be included for the different types of financial products or any requirement of a product even though there are some provisions requiring disclosure of terms and conditions of products. The disclosure requirements in financial consumer protection law do not adequately deal with these issues given the generality of the requirements in provisions e.g. articles 4 and 8.

In banking industry, the banking regulation allows exceptions to maintain secrecy regarding the deposits of any depositor. It includes provisions allowing certain disclosures for tax purposes in relation to deposit and depositor information, to settle a bank's claims (in respect of a depositor) that have been transferred to the Agency for State Loan Settlement and Auction or to the Committee for State Loan Settlement; and to assist in respect of a criminal case involving the depositor; for or the purposes of civil suits; as required by the Anti-Money Laundering Law and a board of directors of a bank may disclose a customer's financial information to other banks.

In capital market industry, capital market institutions can give an impact to investor in investment decision and performance. Therefore, disclosure about these entities is important to give full information about investors' investment and the entity with whom they are doing business. It is recognized in the rule V.H.1 related to investment advisors that need to disclose the information if other entities or parties prepared research reports to their clients.

Related to disclosure and sales practice, financial service institutions should sell their product with accurate, honest, clear and not misleading information about its products and/or services. It is stated in Financial Services Authority regulation No. 1/POJK.07/2013 concerning consumer protection in financial sector article 4. Further, information shall be delivered to the customers regarding their rights and obligations when giving an explanation and making an agreement. Thus, various media through advertisement in print or electronic media should state the information. Still the same regulation article 17, it states that The Financial Services Providers are prohibited to use marketing strategy of the products and/or services that can harm the Consumers by taking advantage of the Consumers' condition which does not have other choice when making a decision.

2.2.3 Financial Literacy and Education

OJK issued Circular Letter PUJK. SEOJK No. 1/SEOJK.7/2014 concerning the Education Implementation Plan to Enhance Financial Literacy towards the Consumer and/or Society stipulates that every financial service institutions have to include education plans in their annual business plan and obliges them to report its implementation to OJK. According to the OJK Commissioner in charge of Consumer Education and Protection, the arrangement of an education plan needs to refer to the Strategy of National Financial Literacy published by the President of Indonesia in November 2013 (Otoritas Jasa Keuangan 2015). All education plans together with annual business plans have to be submitted to the supervisory board of OJK in 2015.

2.2.4 Dispute Resolution Mechanism

There are two statutory dispute settlement systems in financial service sectors, the Consumer Dispute Resolution Board/Badan Penyelesaian Sengketa Konsumen (BPSK) and Central Bank of Indonesia mediation service. BPSK operates under regulation of Ministry of Trade and Industry no. 350/2001 and BI mediation service operates under the Banking Mediation Regulation No. 8/2006.

Further, Indonesia OJK as a regulator provides a procedure to dispute resolution mechanism. On 23 January 2014, OJK issued regulation No. 1/POJK.07/2014 concerning alternative dispute settlement institutions in the financial service sector. This regulation governs the function and the establishment of independent institutions that are appointed by OJK to solve any dispute that has occurred between consumers and Financial Services Institutions or through alternative dispute resolution mechanism. Indonesia also participates in ASEAN committee on Consumer Protection that gives an avenue for consumers to complain and seek compensation for loss.

There are six alternative agencies to manage mediation in financial services sector mandated under OJK regulation No. KEP-01/D.07/2016 dated on 21 January 2016 (Pengumuman 2016), namely Alternative Dispute Resolution (ADR) agencies. The official list of ADR agencies are as follows:

1. The Insurance Arbitration and Mediation Agency (Badan Mediasi dan Arbitrase Asuransi Indonesia—BMAI) is one of service provided by the Life and General Insurance Associations to give a comprehensive mediation and adjudication service.

2. The Indonesian Capital Markets Arbitration Agency (Badan Arbitrase Pasar Modal Indonesia—BAPMI) provides mediation and adjudication service in capital market.
3. The Pension Fund Mediation Agency (Badan Mediasi Dana Pensiun—BMDP) provides mediation service in pension fund.
4. The Indonesian Alternative Dispute Resolution Institution for The Banking Sector (Lembaga Alternatif Penyelesaian Sengketa Perbankan Indonesia—LAPSPI) provides mediation service in banking sector.
5. The Indonesian Arbitration and Mediation Agency for Underwriting Companies (Badan Arbitrase dan Mediasi Perusahaan Penjaminan Indonesia—BAMPPI) provides mediation and arbitration service in underwriting companies.
6. The Indonesian Financing and Pawnshop Mediation Agency (Badan Mediasi Pembiayaan dan Pegadaian Indonesia—BMPPI) provides mediation service in financing and pawnshop companies.

ADR agencies above have their own distinct legal characteristics and implications. These agencies provide mediation, adjudication and arbitration to resolve complaints from consumers. In general, there are two mechanisms to handle the complaints from financial consumers, i.e. Internal Dispute Resolution (IDR) and External Dispute Resolution (EDR).

1. Internal Dispute Resolution (IDR) Mechanism
   This mechanism obliges financial services business players to solve their consumers' complaints through giving the functions or units to deal with the complaints.
2. External Dispute Resolution (EDR) Mechanism
   EDR is needed when consumers fail to reach agreements with financial services business players over their complaints. In this mechanism, consumers can contact one of the following institutions:

   (a) The OJK
   Since 2013, OJK has handled 3832 complaints and resolved 3574 complaints as the following (Table 5):
   (b) Alternative Dispute Resolution Agencies (ADR agencies)

Table 5 Complaints handled by FSA in 2016

Year	No. of Complaints	Cases resolved per year				In progress
		2013	2014	2015	2016	
2013	844	313	429	98	2	
2014	2182		1096	937	96	
2015	734			410	178	
2016	72				15	
Total	**3832**	**313**	**1525**	**1445**	**291**	**258**

Source OJK

Table 6 Cases handled by ADR agencies in 2016

ADR agencies	No. of cases received	In progress	Resolved
BMAI	28	8	20
BAPMI	9	7	2
LAPSPI	9	3	6
BMDP	1	0	1
Total	47	18	29

Source OJK

Consumers can contact ADR agencies to mediate, adjudicate and arbitrage their cases. Since January 2016 to June 2016, ADR agencies has handled 47 cases and resolved 29 cases with the detail as the following (Table 6). The procedure to handle complaints are visualized as the Graph 4.
Under OJK regulation No. 1/POJK.07/2014, every financial services business players have to take further steps and settle all complaints from customers within 20 business days. In some cases, the settlement of complaints may be extended for further 20 business days and consumers must get notification about the time extension. The financial services business players are also required to report to OJK every quarter all complaints received from their consumers and also mechanism used to settle the complaints.

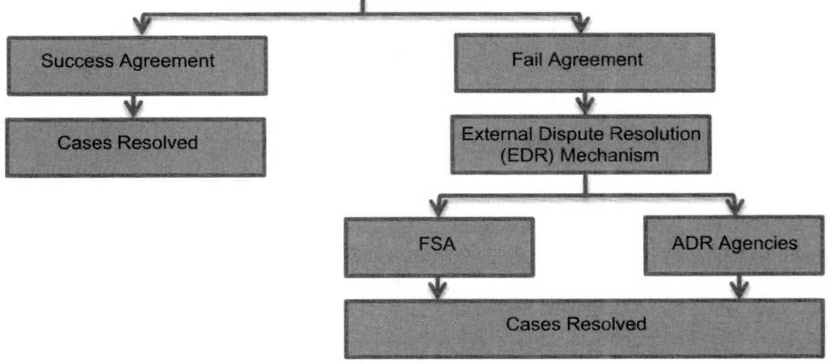

Graph 4 Complaint and dispute resolution procedures. *Source* Author, OJK and other sources

2.2.5 Guarantee Schemes and Insolvency

Indonesia already has a depositor protection scheme. Since 1 January 2014, OJK and The Indonesia Deposit Insurance Corporation (IDIC) became the parties who have empowered to take all measures to protect depositors when a bank proved unable to meet its obligations. Based on IDIC law act No. 24/2004, IDIC has two key functions: to insure customer deposits and to carry out the resolution of failed banks. Moreover, the IDIC law states that IDIC is designated as the insurer, and every commercial and rural bank must be a member of the deposit insurance program and pay a yearly membership fee from its own equity at the end of the previous fiscal year.

Based on IDIC regulation No. 2/PLPS/2010 deposit insurance covers a total of 2 billion rupiah on deposit by any individual in any member bank and maximum fair interest rate on deposit account at 7% for an account denominated in rupiah and 1.5% for an account denominated in foreign currency. The guarantee covers demand deposits, certificates of deposits, saving accounts, time deposits and deposits in other equivalent form on a per customer, per account basis for each bank (Fig. 5).

Related to insolvency, the law No. 24/2004 concerning Indonesia Deposit Insurance Corporation states that depositor will enjoy higher priority compared to other unsecured creditors in the liquidation process of a bank. If the coverage given by IDIC is inadequate, the IDIC law sets out the hierarchy of payments to creditors from the disposal of assets and/or the collection of receivables. The order, stated in article 54, is as follows:

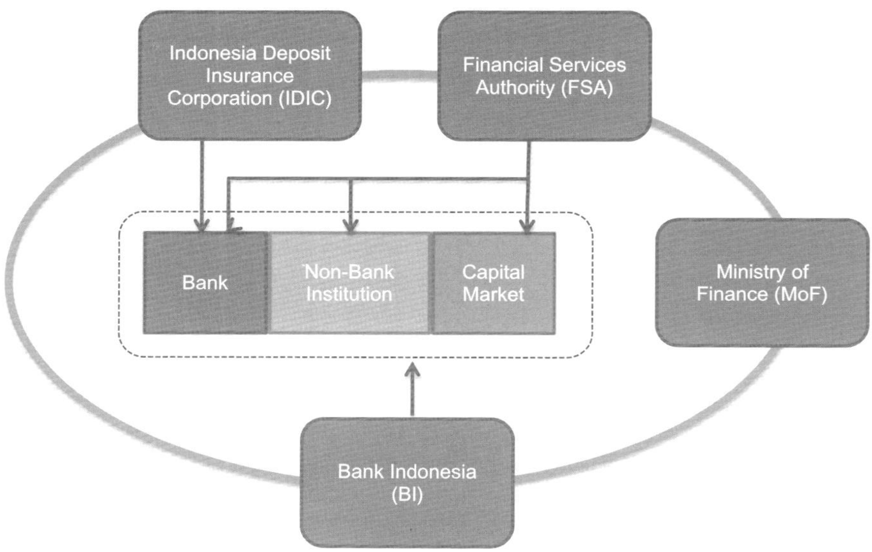

Fig. 5 Financial system coordination forum. *Source* OJK

1. Accrued and unpaid remuneration for staff
2. Severance payment for staff
3. Judicial fees and court charges, cost unpaid auction expenses and cost of operational expenses
4. Resolution cost incurred by the IDIC
5. Unpaid taxes
6. Uninsured portion of deposits and ineligible deposits
7. Other creditors.

Moreover, the IDIC law gives expeditious, cost effective and equitable provisions to enable the maximum timely refund of deposits to depositors.

3 Hard Infrastructure of Indonesian Financial Consumer Protection System

3.1 Indonesia Financial Service Authority (Otoritas Jasa Keuangan)

Otoritas Jasa Keuangan (OJK, hereinafter) is an independent state agency responsible for conducting integrated regulation and supervision system of all activities in the financial service sector including banking, capital market, insurance, pension fund, financing companies, and other type of financial institutions. Since the establishment of OJK by Law Number 21 Year 2011 (Law 21/2011), the capital market and non-bank financial institutions supervision duty has been transferred from Ministry of Finance to OJK on 31 December 2012. Meanwhile, Central Bank's authority to conduct banking supervision has been fully shifted to OJK by 31 December 2013. OJK started to regulate and supervise microfinance institutions since 2015.

The establishment of OJK is expected to improve nation's competitiveness by supporting the development of Indonesia financial service sector. According to Article 4 Law 21/2011, OJK shall be established to create a well organized, fair, transparent, accountable financial service sector and capable to implement a sustainable and stable financial system, as well as to be able to protect the interest of consumers and the community. OJK performs its duties and responsibilities based on good governance principles, namely independency, accountability, responsibility, transparency, and fairness. The consumer protection term is relatively new in the financial sector supervision. OJK is the first financial supervision body in Indonesia that included consumer protection into its main purpose.

OJK implements consumer protection through market conduct regulation and supervision. Market conduct supervision balances the financial sector development and the fulfillment of consumer's right and obligation in order to increase consumer confidence. Market conduct itself is the behavior of financial service providers

(PUJK, hereinafter) in designing, setting, disseminating information, offering, making agreement related to products and/or services as well as dispute resolution and complaint handling. Regarding that matter, consumer protection program led to achieve two main objectives. First, is to increase market confidence in all business activities in the financial service sector. Second, provide opportunities for a fair, efficient and transparent development of financial while also ensuring consumer understanding of their rights and obligations related to financial products and/or services. These two objectives are required to maintain financial stability, growth, efficiency, and innovation in long term.

Several factors underlying the need of market conduct supervision in Indonesia. Low financial literacy index reflects consumer in financial sector have a low level of knowledge regarding financial products and services. In this case, consumers are very prone to asymmetric information problem because financial institutions and consumer are not in the same level of playing field. The probability of misconduct by PUJK is usually higher when consumer has a low financial knowledge, in the end leads to higher probability of default. Some misconduct cases in financial service sector are quite often to be found in Indonesia such as predatory lending, personal information theft, and misleading advertisement. The next part of this chapter will discuss about some sample cases of financial service misconduct in Indonesia. OJK Regulation Number 1 Year 2013 on Consumer Protection in Financial Service Sector (POJK No. 1/2013) and OJK Regulation Number 1 Year 2014 on Alternative Dispute Resolution Body in Financial Service Sector (POJK No. 1/2014) along with OJK form letters on consumer protection are the regulatory frameworks of consumer protection in the financial service sector.

Apart from setting up the regulatory frameworks, Education and Consumer Protection Division in OJK also undertakes financial literacy program. The objectives of conducting education for financial services consumer is to increase the level of consumer understanding of financial products and services. Financial well-literate consumer is a substantial element to increase market confidence and consumer's utility in the financial service sector. PUJK are required to submit financial education activity report to OJK. Financial education activities shall not only include product information but also include education on financial planning, investment planning, preparation of financial statements, or any other type of financial education.

POJK No. 1/2013 also emphasizes on complaint handling and dispute resolution mechanism. Regarding that matter, PUJK are obliged to:

a. Create a division/unit to handle consumer complaints, equipped with reliable adequate personnel and standard operating procedures
b. Submit quarterly report regarding consumer complaint handling

OJK also regulates complain handling through OJK Form Letter Number 2/SEOJK.07/2014 (SE No. 2/SEOJK.07/2014) as follows (Fig. 6).

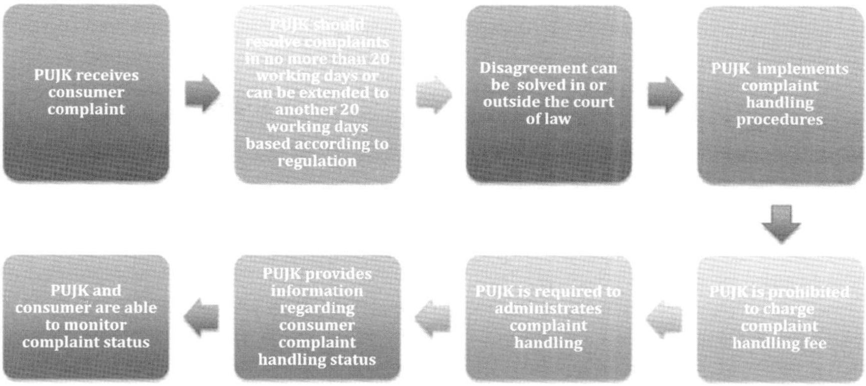

Fig. 6 Complaint handling mechanism according to SE No. 2/SEOJK.07/2014. *Source* OJK

3.2 Central Bank of Indonesia (Bank Indonesia/BI)

Bank Indonesia in an independent central bank as enacted by the new Central Bank Act Number 23 Year 1999 (UU No. 23/1999). As and independent state institution, Bank Indonesia is fully autonomous and free from interference by the government or any other external parties in conducting and implementing its task and policy. Bank Indonesia has a single objective of achieving and maintaining stability of Rupiah. The stability of nation's currency consists of two aspects, currency stability against goods and services, and currency stability against other currencies. The first aspect is reflected in the rate of inflation, while the second aspect is depicted by the Rupiah exchange rate against other currencies. In pursuing its single objective, Bank Indonesia is supported by three main pillars that represent task division. The pillars are formulating and implementing monetary policy, regulating and ensuring a smooth payment system, and financial system stability. Bank Indonesia integrates these three pillars in maintaining a stable value of Rupiah effectively and efficiently (Fig. 7).

This chapter focuses on the second pillar, regulating and ensuring a smooth payment system. In the pursuit of smooth, safe, efficient, and reliable payment system, Bank Indonesia shall also maintain access expansion, consumer protection, and national interest. Bank Indonesia focuses its consumer protection aspect in payment system while OJK focuses in market conduct supervision. The current rapid technological development creates various ranges of innovations that enable people to conduct payment system transactions anywhere and anytime. At the same time, consumer should be provided with adequate and accurate information regarding the benefit and risk of payment system to mitigate misconduct risks. In response to those needs, Bank Indonesia established Payment System Consumer Protection Division in August 2013 and issued the regulatory framework on consumer protection in payment system is PBI No/16/1/PBI/2014 in 2014.

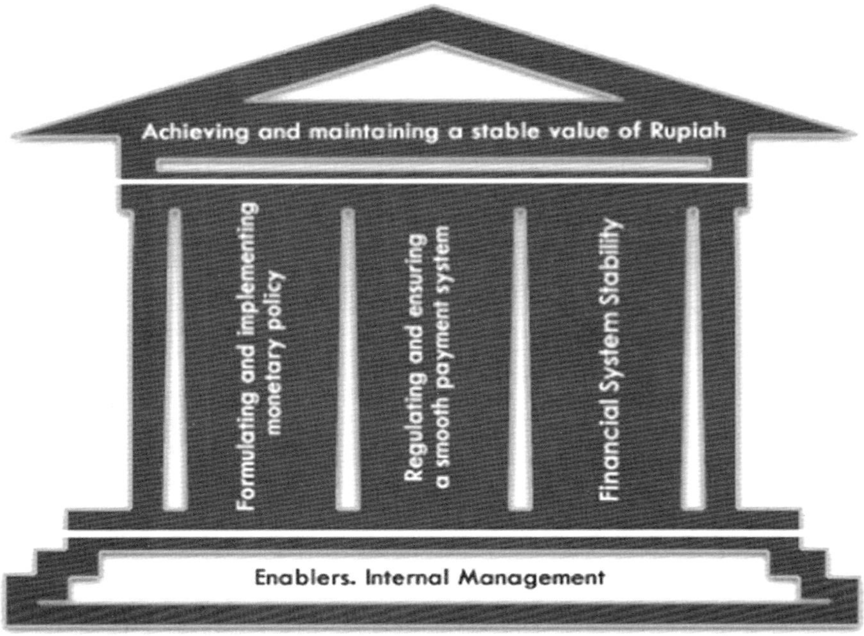

Fig. 7 Objectives and function of Bank Indonesia. *Source* Bank Indonesia (2017a)

The payment system services and/or products within the scope of payment system consumer protection are: (a) issuance of fund transfer instruments and/or withdrawal of funds; (b) funds transfer; (c) card based payment instrument (ATM/ debit card and credit card); (d) electronic money; (e) providing and/or depositing Rupiah banknotes; and (f) other payment system services determined in BI regulations. Payment system consumer protection division has three functions as explained below:

a. Education
   Bank Indonesia conducts education program on payment system products through various media. The education program aimed at academics, students, housewives, payment system providers, and public in general.
b. Consultation
   Bank Indonesia provides consultation on payment system issues from public and payment system providers via telephone, email, mail, and Bank Indonesia offices.
c. Facilitation
   Bank Indonesia facilitates dispute resolution between consumer and payment system provider through mediation between two parties to resolve the problem (Fig. 8).

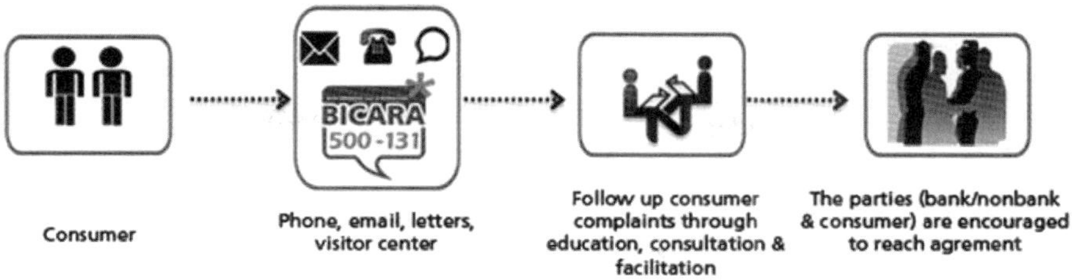

Fig. 8 Payment system consumer protection mechanism

3.3 Indonesia Deposit Insurance Corporation (Lembaga Penjamin Simpanan)

Deposit insurance plays an important role as an element of financial safety net. Deposit insurance acts as a "lender of last resort", to minimize financial and social impact of in the time of banking crisis. The existence of explicit deposit insurance can significantly decrease the likelihood of bank runs or even put an end to runs altogether in countries with solid institutions (McCoy 2007). In addition to that, deposit insurance also provide compensations to small-scale depositors in the case of bank failures (Hoelscher et al. 2006). Many countries in almost all regions have adopted depositor insurance, with a significant increase in the number of adopters in the 1990s and 2000s (Bank Indonesia 2017a, Demirgüç-Kunt et al. 2008).

Prior to the 1997/1998 Asian Financial Crisis, Indonesia government adopted an implicit deposit guarantee. There was no specific institution/agency assigned as deposit insurance at that moment, it was believed that the financial industry was quite strong after the economic boom in 1970s. Under Soeharto's centralized regime, government would provide assistance to save troubled banks in order to maintain country's financial stability. The Asian Financial Crisis apparently has provided valuable lessons for Indonesia. The provision of blanket guarantee, not only created serious moral hazard but also burden for state budget. Considering those two major drawbacks of blanket guarantee schemes and as a part of IMF assistance in rescuing the national financial system, Indonesia implemented an explicit deposit protection schemes in early 2000s. There is a clear difference between implicit and explicit deposit protection schemes. Under the implicit deposit protection schemes, there are no stated rules but only obvious intention by the government to save financial institutions from crisis. On the contrary, explicit deposit protection schemes clearly state terms and conditions of the scheme.

Indonesia government enacted the Indonesia Deposit Corporation (IDIC) Law on 22nd September 2004 after the approval of the parliament. The IDIC was established on 22nd September 2005 with two main responsibilities, providing guarantee of bank's depositors and actively participating in maintaining the stability of the banking system. After its establishment, the level of IDIC coverage was gradually adjusted as follows:

IDIC insures deposits in all conventional banks and Islamic banks operating in the Republic of Indonesia. The IDIC membership is mandatory to all banks including foreign bank branches and subsidiaries. However, IDIC does not cover overseas branches of Indonesian banks. IDIC's coverage including all type of deposits such as saving account, current account, certificate of deposit, and time deposit denominated in Indonesian Rupiah and foreign currencies. IDIC funding comes from initial capital contributed by Indonesia government, membership contribution paid once when a bank becomes IDIC member, and insurance premiums paid twice a year. Until December 2016, there are 104 conventional banks and 13 Islamic banks registered as IDIC members.

The following Table 7 shows deposit distribution in Indonesia based on the amount of deposits in Rupiah. Based on the deposit distribution data on December 2016, 97.84% of the bank accounts in Indonesia have less than Rp100 million in their deposits. This figure shows the characteristic of depositors in Indonesia banking industry that is dominated by small-scale depositors. More than 99% of bank accounts, with deposit up to Rp2 billion, are insured by the IDIC. As of December 2016, the amount of deposit covered by the IDIC reached Rp2.180.713 billion. The deposit guarantee scheme by the IDIC is expected to provide consumer protection, particularly small-scale depositors, in case of a troubled bank.

In order to be eligible-to-be-paid insured deposit, deposit has to meet three main criteria. Firstly, it has to be recorded on bank's book. Secondly, interest rate on the deposit should not be higher than IDIC maximum interest rate limit. IDIC adjusts its interest rate limit frequently to response the changing macroeconomic conditions. Thirdly, the account holder should not be engaged in an action that cause any harm to the bank. In the event of a bank declared as a failed bank IDIC has options to rescue the bank or pay insured deposits. IDIC will do verification and aggregation in 90 days or less to determine eligible depositors and amounts to be paid. Depositors start to receive their payment after the fifth day of verification and aggregation process (Table 8).

Table 7 IDIC coverage amounts

Period	Coverage
22 September 2005–21 March 2006	Full coverage
22 March 2006–21 September 2006	Maximum Rp5 billion
22 September 2006–21 March 2007	Maximum Rp1 billion
22 March 2007–12 October 2008	Maximum Rp100 million
13 October 2008–Onward	Maximum Rp2 billion

Source Lembaga Penjamin Simpanan (2017)

Table 8 Deposit distributions in Indonesia banking sector

Amount of deposits	Number of accounts	%	Amount of deposits (billion 1DR)	%
N < Rpl00 mio	195,002,534	97.84	722,355	14.74
Rupiah	194,238,783	99.61	707,832	97.99
Foreign currency	763,751	0.39	14,523	2.01
Rp100 mio < N $\leq$ Rp200 mio	1,952,583	0.98	274,016	5.59
Rupiah	1,853,513	94.93	259,816	94.82
Foreign currency	99,070	5.07	14,200	5.18
Rp200 mio < N $\leq$ Rp500 mio	1,313,266	0.66	422,787	8.63
Rupiah	1,221,896	93.04	393,947	93.18
Foreign currency	91,370	6.96	28,840	6.82
Rp500 mio < N $\leq$ Rpl bio	527,268	0.26	387,583	7.91
Rupiah	483,987	91.79	357,323	92.19
Foreign currency	43,281	8.21	30,260	7.81
Rpl bio < N $\leq$ Rp2 bio	262,911	0.13	373,972	7.63
Rupiah	236,923	90.12	337,991	90.38
Foreign currency	25,988	9.88	35,981	9.62
Rp2 bio < N $\leq$ Rp5 bio	157,655	0.08	490,816	10.02
Rupiah	141,182	89.55	440,089	89.66
Foreign Currency	16,473	10.45	50,727	10.34
N > Rp5 bio	85,285	0.04	2,228,785	45.48
Rupiah	69,532	81.53	1,661,261	74.54
Foreign currency	15,753	18.47%	567,524	25.46
Total	199,301,502	100.00	4,900,314	100.00
Rupiah	198,245,816	99.47	4,158,259	84.86
Foreign currency	1,055,686	0.53	742,055	15.14

Source Lembaga Penjamin Simpanan (2017)

3.4 Indonesia Securities Investor Protection Fund

As part of OJK's responsibility to create a fair, well-regulated, and efficient capital market and to implement consumer protection in capital market, Indonesia Securities Investor Protection Fund (Indonesia SIPF) was established in 2012. Prior to Indonesia SIPF establishment, a study conducted by OJK recommended that the existence of investor protection fund could boost investor confidence in Indonesia capital market. Investor confidence is one of the important elements in the development of a capital market. Indonesia SIPF was established by three shareholders, consist of Indonesia Stock Exchange, Kliring Penjamin Efek Indonesia, and Kustodian Sentral Efek Indonesia. All of Indonesia SIPF shareholders are self-regulatory organizations in Indonesia capital market. The Indonesia SIPF membership is mandatory to all brokers, dealers, and custodian banks. Members are obliged to pay initial membership fee Rp100 million (only paid once during the registration) and annual membership fee 0.001% of monthly average of investor's assets in the prior year.

Indonesia SIPF's core mission is to intensify the capital market investment security by establishing investor protection fund. Indonesia SIPF protects investors from losing their assets if the custodian banks or brokers/dealers failed to return the assets to the investors. Investors are not charged any fee by Indonesia SIPF to be covered under this protection scheme. In the case of Indonesia SIPF member failed to return investor's asset, investors reserve the right to get up to Rp100 million per investor and custodian banks entitled to claim up to Rp50 billion per bank. Indonesia SIPF sets three main criteria to determine eligible investor in the protection scheme as follows:

a. Investor invests their fund and has an account at SIPF member
b. Investor is registered by SIPF member on a sub-account at KSEI
c. Investors has a single investor identification number from SIPF member.

Indonesia SIPF covers investor assets regardless of investor's nationality or country of residence. As long as investor assets are registered in Indonesia SIPF member account. Indonesia SIPF protection scheme is not applicable to investor that falls into one of these criteria:

a. Investor is engaged in any action that causing the loss of assets;
b. Investor is majority shareholder, board of directors, board of commissioners, or one level below board of directors officials of custodians; and
c. Investor is affiliated to any parties as mentioned in point a and b.

Investors and Indonesia SIPF should report any loss events to OJK, because all SIPF members (brokers/dealers and custodian banks) are under OJK's supervision. OJK verifies the asset loss report using three criteria as follows:

a. Investor asset loss occurs;
b. Custodian failed to repay the lost assets;
c. Custodian is unable to continue its operation and its business license is under consideration to be revoked.

If the event meets those criteria, OJK will issue a legal written statement to Indonesia SIPF. The next step is internal verification by Indonesia SIPF before making payments for asset loss claims. Indonesia SIPF has set the formula to determine the lost asset value as follows:

- Assets in the form of **equity**
  = number of securities (in unit) * average closing price (where transaction exists for the last six months prior to the issuance of OJK written statement
- Assets in the form of **debt instrument or Sukuk**
  = number of securities (in unit) * average fair market price issued by the bond pricing agency in the last six months
- The value of asset in **any form other than the aforementioned** is calculated using **fair asset pricing method**

As of February 3, 2017, Indonesia SIPF has been managing Rp126 billion in investor protection fund. The investor asset value covered by Indonesia SIPF has reached Rp3.576 billion. Indonesia SIPF members consist of 19 custodian banks and 108 brokers/dealers with 660.796 securities sub-accounts (SIPF 2017).

References

Bank Indonesia. 2017a. "Objectives and Tasks of Bank Indonesia." Retrieved from http://www.bi.go.id/en/tentang-bi/fungsi-bi/tujuan/Contents/Default.aspx

Bank Indonesia. 2017b. "Payment System Services Consumer Protection." Retrieved from http://www.bi.go.id/en/sistem-pembayaran/di-indonesia/perlindungan/Contents/Default.aspx

Berlinawati, Santi. 2016. Emerging Insurance Market in Indonesia. http://www.globalindonesianvoices.com/28734/emerging-insurance-market-in-indonesia/

Demirgüç-Kunt, A., Kane, E. J., & Laeven, L. (2008). Determinants of deposit-insurance adoption and design. Journal of Financial Intermediation, 17(3), 407–438.

Financial Services Authority Regulation No. 1/POJK.07/2013 concerning consumer protection in financial services sector.

Garcia, Gillian G. H. 1999. "Deposit Insurance: A Survey of Actual and Best Practices." IMF Working Paper No. 99/54.

Global Business Guide Indonesia. 2012. The Prospects for Indonesia's Insurance Industry.

Hamada, Miki. 2003. Transformation of the Financial Sector in Indonesia. IDE Research Paper No. 6

Hoelscher, David S., Michael Taylor and Ulrich H. Klueh. 2006. The design and implementation of deposit insurance systems. Washington, D.C.: International Monetary Fund.

Indonesia SIPF. 2017. "Investor Protection Fund Statistics as of February 3, 2017." Retrieved from www.indonesiasipf.co.id

Law of The Republic of Indonesia No. 5/1999 concerning the ban on monopolistic practices and unfair business competition.

Lembaga Penjamin Simpanan. 2017. "Deposit Distribution of Indonesian Commercial Banks as of December 2016." Retrieved from http://www.lps.go.id/documents/830952/0/Statistik+%28Website%29-Desember+2016.pdf/92be6225-e599-4f6f-ad6e-951a8f0a9040www.ojk.go.id

Maarif, Syamsul. 2001. Competition Law and Policy in Indonesia. Jakarta

McCoy, Patricia A. 2007. "The Moral Hazard Implications of Deposit Insurance: Theory and Evidence." Presented in Seminar on Current Developments in Monetary and Financial Law Washington, D.C., October 23–27,2006

Otoritas Jasa Keuangan. 2015. "Pemberdayaan Konsumen dan Peningkatan Kapasitas Perlindungan Konsumen di Sektor Jasa Keuangan." Presented in Jakarta, 10 Maret 2015

Otoritas Jasa Keuangan. 2016a. Laporan Triwulanan: Triwulan III - 2016

Otoritas Jasa Keuangan. 2016b. Statistik Perbankan Indonesia. Vol. 14 No. 012.

Otoritas Jasa keuangan. 2016c. Indonesian Financial Services Sector Master Plan 2015–2016: Fostering Growth and Addressing Challenges in the Financial Services Sector, Today and Tomorrow.
Pengumuman No. PENG-1/D-07/2016 tentang Daftar Lembaga Alternatif Penyelesaian Sengketa di Sektor Jasa Keuangan
www.tradingeconomics.com
www.bi.go.id
www.ojk.go.id

Rofikoh Rokhim is an associate professor at the Faculty of Economics and Business, Universitas Indonesia. She holds a Ph.D. in Economics from Université Paris 1 Panthéon-Sorbonne, France. She is one of the founding members of the International Academy of Financial (IAFICO) and Indonesian Financial Association (IFA). Her research interests include capital market, banking, small medium enterprises development, microfinance, financial inclusion as well as financial policy and regulation. Her work has been featured in many academic journals. Apart from academics, she is also serving as advisory board member of Yayasan Cinta Anak Bangsa, a non-profit organization focusing on youth drug prevention programs and women impowerment. She is also advisor of several projects of Indonesian government for enhancing of financial industry and consumer protection.

Wardatul Adawiyah is currently a lecturer and researcher at Faculty of Economics and Business, Universitas Indonesia. She received a master degree in finance from Daegu University, South of Korea. She began her specialization in financial analysis and modeling that led to a seven-year of experiences in several consulting firms and positions as financial analyst, researcher and also involved in various research projects of government and private companies. Her research interests include capital market, financial inclusion and financial consumer protection. Her interest in capital market allowed her to be a part of creator of The Indonesian Capital Market Institute (TICMI) and she prepared the curriculum. She later appointed as a secretary of Indonesia Finance Association (IFA).

Ida Ayu Agung Faradynawati is a lecturer and researcher at the Faculty of Economics and Business, Universitas Indonesia. She received a master degree in Money, Banking, and Finance from University of Birmingham, United Kingdom. She is particularly interested in financial inclusion, infrastructure financing, and SME development topics. She has worked in various research projects with government and private companies.

Chapter 8
Financial Consumers and Applicable Remedies: A European and Italian Framework

Vincenzo Senatore

Abstract In Europe, general legislation requires protection of the economic interests of consumers. This includes, for instance, the consumer protection from financial services, misleading advertising and unfair contract terms. However, only after the global financial crisis, the European Union (EU) has become aware of the lack of transparency, poor handling of conflicts of interest, over-indebtedness, and low awareness of risks of the consumers in dealing with financial services. This paper aims to investigate the financial knowledge and overconfidence in Europe, and to provide an overview of consumer protection policy in EU. Here, it will be analyzed the EU regulatory framework, whose aim is to ensure the stability of the financial markets and to establish specific and common rules for banks and investments companies among the Member States. Furthermore, it deals with protections of financial consumers in the Italian legislation and within a European context. It concludes providing the Italian financial system as best example of crisis management and resolution, by providing out-of-court settlements, collective redress and crisis management procedures, with the aims to establish a systemic stability and financial consumers' confidence in the bank system.

Keywords Financial consumer · Financial consumer protection Literacy, ADR · Out-of-court settlement · Access to justice · Compulsory mediation · Class actions

---

V. Senatore (✉)
GSA Law Firm, Rome, Italy
e-mail: vsenatore@studiolegalegsa.it

© Springer Nature Singapore Pte Ltd. 2018

T.-J. Chen (ed.), *An International Comparison of Financial Consumer Protection*,
https://doi.org/10.1007/978-981-10-8441-6_8

1 Introduction

1.1 The Importance of a Financial Literacy: A General Overview

Economic and technological developments have brought greater global connectedness and the massive changes in communications and financial transactions, as well as in social interactions and consumer behavior. Such changes have made it more important that individuals can interact with financial providers. Consumers often need access to financial services in order to make and receive electronic payments like income, remittances and online transactions, as well as to conduct face-to-face transactions in societies where cash and checks are no longer favored. These trends have transferred the responsibility of major financial decisions to individuals, who are expected to be sufficiently financially literate to take the necessary steps to protect themselves and ensure their financial well-being. Indeed, this scenario is very different.

The recent collapse of the financial markets has highlighted consumers lack financial knowledge that can go unnoticed for long periods of time before exploding on the surface. Accordingly, after the credit crunch, many countries have adopted measures to prevent similar crises in the future. Financial institutions, avoiding the risk of disputes with consumers and loss of reputation, have therefore started to provide detailed financial information to financial consumers about the characteristics and costs of services, ensuring the transparency and correctness of contractual conditions as well as their rights and obligations in the financial transactions.[1] Financial education has therefore become a strong need, through which financial consumers make aware choices and decisions on their investments. Nevertheless, international analysis shows a situation worrying in the baseline financial knowledge levels. A growing body of evidence suggests that many consumers still lack the knowledge they need to evaluate and make decisions about financial transactions and informed decisions.

A report of ABI, the association of Italian banks, informed that according to the World Competitiveness index of 2016 prepared by IMD (International Institute for Management Development), (see the chart below), the problem of financial illiteracy is a global phenomenon.

The IMD World Competitiveness Scoreboard 2016

WCY 2016	Country	WCY 2015	Change
1	China Hong Kong	2	+1 ↗
2	Switzerland	4	+2 ↗
3	USA	1	-2 ↘
4	Singapore	3	-1 ↘
5	Sweden	9	+4 ↗
6	Denmark	8	+2 ↗
7	Ireland	16	+9 ↗
8	Netherlands	15	+7 ↗
9	Norway	7	-2 ↘
10	Canada	5	-5 ↘
11	Luxembourg	6	-5 ↘
12	Germany	10	-2 ↘
13	Qatar	13	- -
14	Taiwan	11	-3 ↘
15	UAE	12	-3 ↘
16	New Zealand	17	+1 ↗
17	Australia	18	+1 ↗
18	United Kingdom	19	+1 ↗
19	Malaysia	14	-5 ↘
20	Finland	20	- -
21	Israel	21	- -
22	Belgium	23	+1 ↗
23	Iceland	24	+1 ↗
24	Austria	26	+2 ↗
25	China Mainland	22	-3 ↘
26	Japan	27	+1 ↗
27	Czech Republic	29	+2 ↗
28	Thailand	30	+2 ↗
29	Korea Rep.	25	-4 ↘
30	Lithuania	28	-2 ↘
31	Estonia	31	- -
32	France	32	- -
33	Poland	33	- -
34	Spain	37	+3 ↗
35	Italy	38	+3 ↗
36	Chile	35	-1 ↘
37	Latvia	43	+6 ↗
38	Turkey	40	+2 ↗
39	Portugal	36	-3 ↘
40	Slovak Republic	46	+6 ↗
41	India	44	+3 ↗
42	Philippines	41	-1 ↘
43	Slovenia	49	+6 ↗
44	Russia	45	+1 ↗
45	Mexico	39	-6 ↘
46	Hungary	48	+2 ↗
47	Kazakhstan	34	-13 ↘
48	Indonesia	42	-6 ↘
49	Romania	47	-2 ↘
50	Bulgaria	55	+5 ↗
51	Colombia	51	- -
52	South Africa	53	+1 ↗
53	Jordan	52	-1 ↘
54	Peru	54	- -
55	Argentina	59	+4 ↗
56	Greece	50	-6 ↘
57	Brazil	56	-1 ↘
58	Croatia	58	- -
59	Ukraine	60	+1 ↗
60	Mongolia	57	-3 ↘
61	Venezuela	61	- -

Source: IMD World Competitiveness Center. IMD World Competitiveness Yearbook 2016 – Copyright © 2016, IMD International, Switzerland, www.imd.org/wcc

This study reveals the difficulties of many countries in this area. According to the IMD world ranking, Italy, for instance, is at the thirty-five places for the dissemination of financial and last among the G8 member states. A Doxa[2] survey conducted in the same year also shows that 50% of young people between 18 and 29 years does not know what is a bond, 83% cannot orientate in asset management, while only 50% of the holders of a counter current can correctly read the own bank statement. According to a research conducted by the European House—Ambrosetti,[3] the average level of financial culture in Italy, according to a scale of 1 to 10, is 3.5 percentage points, against 5.18 in Germany, 4.68 in the UK, 3.87 in France. In the UK, a lack of financial education costs Britain £3.4 bn a year.[4] A research conducted by YouGov's Financial Services team into the financial literacy of the UK reveals that young adults are least likely to understand financial literature, with just 8% of UK 18 to 24-year-olds admitting to having a 'high understanding', compared to at least 20% of older age groups. Generally, half of all UK adults (50%) modestly rate themselves as having some understanding of financial products and services and only 15% say they have a 'very good' understanding. A minority of just 5% admitted to having "no understanding". In addition, that research reveals that online sources are the first port of call for consumers who don't understand a term used in documentation for a financial product, with most respondents (58%) turning to the internet.[5]

1.1.1 The Role of the International Organizations in the Financial Education

The Organization for Economic Co-operation and Development ("OECD"), is one of the most active international institution in the world who has been promoting the importance of financial literacy in the world, recommending that it should start as early as possible. To get this goal, OECD started an inter-governmental project since 2003 with the objective of providing ways to improve financial education and literacy standards through the development of common financial literacy principle, adopting the "Recommendation on Principles and Good Practices for Financial Education and Awareness" (adopted by the OECD Council on July 2005). Alongside these recommendations, the publication "Improving Financial Literacy: Analysis of Issues and Policies" details the reasons for focusing on financial education, and provides a first international overview of financial education work being undertaken in various countries (OECD 2005a). Recognizing the increasingly global nature of financial literacy and education issues, in 2008 the OECD created the International Network on Financial Education (INFE) to facilitate the sharing of experience and expertise among worldwide public experts and to promote the development of both analytical work and policy recommendations. In this regard, the OECD has tested 15-year-olds on their knowledge of personal finances and ability to apply it to their financial problems. This is the first large-scale international study to assess the financial literacy of young people, the data collection was completed in Fall 2015, and the results will be published in the next Program for International Student Assessment ("PISA") study.

1.1.2 European Union and Financial Literacy

The European Commission has provided impetus in the development of financial education in the EU, taking several practical steps towards promoting and involving financial education to improve information and raise awareness of consumer rights and interests. In this regard, on 2007, the European Commission convened an Expert Group on Financial Education with the aim to promote the exchange of ideas, experiences and best practices in the area of financial education.[6] Next, it established a European Database for Financial Education that lists and describes financial education resources that are available within member states.[7] Currently, the European Commission has providing sponsorship/patronage to Member States and private actors in the organization of national or regional conferences and other events, which give visibility and impetus to the promotion of financial education in the EU, and supports the continued development of the Dolceta online resource.[8] This project, started in 2003 and realized in collaboration with European Continuing Education Network and various European universities, has the objectives to educate students, vulnerable adults in the financial arena as well as to reduce the gap to university level and in the protection of academic consumption.

1.1.3 National Strategies: The First Goal

Pursuant to Article 165 of the Treaty on the Functioning of the European Union, EU Member States are responsible for legislating on education. On this ground, several European countries have gained experience in financial education implementing in primary and secondary schools target programs as well as setting forth strategy plans to reduce the financial illiteracy.

In Czech Republic, for instance, the strategy was approved in May 2010 by the Czech Government. The financial education became compulsory in high schools at the beginning of the 2012. The Government is also working with the OECD looking at how to measure financial literacy (pilot program). On the other hand, in Spain there is a national program that covers all the financial sectors, including pension funds, called "*Plan de Educación Financiera*". This initiative is along similar lines to one conducted by the UK's Financial Services Authority, and it is informed by the principles and guidelines of the OECD and European Commission. The Portuguese Parliament has adopted, instead, two acts addressing recommendations to the Government on possible sets of measures aimed at promoting financial literacy. In particular, one of the acts foresees in an express manner the objective that the Government takes into account the content of the *National Plan on Financial Education*, which is a joint initiative of the three-sectorial national supervisory authorities. The Plan has considered the years 2011–2015 and it was decided that its governance model should include, apart from the Co-ordinating Commission (composed by representatives of the financial regulators), two Monitoring Committees and a Consultative Committee (these, including public entities, financial sector associations, consumer representatives, universities as well as other entities aiming at the promotion of financial literacy).

Other European countries are preparing national strategies, and several bills are pending in Parliament awaiting their approvals. In Italy, for instance, the Parliament is at present working on the adoption of a specific Bill on Financial Education, also considering some coordination issues.[9] In the meantime, a recent law (n. 107/2015, so called "Buona Scuola"), concerning the reform of the public school in Italy has, *inter alia*, launched financial education program involving all school grades. In line with international best practice, the project is competence based and designed to help students develop the skills and knowledge necessary to make informed financial decisions.

In Poland, the Polish National Strategy on Financial Education is still in the early stage of development and has not been implemented. On the other hand, in Romania the *Comisia de Supraveghere a Sistemului de Pensii Private* is involved in a working group on development of a national strategy of financial education. The purpose of this strategy is to create a framework that all organizations involved in financial education, and policymaking in this area, will find useful and provide guidelines on developing financial education programs for the next five years.

By contrast, there are some EU countries where there is no national strategy on financial education, although a special body has been set up with the aim to determine principles on financial education initiatives themselves (such as in

Ireland) or with the aim to improve financial literacy (such as in Denmark, Netherland and United Kingdom). In Ireland, the National Steering Group on Financial Education was established by the then Financial Regulator (now Central Bank of Ireland) in late 2006, and included a range of stakeholders with an interest in personal finance and education. The purpose of the Steering Group was to encourage the development of personal finance education in the Republic of Ireland. The group conducted extensive work including a review of current practices and resources in financial education in Ireland and abroad and a financial competency framework was developed. This is a resource development tool that would support the creation of personal finance education initiatives and to define what a financially capable person should know and be able to do. While there is no 'national strategy' per se, the Steering Group published a report "Improving Financial Capability—a multi-stakeholder approach" in mid-2009, making commitments and recommendations intended to foster personal finance education in this country. The report sets out a roadmap for where the Steering Group saw financial education going in the future but there are no specific time spans.

In Belgium, at the beginning of April 2011, a law entered in force introducing the 'Twin Peaks' financial supervisory model. The law provides that the Financial Services and Markets Authority ("FSMA") contributes to the financial literacy and education of financial consumers. The FSMA is currently exploring how it can best implement this new competence and take a coordinating or leading role by developing a network with relevant stakeholders and defining a strategy at national level. In Denmark, instead of launching a national strategy, a board called The Money and Pension Panel was established by the Danish Parliament in June 2007. The aim of the Panel is to further more comprehensive knowledge of and interest in financial matters among consumers. The main tasks of the Panel are from an objective point of view: (i) to provide consumer information about financial products and services; (ii) to carry out and publish financial market studies of e.g. prices, customer services and conditions at diverse financial suppliers; and (iii) to carry out consumer affairs studies thereby achieving a better understanding of consumer views, consumer behavior and consumer affairs with regards to the provision of financial services.

In Luxemburg, financial education is present at two different levels: at the level of continuous vocational training (CVT) and at an academic level. CVT or tailor-made training for the professionals of the financial industry is offered by private companies (such as the "Institut de Formation Bancaire Luxembourg") as well as public institutions such as the Chamber of Commerce or the Chamber of Workers ("Chambre des Salariés"). In the early 1990s, at a time when the Government wanted to emphasize the growing importance of CVT to the economic and social development of Luxembourg, the law of 1st December 1992 created the National Institute for the Development of Continuous Vocational Training (INFPC), which is a state institution under the supervision of the Ministry of Education. The INFPC is responsible for the promotion of CVT and the development of CVT concepts, in association with private partners, such as training companies, and institutional partners, such as social partners. On the other hand, the academic level is developed via education programs and academic research in finance for university students. The Luxembourg School for Finance—created in 2003 as a Department of the Faculty of Law, Economics and Finance at the University of Luxembourg—is offering education programs and conducts academic research in finance at the highest level. It strives to attract students having a previous degree in finance or in a related field, as well as professionals seeking to obtain a greater theoretical foundation in finance to support their career objectives. In Sweden, in 2010, The Swedish Financial Supervisory Authority and several other stakeholders started to build a financial education network, supported by the Swedish Ministry of Finance, for raising self confidence in personal finances.

In UK, the Financial Services & Markets Act 2000 provides for the regulation of financial services and markets, and until 2010 included provision for financial education, by providing a public awareness objective of "promoting public understanding of the financial system". After the 2010, the Financial Services Act ("the ACT") made several amendments regarding the provision of financial education. The Act, which comes into force on 1 April 2013, required to establish a new consumer financial education body (named the Money Advice Service), with the scope to raise the public's understanding and knowledge of financial matters and improve their ability to manage their financial affairs. In addition, the ACT required creating a new regulatory framework for the supervision and management of the UK's banking and financial services industry, giving to the Bank of England macro-prudential responsibility for oversight of the financial system and day-to-day prudential supervision of financial services firms managing significant balance-sheet risk.

2 Good Practices for Consumer Protection

2.1 The European Framework

The European Council adopted its first special program for consumer protection and information policy in 1975,[10] where it defined five fundamental consumer rights: the right to protection of health and safety, the right to protection of economic interests, the right to claim for damages, the right to an education, and the right to legal representation (or the right otherwise to be heard). This program has served as a basis for an ever-growing corpus of directives (that do not apply directly and need to be transposed into the national laws of each EU Member State) and regulations (that are self-executives) in the area of consumer protection.

Currently, around 90 EU directives cover consumer protection issues, and that is why the consumer acquis remains complex and sometimes inconsistent (in the case of the same directive, since it can be transposed into national law differently, but also because of differences between various directives).

2.1.1 The EU Directives in the Financial Sector

One of the pivotal directives in the financial sector is represented by Directive 2004/39/EC on Markets in Financial Instruments Directive ("MiFID").[11] This Directive was adopted by European Union to protect investors/consumers, to promote fair, transparent, efficient and integrated financial markets as well as to safeguard market integrity by establishing harmonized requirements governing the activities of authorized intermediaries. Although the aims of the MiFID are to protect investors, surprisingly it does not contain neither references nor rules to improve the retail investor's procedural position by reversing the burden of proof in their favor. More specific is instead the Directive 2002/65/EC on Distance Marketing of Consumer Financial Services.[12] This latter Directive also refers to consumers,[13] but it leaves to the Member States the possibility of extending the scope of this Directive, and thus the qualification of 'consumer', to non-profit organizations and people making use of financial services in order to become entrepreneurs.[14] Moreover, it rules the burden of proof upon the supplier. As a matter of law, Art. 7, paragraph 3, provides that in those cases where the consumer exercises his right of withdrawal from a distance contract, the supplier may not require the consumer to pay any amount for the service provided, unless he can prove that the consumer was duly informed about the exact amount payable. In addition, Art. 15 provides that the Member States may also shift the burden of proof to the supplier in respect of other suppliers' obligations to inform the consumer's consent to conclusion of the contract and, where appropriate, its performance. Similarly, Art. 33 of the Directive 2007/64/EC on Payment Service provides that the Member States may stipulate that the burden of proof concerning the compliance with the information requirements laid down in this Directive shall lie with the payment service provider.

Another pivotal provision is represented by the Directive 2004/109/EC,[15] concerning the harmonization of transparency requirements in relation to issuer disclosure for those whose securities are listed for trading on a regulated stock market within the EU and further market participants. This Directive guarantees investors a high level of protection and strengthen confidence in the market. Finally, the financial legislative framework is completed by the Directive 2003/71/EC[16] regarding the type of prospectus to be published when securities are offered to the public or admitted to market trading, and by the Directive of the 23th of July 2013, where the European Commission has decided to adopt a revision of the Payment Services Directive (PSD), the so called "PSD2".[17] The scope of the latter Directive is to increase consumer rights when they send transfers and money remittances outside Europe or paying in non-EU currencies (the existing legislation addresses only transfers inside Europe and is limited to currencies of Member States) as well as when they are involved in unauthorized debits. Currently, in fact, the PSD protects rights of consumers in the event of unauthorized debits from an account within certain conditions. In order to enhance consumer protection and promote legal certainty further, the PSD2 will provide an unconditional refund right for consumers. This means that consumers would be allowed to ask for an unconditional refund even in the case of a disputed payment transaction. The only exceptions to this unconditional refund right will relate to cases where the merchant has already fulfilled the contract and the corresponding good or service has already been consumed. Moreover, the consumers will also gain a stronger position in case of disputes with their bank and other payment service providers: the new rules will oblige banks to answer in written form to any complaint within 15 business days. Finally, the PSD2 will oblige Member States to designate competent authorities to handle complaints of payment service users and other interested parties, such as consumer associations, concerning an alleged infringement of payment service providers of the directive. Payment service providers that are covered by this Directive on their side should put in place a complaints procedure for consumers that they can use before seeking out-of-court redress or before launching court proceedings.

On 26 November 2014, the Regulation (EU) No 1286/2014 of the European Parliament and of the Council on key information documents for packaged retail and insurance-based investment products (PRIIPs) was published into the Official Journal of the EU. The Regulation aim is to ensure that retail investors are able to understand the key features and risks of retail investment products as well as and to compare the characteristics of different products levelling the playing field between different manufactures of investment products and those who sell such products. According to this Regulation, that will apply only from 31 December 2016, the investment product manufacturers shall draw up a key information document for each investment product and publish the document on a website before the investment product can be sold to retail investors. The further Directive 2014/65/EU (so-called MiFID 2), on Markets in Financial Instruments deserve also particular attention. The Directive revision of MiFID constitutes, in fact, an integral part of the reforms aimed at establishing a safer, sounder, more transparent and responsible financial system as well as at improving the organization, transparency and oversight of various market segments, especially in those instruments traded mostly over the counter. MiFID 2 amending MiFID includes: (a) a Regulation (MiFIR) setting out, *inter alia*, requirements in relation to the disclosure of trading transparency data to the public and transaction data to competent authorities, specific supervisory action and the provision of services by third-country firms without a branch; and (b) a directive, amending, *inter alia*, specific requirements regarding the provision of investment services.[18]

More specific are instead the two Directives recently adopted by the Council and the Parliament.[19] The first Directive, 2014/92/EU, concerns the 'comparability of fees related to payment accounts, payment account switching and access to payment accounts with basic features' (to be transposed by the Member States by 18 September 2016).[20] The second Directive 2014/17/EU regards the 'credit agreements for consumers relating to residential immovable property' (to be transposed by the Member States by 21 March 2016). All those Directives have the aim of approximate the laws, regulations and administrative provisions of the Member States in the fields concerning the distance marketing of consumer financial services, the minimum requirements regarding the financial information, as well as to protect investors as consumers in the financial market promoting a fair, transparent, efficient and integrated financial market. Under the above-mentioned Directives, however, only natural persons are qualified to be 'consumers', enjoying thus a higher level of protection. Accordingly, are excluded entrepreneurs, no-profit associations, companies and all persons who are acting for their business, trade or profession, except financial investors who, acting as natural person outside the scope of an economic activity, have to be intended as 'consumers'.[21] This interpretation is also followed by the Court of Justice of European Union (CJEU), which has excluded from the definition of 'consumer' start-up contracts, assignments of consumer claims, and mixed contracts.[22] This has been the case of the Directives on doorstep selling (85/577/EEC), consumer credit (2008/48/EC), unfair contract terms (93/13/EC), time shares 2008/122/EC), distance selling (97/7/EC), and consumer sales and guarantees (1999/44/E).

2.2 *Legal Remedies in EU*

2.2.1 Alternative Dispute Resolution (ADR) and the ADR Directive

The ADR Directive ensures that consumers have access to ADR for resolving their contractual disputes with traders.[23] Access to ADR is ensured no matter what product or service they purchased (only disputes regarding health and higher education are excluded), whether the product or service was purchased online or offline and whether the trader is established in the consumer's Member State or in another one. This Directive also established binding quality requirements for dispute resolution bodies offering ADR procedure to consumers. Member States' competent authorities, after their assessment, communicate to the European Commission the list of national dispute resolution bodies. However, these out-of-court mechanisms have been developed differently across the European Union. Some are the fruit of public initiatives both at central level (such as the consumer complaints boards in the Scandinavian countries) and at local level (such as the arbitration courts in Spain), or they may spring from private initiatives (such as the mediators/ombudsmen of the banks or insurance companies). Precisely because of this diversity, the status of the decisions adopted by these bodies differs greatly. Some are mere recommendations (such as in the case of the Scandinavian consumer complaints boards and most of the private ombudsmen), others are binding only on the professional (as in the case of most of the bank ombudsmen); and others are binding on both parties (arbitration).[24]

Recently, the European Commission has developed a web-based platform called The Online Dispute Resolution platform (ODR platform). The ODR platform's objective is to help consumers and traders resolve their contractual disputes about online purchases of goods and services out-of-court at a low cost in a simple and fast way, and establishes a common framework for ADR in the EU member states by setting out common minimum quality principles in order to ensure that all ADR-entities are impartial, independent, transparent and efficient. It allows consumers to submit their disputes online in any of the 23 official languages of the EU, and to transmit the disputes only to the quality dispute resolution bodies communicated by Member States. The ODR platform is accessible to consumers and traders since 15 February 2016.

Another financial dispute resolution network of national out-of-court complaint schemes in the European Economic Area countries (the European Union Member States plus Iceland, Liechtenstein and Norway) is FIN-NET. This network, launched by the European Commission in 2001, is responsible for handling disputes between consumers and financial services providers. Within FIN-NET, the schemes cooperate to provide consumers with easy access to out-of-court complaint procedures in cross-border cases. If a consumer in one country has a dispute with a financial services provider from another country, FIN-NET members will put the consumer in touch with the relevant out-of court complaint scheme and provide the necessary information about it.

3 The Italian Scenario and the Common European Framework

The principal source of rules and regulations for the banking and financial sector is EU legislation. The tools used by the EU—regulations, directives, decisions, recommendations and opinions—vary depending on whether they are binding and on how they are applied in the member states as described in Article 288 of the Treaty on the Functioning of the European Union. Regulations have general application, are binding in their entirety and are directly applicable in the member states without the need for transposition. They are therefore the preferred tool for achieving full harmonization and for limiting national discretion, in part to avoid distortions in competition between economic actors caused by differences in legislation across member states. Directives are binding on member states as to the results to be achieved, but leave the choice of forms and methods to the national authorities. Regulatory and implementing technical standards play an increasingly important role in banking and financial regulation. They are developed by European supervisory authorities and adopted by the European Commission via regulations. The standards seek to harmonize the most complex and detailed aspects to create a complete, homogeneous and unified system of rules for the single market.

The main European legislation governing the supervisory duties of the Bank of Italy is Regulation (EU) No. 575/2013 and Directive 2013/36/EU. Regulation (EU) No. 575/2013 (the Capital Requirements Regulation—CRR) introduced prudential supervision rules directly applicable to all European banks and investment firms. The Bank of Italy's regulatory powers over the subject matter are governed by the CRR (capital, minimum capital requirements and public disclosure) and therefore confined to those areas where the Regulation allows it very limited discretion to make the necessary adjustments for integration with Italy's law and specific circumstances. Directive 2013/36/EU (the Capital Requirements Directive IV—CRD IV) establishes the conditions for access to the activity of banks; the freedom of establishment of banks in the EU and freedom for them to provide their services; prudential control; additional capital buffers; and bank corporate governance. The Law No. 154 of the 7th of October 2014, named "Legge di delegazione europea 2013-*bis*", was enacted to implement the above EU directives, and thus the EU framework, into the Italian financial services sector.

3.1 *Financial Services and Applicable Consumer Protection Provisions*

The Italian financial services[25] sector is governed either by general consumer law or special provisions contained in the "Testo Unico Bancario"[26] (Consolidated Law on Banking) and in the "Testo Unico della Finanza" (Consolidated Law on Finance).[27] In addition, related regulations issued by the "Banca d'Italia" (Bank of Italy) and by the Italian Securities and Exchange Commission (Consob) provide further guidance. Finally, the Italian legislative decree No. 206/2005, a consolidated Act called "Consumers' Code",[28] also plays an important role within the financial services scenario, ensuring a high level of protection to the consumers involved in financial transactions and banking practices.

3.1.1 The Consolidated Law on Banking

The Consolidated Law on Banking is the main legislative source for the framework of the powers and liabilities of the regulatory authorities in Italy. It contains principles relating the carrying out of business by banks, other financial intermediaries, as well as by other entities operating in the banking sector. Part of the Consolidated Law on Banking provisions are addressed to all bank clients, such as corporates, bodies having a contractual relationship with the bank, professionals, whilst regulations on consumer credit concern only consumers. In order to increase the consumer protection, the Legislative Decree No. 141/2010, which has implemented the EU Consumer Credit Directive (2008/48/EC) on Credit Agreements for Consumers, has introduced a set of provisions in the Consolidated Law on Banking regulating, *inter alia*, pre-contractual transparency duties, verification of the creditworthiness of consumers and the rights of consumers in case of withdrawal.[29]

The new rules on pre-contractual duties impose certain information obligations on lenders or intermediaries to make potential consumers aware of the terms of the proposed loan, or credit agreement, and its consistency with their needs. Such information must be provided in a specific format, including the standard European consumer credit information form.[30] Furthermore, those rules declare void all contractual clauses that impose costs on the consumers that are not fully included in the annual percentage rate disclosed in the pre-contractual documentation, providing also a series of consumers rights such as: (a) a right of withdrawal (which can be exercised within 14-days of the signing of the credit agreement or the consumer's receipt of all the required pre-contractual information, if such information is provided after the agreement is signed); (b) a right of early termination if the supplier connected with the credit agreement breaches its terms (if such a right is exercised, the lender must reimburse the instalments already repaid by the consumer, plus any additional charges); and (c) a right of early repayment at any time, with a reduction in the total cost of the credit equal to the interest and charges that would otherwise have fallen due during the remainder of the agreement. Moreover, regarding the consumer credit, consumers are also entitled to consult and obtain by the bank, or other regulatory authority, copies of all special information sheets containing details of the bank, the characteristics and inherent risks of the transaction or service concerned, the terms and conditions applying thereto as well as the most significant contract clauses. In addition, they are also entitled to receive paper or other hard copies of this notice and of the information sheets relevant to the transaction or service concerned if the bank uses remote communication techniques. Before signing it and subject to no conditions of any sort, the consumers may obtain a copy of the full contract as well as a summary of the terms, financial and otherwise, applying thereto to allow for a careful assessment of the same and on the understanding that delivery of such a copy does not entail an obligation on the part of the bank (or the customer) to conclude the contract. After the contract has been signed, the consumers are entitled to receive regular updates on the status and performance of their account—at the end of the contract period and once a year at a minimum—in the guise of a formal statement along with a summary of the contract's terms and conditions as well to be informed about any unfavorable changes to the contract's terms and conditions. In the event of any unfavorable changes in rates, prices or other conditions, the consumers are entitled to withdraw from the contract within 60 days of receiving the bank's notice thereof—in writing or by any other authorized means—without incurring any penalties and on the same conditions as were applied beforehand.[31] Finally, they are also entitled to obtain within a maximum period of 90 days a copy of the documentation relevant to any transaction executed with the bank during the previous ten years. If a bank, instead, is involved in the placement of government bonds and certificates, in addition to ensure the existence of disclosure, transparency and advertising rules, it must allow to the clients full understanding of such secured transaction. In addition, if an offer is made in a place other than the bank's central or branch offices, the customer shall be given copies of this notice and of the information sheets relevant to the transaction or service concerned before signing the contract. The customer is, furthermore, entitled to receive all relevant information sheet before subscribing any structured securities. If the customer is a 'consumer', instead, he shall be supplied with the relevant information sheet before finalizing the purchase of any complex financial products; any contract clause providing for the interest rate or any other prices or terms to be modified to the consumer's detriment must be expressly approved as well as any contract clause relating to the capitalization of interest.

Credit and debit interest accruing on current accounts shall be calculated at the same intervals, and any contract clauses purporting to set the interest rate or any other prices or terms by reference to custom shall be null and void, as will any clauses stipulating less favorable rates, prices or terms than those advertised in the relevant information sheets. Such clauses shall be replaced automatically by applying the conditions and prices that are foreseen by the law.

3.1.2 The Consolidated Law on Finance

The Italian securities regulations are instead provided for by the Consolidated Law on Finance and by the Consob under the Regulation No. 11522/98. The Consolidated Law on Finance provisions have the aim to provide protection for a general category of financial consumers related to authorized intermediaries against unreliable financial investments going beyond ordinary risk standards proper to these types of transactions, respecting the duties of care and fairness, and, more generally, contributing to the efficient functioning of financial markets.[32]

According to Art. 21, paragraph 1, of the Consolidated Law on Finance, as amended by article 14 of Law 262/2005, authorized intermediaries shall conduct an independent, sound and prudent management and make appropriate arrangements for safeguarding the rights of customers[33] in respect of the assets entrusted to them. In doing this, they must act diligently, fairly and transparently in the interests of customers and the integrity of the market classifying, according to the minimum general criteria to be set forth in a specific regulation issued by Consob, the risk inherent in financial products[34] and individually managed investment portfolio. At the same time, they shall do acquire the necessary information from customers and operate in such a way that they are always adequately informed; in addition, they shall use publicity and promotional communications which are correct, clear and not misleading, and have resources and procedures, including internal control mechanisms, suitable for ensuring the efficient provision of services and activities. Moreover, the authorized intermediaries in conducting financial investments shall: (a) adopt all reasonable measures to identify and manage conflict of interest which may arise with the customer or between customers, also by the adoption of appropriate organizational measures, in order to avoid a negative impact on the interests of the customer; (b) clearly inform customers, prior to acting on their behalf, of the general nature and/or sources of conflict of interest where measures taken pursuant are not sufficient to ensure, with reasonable certainty, that the risk of damaging the interests of the customer is avoided; (c) perform independent, sound and prudent management and take measures to safeguard the rights of customers with regard to their assets.

Finally, in recommending the transaction to investors they shall also do evaluate the profile of each customer. In doing this, they shall check the customer experience (concerning investments in financial products), his financial situations as well as his investments objectives and the possibility to incur risks. In any case, the orders expressly given by the customer in writing or by telephone or electronic means shall be valid and binding for the intermediaries, on condition that, pursuant to Art. 21 of the Consolidated Law on Finance, procedures ensuring the possibility of ascertaining the provenance of the orders and retention of the related documentation. Art. 23, concerning the discipline applicable to contracts for the provision of investment services or non-core services, provides for that such contracts under penalty of nullity shall be reduced to writing and a copy given to customers.

3.1.3 The Bank of Italy and the CONSOB

The implementation of the Consolidated Law on Finance and Banking is granted by secondary legislation enacted by the Bank of Italy and by the Consob, which have equivalent powers of control and supervision over financial markets.

The Bank of Italy requires intermediaries (banks and financial intermediaries) to comply with principles of transparency and correctness in their relations with customers. In carrying out this task, the Bank of Italy has adopted several regulations governing the requirement for the pre-contractual transparency, the organization and effectiveness of the alternative dispute resolution system provided by the Consolidated Law on Banking, the authorization and supervision procedures over all supervised entities. One of those is the Regulation issued on 29 July 2009 for "Transparency of Banking and Financial Operations and Services" and for the "Correctness in Relations between Intermediaries and Clients" containing the new regulation on transparency in banking and financial services. Under this Regulation, Bank of Italy provides a series of graduated measures in relation to the nature of the services provided and the characteristics of the clientele to which they are targeted. On the basis of the principle of proportionality, duties differ according to the features of services provided and their recipients, who-taking into consideration the varying intensity of the degree of protection-can be identified as follow: (a) 'consumer', namely the natural person who is acting for purposes which can be regarded as outside his trade or profession; (b) 'retail clients', understood as consumers, non-profit entities and businesses having total revenues lower than Euro 5 million and fewer than 10 employees[35]; (c) 'client', that is every natural person or legal person that has a contractual relationship, or that is willing to enter into such, with an intermediary. The status of 'consumer' or 'retail clients' must be verified by intermediaries before the conclusion of the contract, since some provisions apply exclusively to contracts entered into with consumers or 'retail clients'.

On 17th June 2013, the Bank of Italy launched a public consultation concerning some changes to the provisions on transparency of banking and financial services and transactions, as well as on the correctness of the relationships between intermediaries and customers. The proposed changes are aimed at establishing a sort of balance between efficiency needs and solidity of the banking and financial systems, on the one hand, and the protection of clients on the other, simplifying the disclosure of the documentation to be provided to clients and clarifying the relevant requirements for banks and financial intermediaries.

The Consob, instead, is the public authority responsible for regulating the Italian securities market. It exercises its supervisory powers to ensure transparency and correct application of the rules of conduct of business by the banks and investment firms in the provision of investment services and activities. Pursuant to Art. 74, paragraph 1 and 3, of the Consolidated Law on Finance, the Consob shall supervise regulated markets with the aim of ensuring the transparency of the markets, the orderly conduct of trading and the protection of investors, by adopting, in cases of necessity and as a matter of urgency, all the measures required for the above-mentioned purposes.

In the financial market scenario, the Consob also plays an important role adopting proper measures either setting restrictions on short sale of shares issued by banks and insurance companies with the aim of ensuring the transparency, the orderly conduct of trading and the protection of investors,[36] or setting provisions ensuring adequacy evaluation about the investment services and financial instruments suited to the customers, or potential customers.[37] In this regard, the Consob provide the intermediaries, in recommending investment services and financial instruments, shall obtain necessary details from their customers or potential customers in relation: (a) to awareness and experience of the investment sector relevant to the type of instrument or service; (b) the nature, volume and frequency of financial instrument transactions performed by the customer and the period in which such transactions were executed. In addition, they must obtain necessary information on the level of education, profession or, if relevant, the former profession of the customers; (c) the data on the period for which the customer wishes to retain the investment, his preferences in relation to risk, his own risk profile and investment aims, where relevant. Where intermediaries providing investment consultancy or portfolio management services are unable to obtain the information required, they shall abstain from providing said services and to carry on.[38] Further, duties arise upon intermediaries in the case the customers give all information required. As a matter of law, even if the intermediaries receive in full all details and information from the customer, they shall, however, assess whether the specific transaction recommended or executed as part of the provision of portfolio management services satisfies the correspondence with the customer's investment objectives.[39] Moreover, the intermediaries shall verify the customer have necessary experience and awareness of the nature of that transaction to understand the risks involved in such a transaction or management of the portfolio. However, where investment consultancy or portfolio management services are provided to professional customers, not qualified as consumers, intermediaries may presume that they are financially able to face any investment risk compatible with their investment objectives, since those have the necessary level of experience and awareness in conducting such transactions.

The complex structure of the Italian banking and finance system represent, however, a veritable legislative labyrinth for the investors who, in conducting a specific transaction with the banking/financial institutions, must be first wondering whether they are acting as 'consumers' or 'retail investors'. The notion of 'investor' in the financial market must be thus accordingly defined to apply the proper law, and to ascertain whether that individual will enjoy of the higher level of protection, under the provisions of the consumer law, or no.

3.1.4 The Consumer Code

The EU consumer protection legislation has been collected into the Italian legislative decree No. 206/2005, a consolidated act called "Consumers' Code". The Consumers' Code harmonizes and consolidates the laws of purchase and consumption, in accordance with the principles of the EU legislation, to ensure a high level of protection to consumer and users in all contractual processes they take part in. Following the Consumer Code, the Italian Government approved a package of measures, designed by the Minister of Economic Development, with benefits to 'citizens-consumers' exploiting the effects of the liberalization processes on the national market.[40]

Art. 2 of the Consumer Code lists all the fundamental rights of consumers,[41] while Arts. 40–43 grant the consumers special protection in consumer credit contracts and financial services,[42] where consumer is meant to be a "natural person who is acting for purposes which can be regarded as outside his trade or profession".[43] Here, for example, when marketing at a distance involves 'consumers', due account must be taken and the relevant Consumer Code provisions apply. Among those contained in the section regarding the distance marketing of investment services and activities and financial products, it is worth mentioning: (a) Art. 67*quater*, which indicates the information on the service provider to be supplied to the consumer prior to the conclusion of the distance contract or offer. Such information concern (i) the identity and the main business of the supplier, the geographical address at which the supplier is established and any other geographical address relevant for the customer's relations with the supplier, (ii) the identity of the representative of the supplier established in the consumer's Member State of residence, if any, and the geographical address relevant for the customer's relations with the representative, (iii) when the consumer's dealings are with any professional other than the supplier, the identity of this professional, the capacity in which he is acting vis-à-vis the consumer, and the geographical address relevant for the customer's relations with this professional, (iv) where the supplier is registered in a trade or similar public register, the trade register in which the supplier is entered and his registration number or an equivalent means of identification in that register, (v) where the supplier's activity is subject to an authorization scheme, the particulars of the relevant supervisory authority; (b) Art. 67*sexies* lists the information to be provided in respect of the financial service offered, such as (i) a description of the main characteristics of the financial service, (ii) the total price to be paid by the consumer to the supplier for the financial service, including all related fees, charges and expenses, and all taxes paid via the supplier or, when an exact price cannot be indicated, the basis for the calculation of the price enabling the consumer to verify it, (iii) where relevant notice indicating that the financial service is related to instruments involving special risks related to their specific features or the operations to be executed or whose price depends on fluctuations in the financial markets outside the supplier's control and that historical performances are no indicators for future performances, (iv) notice of the possibility that other taxes and/or costs may exist that are not paid via the supplier or imposed by him, (v) any limitations of the period for which the information provided is valid, (vi) the arrangements for payment and for performance, (vii) any specific additional cost for the consumer of using the means of distance communication, if such additional cost is charged; (c) Art. 67*sexies*, concerning the distance contract itself, requesting the provider to supply information on (i) the existence or absence of a right of withdrawal and, where the right of withdrawal exists, its duration and the conditions for exercising it, including information on the amount which the consumer may be required to pay, as well as the consequences of non-exercise of that right, (ii) the minimum duration of the distance contract in the case of financial services to be performed permanently or recurrently, (iii) information on any rights the parties may have to terminate the contract early or unilaterally by virtue of the terms of the distance contract, including any penalties imposed by the contract in such cases, (iv) practical instructions for exercising the right of withdrawal indicating, inter alia, the address to which the notification of a withdrawal should be sent, (v) the Member State or States whose laws are taken by the supplier as a basis for the establishment of relations with the consumer prior to the conclusion of the distance contract, (vi) any contractual clause on law applicable to the distance contract and/or on competent Court, (vii) in which language, or languages, the contractual terms and conditions, and the prior information referred to in such article are supplied, and furthermore in which language, or languages, the supplier, with the agreement of the consumer, undertakes to communicate during the duration of this distance contract; (d) Art. 67-*octies*, on the redress mechanism (i.e. information on whether or not there is an out-of-court complaint and redress procedure for the consumer that is party to the distance contract and, if so, the methods for having access to it, and the existence of guarantee funds or other compensation arrangements).

4 Consumer's Financial Definition

4.1 Acting Outside Trade or Profession

4.1.1 The Notion of 'Consumer'

As we have seen, the "client-consumer" that purchases a consumer credit contract is protected by special legislation provided either by the Consumer Code or by the Consolidated Laws. Both legislations, however, make the identification of the 'consumer' quite confusing.[44] As a matter of fact, the Consolidated Law on Banking contains general rules protecting the 'client' and some specific provisions on the 'consumer' applicable on the basis of the consumer's definition. Moreover,

Art. 121 of the Consolidated Law on Banking[45] repeats at the first paragraph the definition proposed by the Consumer Code in Art. 3, by which consumer is identified as a "*natural person who is acting for purposes which can be regarded as outside his trade or profession*".[46]

At the same time, the fourth paragraph of the Art. 121 enumerates those cases excluded from its range of application. Letter a), for example, refers to "financing instruments that have an aggregate value inferior or superior to limits imposed by the Interministerial Committee for Credit and Savings (CICR)". Consequently, if the person that received the financing is a "natural person who is acting for purposes which can be regarded as outside his trade or profession", but the financial operation has a greater value of the limits imposed by the CICR, the contract may no longer be regulated by consumer rules. It means, although a consumer is a natural person who is acting for purposes that can be regarded as outside one's trade or profession, under certain circumstances that 'natural person' cannot be qualified as consumer, and the proper consumer rules do not apply.

4.1.2 Extension to Business-Persons

Some Courts propounded the view for a time, that a person should be protected as a consumer, if the relevant transaction does not belong to his core business activities.[47] The Italian Supreme Court, however, rejected this variant establishing a narrow definition of consumer, ruling that consumer is that person who is acting also for related purposes to his business activity.[48]

The definition of consumer thus appears to distinguish between two different types of information: the first is that a consumer can only be a physical person; the second is that the purpose of the activity concerned must be non-professional, that means the scope of the activity must be the satisfaction of some personal or family need. Having regard to the first condition, Italian experts have increasingly proposed the extension of consumer protection to legal persons, in particular to corporate entities, paying particular attention to those having a not-for-profit purpose, such as associations, committees and consortia carrying out both external and internal activities.[49] This way, it would be possible to provide a more coherent definition of the "weaker" contractual party. However, this interpretation has been rejected both by the Italian Constitutional Court[50] which clarified that an extension of protection to legal persons is not provided for in Italian constitutional law, and by the Italian Supreme Court,[51] who have invoked the need for coherence towards European policy.

Nevertheless, recently the United Sections of the Italian Supreme Court[52] has extended the scope of consumer protection provisions under the Consolidated Law on Finance issuing a decision concerning the obligation for banks and financial intermediaries, engaging in "door-to-door" selling of financial instruments. The Court provided a withdrawal right to be exercised by retail clients within seven days of the signing of the relevant contract. This decision is important because it extends such obligation, originally provided by Art. 30, paragraph 6, of the Consolidated

Law on Finance only in relation to the placement of financial instruments and portfolio management contracts entered into outside the registered office/place of business, also to other types of financial services and in particular to all investment services performed by financial salesmen through home visit whereas that need for investor's protection, resulting from the "surprise effect" and "traditionally" typical and inherent in the placing of financial instruments investment service, effectively occurs. The regulatory framework is provided by Art. 30, paragraph 6, of the Consolidated Law on Finance according to which: "The enforceability of contracts for placing of financial instruments or the portfolio management concluded outside the registered office shall be suspended for a period of seven days beginning on the date of subscription by the investor. Within that period the investor may notify his withdrawal from the contract at no expense and without any compensation for the approved person or the authorized person. This possibility shall be mentioned in the forms given to the investor. The same rules shall apply to contract proposals effected outside the registered office", and the following paragraph 7, under which "failure to indicate the right of withdrawal in forms shall result in the nullity of the related contracts, which may be enforced only by the customer". Regarding the scope of those provisions, two opposite interpretative orientations, either in doctrine and in case law, were formed over time, necessarily leading to the referral of the matter from the Supreme Court's First Civil Section, by order of April 2012, to the United Sections, in order to reconcile the contrast. In particular, the dispute was related to the concept of "contract for placing of financial instruments". The first orientation—prevailing, also because supported by two recent legitimacy judgments[53] and reassured by the concerned supervisory authority[54]—was upholding the technical and restrictive interpretation of the contract for the investment service of "placing of financial instruments" (service defined by Art. 1, paragraph 5, Consolidated Law on Finance) concept, recalled in article 30, paragraph 6, Consolidated Law on Finance. Consequently, that provision was held to be unenforceable for the other investment services of a typical "executive" nature, as, dealing on own account, execution of orders on behalf of clients and reception and transmission of orders.

Otherwise stated, the prevailing interpretation, adhering to the wording of the provision, was restricting the scope of application to the sales of financial instruments and products carried out by the intermediary on the basis of a mandate of placing of financial instruments conferred by the issuer or the offeror, on the assumption that the reason of the *ius poenitendi*[55] was to be inferred from the door-to-door selling of a contract promoted by the intermediary, with possible "surprise effect" for the client. On the contrary, the second and minority orientation, assuming that the Legislator had wanted to convey a "nontechnical" meaning to the term "placing", was upholding an application of the *ius poenitendi* extended also to investment services different from that of placing of financial instruments and portfolio management explicitly recalled by the concerned provision. In this regard, the minority orientation was giving a broad interpretation to the concept of "placing of financial instruments" provided by Art. 30, paragraph 6, Consolidated Law on Finance, thus supporting the applicability of that provision also to the investment services of dealing on own account, execution of orders on behalf of clients and reception and transmission of orders, when promoted door-to-door by the intermediary. In this scenario, the United Sections of the Supreme Court, diverging from the recalled recent legitimacy judgments and also disregarding the Consob, have joined the minority interpretation, stating the principle according to which the *ius poenitendi* granted to the investor by Art. 30, paragraph 6, Consolidated Law on Finance, and the prescription of nullity of the contracts in which that right has not been provided (as per paragraph 7) should be applied not only when the door-to-door selling of financial instruments by the intermediary has taken place within a placement carried out by the intermediary itself in favor of the issuer or offeror of such financial instruments, but also when the same door-to-door selling has taken place in the execution of a different investment service, where the same investor's need of protection occurs.

The United Sections ruling will be influencing the decisions that must be taken by national courts in cases relating to the provision of any sort of investment service having been accompanied by promotional activities by the intermediary (in particular, it has to be emphasized, would fall within this category also the combination of investment advice service with a typically "executive" investment service). Moreover, the principle expressed in the judgment in question would apply not only to the retail clients but also in respect of certain corporate investors and local entities.

5 Remedies

5.1 Alternative Dispute Resolution (ADR) and Access to Justice in the Italian Financial Sector

The European legislation on consumer credit and distance contracts for financial services as well as the compelling need of protection of investors against unfair terms in consumer contracts and against unlawful conducts perpetrated by financial intermediaries, have recently led the Italian Government to introduce either alternative, fast and cheap methods of dispute resolution as out-of-court dispute resolution processes or new remedies to access to justice.[56]

The Consolidated Law on Finance and the Consob lack, in fact, to state clearly what remedies are available to the investors in case the investment firm should breach any of its duties.[57] This omission explains why Italian Lower Courts have recognized different remedies in case of individual lawsuits: (a) reliance damages deriving from pre-contractual liability[58]; (b) expectation damages deriving from breach of the financial contract[59]; (c) invalidity of the financial contract absent the required written form or due to the violation of mandatory rules.[60]

In order to avoid this fragmentation, and also in compliance with the guidelines issued by the European legislation, the Italian Government updated the legislation for protecting savings and regulating financial markets enacting the Law no. 262/2005. Accordingly, it introduced two difference remedies available to investors: (i) the guarantee indemnification fund within the settlement procedure and the Conciliation and Arbitration Chamber, and the (ii) no-fault indemnification fund.[61]

5.2 *Out-of-Court Remedies*

5.2.1 The Guarantee Indemnification Fund Within the Settlement Procedure and the Conciliation and Arbitration Chamber

The Conciliation and Arbitration Chamber housed on Consob premises was founded on the provisions of the Italian Investment Protection Law (no. 262/2005), enacted by Legislative Decree 179/2007, and later governed in organizational and procedures terms first by Consob Regulation No. 16763 of 29th December 2008 (expired on 1st August 2012) and then by Consob Regulation No. 18275 of 18th July 2012.[62] With Resolution No. 18310 of 5 September 2012, the Commission approved new rules for the organization and operation of the Conciliation and Arbitration Chamber at the Consob. The Chamber[63] is the organization responsible for the administration of conciliation and arbitration proceedings involving disputes arising between investors[64] and financial intermediaries[65] regarding compliance with disclosure obligations, correctness and transparency as envisaged in the contractual relations with customers and concerning investment or asset management services. It is composed of a President and two members, appointed by the Consob, chosen from amongst Consob employees who find themselves in a senior management position.

i. ***Out-of-Court Settlement***

A petition to initiate the conciliation procedure may be presented exclusively by the investor when, in relation to the dispute no other conciliation procedures have been initiated, including by the initiative of the intermediary the investor used. In addition, a complaint has to be presented to the intermediary to which a specific response was provided, and a period of ninety days or any shorter period set by the intermediary for handling of the complaint has elapsed without the investor having received a response. Once the petition has been submitted, the Chamber appoints without delay a conciliator from among those listed. The conciliator shall conduct the meetings without procedural formalities and without the obligation to take minutes, in the way he considers most appropriate given the circumstances of the case, the willingness of the parties and the necessity of reaching a solution to the dispute quickly. He also may hear the parties separately or conduct a cross-examination in order to better clarify the dispute and identify the points on which there is agreement, and may order the intervention of third parties, provided the parties agree to this and to covering the relative expenses.[66]

If conciliation proves successful, the content of the agreement shall be drafted in the form of a special report signed by the conciliator and the parties involved. Should the parties fail to immediately implement the conciliatory measures, subject to confirmation of its formal consistency, the report shall be approved by decree of the President of the Court with jurisdiction over the district in which conciliation proceedings were held, and shall constitute a writ of execution for enforced expropriation, enforcement of specific performance and for registration as mortgage by order of the court. By contrast, where no agreement is reached and in the event of non-conciliation, at the joint request of all parties the conciliator shall formulate a proposal to which each party shall indicate its final position (i.e. the terms under which the party is willing to conciliate). The conciliator shall note these final positions in a special "conciliation failed" report.

ii. ***Arbitration***

In case of breach of disclosure, required by Art. 21 of the Consolidated Law on Financial, investors may also ask for an arbitration redress procedure held by the Consob. In this regard, the parties may submit a joint written application to start an arbitration proceeding, which will be administrated by the Chamber under the provisions of the Consolidate Law on Finance and Consob enactment provisions. Disputes shall be settled by a single arbitrator, selected from among entries on the list held by the Chamber, unless the parties decide to refer the dispute to a panel of three arbitrators, with proceedings as indicated in Art. 810, subsection 1 of the Italian Code of Civil Procedure.[67] During their first meeting, the arbitrators shall ask the parties to deposit a sum as payment on account of arbitrator fees and defense costs to be incurred by the parties in order to obtain the award, deciding also the criteria for distribution of costs between the parties. The payment on account shall be determined by the Chamber on recommendation from the arbitrators.

The arbitrators shall pronounce the award within one hundred and twenty days of acceptance of the appointment. However, this deadline may be extended prior to its expiry for a period not exceeding one hundred and twenty days by the Chamber, following justified application from one of the parties or arbitrators, after consulting the other parties involved, or the by joint written declarations of the parties. The investor, however, can also opt for a fast-track arbitration procedure, which will be based solely on evidence submitted in advance by the parties with the application for arbitration and it more fast than the "full" arbitration. The option of recourse to fast-track arbitration must be expressly indicated in the arbitration agreement, and the application cannot be accepted if as part of the same dispute no complaint was issued to the intermediary to which specific response was provided, or if ninety days have lapsed, or shorter term as established by the intermediary for handling of the complaint, in which time the investor has received no response.

The fast-track arbitration shall be settled before a single arbitrator appointed by a joint application by the parties among entries on the list held by the Chamber, and has the aim to compensate the equity damages suffered by the investor as a result of intermediary default in terms of disclosure, correctness and transparency obligations envisaged in contractual relations with investors. The equity compensation will be determinate on the base of the documentary evidence provided, and consists of a lump sum appropriate to compensate the equity damages suffered as an immediate and direct consequence of default by the intermediary. This is an alternative redress. Should the claimant be unsatisfied with the arbitration decision, he, however, may file claim before the ordinary courts that will award all damages suffered by investors in addition to the equity damages eventually recognized.

5.2.2 No-Fault Indemnification Fund

The second remedy has been introduced by the Law No. 23/2006, then implemented by the Law No. 179/2007, which has established new procedures for the conciliation and arbitration system of compensation and guarantee fund for investors. This provision consists of a no-fault indemnification fund based on the unlawful brokerage activities. To have access to this "fund" investors must demonstrate their economic loss and provide evidence of the breach of broker's duties as stated in Part II of the Consolidated Law on Finance.

This means that the broker's activities are already judged as unlawful by an ordinary court or arbitrator, and the final judgment of the court or the arbitration award is not more subjected to appeal. The Fund, managed by the Consob, is exclusively created by collecting half of the total amount deriving from criminal fines eventually paid by financial brokers.

5.2.3 Mediation in Consumer and Financial Litigation

The mediation proceeding provided for by the Legislative Decree No. 28/2010 (Mediation Law)[68] which implemented the Mediation Directive (2008/52/EC),[69] and it is administered by a qualified mediation body, registered on a list kept by the Italian Ministry of Justice. Both the mediation bodies and the mediators themselves must, furthermore, meet some requirements to be qualified. As for the mediators, they must hold a university degree (not necessarily in law), or at least be enrolled in a professional association; moreover, they must have a certificate of good standing issued by their professional association and have attended a specific training on mediation theory and techniques.[70] The Mediation Law provides three forms of mediation: (a) voluntary mediation, spontaneously decide to avail themselves of mediation services; (b) delegated mediation (whenever deemed necessary, the judge may refer the parties to mediation); and (c) mandatory mediation. In this latter case, a large range of disputes[71] cannot be brought before civil courts unless the plaintiff had first attempts the mediation procedure.

The Italian Constitutional Court was called several times to judge on compliance of mandatory mediation attempts with Arts. 24, 25 and 111 of the Italian Constitution, according to which anybody has the right to access State justice. In at least three consistent judgments[72] the Court, considering that after mandatory mediation attempt parties can refer their dispute to the State judge, affirmed such compliance. Despite this, also a cause of many criticisms and protests, the law was challenged on various grounds before the Italian Constitutional Court.[73]

Nearly six months after its entry into force, the Italian Constitutional Court made invalid Art. 5 of the Mediation Law, finding it in breach of Art. 76 of the Italian Constitution. Relying on technical grounds, the Court found that by enacting the law, the government had exceeded the scope of both the Mediation Directive and Law No. 69/2009, which empowered the government to adopt a legislative decree introducing administered mediation procedures. The overall rationale embodied in the preamble to the directive was identified as follows: "Mediation can provide a cost-effective and quick extrajudicial resolution of disputes in civil and commercial matters through processes tailored to the needs of the parties. Agreements resulting from mediation are more likely to be complied with voluntarily and are more likely to preserve an amicable and sustainable relationship between the parties. These benefits become even more pronounced in situations displaying cross-border elements." The Mediation Directive, thus, defines 'mediation' as "extrajudicial resolution of disputes", whereas the Italian government had conceived in mediation as a compulsory preliminary step of judicial litigation. Further confirmation of this misunderstanding is to be found in Art. 60 of Law No. 69/2009, which officially recognized mediation in civil and commercial disputes and delegated power to the Italian government to issue a Legislative Decree on mediation to implement the provisions of Mediation Directive. For this reason, the Italian Constitutional Court ruled that compulsory mediation was implemented in Italy in order to reduce the congestion of tribunals, rather than to create an alternative (i.e. more rapid and less expensive) form of dispute resolution and that mediation was pushed beyond its natural scope in an attempt to achieve economies in the administration of justice. At the same time, the Constitutional Court decision represents a setback for the promotion of alternative dispute resolution, which in a litigation-friendly country such as Italy would benefit individuals and businesses.

Nevertheless, on 15 June 2013, the Italian government issued a Law Decree (so called "Decreto del Fare"), then converted in Law No. 98, on 9 August 2013, providing urgent measures that also involve important changes to Italian litigation system.[74] It resurrected the mediation provision by announcing a new mandatory mediation for a wide range of classes of disputes, including banking and financial agreements.

5.2.4 Conciliation in Consumer and Financial Litigation

The Consob conciliation procedure is modelled upon state-sponsored out-of-court commercial mediation (Legislative Decree No. 3/2005). Benefits of the procedure include the judicial enforceability of the settlement agreement and exemption from stamp duty. Confidentiality is strictly protected, and the mediator can meet the parties separately. If the parties agree in advance, the mediator can make a final settlement proposal on which both the investor and the financial intermediary should take a stance, also stating under what conditions they could sign an agreement. This last proposal, together with the parties' positions, is recorded in the minutes, and could be taken subsequently into account by a judge to rule on the costs of judgment.

5.2.5 Banking and Financial Arbitrator

In the banking sector, a different—albeit similar in several respects—procedure has been introduced by article 128*bis* of the Consolidated Law on Banking, introduced in 2005 following the financial scandals of Cirio, Parmalat and the Argentinean Bonds, and then amended by the Legislative Decree No. 28 of 4 March 2010, and subsequently by the Law 9th August 2013, No. 98.

Article 128*bis* provides for a special alternative dispute resolution procedure (the Arbitro Bancario Finanziario, or ABF) applicable to all disputes arising between banks (and financial intermediaries) and clients in the context of banking and financial services/products (with the exclusion of investment services). The procedure applies to all bank-client litigation whether or not the client qualifies as a 'consumer'; only clients that are financial intermediaries themselves are excluded. The procedure applies to all disputes relating to rights and obligations regardless of the monetary value of the underlying contractual relationship. However, if the litigated matter includes a request for money, the procedure only applies if the requested sum does not exceed €100,000.

Access to the procedure is voluntary for clients but mandatory for intermediaries. The procedure is managed by an Arbitration Tribunal which comprises five arbitrators appointed as follows: one each by intermediaries and consumers' associations respectively, and three (including the President) by the Bank of Italy. The procedure can only be initiated by clients, and the action starts with a complaint and then follows a typical litigation path. The possible outcomes of the procedure, however, are peculiar in several respects. The litigated matter is limited to the claims brought about by the client; the intermediary can defend itself but, it seems, cannot advance counterclaims. If the tribunal upholds the client's complaint, it orders the intermediary to comply with its decision within a fixed date.

The ABF's decisions, however, are not binding as those of a court judge, and therefore if the broker fails to comply with the above-mentioned decisions, this bad behavior is made public both either through the ABF's website or through two national newspapers, at the intermediary's own expense. The law does not expressly provide for any appeal against the ABF's decisions. It does provide, however, that the decision does not prevent either party from returning to court or any other applicable dispute resolution system. This, together with the general, constitutionally granted right to justice, seems to imply that the intermediaries may request the redress of damages caused by the publication of their non-compliance to a decision if they can make a successful case that it was wrong on the merits.

5.2.6 The Banking and Financial Ombudsman

The Banking and Financial Ombudsman was set up in 1993 under an interbank agreement of 1992. It is an alternative Court, composed by five members, where the customer can try to resolve disputes with banks and financial intermediaries for free. The Ombudsman's powers are limited to matters relating to operations and investment services as well as other types of operations not covered by Title VI of the Consolidated Law on Banking (i.e. consumer credit and payment services), and its value jurisdiction is up €100,000.

To start the procedure, the consumer has to submit a written application to the ombudsman's offices. The application must be signed by the consumer who may, if he so wishes, be assisted by a lawyer, an accountant or an adviser. Before lodging a complaint with the Ombudsman, the consumer must first lodge a complaint with the bank concerned. However, if this procedure has not been followed, the Ombudsman's office will forward the complaint to the bank which has 60 days (90 in the event of financial transactions) to respond. The Ombudsman has unofficial investigatory powers so it draws up an adversarial report with the bank and obtains all the documentation considered necessary. After evaluated all documents the Ombudsman issues a reasoned decision which may concern only compensation for damages sustained by the applicant. The decision is not binding between the parties, who are however free, if unsatisfied, to apply before the ordinary courts.

The arrangements for financial out-of-court redress, however, vary from country to country—and there are some significant gaps. Most other member states still have separate ombudsmen schemes for the various areas of financial services. In Belgium, for example, there are two banking ombudsmen, because they have a post-office bank as well as ordinary banks. But the most complicated is Germany, where they have four different types of banks with redress schemes at federal and regional levels. Altogether, they have 14 different banking ombudsman schemes. Although complaint-handling is generally quite well-developed for banking—it's often less so for insurance and investment. So, it's in those sectors that there are still quite a lot of gaps.

5.3 Court Remedies

The Italian legal system provides not only individual actions to ascertain and block the unlawful broker's activities, but also different kinds of collective remedies with the aim to handle those claims that concern a plurality of individuals. Further to the cumulative action, where multiple plaintiffs may grant the same lawyer proxies to act on their behalf against the same defendant in the same proceedings, the Consumer Code sets forth rules for both an injunctive Class Action and for a Class Action for monetary recovery. As a matter of law, pursuant to Art. 140 of the Consumer Code, consumer associations can bring representative action for injunctive relief in favor of all consumers (not only association members), asking for the cessation of unlawful conduct (the so called "Representative Action");

moreover, pursuant to Art. 140*bis* of the Consumer Code, each member of the same category may start a Class Action seeking compensation for damages and/or restitution of undue payments.

5.3.1 Collective Injunctions

Highly recommended by the European legislation,[75] collective injunctions represent an efficient alternative redress to ordinary individual claims. The Directive on Injunctions (Directive No. 2009/22/EC) ensures the defense of the collective interests of consumers in the internal market by providing means to bring action for the cessation of infringements of consumer rights.[76] The consumers (that is, consumer representative body, excluding individual claimants) can thus claim interest damaged by unlawful practices carried out by professionals infringing European law, asking for the cessation or prohibiting defendants from any infringement, requiring accordingly adequate measures to eliminate the effects caused by that infringement as well as compensation for damages and loss suffered.

By contrast, the Italian financial legislation grants standing to consumer associations representing collective consumer interests against any violations of investment services activities. So, for instance, Art. 32*bis* of the Consolidated Law on Finance refers to Arts. 139 and 140 of the Italian Consumer Code, and both provisions regulate collective injunctions issued as redress for damages.

i. ***Area of application***

Consumer associations (officially registered with the Ministry of the Economic Development) may initiate representative actions to stop behavior prejudicial to the interests of the consumers and users and/or to adopt the measures aimed at amending and/or removing the harmful effect. Pursuant to Art. 37 of the Consumer Code, a representative action may be further started to obtain the cessation of the use of unfair terms and conditions in consumer contracts causing a significant imbalance in the parties' rights and obligations, to the disadvantage of consumers. The procedure starts with a formal warning notice, sent by the consumer associations, in which has given a term of at least 15 days to cease the challenged behavior. The procedure is the one of an ordinary civil trial; accordingly, class actions for injunctive relief are tried and decided by a single Judge. The extension of the class is defined by the plaintiff claim and the Judge can also order interim and urgency measures anticipating the decision. It worth to notice that the only reliefs available in the class actions are injunctive reliefs, whilst monetary compensation is not possible. The decision has effect on all the class members.

5.3.2 Class Actions

The class action came into force since the beginning of 2010. This new legal institute allows each consumer to act for the protection of a determined class of persons' rights, also through consumer associations. Art. 49 of Law no. 99/2009 amending article 140*bis* of Consumers' Code,[77] regulates the class action. The same article also provides that the abovementioned action can be applied only regarding the offenses completed after the date of entry into force of Law No. 99/2009 (therefore, after 15 August 2009). As a preliminary matter, it should be highlighted that Art. 140*bis* Consumer Code sufficiently defines the range of application of the collective redress procedure: the subjective range is restricted to "consumers and users of public services", whilst the objective range of application is limited only to specific situations. It had been argued whether investors might be included under the definition of 'consumer' (as intended by Art. 3 of the Consumer Code), and thus under the range of subjective application of class actions, or no. While previous drafts of the law dealing with class actions did contain a clear reference to investors, in the present version of Art. 140*bis*, all references to investors have been removed.

i. ***Area of Application***

Pursuant to Art. 140*bis* of the Consumer Code, the Class Action aims to protect: (a) the contractual rights of a plurality of consumers and users who find themselves in an identical situation vis-à-vis the same defendant, including the rights related to agreements entered into through standard forms and conditions; (b) the identical rights that end-users of a certain product have vis-à-vis the related manufacturer, even without any direct contractual relationship (such as product liability); and (c) the identical rights to compensation for the prejudice suffered by the same consumers and users as a consequence of unfair business practices or unfair competition".

It is argued whether the extension of the Class Action is applicable to the financial products, and therefore to the investors. As a matter of law, the investors have their own regulation (the Consolidated Law on Finance), and there is no sense to provide this 'category' of another redress. However, Art. 32*bis* of the Consolidated Law on Finance refers to "collective injunctions" (orders), rather to "class actions for damages". By the same token, consumer credit statutory regulations are dealt with under Arts. 121 and ss. of the Consolidated Law on Finance, thus remaining outside the coverage range of class actions under the Consumer Code. Although the literal meaning - as well as the overall framework of the statutory provisions—do not leave any further objection to the argument excluding investors from class actions, this argument is nonetheless still not convincing.[78] However, since the provisions concerning the distance marketing of consumer financial services has been introduced into the Consumer Code, accordingly the financial services providing the distance selling methods should implicitly be included within the area of application of Art. 140*bis* of Consumer Code, and a Class Actions concerning that services can be thus brought.

ii. ***The Procedure***

Pursuant to Art. 140*bis* of the Consumer Code, all class members may start a Class Action acting as a class representative, also through consumers' associations or committees. The claim is put forward with a writ of summons, notified also to the office of the Public Prosecutor at the Court in charge, who may only intervene for the judgment on admissibility. Upon first hearing, the Court shall decide by order on the admissibility of the claim; however, it may suspend judgment when there is an ongoing inquest before an independent Authority on the facts which are relevant to the decision, or a trial before the administrative judge. The claim is declared inadmissible if clearly unfounded or there is a conflict of interest, if the judge does not recognize the identity of the individual rights, and when the proposing party seems incapable of adequately protecting the class's interests.[79] If instead the claim is declared admissible, the Court sets the terms and methods of the most appropriate form of public notice in the order with which it admits the action, so that those belonging to the class can join promptly. By the same order the Court: (a) determine the characteristics of the individual rights involved in the judgment, specifying the criteria according to which individuals seeking to join are included in the class or must be regarded as excluded from the lawsuit; (b) establish a peremptory time limit that does not exceed one hundred and twenty days from the deadline for public notification. By this date, the adhesion contracts shall be lodged at the registry, even by the claimant.[80]

The order with which the Court admits the action also determines the course of the procedure. In the same or subsequent order, which can be modified or revoked at any time, the Court may prescribe measures aimed at preventing undue repetitions or complications in the presentation of evidence or arguments. If the Court grants the claim, it shall issue a verdict by which the final amounts due to those who have joined the act shall be paid, or shall establish the homogeneous calculation criterion to pay these sums. As far as the kind of recoverable damages possible, the Italian legal system aims at consenting the full recovery of all the suffered damages, both economical (pecuniary loss, out-of-pocket expenses, loss of profit) and non-economical. Under the Italian law, non-economic damages include: (a) biological damages (which represent all damages to the psycho-physical integrity of a person, directly relating to the health of such person and as such can be proven by way of medical assessments), (b) moral damages (pain and sufferance), and (c) the so-called "existential damages" (any event which impacts on the normal life or on the relationships of a person and which negatively affects the existence of such person in a consistent manner).

Moral and existential damages are recoverable only in cases provided for by the law, mainly in cases of criminal offences (Art. 2059 of the Italian Civil Code) or breach of human rights recognized by the Italian Constitution. All damages suffered, however, have to be a direct consequence of the defendant's behavior, so 'indirect' damages are not recoverable. The decision becomes enforceable one hundred and eighty days from publication, and the ruling establishes that the trial is also binding upon the members. After the decision, no further class action can be put forward for the same facts and against the same company after the closing date for joining assigned by the judge, but single action of those individuals who do not join collective action can be brought without any prejudice.

5.4 A Way Forward for the Italian Financial Framework in EU?

It seems that in the Italian system we find a growing need for protection of weaker parties, also as regards financial contracts. Different remedies have thus been introduced in order to provide adequate investor protection. On the one hand, in fact, case law shows a certain tendency to act against non-transparent behavior by economic actors/operators and, on the other, of the legislator (or delegated authorities) to establish a set of rules allowing consumers to attack the "stronghold" of banking interests. In the same vein, several legislative provisions, such as the so-called "Decreto Bersani-bis" successively confirmed by a Parliamentary Act (Law n° 126/2008), introduced important changes concerning loans by giving a new basis to the relationship between the client and the bank, by granting the former new advantages. Class actions have thus been allowed under Article 32-bis of the T.U.F. applying Articles 139 and 140 of the Consumer Code to consumer associations. Finally, recent legislative and regulatory provisions have introduced an indemnity guarantee fund as well as a no-fault fund, thus creating an alternative compensatory system aimed at compensating damages suffered by a general category defined as "non professional" savers/investors (L. n° 262, 28 December 2005, n. 262 Disposizioni per la tutela del risparmio e la disciplina dei mercati finanziari, as implemented by D.lgs. n. 179/2007 and by Consob Regulation n. 16190/2007).

All these provisions have lead the Italian financial framework to an efficient and well-regulated system, providing consumers with five key elements: (i) Transparency, by providing full, plain, adequate and comparable (and understandable) information about the prices, terms and conditions (and inherent risks) of financial products and services; (ii) Choice, by ensuring fair, non-coercive and reasonable practices in the selling and advertising of financial products and services, and collection of payments; (iii) Redress, by providing inexpensive and speedy mechanisms to address complaints and resolve disputes; (iv) Privacy, by ensuring protection over third-party access to personal financial information; and (v) Trust, by ensuring that financial firms act professionally and deliver what they promise, (vi) Financial education, by providing consumers the knowledge needed to an appropriate use of financial products and services; (vi) ADR, providing several out-of-court procedures.

6 Final Remarks

The global financial crisis and its origins revealed some fundamental flaws in financial consumer protection frameworks. One of the main reasons for the negative development of the financial services market was the lack of consumer confidence. In turn, the main reason for lack of consumer confidence in the financial service scenario was a lack of mechanisms for protection of consumer rights. Based on an assessment of the current situation, this paper has shown alternatives ways and mechanisms for the protection of consumer provisions, with respect to financial services in the bank sector. In analyzing the current situation and listing a set of effective mechanisms for protection of financial consumers, this paper has also discussed the main impact on the Italian system of the European legislation concerning financial markets. Such impact has consisted in rendering financial institutions more transparent and therefore more trustworthy, and in improving the relationship between public institutions and citizens.

However, it is argued that the Italian's mechanism for financial consumer protection cannot be the function of one actor alone, it must be based on the common development of multiple market actors. Different actors, thus, must work together in establishing a framework for the protection of financial consumers' rights, build a system that will be effective in the long run, restore consumers' confidence in the financial sector, improve its public reputation, and finally, to shift the development model of the insurance sector from one of expansion to one of intensification. The courts will also play a very significant role since they will be called to decide, in case of litigation, whether the granting of credit was responsible or not. The supervisory authorities, also, will play a crucial part concerning the supervision of compliance with these provisions and the imposition of sanctions in case of infringements of the national provisions. In this regard, Governments, financial institutions and agencies of Member States, should call for the establishment of an unified European agency or advisor board with the aims to require to financial institutions of Member States to regularly demonstrate, through third-party testing of random samples of their customers, that a good proportion of their customers know, at the time of the transaction, the key pertinent "costs, benefits, and risks" of the products they are buying. This preliminary investigation, in fact, can demonstrate both the customer comprehension the financial products involved and bought, and a precondition for the financial institution that must meet before enforcing burden terms to consumers.

Notes

1. For the scope of this paper financial transactions mean banking and financial products.
2. Italian Institute of Statistical Research and Public Opinion Analysis.
3. The European House-Ambrosetti-Consorzio Patti Chiari: L'educazione finanziaria in Italia: La prima misurazione del livello di cultura finanziaria degli italiani. Roma 25 November 2008.
4. The Telegraph Journal, finance section, 7 January 2013.
5. See https://yougov.co.uk/news/2012/06/07/britains-financial-literacy/.
6. You can get information on the EU Expert Group on http://www.ec.europa.eu/.
7. The EDFE was discontinued and taken offline on 17 June 2011. However, a survey of financial literacy schemes in the EU is available at: http://ec.europa.eu/internal_market/finservices-retail/docs/capability/report_survey_en.pdf.

8. The Commission's on-line consumer education website to help teachers to incorporate financial matters into the school curriculum. With respect to consumer education in schools, the Commission will promote the sharing of best practices through an interactive community site for teachers. This new community site will replace the dolceta.eu site, and offer a platform for exchange of experiences, dialogue and teaching materials on consumer education.
9. Senate Bill n. 1288, XVI Legislature, filed on 17 December 2008, assigned to the 10th Permanent Commission (Trade, Tourism and Industry) on 4 February 2009.
10. Council Resolution on a preliminary program of the European Economic Community for a consumer protection and information policy, OJ C-092, 25 April 1975.
11. The Directive 2004/39/EC of the European Parliament and of the Council of 21 April 2004 on Markets in Financial Instruments has recently been recast in the framework of Directive 2014/65/EU (so-called MiFID 2), in an effort to incorporate the significant amendments made to the text. MiFID 2 provides for a new legal framework that better regulates trading activities on financial markets and enhances investor protection. The new rules revise the legislation currently in place and will apply from January 2017.
12. The Directive 2002/65/EC of the European Parliament and of the Council of 23 September 2002 concerning the Distance Marketing of Consumer Financial Services, and whose text contains a direct obligation to inform customers of any risks involved in the financial services being offered, has been amended by the Directive 2005/29/EC of the European Parliament and of the Council of 11 May 2005, concerning unfair business-to-consumer commercial practices in the internal market. In this regard, Article 9 (Unsolicited services) of Directive 2002/65/EC has been replaced by the following Article 9 of the Directive 2005/29/EC: "*Given the prohibition of inertia selling practices laid down in Directive 2005/29/EC of 11 May 2005 of the European Parliament and of the Council concerning unfair business-to-consumer commercial practices in the internal market and without prejudice to the provisions of Member States' legislation on the tacit renewal of distance contracts, when such rules permit tacit renewal, Member States shall take measures to exempt the consumer from any obligation in the event of unsolicited supplies, the absence of a reply not constituting consent*. Moreover, the Directive 2002/65/EC has been amended by the Directive 2007/64/EC of the European Parliament and of the Council of 13 November 2007 on payment services in the internal market. In this regard, Article 4 of the Directive 2002/65/EC has been added: "*Where Directive 2007/64/EC of the European Parliament and of the Council of 13 November 2007 on payment services in the internal market is also applicable, the information provisions under Article 3(1) of this Directive, with the exception of paragraphs (2)(c) to (g), (3)(a), (d) and (e), and (4)(b), shall be replaced with Articles 36, 37, 41 and 42 of that Directive*". Additionally, Article 8 ("Payment by card") of the Directive 2002/65/EC has been deleted.

13. Pursuant to the Directive 2002/65, art. 2d) consumer means "any natural person who, in distance contracts covered by this Directive, is acting for purposes which are outside his trade, business or profession".
14. Recital 29 states: "This Directive is without prejudice to extension by Member States, in accordance with Community law, of the protection provided by this Directive to non-profit organizations and persons making use of financial services in order to become entrepreneurs".
15. The aim of the Directive 2004/109/EC of the European Parliament and of the Council of 15 December 2004 is to establish minimum requirements regarding to the financial information distribution all over the European Union and an increase in transparency at the capital markets and in investor protection to meet information deficits in a developing financial market environment. This Directive has been amended by the Directive 2010/78/EU of the European Parliament and of the Council of 24 November 2010 establishing a European System of Financial Supervisors (ESFS), consisting of a network of national financial supervisors working in tandem with new European Supervisory Authorities (ESAs), created by transforming the existing European supervisory committees into a European Banking Authority (EBA), a European Insurance and Occupational Pensions Authority (EIOPA), and a European Securities and Markets Authority (ESMA), thereby combining the advantages of an overarching European framework for financial supervision with the expertise of local micro-prudential supervisory bodies that are closest to the institutions operating in their jurisdictions. In addition, this Directive has established a European Systemic Risk Board (ESRB), to monitor and assess potential threats to financial stability that arise from macro-economic developments and from developments within the financial system as a whole. The ESRB provides an early warning of system-wide risks that may be building up and, where necessary, issue recommendations for action to deal with these risks.
16. The Directive 2003/71/EC of the European Parliament and of the Council on the prospectus to be published when securities are offered to the public or omitted to trading came into effect on 31 December 2003, has been also amended by the Directive 2010/78/EU.
17. See http://ec.europa.eu/finance/payments/framework/index_en.htm (last access: 15 March 2016).
18. On 10 February 2016, the European Commission has proposed a one-year extension to the entry into application of the revised Markets in Financial Instruments Directive (MiFID II). *See* http://europa.eu/rapid/press-release_IP-16-265_en.htm?locale=en (last access 15 March 2016).
19. Older legislation in this area: Directive 2002/65/EC concerning distance marketing of consumer financial services, and Directive 2008/48/EC on credit agreements for consumers, are already in force.
20. In 2011, the Commission issued a Recommendation on access to a basic payment account, where it presented general principles regarding access to basic payment accounts by European consumers in all European Union

countries, stating that access should not be made conditional on the purchase of additional services.

21. However, the Directive 2002/65/EC makes clear in Recital 13 that Member States should remain competent, in accordance with Union law, to apply the provisions of this Directive to areas not falling within its scope. Member States may therefore maintain or introduce national legislation corresponding to the provisions of this Directive, or certain of its provisions, in relation to contracts that fall outside the scope of this Directive. This goes on to provide a number of examples, which include extending the application of the Directive to persons falling outside the Directive's definition of "consumer", such as small and medium-sized enterprises.
22. ECJ judgment of 14 March 2003, C-361/89—*Criminal proceedings v Patrice Di Pinto* [1991] ECR I-01189. See also *Cape Snc v Idealservice Srl*, C—541/99 [2002] All ER (EC) 657, [2003] 1 CMLR 42, [2002] ECR 1–9049.
23. Directive 2013/11/EU of the European Parliament and of the Council of 21 May 2013 on alternative dispute resolution for consumer disputes and amending Regulation (EC) No 2006/2004 and Directive 2009/22/EC (Directive on consumer ADR) OJ L 165/63.
24. The Necessity of Alternative Dispute Resolution systems in Romania Best practices in the Member States. How to build up confidence between consumers and businesses? Report of 14 May, 2009. Available at: www.eccromania.ro/media/pdf/raport_conferinta_adr_en.pdf.
25. Italian financial regulation has been traditionally organized along functional lines. Financial services activities are divided among four main industries: banking, investment services, asset management, and insurance. Each industry has its own supervisor, legal framework, and rules. For the scope of this paper the banking sector will be dealt with only.
26. Legislative Decree No. 385/1993. A Legislative Decree under the Italian legislation is act having force of law adopted by the Government under authorization of the Parliament (Art. 76, Italian Constitution). It is often usually employed in cases of highly technical matters.
27. Legislative Decree No. 58/1998, as amended by Law no. 208 of 28 December 2015.
28. The text was approved by the Italian Council of Ministers of 22 July 2005 and promulgated on 6 September 2005 (published in Italian Official Gazette on 8 October 2005, entered in force since 23 October 2005).
29. See Art. 124*bis* and Art. 125 of the Consolidated Law on Banking.
30. The form includes key details such as the type of credit, the annual percentage rate, the number and frequency of payments, the total amount owed etc. Receiving the same form from each credit provider will allow consumers to easily compare and choose the best credit offered.
31. See Art. 118, paragraph 2, of the Consolidated Law on Banking.
32. Pursuant to Art. 1, lett. r), of the Consolidated Law on Finance "authorized intermediaries" means investment companies (SIM), EU investment companies with branches in Italy, non-EU investment companies, asset management

companies, harmonized asset management companies with branch in Italy, SICAVs and financial intermediaries entered in the register referred to in Art. 107 of the Consolidated Law on Banking and Italian banks, EU banks with branches in Italy and non-EU banks, authorized to engage in investment services or activities.

33. In this context, the term 'customers' include either consumers or professionals.
34. 'Financial products' shall mean financial instruments and any other form of investment of financial nature as provided for in article 1, letter u), of the Consolidated Law on Finance.
35. In fact, the Consolidated Law on Banking contains general rules protecting the "client", and some specific provisions on the "consumer" applicable on the basis of the consumer definition.
36. See Consob Resolution No. 16622/2008 on "Measures on short sales of securities aimed at ensuring the orderly conduct of trading and the integrity of the market".
37. See Consob Resolution No. 16190/07. This Resolution and annexed regulation were published in ordinary section no. 222 of Official Gazette no. 255 of 2.11.2007 and in CONSOB, Fortnightly Bulletin 10.2, October 2007. The Consob Resolution No. 16190/07 was later amended by Resolutions no. 16736 of 18 December 2008, no. 17581 of 3 December 2010 and no. 18210 of 9 May 2012, and no. 19094 of 8 January 2015).
38. See Art. 39 Consob Resolution No. 16190/07.
39. See Art. 40 Consob Resolution No. 16190/07.
40. Decree-Law No. 7 dated 31 January 2007, converted in Law No. 40, dated 2 April 2007.
41. Pursuant to Art. 2 of the Consumer Code the fundamental rights of the consumers are: (a) health protection; (b) product and service safety; (c) adequate information and correct advertising; (c-*bis*) exercise of commercial practices according to principles of good faith, correctness and loyalty; (d) education to consumption; (e) correctness, transparency and equity in contractual relations; (f) promotion and development of free associations between consumers and users; (g) delivery of quality and efficient public services.
42. The Directive 2002/65/CE concerning the Distance Marketing of Consumer Financial Services has been directly inserted as a new section of the Consumer Code (Section IV-*bis* of Chapter I of Title III of Part III: Art. 67*bis* to 67*vicies-bis*). The beneficiary (Art. 67*ter* 1ett.d) of this protective legislation is thus the "consumer".
43. Pursuant to Art. 3, paragraph 1, sub-paragraph a), of the Consumer Code, "consumer" means "any natural person who is acting for purposes which are outside his trade, business or profession".
44. Amato, C., Perfumi, C. *Financial Investors as Consumers and their protection: Recent Italian legislation from a European perspective.* In Op. J. Vol. 3/2010, Paper n. 3. (2010), pp. 6–24.

45. Art. 121, letter (b), of the Consolidated Law on Banking defines consumer: "any natural person who is acting for purposes which are outside his own trade, business and profession".
46. The same definition is contained in the Art. 1469*bis* of the Italian Civil Code: "a consumer is any natural person who, in contracts covered by this provision, is acting for purposes which are outside his trade, business or profession". This interpretation run in accordance with the purpose of the Directive 93/13/CEE on Unfair Terms in Consumer Contracts that expressly applies only to the persons acting for purposes which are outside trade, business or profession.
47. Tribunale Roma, 20 of October 1999, Giustizia civile 2000, I, 2117.
48. Supreme Court, 25 July 2001, No. 10127, I Contratti 2002, 338.
49. Ebers. M. *The Notion of "Consumer"*. Consumer Law. Compendium, Part III. (2007), p. 13.
50. Corte Costituzionale, 22 November 2002, No. 469, Giustizia civile 2003, 290 *et seq.*
51. Cass. 14 April 2000, n. 4843, in Foro Italiano, (2000), I, 3196; Cass. 25 July 2001, n. 10127, in Giurisprudenza italiana, (2002), 543.
52. The United Sections of the Italian Supreme Court, sentence n. 13905 of 3 June 2013.
53. See Supreme Court of Cassation, February 14, 2012, no. 2065, and March 22, 2012, no. 4564.
54. See Consob Communication no. DIN/12030993 of April 19, 2012.
55. *Jus Poenitendi* is the right of rescission or cancellation. The Consumer is the sole party entitled to cancel any order under a Contract in accordance with the Consumer Code, Art. 64 *et seq.* and obtain repayment of the sums paid at the moment of purchase. A Professional is not entitled to any such cancellation right.
56. Most of the Italian contemporary legislation on ADR—except for labor mediation and judicial conciliation in civil litigation—has its origin in Institutions of the European Community. One of the main document in this path may be identified in the "Commission Green Paper on access of consumers to justice and the settlement of consumer disputes in the single market" of 16 November 1993. This document conceived with the official purpose "to enable all the Community's consumers to gain access to justice and to deal with cross-border disputes" focused on both in-court and out-of-court dispute resolution procedures.
57. Amato, C. *Financial Investors as Consumers in a European Perspective* (2012), p. 8.
58. See Tribunale Udine, decision No. 376 of 5 March 2010.
59. See Corte di Appello di Torino, decision No. 615 of 10 April 2012.
60. See Tribunale Ravenna, decision 29 May 2010, available at: http://www.unijuris.it/sites/default/files/sentenze/Tribunale%20di%20Ravenna%2029%20maggio%202010.pdf.

61. On 4th September 2012, the Bank of Italy published a consultation paper containing new rules on prudential supervision and risk containment for banks, which include, *inter alia*: (i) the establishment of an internal alert procedure; (ii) clearer provisions on the role of the chief risk officer; and (iii) the assignment to the banks' board of tasks originally belonging to the surveillance committee established pursuant to Legislative Decree 8th June 2001, No. 231. As result of the public consultation, some additional chapters (namely, nos. 7 ("Internal controls system"), 8 ("Informative system") and 9 ("Business continuity")) have been introduced in the Bank of Italy Circular 27th December 2006, No. 263 ("New Regulations for the Prudential Supervision of Banks on Highly Significant Transactions"), laying down new prudential supervisory instructions for Banks (See Bank of Italy on 2 July 2013 with the 15th amendment of Circular No. 263 of 27th December 2006).
62. The Resolution and annexed regulation were published in the Official Gazette No. 176 of 30 July 2012 and in CONSOB's fortnightly bulletin No. 7, 2nd July 2012.
63. Pursuant to the opinion of the Council of State of 20 October 2011, the Chamber without subjectivity, is "classified [...] as a technical body, instrumental to Consob but not separate to it" and whose functions, provided autonomously, in any case belong to Consob, which is the final arbiter of the related effects. The regulatory changes introduced in the more general system of civil mediation aimed at conciliation pursuant to Italian Legislative Decree No. 28 of 4 March 2010, the related enactment decrees of the Ministry of Justice, and the experience accrued in the overall Chamber activities derive from Consob.
64. Under Art. 1, lett. b), of the Consob Resolution No. 16763, of 29 December 2008 (as amended by Consob with Resolution no. 18275 of 18 July 2012), "investors" shall mean investors other than the counterparties defined under Art. 6, paragraph 2*quater* d) and the professional clients under paragraphs 2*quinquies* and 2*sexies* of Consolidated Law on Finance as amended.
65. Under Art. 1, lett. c), of the Consob Resolution No. 16763, of 29 December 2008 (as amended by Consob with Resolution no. 18275 of 18 July 2012), "Intermediaries" shall mean the persons entitled pursuant to Art. 1, paragraph 1, let. r), of Consolidate Law on Finance, as amended, and the company Poste Italiane - Divisione Servizi di Banco Posta—authorized pursuant to Art. 2 of Italian Presidential Decree No. 144 of 14 March 2001.
66. See Art. 12 of the Consob Resolution No. 16763 of 29 December 2008, as amended.
67. Pursuant to Art. 810 (Appointment of the Arbitrators) of the Italian Code of Civil Procedure: "Where, in accordance with the provisions of the submission to arbitration or of the arbitration clause, the arbitrators are to be appointed by the parties, each party, by means of a bailiff's notification may inform the other party of its appointment of an arbitrator or arbitrators and request said other party to name its own arbitrators. The party so requested shall, within twenty days, serve notice of the personal data regarding the arbitrator or arbitrators

appointed by it. Failing this, the party which has made the request may petition the President of the Court in whose district the arbitration has its seat, to make the appointment. If the parties have not yet determined the seat of arbitration, the petition is presented to the President of the Court in the place where the submission to arbitration or the contract to which the arbitration clause refers has been executed or, if such place is abroad, to the President of the Court of Rome. The President, having heard the other party where necessary, shall issue his order against which there shall be no recourse. The same provision is applied where the submission to arbitration or the arbitration clause has entrusted the appointment of one or more arbitrators to the judicial authority or where, if entrusted to a third party, that third party has failed to act".

68. The Legislative Decree No. 28/2010 has been amended by the Law 9th August 2013, No. 98, converting the Law-Decree 21st June 2013, No. 69 (the so-called "Decreto del Fare"). The main changes concern, *inter alia*,: (i) the introduction (based on decision no. 13905 of the Joint Chambers of the Supreme Court of Cassation of 3rd June 2013) in Sect. 30, paragraph 6, of the Consolidated Law on Finance – which provides a withdrawal right for investors (the so-called "*jus poenitendi*") in case of door-to-door selling - of a new period according to which the mentioned regime is applicable, as from 1st September 2013, not only to the services of placement of financial instruments and portfolio management, but also to the dealing for own account (pursuant to Sect. 1, paragraph 5, lett. a), of the Consolidated Law on Finance); (ii) the reintroduction, as from 20th September 2013, of the mandatory mediation in civil and commercial disputes (including those related to banking, financial and insurance contracts). As a result, the parties to a dispute must resort (assisted by a lawyer) to a mediator in an attempt to reach an out-of-court settlement.
69. The European Council has in late April 2013 adopted two key legislative measures regarding dispute resolution. This includes a Directive on alternative dispute resolution and a Regulation on online dispute resolution. The aim is to offer consumers fast and cost- effective means to resolve disputes with businesses.
70. See Art. 4 Ministerial Decree No. 180/2010 (as amended by the Ministerial Decree No. 145/2011) which entrusts the examination of applicants' professionalism and efficiency to the person in charge.
71. Those matters include: (i) banking and financial agreements; (ii) rights *in rem*; (iii) division of assets; (iv) inheritance; (v) family estates; (vi) eases of real property or going concerns; (vii) gratuitous loans for use; (viii) medical liability; (ix) defamation in the press and other media; (x) insurance.
72. See Italian Constitutional Court, decisions No. 82/1992, No. 376/2000 and No. 403/2007.
73. The case was heard before the Italian Constitutional Court on 23rd October 2012, and on 6th December 2012 the decision was issued.
74. A decree-law is issued in special and urgent cases by the Government. It must be presented on the same day to Parliament for conversion into law, if it is not converted within sixty days of its publication it loses validity retroactively, but

the Parliament may regulate by means of law any relation that have arisen by virtue of unconverted decree.

75. See Directive on Injunctions 2009/22/EC.
76. For the purposes of the Directive 2009/22/EC an infringement means any act contrary to the Directives listed in Annex I, as transposed into the internal legal order of the Member States which harms the collective interests. The Annex I includes the Directive on distance marketing of financial services, but any other violations of financial services legislation are not mentioned.
77. Art. 140*bis* of the Italian Consumer Code was introduced by Art. 2, paragraph 446, of Law No. 244/2007.
78. Amato, C., Perfumi, C. *Financial Investors as Consumers and their protection: Recent Italian legislation from a European perspective.* In Op. J. Vol. 3/2010, Paper n. 3. (2010), p. 10.
79. See Tribunale of Torino, 27 May 2010, ord.—Est. Panzani—R. rappresentato da Codacons c. Intesa Sanpaolo s.p.a.
80. See Art. 140*bis*, paragraph 9, Consumer Code.

Vincenzo Senatore is an Italian licensed Attorney, an English Solicitor of the Senior Courts of England & Wales, and a Notary Public for the State of California. He is the founding partner of GSA Law Firm, with main office in Rome. Vincenzo graduated from the University of Naples "Federico II" (Italy), Law School, and University of Salzburg (Austria), and obtained his LL.M. degree in International Business Transaction and Trade Law at the Catholic University of America, Washington D.C. Vincenzo research touches on various aspects related to Financial Consumer Protection and Workers' Compensation Insurance in Europe.

Chapter 9
Financial Consumer Protection in Japan

Hongmu Lee and Satoshi Nakaide

1 Financial Consumer

1.1 General Introduction

Financial services play a critical role in society at large, enabling individuals, families and businesses to thrive. When a buyer utilizes services from a financial institution, there is a monetary transaction that takes place with an expectation to gain a profit in the future. There are various risks inherent in the process based on the time between paying and receiving money. It is often very difficult for consumers to understand the details and risks involved in these transactions[1] and as a result, protection for financial consumers is a very important issue. The goal of financial protection is not easily attained through free competition in the marketplace. Thus, the government is justified to intervene in the market and regulate the conduct of the players in the market.

In general, there is no comprehensive Act or law[2] for the protection of financial consumers in Japan. Various laws regulate relevant aspects of financial services from the viewpoint of protecting financial consumers. Acts regulating financial business, such as the Insurance Business Act or the Banking Act, contain some rules governing the protection of financial consumers. For example, the Financial Instruments and Exchange Act and other Acts set out rules on the sales of financial products for the protection of financial consumers. The Consumer Contract Act is an Act to regulate contractual matters to protect consumers; it also applies to financial services contracts. The Insurance Act regulates insurance contracts and contains rules to protect consumers.

H. Lee · S. Nakaide (✉)
Waseda University, Tokyo, Japan
e-mail: nakaide@waseda.jp

© Springer Nature Singapore Pte Ltd. 2018

T.-J. Chen (ed.), *An International Comparison of Financial Consumer Protection*,
https://doi.org/10.1007/978-981-10-8441-6_9

The Financial Services Agency (FSA) is a regulatory body whose primary function is to protect the financial consumer. The FSA responsibilities include supervision of financial services, declaring that the protection of depositors, policyholders, investors in the securities and others exist at the core of its responsibility.[3]

There is no legal definition for the term 'financial consumer' in Japan, as there is no comprehensive Act on the protection of financial consumers. In various Acts, more specific words are used to designate the user of financial services, such as customer, depositor, policyholder, assured and investor, to denote the requirement of the law more precisely.

1.2 Population and Ageing Society

It is important to review the demographic data of Japan's population in order to understand the needs of protecting the consumer of financial services.

The population of Japan is 126.9 million as of the 1st December 2016.[4] Among them, shares of the people from 0 to 14 years old is 12.5%, from 15 to 64 is 60.8%, over 65 is 27.1%. It is anticipated that the ratio of the population aged over 65 years will continue to rise in the future and will reach 33.4% in 2035.[5] This means that one among three will be a person aged over 65 years in Japan.

The number of people over 100 years is 65,692 as of September 2016.[6] The average life span is 80.79 years for a man and 87.05 years for a woman and it is during this span of years that the trend is rising as shown in Fig. 1.

The ageing population depends heavily on various financial services including pension. The older population tends to be more vulnerable to fraud or other mischiefs. The number of frauds on financial consumers is regrettably increasing in

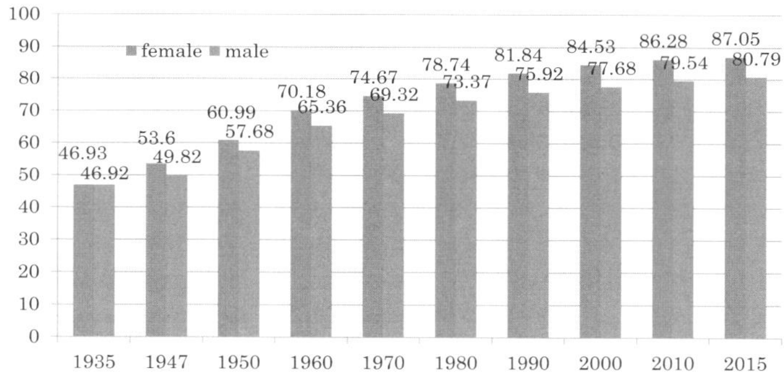

Fig. 1 Trend of the average life span. *Note* The chart is made by the authors using the data of the ministry of health, labor and welfare

Japan and there are many complaints and claims on the selling of financial services. These complaints urge regulators to strengthen their policies in order to protect financial consumers.

2 Financial Consumer Protection System (Software)

2.1 Overview

As stated above, there exists no comprehensive Act on the protection for financial consumers. Instead, various Acts regulate the business and conduct of financial institutions, as well as their financial services and contracts. These Acts are classified as an Act governing financial services in general or as a specific Act overseeing a certain type of financial service.[7] In both areas and as a general trend, Acts are amended periodically to reinforce the protection of financial consumers. In addition to the various Acts, regulations, guidelines and manuals on the business of financial services issued by the relevant offices of the Ministry play an important role. The following are the major Acts relating to the protection of financial consumers.[8]

2.2 Consumer Contract Act

In 2000, the Consumer Contract Act was enacted[9] and it applies to any type of consumer contract except a labour contract. Therefore, it applies to any contract offering a financial service that is accepted by a consumer. The Act protects the interests of consumers,[10] by permitting a consumer to rescind the manifestation of its intention to offer or accept a contract when the consumer has misunderstood or was distressed by certain acts of business operators,[11] and by nullifying any clause that exempts business operators from liability for damages or that otherwise unfairly harm the interests of consumers. In addition, the Act gives to qualified consumer organizations the right to demand an injunction against a business operator in certain situations.

2.2.1 Rescission of Consumer Contract (Article 4)

The Act gives consumers a right to rescind the manifestation of the consumer's intention to offer or accept a consumer contract if either of the actions listed below caused the consumer to have a mistaken belief:

(i) Misrepresentation of an important matter,[12] such as a mistaken belief that the said misrepresentation is true or
(ii) Providing conclusive evaluations of future prices, amounts of money to be received and other uncertain items, including a mistaken belief that the content of the said conclusive evaluations is certain.

Consumers may also rescind the contract if a business operator shows only the advantages of an important matter and intentionally omits disadvantageous facts, causing the consumer to mistakenly believe the non-existence of such facts.

In addition to the above, consumers may rescind the contract if distressed because of (i) the business operator's failure to leave a consumer's residence or place of business or (ii) preventing a consumer from leaving a place.

2.2.2 Nullity of Consumer Contract Clauses (Article 8)

The following clauses in consumer contracts are void:

(i) Clauses which totally exempt a business operator from liability to compensate a consumer for damages arising from default by the business operator; or
(ii) Clauses which partially exempt a business operator from liability for damages arising from default by the business operator; or
(iii) Clauses which totally exempt a business operator from liability for damages to a consumer which arise from a tort pursuant to the provisions of the Civil Code; or
(iv) Clauses which partially exempt a business operator from liability for damages to a consumer arising from a tort pursuant to the provisions of the Civil Code; or
(v) Where a consumer contract is a contract for value and there exists a latent defect in the subject matter of the consumer contract the clause that totally excludes a business operator from liability to compensate a consumer for damages caused by such defect.

The Act makes certain clauses in the consumer contract void if:

(i) a clause stipulates an amount of liquidated damages and/or establishes a fixed penalty in the event of cancellation, wherein the total amount of damages and/or penalty exceed the normal amount of damages that would be caused to a business operator by the cancellation of a contract of the same type in accordance with the reason for the cancellation, the time of the cancellation, etc.; or
(ii) a clause that stipulates an amount of liquidated damages and/or establishes a fixed penalty in the event of a total or partial default by the customer, wherein

the total amount of damages and/or penalty exceeds the amount calculated by deducting the amount actually paid from the amount that should have been paid on the due date and multiplying the result by 14.6% per year in accordance with the number of days from the due date to the day on which the money is actually paid.

In addition, Article 10 nullifies any consumer contract clause that restricts the rights or expands the duties of the consumer more than the application of provisions unrelated to public order in the Civil Code, the Commercial Code (Act No. 48 of 1899) and any other laws and regulations that unilaterally impairs the interests of the consumer in violation of the principle of good faith.

2.2.3 Right to Demand an Injunction (Article 12)

In 2006, the Act was amended to introduce a remedy for group litigation by qualified consumer organizations. The Act was further amended in 2008 to widen its coverage. The method of group litigation aims at preventing the act of a business operator who may cause harm or similar losses to a number of consumers, even though the amount in each transaction is relatively small.

Where a business operator engages in or is likely to engage in such acts of soliciting many consumers, qualified consumer organizations are entitled to demand the operator in question to stop or prevent such acts. In order to stop or prevent such acts, qualified consumer organizations need to first make a written request to the business operator to cease making contracts or solicitations. One week after this formal written request, the qualified consumer organizations are allowed to bring litigation against the operator. If the business operator accepts the request within one week, the qualified consumer organizations are not allowed to file a lawsuit. Remedies for the qualified consumer organizations are limited to the injunction only—i.e. a demand to stop or prevent further actions. They are not allowed to bring litigation for damages against the business operator.

Qualified consumer organizations need to be approved by the Prime Minister and owe certain duties as stated in the Act.

2.3 Act on Sales, etc. of Financial Instruments

2.3.1 Overview

The Act on Sales, etc. of Financial Instruments[13] was enacted in 2000 to protect financial consumers. In the 1990s, a variety of financial products were introduced in the market along with the development of financial techniques, including foreign currency deposit, monetary trust, and derivatives. At the same time, the number of complaints from the customers of financial services increased partly because of the lack of adequate explanation of the products. While the regulatory law on banking or insurance business regulates the conduct of providers, it does not afford a remedy for the customer. For example, a customer could utilize tort law and claim damages under the Civil Code Article 709; however, the customer endured a long period of damages or harm before having the right to pursue legal action. The process for the consumer to pursue a claim was very difficult because it was necessary for the customer to prove the negligence of the financial service provider, the loss suffered, and causation between the negligence and the loss.

The Act made it a duty for a seller, or a provider, of financial products of various types[14] to explain material facts—i.e. risks involved in the relevant financial product. If a seller fails in the duty of explanation, the seller will be held liable for the loss to the customer. In addition, the Act made it an obligation for the seller to clearly state its policy in the sales of the financial products and to make it public. These rules are further explained below.

2.3.2 Duty to Explain Material Facts

Under the Act, the seller and any agent or intermediary has a duty to explain the following risks to the customer:

(i) Market risk: if the products involve any risk of deficit by the fluctuations of interest rate, exchange rate, stock market etc., the seller needs to explain its risk;
(ii) Credit risk: the seller needs to explain a bankruptcy risk if the product has such a risk; and
(iii) Period of execution right/limit of period for cancellation: if the period for executing a right or making a cancellation is confirmed, then the seller needs to explain it to the customer.

In addition to the above, a seller must not make any conclusive evaluation on uncertain matters or mislead the customer to believe the above risk matter as certain.

2.3.3 A Right to Claim Damages

The customer is entitled to claim damages against the seller if the seller fails to explain the above material facts and the customer suffers loss. The customer is entitled to damages if he/she proves the failure of explanation and the loss. The Act does not require the claimant to show the causation between the failure and the loss. The loss of principal is presumed to be the amount of loss suffered by the customer.

2.3.4 Solicitation Policy

The Act made it a duty for the seller of financial products to make a solicitation policy and make it open to the public. The policy must contain the following:

(i) Items to be considered in view of the knowledge, experience and asset of the customer.
(ii) Items to be considered as relating to the method of selling and time of selling.
(iii) Other items necessary to secure the sound transaction.

The seller needs to pay a non-penal fine if it fails this duty. It is expected that the seller would make an improvement in the sales of financial products as the solicitation policy may work as an important factor for the customer in choosing the seller.[15]

2.4 *Financial Instruments and Exchange Act*

2.4.1 Overview

In 1948, the Financial Instruments and Exchange Act was enacted[16] to regulate the financial markets in Japan. It was largely amended in 2006[17] to modernize the law and comprehensively cover various financial products.

The Act regulates the duty of disclosure of corporate affairs and other related matters. Furthermore, it regulates the necessary matters relating to persons who engage in financial instruments business and secures appropriate operation of financial instrument exchanges. The Act aims to ensure fairness in the issuance of the securities and transactions of financial instruments and facilitates the smooth distribution of securities as well as the fair price formation of financial instruments.

The Act covers a wide range of financial instruments including swap of currency, weather derivatives, etc. However, the rules on the deposit of foreign currency and variable pension insurance are excluded since they are stated in the Banking Act and Insurance Business Act, respectively, along with the rules laid down in the Financial Instruments and Exchange Act.

2.4.2 Main Regulations on the Process of Sales, Solicitation and Effecting Contracts

The following are the main points of the rules:

Principle or duty	Explanations
Principle of suitability	–Duty to sell the product which matches with the customer –Duty not to make any improper solicitation or any other improper conducts in the light of the knowledge, experience, asset and the purpose of the contract
Restrictions on advertisement	–Duty to not make any representation which differs from the facts on the prospect of profits significantly or any representations that greatly mislead the customer
Duty to provide document	–Duty to provide a document showing the structure of the financial product, risk involved, outlines of the contract, rough figure of commissions –Duty to state the risk in the document to state if the product involves a risk of incurring loss or a risk that the loss would exceed the amount of deposit or guarantee provided by the customer
Prohibited conducts	–Prohibition of the act to make a false statement or the act to solicit by providing a firm view on uncertain issues –Prohibition of the visit or phone call to the client who has not requested solicitation –Prohibition of the continuing solicitation to the client who expressed an intention to not enter into a contract
Prohibition of the loss compensation	–Prohibition of the compensation of the loss incurred by the transaction

Most of the rules in the Act of protecting customers are for the general investors and they do not apply to professional investors. Under the Act, an individual can be treated as a professional investor if he or she has more than one year of investment experience, possesses net assets exceeding 3 billion yen and has financial assets of investment nature of at least 3 billion yen.

The Act also introduced a duty for a company to publicize the quarterly reports and a duty to provide a confirmation document to guarantee the properness of the statements in the report.

The Act strengthened the penalty for the breach of the duty by introducing a criminal offence, fines, or surcharge depending on the breach.

2.5 The Act Concerning Protection of Personal Information

The Act concerning Protection of Personal Information[18] was introduced to protect personal information and extends protection to financial consumers. Any financial provider that possesses personal data exceeding 5,000 is not allowed to sell, transfer, or handle any other information beyond the extent that is necessary for achieving the purpose specified under the Act. The financial provider needs to obtain consent from the individual to use the data. In addition, the financial provider is required to maintain and protect accurate data.

2.6 *Duty of Explanation Under the General Law of the Civil Code*

Apart from the above Acts, the case law and academic theory are developing to protect the legal position of financial consumers in Japan. For example, variable life insurance policies were sold using bank loans and several judgements were issued against the sellers of those products based on the principle of good faith under the Civil Code. It is now generally accepted that the seller of financial products owes a duty of explanation because it largely affects the determination of the buyer who is reviewing information that may be asymmetric. As a remedy, the buyer will be entitled to claim damages in tort against the negligent seller after proving negligence of the seller, loss, and its causation. If the buyer is co-negligent, the amount of damages is reduced proportionally with the ratio of contributory negligence.

2.7 *Insurance Business Act*

2.7.1 Overview

The Insurance Business Act is a law regulating the insurance business and markets in Japan. One of the main purposes of the Insurance Business Act is the protection of the policyholder, the insured and beneficiary, hereafter referred to as 'policyholder'. Insurance is a very important financial service; however, it is complicated and difficult for the consumer to understand. There exists a certain asymmetry of information on the products between the seller of insurance and the consumer. Protection of the policyholder, especially the consumer, has been an important issue in the insurance business. The Insurance Business Act lays down various rules to protect the policyholder. Among them, it is worth mentioning the rules on the sales of insurance, liability of insurance agents and the right of 'cooling off' on a contract for the policyholder.

2.7.2 Prohibitions of Certain Conducts in the Solicitation of Insurance

The Act prohibits certain conduct of sellers in the process of solicitation of insurance. These prohibitions apply to the solicitation of any insurance and are not limited to the solicitation of consumers[19]:

(i) False explanation.
(ii) Omission to explain material facts on the insurance contract.
(iii) Act to recommend not to disclose material facts to the insurer.
(iv) Act to recommend an alteration of insurance products without revealing its disadvantage.
(v) Act to give special benefit in return for contracting.
(vi) Act to provide misleading information on the comparison of products.
(vii) Act to lead policyholder to misunderstand uncertain return as certain.
(viii) Any other acts to be harmful for the policyholder.

Breach of the prohibition may amount to criminal sanction depending on the type of the rule violated.

2.7.3 Duty of Providing Information and Confirming Intention

In addition to the above prohibitions, the Insurance Business Act makes it a duty for the insurer, its agent, broker or another seller of insurance to provide the policyholder with information on the content of the insurance contract and other information that should serve as reference for them to conclude an insurance contract.[20] The insurance contract must be outlined with relevant information so that the policyholder can understand its significance. The provision of the above information to the policyholder is, in principle, to be made by way of providing documents containing all necessary information.

2.7.4 Duty of Ascertaining the Customer's Intention, etc.

Article 294-2 of the Insurance Business Act makes it a duty for the insurance company, its agent, broker, or the other seller of insurance, when they are to conclude an insurance contract, to ascertain the customer's intention. In doing so, they must propose an insurance contract in line with the customer's intention and explain the contents of the relevant insurance contract. They also must provide the customer with the opportunity to confirm that the customer's intention at the time of the conclusion of an insurance contract is in accord with the contents of the relevant insurance contract.

2.7.5 Duty of Creating System to Secure Sound Operation in Insurance Solicitations

In addition to the duty of the insurance company, agent, broker, etc. as to their conduct, the Insurance Business Act makes it a duty for them to take measures to ensure sound and appropriate operations of the business of insurance solicitations.[21] This means that the organization of the seller needs to establish a compliance system to secure sound transactions.

2.7.6 Sanctions Against the Breach of Duty Under Insurance Business Act

The Insurance Business Act regulates the conducts of the seller of the insurance. It affords a wide range of authority to the Ministry and the Financial Services Agency (FSA). The violation of the Act will allow the authority to make an order against the insurance company, agent, broker or any other party to improve its operation or suspend certain business. The FSA also has the ability to revoke the licence of the insurance business in Japan.

As stated above, violation of the law of certain Articles in the Act will amount to criminal sanctions. In turn, violation on some articles amounts to the payment of administrative charges.

2.7.7 Liability of Insurance Company

In Japan, the major channel for selling life insurance has been the sales representatives of life insurance company. In recent years, sales by insurance agents and banks are increasing. For general insurance, insurance agents entrusted by insurance companies sell more than 90%.

Under tort law, policyholders or the assureds may claim damages against the person or company when they suffer a loss because of the negligence of the seller.

When an employee of an insurance company is found to be negligent, the employer is also responsible for the conduct of its employees under the Civil Code. On the other hand, if the insurance agent is an independent merchant, the insurance company that entrusted agency business to the agent is not held responsible for the negligence of the agent unless the insurance company is concurrently found negligent under the Civil Code.

This legal position of the agent in general law is modified in the case of negligence of the insurance agent. The Insurance Business Act reinforces the responsibility of the insurance company. Under the Act, when the insurance agent owes liability against a policyholder or the assured in its insurance business, the insurance company will also be directly held responsible to the policyholder or the assured.[22] The insurance company, which compensated a loss for the policyholder, is entitled to make a recovery claim against the responsible agent.[23]

2.7.8 Cooling Off

The Insurance Business Act introduced a right for consumers to revoke or cancel the offer of certain insurance contracts, so-called 'cooling off'.[24]

The revocation must be made in writing within 8 days after making an insurance contract. Revocation of an insurance contract is allowed if a contract's period exceeds 1 year. Most general insurance contracts are for 1 year or less, making them ineligible for revocation.

2.8 *Insurance Act*

The Insurance Act was enacted in 2008 as an independent and comprehensive Act applying to insurance contracts of any type irrespective of the name of the service or the type of provider. Before its enactment, the law on insurance contracts was stated in the Commercial Code. By the enactment of the Insurance Act, provisions on the insurance contract in the Commercial Code were abolished, except those on marine insurance contracts.[25] One of the main purposes of the new Insurance Act was the protection of consumers. The Act introduced unilateral mandatory provisions that do not allow any agreement less favourable to the policyholder, insured, or beneficiary than under the rules of the Act.

2.9 *Banking Act*

The Banking Act[26] also sets up various rules to protect financial consumers. The following are major rules related to the protection of financial consumers.[27]

2.9.1 Duty of Providing Information

For the protection of depositors and pursuant to the provisions of the Cabinet Office Ordinance, the Bank must provide helpful information in the content of contracts with respect to deposits, instalment savings, and other information to the depositors.[28]

In addition, the Bank must explain important matters pertaining to its business to customers, appropriately handle customer information acquired in relation to its business, take measures to ensure precise execution of that business and other sound and appropriate management in the case of entrusting its business to a third party, pursuant to the provisions of Cabinet Office Ordinance.

2.9.2 Prohibited Acts

Banks are prohibited to perform certain acts. They include[29]:

(i) An act of providing false information to customers;
(ii) An act of providing a customer with any conclusive judgment with respect to an uncertain matter or giving information that is likely to have the customer mistakenly believe an uncertain matter for being certain;
(iii) An act of granting of credit or promising granting of credit to customers on the condition that the customers carry out transactions related to the business operated by that bank, a specified related person of that bank or any other

person with a close relationship thereto as specified by Cabinet Office Ordinance; and

(iv) Other acts specified by Cabinet Office Ordinance as those that have a risk of lacking customer protection.

2.9.3 Duty of Establishing a System to Protect Customers

The Bank owes a duty to establish a system for properly supervising the status of implementation of the business or taking any other measures necessary so that the interests of the customer will not be unjustly impaired.[30]

2.10 Laws Restricting the Interest Rate for Loans

As shown below, any money loan with an interest rate exceeding a certain limit is prohibited in Japan. If the moneylender violates the limit, it will be punished, and the contract will be void in full or in part, based on the Act.

2.10.1 Act Regulating the Receipt of Contributions, Receipt of Deposits and Interest Rates

The Act[31] restricts the rate of interest. When a moneylender, through its business, creates a contract for a loan to receive interest at a rate of over 20% per annum, it will be subject to a criminal offence facing a maximum of 5 years imprisonment with labour and/or a fine not exceeding 10,000,000 yen (Article 5(2)).

2.10.2 Interest Rate Restriction Act

Article 1 of the Act[32] prohibits placing interest on a loan exceeding the amount stated in the Act and makes any contract void in relation to the portion of interest that exceeds those respective amounts:

(i) where the amount of the principal must be appropriated to the satisfaction of the principal, principal is less than 100,000 yen (20% per annum);

(ii) where the amount of the principal is 100,000 yen or more but less than 1,000,000 yen (18% per annum); or

(iii) where the amount of the principal is 1,000,000 yen or more (15% per annum).

When the moneylender violates the Act, it will be punished under the Act Regulating the Receipt of Contributions, Receipt of Deposits and Interest Rates. The borrower of the money will be entitled to recover the money overpaid based on the law of restitution.

2.10.3 Money Lending Business Act

The Act[33] governs contracts made by any moneylender with an interest rate exceeding 109.5% as void (Article 42–2). If the borrower has entered into such a contract, the borrower does not need to return any interest.

3 Financial Consumer Protection System (Hardware)

3.1 Consumer Affairs Agency (CAA)

In 2009, the Consumer Affairs Agency (CAA) was established as one of the cabinet agencies to strengthen consumer protection. In addition, the National Consumer Affairs Center of Japan was established as an incorporated administrative agency supervised by the CAA as a core organization for consumer affairs administration purposes. Its main activities include the following:

(i) advising on how to handle cases brought by consumers;
(ii) receiving consultation from consumers who were unable to reach the nearest Consumer Affairs Center;
(iii) collecting information on consumer affair cases;
(iv) educating and raising awareness of consumers;
(v) issuing requests and supplying information to governmental bodies and trade associations;
(vi) providing training sessions; and
(vii) implementing dispute resolution procedures for consumers.

CAA covers various issues for consumer protection and handles issues for financial consumers as well.

3.2 Financial Services Agency (FSA)

The FSA was established to ensure the stability of Japan's financial system, protection of depositors, insurance policyholders, and securities investors. In 2001, through the reorganization of the ministries, the FSA became an external organization of the Cabinet Office. The FSA took over the roles concerning disposition of failed financial institutions with the abolishment of the Financial Reconstruction Commission that had been established in 1998.

Responsibilities of the FSA include planning and policymaking of the financial system, inspection and supervision of the private sector, establishment of rules for trading in the market, establishment of business accounting standards, supervision of certified public accountants and surveillance of compliance of rules in the market.

There are three bureaus in the FSA. The Planning and Coordination Bureau makes various plans and bills to regulate financial markets and rules for the financial institutions. The Inspection Bureau conducts inspections on the financial institutions. The Supervisory Bureau supervises the financial institutions. In addition to various regulatory laws, the FSA issues supervisory guidelines and manuals for inspection of each financial sector that are also important as 'soft law'. In addition, the FSA includes the Securities and Exchange Surveillance Commission and the Certified Accountants and Auditing Oversight Board.

4 Ex-post Protections

4.1 Financial ADR

To utilize means other than judicial courts for the settlement of disputes, the Act on Promotion of Use of Alternative Dispute Resolution (ADR)[34] was enacted in 2004 and became law as of 2007. Under the Act, the Ministry of Justice approves and certifies the organizations that make intermediate reconciliation between parties if they meet with the standard conditions set out in the Act. In 2009, an amendment was enacted under the Financial Instruments and Exchange Act that made it compulsory for financial institutions to use ADR institutions as of 2010.

As of February 2017, 8 institutions are recognized as the financial ADR in Japan[35]:

(1) The Japanese Bankers Association
(2) The Life Insurance Association of Japan, Inc.
(3) The General Insurance Association of Japan, Inc.
(4) The Small Amount and Short Term Insurance Provider Association of Japan

Insurance Ombudsman

(5) *Hoken-ombudsman* (Insurance Ombudsman)
(6) Trust Companies Association of Japan
(7) Japan Financial Services Association
(8) Financial Instruments Mediation Assistance Center (FINMAC)

Each financial sector establishes its own ADR institution as the recognized ADR organization included in all financial contracts. Under each contract, financial institutions must follow the dispute procedure when the recognized ADR or its member requests the financial institution to accept this dispute procedure.[36] Financial institutions must provide any documents or evidence if required by the dispute resolution member.[37] The dispute resolution member has the power to make a settlement plan and request the parties to accept. In certain situations, it has also a power to provide a special mediation proposal.[38] Financial institutions must accept a special mediation plan by the dispute resolution member with the exception in certain cases.[39] The procedures in the financial ADR are in principle treated as confidential.[40]

4.2 Protection in Case of Bankruptcy of a Financial Institution

4.2.1 Banks

In 1971, the Deposit Insurance Law was enacted to create a deposit insurance system in Japan. The deposit insurance system aims at protecting the depositor and other parties by attempting to guarantee the fund settlement when a financial institution becomes unable to repay their deposit. Under this Act, the Deposit Insurance Corporation of Japan (DICJ) was established with the funding of the Japanese Government, Bank of Japan, and private financial institutions.[41]

The main responsibilities of DICF are to operate the deposit insurance system, oversee asset management of any failed financial institutions, collect on loans that have defaulted payment, inject capital into failing financial institutions, and pursue legal actions that result in liability of the management of failed institutions.

Financial institutions that are under this insurance programme are banks, long-term credit banks, Shinkin Banks, Labour Banks, Shinkin Central Bank, Shinkumi Federation Bank, and Rokinren Bank.[42] It is compulsory for these institutions to enter into DICF and its insurance coverage starts as soon as the banks accept deposits. The financial institutions pay the insurance premium of this deposit insurance annually and the premium is based on the amount of the deposit. Branch offices that exist abroad are excluded from insurance coverage in addition to any deposits made by foreign financial institutions to these branch offices.

The deposits covered by this insurance include instalment savings, instalment contributions, or other types of deposits. The amount of coverage varies with the type of deposit. Examples include the following:

(i) Current deposits, ordinary deposits, specified deposits;
(ii) Full coverage for payment and settlement purposes with no interest rate;
(iii) Time deposits and instalment savings with a maximum principal of ¥10 million plus accrued interest. However, the portion in excess of ¥10 million can be paid, depending on the state of assets of a failed financial institution.
(iv) Foreign currency deposits, negotiable certificates of deposit, and money trusts that are under no guarantee of principal are considered outside the insurance coverage. However, some portion of the principal can be payable depending on the state of assets of a failed financial institution.

4.2.2 Insurance Company

In order to foster competition through deregulation while protecting policyholders at the same time, the Insurance Business Act was amended in 1996. The revised Act introduced a scheme for establishing two protection funds; they included life insurance and non-life insurance. However, the schemes were inherently weak because they did not operate when there was no relief insurance company. To overcome this weakness, the Insurance Business Act was amended in 1998 to establish the Life Insurance Policyholders Protection Corporation of Japan and the Non-life Insurance Policyholders Protection Corporation of Japan.

Any Japanese businesses that operate either life insurance or non-life insurance companies are members of one of these two corporations. There are certain exceptions such as re-insurance companies or other companies who are exempted under the Insurance Business Act. In addition, short-term and small amount insurance companies regulated by the Insurance Business Act and various cooperatives called *Kyosai* are regulated by other Acts and are not members of these protection corporations.

If a member insurance company goes bankrupt and there is a relief insurance company in place, the protection corporation will give financial assistance to the relief company. In this case, insurance contracts continue to exist with the relief company. Where there is no relief insurance company, the protection corporation will establish a successor insurance company as its subsidiary. The successor insurance company will manage the insurance contracts held by the failed insurance company while simultaneously looking to secure a relief insurance company. If there is no relief company to handle the contracts with the policyholders, the successor insurance company continues to insure the contracts.

Under this scheme, the insurance payment or coverage will be reduced or restricted to a certain extent based on the Insurance Business Act. The extent of such reductions depends on the type and nature of insurance pursuant to the rules stated in the Insurance Business Act and its ordinances.

4.2.3 Securities Company

Under the Securities and Exchange Act, securities firms must manage the money, shares, bonds, and other securities entrusted by customers separately from their own assets. Customers are able to recover any of their assets even where a securities firm goes bankrupt. Japan introduced the dual security system to protect customers in cases where failing securities companies file bankruptcy.

In 1968, the Entrusted Securities Indemnity Fund was established, and in 1998 it was reorganized as the Japan Investor Protection Fund (JIPF) under the revised Securities and Exchange Act.[43]

All the securities companies in Japan must be a member of JIPF and must pay the membership fee. The protection of assets is up to ¥10 million per customer. Customers entitled to compensation from JIPF are limited to general customers. Financial institutions and any other institutional investors including local government are regarded as 'professional investors' and are outside this protection.

Transactions covered by this scheme are stated in the Financial Instruments and Exchange Act and they are money, securities, shares, public and corporate bonds, investment trust transactions, deposits concerning margin transactions of shares and others. On the other hand, over-the-counter securities derivatives transactions, market securities derivatives transactions on overseas exchanges, on-exchange currency transactions, foreign exchange margin transactions (FX transactions) and others are outside the scope of this scheme, because they are handled by professionals normally.

Notes

1. See Mitsuru Taniuchi, *Nyumon Kinyu no Genjitsu to Riron* [Introduction: Reality and Theory of Finance] 2nd ed., p.27, Dobunkan, 2013.
2. In this article, Act means a specific legislation and law means law more in general.
3. See homepage of the Financial Services Agency.
4. Based on the Statistics of the Statistic Bureau, Ministry of Internal Affairs and Communications.
5. Based on the analysis of the National Institute of Population and Social Security Research.
6. Ibid.
7. In this article, the writer relies on 'The Japanese Law Translation' of the Ministry of Justice, Japan to show the law in English. However, the writer has changed words in many parts so that the reader may understand outlines better.
8. This is not an exhaustive list of Acts. Explanations are made to give an overview on the main points. The Act always contains certain conditions and exclusions. The writer does not state these detailed provisions. When necessary, please check the article of the relevant Act.
9. Act No. 61 of May 12, 2000.
10. 'Consumer' is defined in the Act as an individual.
11. 'Business operator' in the Act is defined as a corporation or association, or an individual who becomes a party to a contract as a business enterprise or for the purposes of a business enterprise.
12. 'Important matter' is defined in the Act.
13. Act No. 101 of May 31, 2000.
14. The Act applies to deposit, trust fund, insurance, commodity funds, foreign currency dealings, futures, derivative, and other financial products. However, it does not apply to domestic commodity future trading, since it is a sales contract based on commodity in essence and is covered by another Act.
15. This is the original objective of the rule. However, the writer doubts whether such solicitation policy operates to improve the solicitation in practice because the writer finds no significant difference in the wordings of the solicitation policies among various banks, insurance companies etc. Consumers are more interested in the quality and price of the service provided in practice rather than the wordings of the sales policy of the institution.
16. Act No. 25 of 1948.
17. Act No. 109 of 2006.
18. Law No. 57 of 2003.

19. Insurance Business Act, Article 300.
20. Insurance Business Act, Article 294(1).
21. Insurance Business Act Article 294-3.
22. Insurance Business Act, Article 283(1). If the insurance company proves that it took reasonable care in entrusting the agency and supervised it properly, it is relieved from liability. However, this is very difficult to prove for the insurer.
23. Insurance Business Act, Article 283(4).
24. Insurance Business Act, Article 309.
25. At the time of this writing, the government is in the process of modernizing the law on marine insurance.
26. Banking Act. Law No. 59 of 1981. Latest revision Law No. 62 of 2016.
27. These are not an exhaustive list. The Banking Act does not define the meaning of 'customer'.
28. Banking Act, Article 12-2.
29. Banking Act, Article 13-3.
30. Banking Act, Article 13-3-2.
31. Act No.195, 1954.
32. Act No. 100, 1954.
33. Act No. 32, 1983 as amended in 2003.
34. Law No. 151, 2004.
35. FSA web site.
36. Financial Instruments and Exchange Act. Art.156-4(2)2 etc.
37. Financial Instruments and Exchange Act. Art.156-44(2)3 etc.
38. Financial Instruments and Exchange Act. Art.155-50(6) etc.
39. Financial Instruments and Exchange Act. Art.156-44(6) etc.
40. Financial Instruments and Exchange Act. Art.155条-50(7) etc.
41. Following explanations are derived from 'A Guide to the Deposit Insurance System' issued in 2015 of DICF.
42. Norinchukin Bank, Agricultural Cooperatives, Fishermen's Cooperatives, Seafood Processing Cooperatives, etc., are covered by the 'Savings Insurance System of the Agricultural and Fisheries Cooperative Savings Insurance Corporation'. The government guarantees postal savings at Japan Post.
43. The Securities and Exchange Act was revised to the Financial Instruments and Exchange Act in 2007.

Hongmu Lee is a professor of risk management and insurance at the Waseda University, Tokyo in Japan. He received his Ph.D. from the Waseda University. He is also Associate Dean of Graduate School of Commerce at the Waseda University and the President of the Insurance and Risk Management Institute of Waseda University. This Insurance and Risk Management Institute is aiming the research with cooperation between industry and the academic world internationally on the insurance and risk management. He has authored several books and articles in academic and professional journals mainly Korea and Japan.

Satoshi Nakaide is a Professor at Waseda University, Tokyo. He is specialized in insurance law including insurance regulatory law and has published many articles and books on insurance. He was awarded with an academic prize on his book in 2016 as well as two other prizes on his co-authored books in 2012. Prior to taking the professorship, he worked for Tokio Marine and Fire Insurance Company for 28 years. He obtained LL.M. from University of London, LSE, Graduate Diploma in Legal Studies from Cambridge University and a higher doctorate degree of commerce from Waseda University.

Chapter 10
Financial Consumer Protection in Korea

Hongjoo Jung, Misoo Choi and Youkyung Huh

1 Financial Consumer

1.1 Legal Meaning of Financial Consumer

Although not in adopted in any law in Korea yet, the term 'financial consumer', has been widely and increasingly used by the government, policy circles and the financial industry in Korea since 2010, when the Korean Academy of Financial Consumers (hereinafter "KAFC") was set up probably for the first time in its kind in the world. The then new expression, 'financial consumer' was academically attacked by several scholars who believe that to consume finance or investment was irrational or illogical, as finance or investment is to keep its original value or more that is different from consumption that phases away as time goes by.

Basically there were two reasons why the new and controversial expression was adopted in the academic society's official name. The one is a wide spread Financial scandal arising out of financial crisis of the 2008, and the other is the fact that most of the victims of the scandal was average financial users of the financial service institutions, some of which were saved by regulators for the sake of financial system protection.

The unexpected and unwanted event anyhow triggered an institutional innovation for financial consumers in every possible public and private domain in Korean financial system. In public sector, an initiative was developed to enact a new law to

H. Jung
SungKyunKwan University, Seoul, South Korea

M. Choi (✉)
Seoul Digital University, Seoul, South Korea
e-mail: cms@sdu.ac.kr

Y. Huh
University of Virginia, Charlottesville, USA

© Springer Nature Singapore Pte Ltd. 2018

T.-J. Chen (ed.), *An International Comparison of Financial Consumer Protection*,
https://doi.org/10.1007/978-981-10-8441-6_10

protect financial consumers as well as to treat every financial institution, when selling a similar product, in an equitable way regardless of its sector to belong. At that time, expansionary strategies of banks, insurers, and security brokers has led to a similar product composition to much degree except a few core products, a natural legacy in turn producing little specialization or expertise in their own area and thus a number of complaints among consumers.

In 2012, following the creation of the KAFC, the "Financial Consumer Protection Bureau," a division dedicated to financial consumer protection, led by a deputy governor within the Financial Supervisory Service (hereinafter "FSS"), Korea's consolidated financial supervisory authority,[1] was established. Following a major reorganization in February 2016, financial consumer protection functions were significantly augmented within the FSS, by doubling the staff, and now to be led by the Vice Chairperson of the FSS.

Meanwhile, the private sector was also affected by the growing popularity of the regulatory agenda to enhance financial consumer protection. The financial industry has engaged in defensive management practices, which includes the compulsory establishment of a financial consumer compliance officer in every major financial institution.

Under Korean law, both legislators and the administration enjoy the privilege to propose legislative bills. Numerous unsuccessful bills have been submitted by major political parties and previous administrations since 2010. Lack of consensus on any proposed bill, however, has made it impossible to reach an agreement to move forward to and enact a new law. Recently, however, most issues have been reconciled, with the exception of one issue- how to restructure the existing structure of financial supervisory bodies, an issue which has the potential to jeopardize final enactment of the bill.[2]

Here we briefly introduce the most recent bill submitted by the government for the enactment of the "Foundational Law on Financial Consumer Protection" (the "Proposed Bill").[3]

The Proposed Bill, for the first time in Korean legislative history formally introduces a new statutory definition of "financial consumer," who is defined as (i) a counterparty of a financial institution who sells or brokers a financial product or (ii) a counterparty of a registered adviser to a financial product sales/brokerage agreement."[4] In essence, a "financial consumer" is anyone who conducts any financial transaction with a financial institution. To modify this broad definition, the Proposed Bill further divides financial consumers into two groups: (i) "professional financial consumers" who have sophistication, assets and risk tolerance abilities (i.e., the Korean government, the Bank of Korea, financial and listed companies, and other persons to be determined by further rulemaking),[5] and (ii) "non-professional financial consumers" who are defined as persons who do not fall under the category of "professional financial consumers."[6] The FCP Bill also defers to further rulemaking allowing carve-out provisions in cases where consumer protection is deemed unnecessary.

The Proposed Bill, among others, (i) enhances the regulatory power of the FSS by increasing the maximum amount of administrative fines that can be assessed,[7]

(ii) introduces financial consumers' right to terminate or revoke financial contracts,[8] (iii) expands regulation[9] and sanctions[10] related to sales of financial products, (iv) enhances pre-sale disclosure obligations to financial consumers,[11] (v) enhances consumers' rights to damages by augmenting liability of financial companies,[12] (vi) and classifies financial products and their services into four types according to their practical functions. Specifically, these four types are: (i) deposit-type products (products that guarantee the principal investment amount, such as time deposits); (ii) investment-type products (products that do not guarantee the principal investment amount, but generate return on the investment); (iii) insurance-type products (products that pay out insurance payments for certain insured events after the policyholder have paid insurance premiums for a long period); and (iv) loan-type products (a financial company provides a loan and the borrower repays the principal amount of the loan and accrued interest thereon).[13]

The Proposed Bill stipulates, as a declarative provision, the basic rights of financial consumers as follows[14]:

- Right to be protected from any loss or damage of their property arising out of financial products
- Right to be informed of knowledge or information in the course of selection and consumption of financial products
- Right to be heard of their opinions in the national or provincial policy that may influence the financial consumption life
- Right to be compensated from any loss or damage from consumption of financial products in a quick and fair process
- Right to be educated necessary for rational life of financial consumption
- Right to organize entity to promote their privilege and value and to act through the organization

Corresponding to the rights of consumers, the Proposed Bill also stipulates the duties of financial consumers corresponding to their rights, that the consumers should, recognize themselves as a participant of the financial market, alongside financial companies; thus are required to properly choose financial products, and to exercise basic rights of financial consumers.

As the Proposed Bill is drafted by the Financial Service Committee, which is also subject to possibility of its own restructuring, is up on the air regarding its enactment as of January 2017.

1.2 Economic Situation of Financial Consumer

The Republic of Korea, or the South Korea, is populated by just over 50 million people with very low birth rate, 0.17, coupled with late marriage trend among youngsters and so-called difficulty in raising child in terms of housing, education, employment condition. The low birth rate as well as increasing longevity has accelerated the aging speed of Korean society in such a way to change a number of policies in political, economic, social, and cultural respects. A policy example is a generous immigration policy toward blue collar Asian workers in particular leading to a multi-cultural society.

The country is expected to record the fewest years to become an aged society (12% of the 65 or older people) in the year 2020 and a super aged society (20% of the 65 or older people) in the year 2030 after reaching an aging society (6% of the 65 or older people) in the year 2012 (Figs. 1, 2 and 3; Table 1).

Obviously adverse demographic change results in increasing social security payment as with higher dependency ratio. Social security, comprising of social support, social insurance and social service in Korea, has dramatically been increasing, although in a different level among those individual instruments.

When it comes to social insurance, which covers national pension, national health insurance, workers compensation, unemployment insurance, and last but not the least long-term care, a few of them are reportedly suffering from a lack of serious financial soundness. For instance, national pension, being operated by a partial funding system, will be running out of its reserve in year 2040, due to

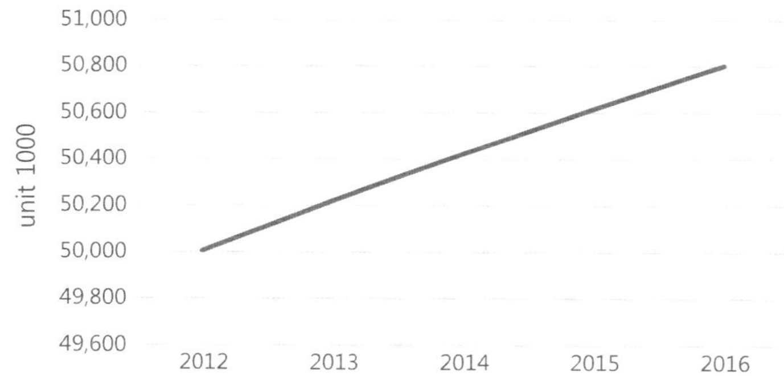

Fig. 1 Population (2012–2016). *Source* Korean Statistical Information Service

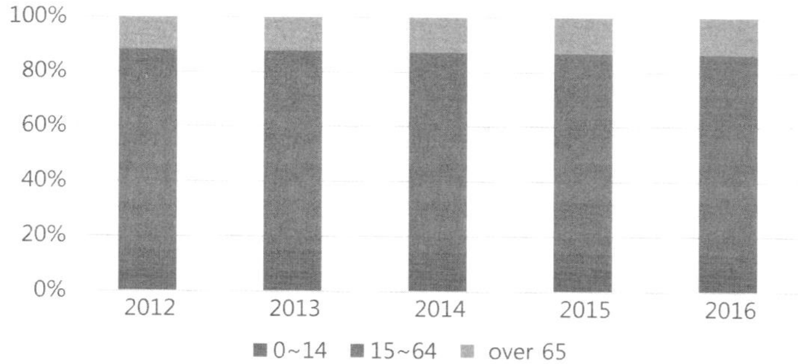

Fig. 2 Age structure. *Source* Korean Statistical Information Service

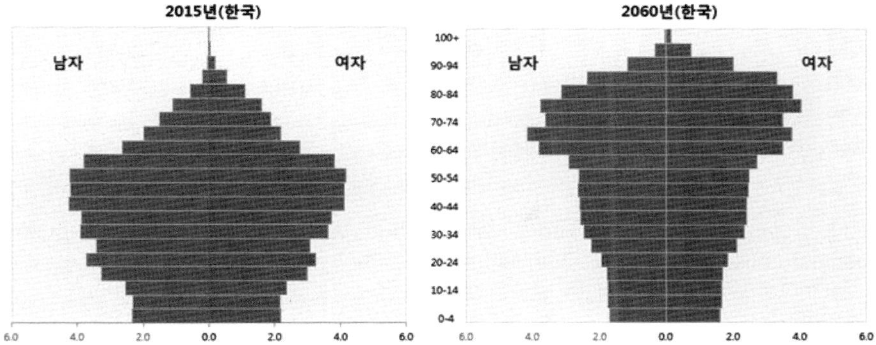

Fig. 3 Expected change in demography from 2105 to 2060. *Source* Population Projections for Korea, Statistics Korea

Table 1 Social spending

Name	2013	2014	2015
Social spending, public, % of GDP	9.332	9.718	10.108
Social spending private, % of GDP	2.196	2.146	–

Source Korean Statistical Information Service

Table 2 Pension spending

Name	2009	2010	2011
Pension spending, public, % of GDP	2.149	2.186	2.238
Pension spending, private,% of GDP	1.01	1.334	1.279

Source Korean Statistical Information Service

Table 3 Social benefits

Name	2013	2014	2015
Social benefits to households In cash,% of GDP	4.714	5.076	5.449

Source Korean Statistical Information Service

continuing longevity and too generous income payment ratio for the current generation and against the incoming generation. From the same reason, government employee pension system, covering a special area of workers, has been restructured in parameter level in 2015 before the same kind of change was done in private teachers' pension system in a few months after. Moreover, workers compensation insurance and national healthcare are also problematic in financial operation, in spite of seemingly sound operation at the moment as the former has too benign benefit level to the disabled people while the latter faces the inflationary pressure in medical expense and ever increasing usage of medical services among the elderly group of people. Those financial issues in social insurance can generate conflicts

Table 4 Public spending

Name	2011	2012	2013
Public spending on incapacity Total, % of GDP	0.583	0.614	0.609

Source Korean Statistical Information Service

between generations and restrict consumption capacity of the upcoming new financial consumers (Tables 2, 3 and 4).

1.3 Financial Service Industry in Landscape

Over the last two decades, Korean financial service sector has observed a shift from the traditional strong regulatory culture, characterized by a limited new business license and active involvement of supervision system. For example, no new license has been issued in insurance area since 1990s when the US successfully asked for liberalization in Korean insurance market. And the neo liberalism in economic policy has expanded its realm into monetary policy and financial policy from the middle of 1990s. It is about that period when the Bank of Korea, the central bank could begin to exercise and enjoy its independent monetary policy freed from government hand. In addition to that, commercial banks, security brokers, and insurance companies were given free marketing options in product development, pricing, ways of promotion, and placement.

One of the driving forces in financial innovation was the development of information technology including internet and mobile phones. Internet has been rapidly expanding in Korea right after the beginning of 21st century thanks to American development, resulting in popularity in internet banking, internet security transaction, and internet purchase of insurance products centering on automobile insurance. Major changes took place in security brokers above banking or insurance sector so that most of the traditional stock brokerage lost its market shares to new internet brokers whereas traditional banks and insurers could slowly adjust their business strategies. Most of those rapid changes may be partially attributable to Korean financial consumers' culture favoring innovation and speed especially among young generation.

Industry structure of Korean financial service sector can be characterized by an oligopoly system mainly thanks to strong government control of new entry. The system may has helped the captive value of the incumbent companies, not the consumer surplus nor stability of financial system, as we observed the 1997 financial crisis or 2000 credit card crisis in Korea. The strict licensing system could contribute to easy merger and acquisition of financially troubled companies to some degree as there were no other option to enter the industry than buying those companies.

One of the great misfortune that Korean economy has had, was the foreign exchange crisis in the late 1997 that prevailed in Asian region which required most of Korean commercial banks to be sold to foreign investors. As a response to shortage of foreign exchange reserve at that time, Korea could not help accepting the proposal of the International Monetary Fund to raise interest rate and to attract foreign capital in a short period. This unusual treatment, which has never been exercised elsewhere in the world since then, had brought many bankruptcies of major industrial companies and consequently commercial banks with non-performing loans to those companies.

After the crisis, which was reportedly overcome very fast but painfully, Korean companies and financial institutions' financial leverage has dramatically reduced but with a balloon effect increasing the debt ration of household on the other hand. Introduction of prudential regulation and its strict standards has reduced debt ratios of major Chaebols and financial institutions previously holding aggressive growth

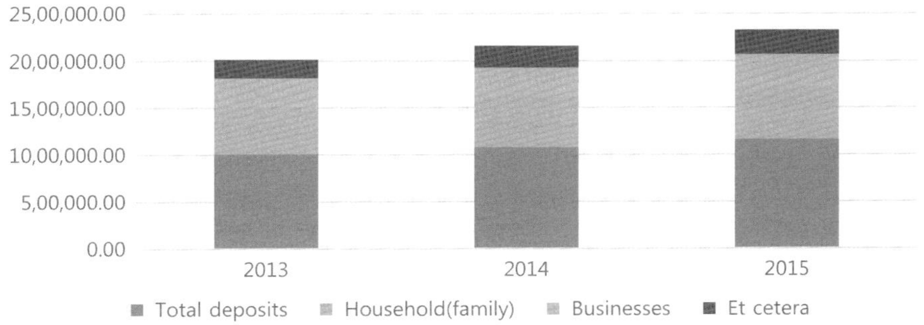

Fig. 4 Account holder per bank deposit (A billion won). *Source* Economic Statistics System, The Bank of Korea

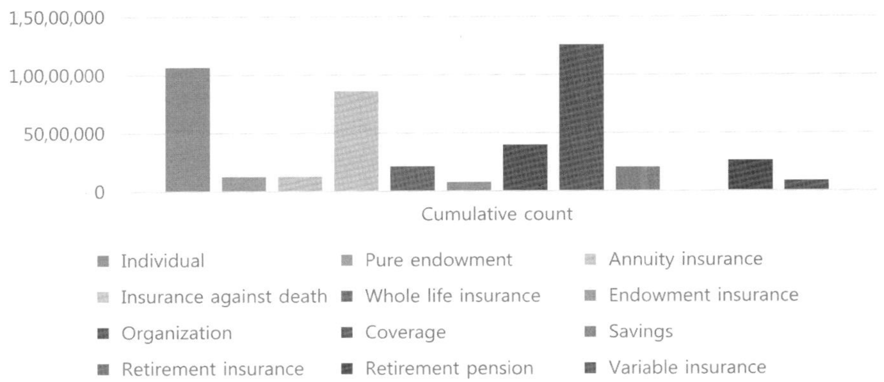

Fig. 5 Life Insurance company's new business (CY'15) (one million won, unit). *Source* Insurance Statistics Information Services, Korea Insurance Development Institute

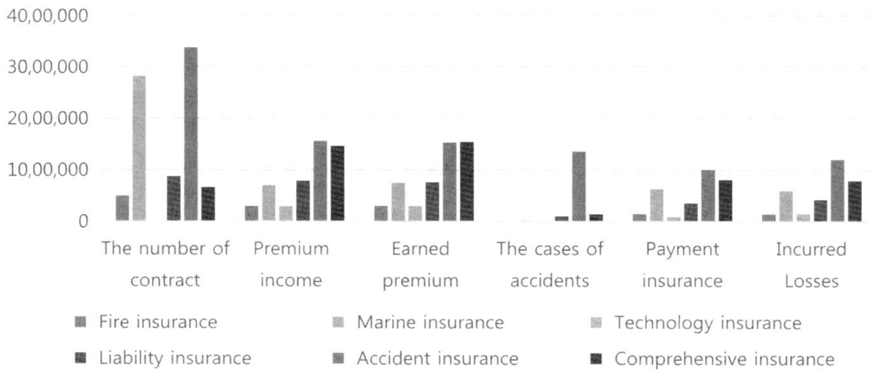

Fig. 6 Non-life insurance major perfomance status (CY'15) (one million won, unit). *Source* Insurance Statistics Information Services, Korea Insurance Development Institute

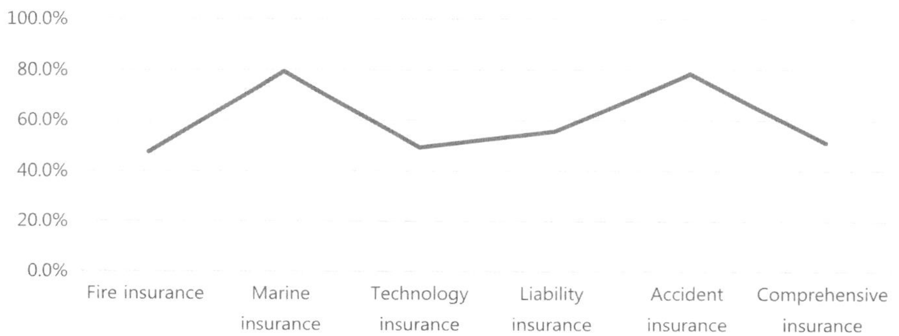

Fig. 7 Loss ratio. *Source* Insurance Statistics Information Services, Korea Insurance Development Institute

policies. Nevertheless, Korean government shifted its growth engine to household consumption by allowing them to borrow more for consumption or investment on real estate, inevitably resulting in credit card crisis in early 2000s and contemporary household debt issues in 2010s. As of 2017, total debt of household amounts to annual Gross Domestic Product level (Figs. 4, 5, 6 and 7).

2 Financial Consumer Protection System (Software)

2.1 Relevant Laws and Rules

As in the most of industrialized countries, Korea has introduced various types of financial services and enacted corresponding laws and rules. The laws and rules are too detailed to be introduced here in its entirety, but the recent revisions briefly represented here, show a strong propensity to increase and formalize consumer protection provisions and that the main goals of the laws have changed over the decades along with the development of Korean economy. Previously, finance has played a subordinate role to support economic development in Korea, but more recently, more laws have begun to acknowledge the rights of consumers and the means to protect them.

Currently there is no single general law overseeing all aspects of financial consumer protection.[15] Rather, financial consumer protection provisions regarding mandatory disclosure requirements, financial education, dispute resolution, etc., are scattered across various sector-based statutes. For example, securities and derivatives are regulated by the Financial Investment Services and Capital Markets Act (hereinafter "Capital Markets Act"),[16] deposits and savings by the Banking Act,[17] and insurance products by the Insurance Business Act,[18] and credit card services by the Specialized Credit Financial Business Act.[19] In addition to sector-based acts, specialized statutes stipulate specific aspects of financial consumer protection such as consumer credit information (including credit ratings),[20] and debt collection.[21]

2.1.1 Banking

All the commercial banks, fully owned and controlled by government up to 1980, used to play a pivotal role in economic development as a compulsory platform of national saving. That is, commercial banks were an official channel to attract savings from household at lower rate than market interest rate or black market rate in order to provide a low rate of commercial loan to major industrialized corporations. And other types of deposit taking institutions were additional banks, or so called savings bank with offering higher lending and borrowing rates than normal banks.

As with change of the Banking law, banks were privatized in terms of ownership as early as 1980s, following global trend of financial liberalization and internal necessity to foster managerial efficiency, and beginning to liberalize interest rates among banks. As the deposit interest rates were so low, considering inflation rate or economic growth rate, that depositors should in fact sacrifice their wealth to the national economic development or growth of large sized conglomerates.

The privatization and liberalization of banking sector had enjoyed a historic economic boom at the later 1980s to see the economic downturn in the 1990s when Korea celebrated the complete political freedom from military dictatorship and membership of the OECD, which was followed by a economic crisis in the 1997.

After the entire major banks went into insolvency and recapitalized at the end of 1998 crisis, government gave banks more freedom to choose for their management and extra service domain as their business area while solvency regulation got more tightened than before. As a way to support bank's profitability as well as to meet a global trend of financial integration, the big brothers in the financial sector were permitted to sell insurance products and investment products one after another. The amendment of banking law for the bancassurance faced no serious difficulty in getting governmental endorsement, partially thanks to banks' reputational advantage over insurance companies in public as well as to dominance in terms of industry size.

The banking law used to stipulate that the banks had been representative 'financial institutions' up to year 2010 when the law was amended to include other types of institutions in the FIs category.

Previously, the detailed provisions for financial consumer protection were not stipulated in formal statutes or enforcement rules, but rather, in supervisory guidelines of the FSS, or self-regulatory rules enacted by the self-regulatory organizations. Recently, however, to reflect the surge of consumer protection initiatives that took place in the financial sector following the financial crisis of 2008, the traditional sector-based laws are incorporating more consumer protection provisions. As such, most of the banking sector financial consumer protection statutes introduced here have been stipulated in the Banking Act on or after 2010.

(1) **Disclosures and Advertisements**

Under the Banking Act, banks are required disclose to their customers, information about the financial products and its transaction terms and conditions as prescribed by the laws and regulations. Specifically, a bank is required to disclose, interest rates, matters related to contract termination, deposit insurance and other matters necessary for the protection of consumers.[22] Banks are also required to explain details of financial contracts in each stage of a financial transaction as follows: (i) when soliciting a contract: major terms and conditions of the contract including costs of transaction; (ii) When a bank customer applies for a contract: Standard terms and conditions; when executing a contract: contract documents.[23] Details also differs depending on the types of financial services provided (i.e. deposit accounts, loans, derivatives).[24]

Likewise, when a bank advertises its bank products, it is required to include the name of the bank, details of banking products, transaction terms and conditions.[25] A bank shall clearly indicate the scope of interest rates and methods of calculating of them, the timing of paying and imposing interest, additional benefits and expenses, to ensure bank users to make reasonable decisions on banking products.[26]

(2) **Prohibition of Mis-selling**

The Banking Act and related regulations prohibit certain unfair bank sales practices. Specifically, in connection with credit provision, a bank is prohibited from, (i) coercing a borrower to purchase bank products, such as deposits contrary to his/her intent, (ii) restricting cancellation or withdrawal of bank products, such as deposits and installment savings, (iii) requesting a borrower or any third person to provide comprehensive collateral security or comprehensive collateral guarantee, without any justifiable grounds, (iv) requesting joint guarantee to a third person who provides security, (v) coercing related persons of a borrower, such as the representative, executive officers, etc. of a small and medium enterprise to purchase bank products contrary to their intent, (vi) selling bank products, in connection with credit transactions, to a small and medium enterprise which is a borrower, or related persons of such borrowers.[27]

(3) **Recent Revisions**

In 2016, the Banking Act added new provisions prohibiting unsound business activities,[28] and requiring banks to prepare measures such as managing internal controls to prevent financial accidents, protect information of bank users, and making procedures to deal with high- risk electronic transactions, requiring banks to report to the public (i.e. on its website) for high-impact financial fraud or accidents.[29]

2.1.2 Securities

The Korean financial system is traditionally well known for its bank based system. More recently, the nation has strived to transition into a market based system, which is considered to be more efficient, diversifiable, innovative and has more advanced consumer protection mechanisms.

The now-defunct Securities and Exchange Act (SEA),[30] which was enacted in 1964 had played a crucial role in regulating the secondary market of securities. The Act stipulated mandatory disclosure requirements for listed companies, and prohibited unfair practices such as market manipulation and the use of nonpublic information. However, the SEA was found insufficient to meet the needs to regulate the increasing variety of securities, growth of the primary market, and protect financial consumers in equal footing.

In February 2009, Korea's financial regulatory structure witnessed a fundamental change in this landscape as the Capital Markets Act came into effect. Enacted in 2007 to promote fair market competition, support financial innovation and to introduce systematic and more stringent investor protection, the Capital Markets Act drastically overhauled the regulatory framework of the Korean capital market.[31] The law was the first major initiative with an ambitious vision to create a global size of investment banks in Korea, and to enhance profitability of securities brokers. The following are a brief introduction of representative provisions of the Capital Market Act that are relevant to investor protection.

(1) Duty to Explain and Advertisement Rules

When a financial investment business entity (hereinafter "Financial Company")[32] is making an investment recommendation to an ordinary investor,[33] the seller is required to explain, to the investor, the details of the financial investment product,[34] the risks contingent upon the investment, the structure and characteristics of the investment, the fees, and terms and conditions related to early termination.[35] A Financial Company is required to obtain a confirmation from each ordinary investor, stating that he/she has understood such aforementioned details.[36]

When advertising its financial investment products, a Financial Company is required to, include the name of the company, descriptions of the financial investment instruments, the risks contingent upon the investment, and other matters[37] For certain types of investment products (i.e. collective investment securities[38]), a Financial Company is required to include information in the advertisement to allow the investor to be cognizant of the risks entailed to the investment. Such information includes, a statement recommending that the investor read the investment prospectus before acquiring the, a statement indicating the fact that there is a risk of loss, a statement that the past performance of the collective investment scheme does not guarantee a return on investment for the future.[39]

Regulations also requires every investment trader or broker to provide continuous information to the customer in forms of monthly reports on sales of securities, of the details of monthly trading and earnings and losses, the current status of balance and remaining volume as at the end of each month, the current status of unsettled agreements for derivatives as at the end of each month, the current status of balance of deposited property and the required amount of margin deposit, and other relevant matters.[40]

(2) Know-Your-Customer and Suitability Rules

The Capital Market Act requires a Financial Company to assess the investor and, make investment recommendations that are suitable to the investor. Specifically, each Financial Company shall first (i) ascertain whether the investor is an ordinary investor or a professional investor, (ii) and if the investor falls into the 'ordinary investor' category, the Financial Company shall obtain information about the investment purpose, status of property, experience in investment, etc. of an ordinary investor through interviews, inquiries, etc. before recommending him/her to make an investment.

In the case of derivatives and other types of high-risk investments, the Financial Company shall obtain information about ordinary investor through interviews and inquiries,[41] and if the high- risk investment is deemed *not* adequate for an ordinary investor taking into consideration of the information obtained from the investor, the Financial Company shall notify the investor of that fact.[42]

(3) Prohibition of Mis-selling and Rules on Conflicts of Interest

Providing false information, misleading information or decisive judgment on uncertain matters, when making an investment recommendation, are prohibited under the Capital Markets Act.[43] Unless there is a justifiable ground, promising in advance to compensate, or compensating after the fact, for all or part of losses that an investor may (or has) sustained is prohibited.[44]

Investment traders and brokers are also prohibited from front-running, that is, a broker or dealer trading in his personal account based on advanced knowledge of pending orders from the clients; or, within 24 h of public disclosure of certain research and analysis data.[45] Paying to a person in charge of the preparation of research and analysis, any contingent remuneration in connection to corporate finance, is also prohibited.[46]

2.1.3 Insurance

Insurance laws in Korea are twofold, the fist being insurance contract law, a body of private law which is incorporated as a chapter in the Korean Commercial Act.[47] Insurance contract law deals with the relations between individuals or institutions in insurance contracts by dictating matters on entering into, and interpreting insurance contracts. The insurance contract law provisions have been amended less often than the Insurance Business Act, which has reflected several technological and product innovations that took place in the industry.

Separate from the insurance contract law provisions, is the Insurance Business Act which is a public law directly regulating all the insurance companies' activities, from licensing, capital requirements, dissolution to business conduct regulation. Although both insurance contract laws and the Insurance Business Act have commonalities in that they pursue consumer protection at a higher level, the latter has been amended to incorporate provisions which have a more direct effect on consumer protection. More recent revisions since 2010 have reflected heightened consumer protection significance and legislative efforts by including provisions such as the duty to explain and suitability rules first introduced in the Capital Markets Act.

The following are a brief introduction of representative provisions of the Insurance Business Act that are relevant to consumer protection.

(1) **Disclosure and Advertisement Rules**

Insurance companies are required to include in their insurance prospectuses used for solicitation, certain matters such as, (i) the insurance company or agent's name, (ii) important matters concerning rights and duties of the holder of the insurance contract, (iii) matters concerning on what is being insured under insurance policies, (iv) matters concerning restriction of payment of insurance proceeds, (v) matters on refunds from insurance contract cancellation, (vi) matters concerning depositor protection.[48] Insurance companies (or persons engaged in insurance solicitation) are also required to explain to the consumer, important matters concerning insurance contracts, such as the premium, scope of coverage, grounds for restricting the payment of insurance proceeds, and other relevant matters to an ordinary policy-holder in an understandable manner.[49]

The Act mandates certain matters to be included in an advertisement for an insurance contract, such as, (i) details recommending to read a product description and terms and conditions before concluding an insurance contract, and (ii) details stating that insurance underwriting may be rejected, premiums may be increased, or details of coverage may change where a policyholder concludes another insurance contract after cancelling a pre-existing insurance contract.[50] An advertisement shall not include certain matters such as, (i) misleading the policyholder that he/she may receive insurance proceeds without any restrictions regardless of contractual restrictions on payment or exemption clauses, (ii) misleading a policyholder by emphasizing/exaggerating certain details or introducing example cases in which a policyholder has received a large amount of insurance proceeds or (iii) misleading a policyholder into underestimate the price of premiums by insufficiently explaining the calculation standards of premiums.[51]

(2) **Know-Your-Customer and Suitability Rules, Duty to Verify Dual Contracts**

Similar to the Capital Market Act, the Insurance Business Act has incorporated suitability rules in insurance contract solicitation by requiring an insurance company to assess the prospective policyholder, and make recommendations that are suitable to the policyholder. Specifically, an insurance company shall, first assess the age and property status of the policyholder, the reason the policyholder buys insurance, and other relevant matters by interviewing or questioning the policyholder.[52] The insurance company is then prohibited from soliciting an ordinary policyholder[53] to enter into an insurance contract which is deemed inappropriate for the ordinary policyholder in light of the information collected in the aforementioned manner.[54] An insurance company is also required to verify, after obtaining consent thereof of the policyholder, whether a potential policyholder has entered into an insurance contract which covers the same risk as that to be covered by the insurance contract he/she or it intends to solicit, before soliciting certain insurance contracts.[55]

(3) **Prohibition of Mis-selling and other Illegal Activities**

Some examples of acts that are prohibited under the Insurance Business Act in relation to consumer protection, are as follows: (i) providing false information about the details of the insurance contract, or failure to provide important details of the contract, (ii) comparing an insurance contract with another without objective standards, obstructing a policyholder from notifying the insurance company about important matters about his/her insurance contract, (iii) inducing a policy holder to provide false information to his/her insurance company, (iv) unduly inducing a policyholder to enter into a new insurance contract by cancelling an pre-existing insurance contract, (v) entering into an insurance contract without the consent of a person, (vi) placing false signature of a policyholder, (vii) soliciting insurance contracts in the name of a person other than who is actually engaged in insurance solicitation, (vii) requiring a policyholder to enter into an insurance contract in relation to a loan, (viii) refusing insurance subscription by a disabled person.[56]

2.2 Rationale and Direction of FCP

Financial consumer protection has been one of a few goals that financial regulators have always pursued, as they seek the goal as well as growth of financial service institutions, since they believed in their capacity to achieve both goals in one hand. As a result, the official name of the regulator is the Financial Services Commission, which was renamed from the Financial Supervisory Commission in 2008, and its dual roles have been under skepticism over its sustainability as well as feasibility, facing a pressure to introduce the Australian style of twin peak system.

In line with international practice, there are two, mutually independent but sometimes conflicting, ways in Korea to protect financial consumers—prudential regulation and business conduct regulation. As the former is to monitor financial soundness of financial institutions while the latter to regulate market activities in general, traditionally the former has been considered as more fundamental and critical than the latter in Korea. It is due to the fact that any bank's failure can influence most of deposit holders while any deceptive sales can impact some depositors in particular, for example. Moreover, the fact that most of financial intermediaries in Korea lack in capital adequacy also makes the prudential regulation more seriously taken than the other. Since the financial crisis in 2008 took place combined with underperforming regulation of market conduct, demand for stricter conduct regulation or consumer protection has been made. Some reformers have proposed to create a dedicated supervisory body for each goal (i.e. one for prudential supervision, and one for conduct supervision).

Because of the weak market conduct regulation in Korea, financial consumer protection is usually referred to as the regulation, excluding the prudential regulation in the regulatory expression. That is, financial regulation in Korea is divided into the prudential regulation and consumer protection regulation, so to speak. The financial consumer protection is so mis-named that the prudential regulation might be understood in some cases to protect financial intermediaries rather than financial consumers.

The market conduct regulator, the newly established division (i.e. Financial Consumer Protection Bureau) established within the financial regulators, has not been so strong or popular at the integrated regulatory body in Korea. It has never been empowered by the top management of the supervisory body nor highly appreciated by consumer activists, while the prudential regulators has enjoyed a rather strong position or treatment from the industry. Also counterpart of the consumer regulators are complaining consumers, while that of the prudential regulators are benign industry people. Nevertheless, the emerging regulatory function is getting more power and popularity in Korean regulatory landscape, as the organizational change is ongoing and the part is taking more regulatory resources as time goes by.

When it comes to supervision method, which can be divided into active one, principle-based one, and disclosure-based one, Korea is now gradually shifting from the first method to the others, by flavoring the second or the third ones little by little. Traditionally, Korean regulator has had such a strong position to maintain the active one that it might involve every detail of business management of financial intermediaries, leading to inefficacy of management and continuing dependence on regulators, in spite of persistent request for more freedom in management. It is not until recently that the big brother spirit, kept by regulators, and undergrown self-independence of industry people are being weakened and changing by other system such as principle based system of disclosure based system.

As to types of consumers, financial intermediaries like to divide them into good common consumers and malicious special ones with a wrongful intention and unacceptable behavior for their own sake. Existence of the latter type of consumers is told to be a rationale for the industry people not to pay whole respect to entire consumers, under information asymmetry of the type of consumers. The supply side people argue against strengthened protection system for consumers due to the likely increasing type 2 error out of the change. Nevertheless, there is no consensus on the relative size of the so called black consumers over the while consumers, despite both industry and some regulators insist that the negative impact of the malicious consumers cannot be overemphasized. Meanwhile, recently the anti-fraud law of insurance has become effective in Korea where as the consumer protection law has not be enacted yet.

2.3 Consumer Protection System

2.3.1 Ex-Ante Protection

Ex-ante protection for consumers are manifold as follows.

- Consumer Literacy Education:
  The consumer education programs are developed and run by supervision agents and major financial institutions, as stakeholders of the financial market, as well as consumer unions sponsored by government (fair trade commission). Interestingly, the Korean consumer activists usually lack in financial resources due to low support from consumers to rely on governmental support.
- Product and Price controls,
  Those controls have existed in order to protect consumers by enabling them to purchase safe and sound products with reasonable prices, but limiting innovation and competition among financial consumers. The controls were substantially lifted in 2015 by the financial regulator believing that their disadvantages outweigh the advantages no more.
- Salesperson license and qualification systems available but not so stringent
  Information Disclosure system: The license or registration systems exist for the salespersons to hold a minimum required knowledge and business ethics. They have been tightened year by year by law and rule, nevertheless lagging behind

ever increasing product complexity, bringing more complaint filings than before.

- Appropriation principle applied to a limited product line
  The principle requires salespersons of financial products to check the consumers' need and capacity to purchase the product in such product lines of major importance or risk for consumers' standpoint as loan or savings with risk elements. Feeling it difficult or unreasonable to obey the principle, some financial intermediaries do lobby to limit the application of the principle.
- Good faith and fair treatment rule not applied yet as in U.S.
  The rule, now popular in the U.S., has not been available in Korea. Some insurance companies exercise their power to refrain from consumers' legal action against them.
- Anti Competition law
  The law as well as segmented business laws governs financial transaction, mostly up to the contractual clauses and pricing.

2.3.2 Ex-Post Protection

- Complaints and Dispute settlement
  The system takes place as an in-house division of the FSS yet, but being subject to majority expert opinion to separate the semi-judicial function from the rather administrative organization. Inconsistency of decision and impartiality of the settlement system has been at issue.
- Deposit insurance scheme
  Korean deposit insurance system is well known for its integrated body to cover all the financial sectors in one hand, regardless of divisional difference among banks, security brokers, and insurers. The system runs a prepayment system with a different rate for each financial sector but not different rate for each company. The public company operating the insurance system shows an expansive coverage compared to other countries.

3 Financial Consumer Protection Institution (Hardware)

3.1 Financial Supervision Organization

3.1.1 History

The Financial Supervisory Service (FSS) was established on January 2, 1999, as Korea's fully integrated supervisory authority under the Act on the Establishment of Financial Supervisory Organizations (the "Establishment Act") that the National Assembly approved on December 29, 1997. The Establishment Act created the FSS as a specially legislated quasi-government supervisory authority and charged it with financial supervision across the entire financial sector.

Prior to the creation of the FSS, financial supervision was carried out by four separate sector-based authorities with the finance ministry exercising significant overarching powers. For banking sector supervision, the Office of Banking Supervision under the Bank of Korea conducted examination of commercial banks and foreign bank branches, while the finance ministry assumed the primary responsibility for the oversight of government-affiliated policy banks and nonbank credit institutions. Similarly, securities sector supervision was shared by the Securities Supervisory Board and the finance ministry, and insurance sector supervision by the Insurance Supervisory Board and the finance ministry. Supervision of other nonbank financial companies was generally divided between the finance ministry and the Bank of Korea's Office of Banking Supervision.

Although institutional and systemic shortcomings that came to light during the 1997 Asian financial crisis reinforced the need for reform of the regulatory and supervisory structures and frameworks, there was a broad recognition even before the crisis of changes needed to deal with the evolving financial market landscape. These ranged from the accelerating convergence of financial services to the blurring of the traditional boundaries between banking and nonbanking activities. The confluence of financial market liberalization, deregulation, and globalization that were gathering momentum across countries at the time also pointed to the need for bold systemic reform to drastically improve the effectiveness of Korea's financial regulation and supervision.

Recognizing the exigency of reform, the government set up a presidential committee in January 1997 to explore ways to bring about more efficient and more robust financial regulation and supervision. The committee followed up with recommendations that culminated in the creation of the Financial Supervisory Commission—predecessor to the Financial Services Commission—as the integrated regulatory authority on April 1, 1998, and the creation of the FSS as the integrated supervisory authority on January 2, 1999. As part of major government reorganization, the Financial Supervisory Commission consolidated the Financial Policy Bureau under the Ministry of Strategy and Finance (formerly Ministry of Finance and Economy) and became the Financial Services Commission (FSC) on February 29, 2008. In addition, the name of the Establishment Act, formerly the Act on the Establishment of Financial Supervisory Organizations, was changed to the Act on the Establishment of the Financial Services Commission.

As a result of the two-tier system created by the law, the FSC assumes the primary responsibility for rulemaking and licensing while the FSS principally conducts prudential supervision, capital market supervision, consumer protection, and other oversight and enforcement activities as delegated or charged by the FSC. As the government regulatory authority, the FSC is staffed by civil servants, but the FSS as a specially legislated supervisory authority is staffed by private sector employees who are not part of the government civil service system.

3.1.2 Organization

(1) **Divisions and Departments**
Following a major reorganization on February 2, 2016, with significantly augmented consumer protection, the FSS was restructured into nine divisions comprising 44 departments and 15 offices. Each of the departments and offices under the nine divisions is charged with specific functions, tasks, and responsibilities ranging from administrative support and examination to consumer protection endeavors. Each of the nine divisions is headed by a deputy governor and each of the 44 departments by a director general. In addition to its headquarters in Seoul, the FSS maintains ten regional and district offices nationwide and eight representative offices overseas. The Office of the Chief Executive Auditor, which comprises an internal audit office and an inspection office, is responsible for internal audit, inspection, and compliance.

(2) **Sources of Operating Funds**
Fees collected from financial institutions and securities issuers and appropriation from the Bank of Korea comprise most of the operating budget for the FSS. The relative share of fees to be contributed by the regulated financial institutions is determined annually by the FSC based on the total amount of liabilities at the end of the previous fiscal year, subject to certain restrictions. The relative share to be collected from securities issuers is also determined by the FSC based on the total amount of securities issued. When approving the budget for a fiscal year, the FSC takes into account the current funding level, assets, and other financial factors and conditions.

3.1.3 Supervision

(1) **Financial Institutions**

(a) FSS-Supervised Financial Institutions
As the integrated supervisory authority, the FSS oversees financial services firms across the entire financial sectors. For supervision purposes, the FSS classifies financial services firms it supervises into four general types: banks, nonbank financial companies, financial investment services providers, and insurance companies.

(b) Entry and Exit Supervision
Financial services businesses are regulated enterprises, and financial services companies are incorporated in accordance with established rules and standards as provided under the law.

Ownership of financial services companies is regulated in accordance with the principle of the separation of banking and commerce to prevent financial services companies from operating under the undue influence of a select few individuals, companies, or business groups. On the other hand, non-depository financial services companies such as financial investment services providers and specialized credit finance companies are not subject to any material ownership restrictions. Small-scale depositary institutions such as mutual savings banks and credit unions that are not particularly susceptible to abuse by the controlling shareholders are also subject to less stringent ownership regulations.

The board of directors of a financial services company comprises executive directors, non-executive directors (non-executive inside directors), and outside directors (non-executive outside directors). Non-executive directors and outside directors are mutually exclusive. Non-executive directors do not take part in the day-to-day management decisions. Outside directors are independent of the management. They are appointed at the general shareholders' meeting with the recommendation of the board's director selection committee; outside directors must make up the majority of the director selection committee.

(c) Prudential Regulation and Supervision
For supervision purposes, financial services that financial services firms engage in are broadly classified into primary business, secondary business, and concurrent business.

- Banks
- Nonbank Financial Companies
- Financial Investment Services Providers
- Insurance Companies

The business activities of financial institutions are subject to certain restrictions and prohibitions that are intended to prevent illegal or anti-competitive activities while promoting sound business practices, competition, and consumer protection.

(d) Supervisory Evaluation and Rating

The FSS periodically evaluates financial institutions' financial health and operations and assigns an overall rating. Supervisory rating was first introduced for banks in October 1996 following Korea's membership in the Organization for Economic Co-operation and Development (OECD) and Bank for International Settlements (BIS). The rating system was soon expanded to other types of financial institutions. It took effect for securities companies in January 1999, insurance companies and specialized credit finance companies in January 2000, mutual savings banks and specialized banks in July and August, respectively, of 2000, and financial holding companies in December 2000, and asset management companies in July 2001.

(2) **Examination**

The Financial Supervisory Service examines financial institutions pursuant to authority conferred by article 37 of the Act on the Establishment, etc. of Financial Services Commission (the "Establishment Act")—formerly the Act on the

Establishment, etc. of Financial Supervisory Organizations— and other financial statutes.

FSS examiners perform full-scope and targeted examinations of financial institutions to help ensure their safety and soundness and compliance with laws and regulations. FSS examiners conduct full-scope examination to evaluate financial institutions' overall financial, management, operational, and compliance performance. The selection of financial institutions that are to undergo a full-scope examination is made in advance during the annual examination planning. The determination of the timing and duration of a full-scope examination and the number of examiners to be assigned is normally made with due consideration given to the size, the complexity, and the risk profiles of the subject institution, findings from the previous examination, and issues of supervisory concerns that have been raised from off-site monitoring.

A targeted examination is limited in scope and is intended to address a narrow range of supervision matters and concerns such as incidents of irregularity and unsound business activity.

Off-site monitoring also constitutes an important component of financial institution examination that complements on-site examination. For normal off-site monitoring, FSS examiners analyze financial and operational reporting from financial institutions, evaluates quantitative safety and soundness measures, and work to identify areas of weaknesses and risks in need of supervision action. If necessary, FSS examiners conduct an on-site inspection and meet with the subject institution's senior executives to address issues of supervisory concern.

(3) **Capital Markets**

(a) Corporate Disclosure

The Financial Investment Services and Capital Markets Act (FSCMA) provides for fair and transparent corporate disclosure in order to protect investors and ensure an efficient and well-functioning securities market. The FSCMA provides for three general types of corporate disclosure: disclosure for new securities issuance, disclosure for listed companies, and disclosure for significant event.

Disclosure for new securities offering pertains to information that an issuer must file with the FSC/FSS about an investment to be offered for sale to the public. The disclosure is made in the form of registration statement and prospectus. Registration statement is filed by a prospective securities issuer about to make a public offering, while prospectus is a document the issuer prepares with facts about the offering to help investors make an informed investment decision.

Disclosure for listed companies refers to information about business operation and financial conditions that listed companies must file with the FSS periodically and as needed or appropriate. Disclosure for listed companies consists of business report—the quarterly, semiannual, and annual regulatory filings publicly companies are required submit to the FSS about their business operations, financial conditions, and other major aspects about their business—and material disclosure, which must be filed for any major business decision or external event that has a material effect on the company's ongoing business operation.

In addition to disclosures applicable to new securities offering and listed companies, disclosure for significant event must be filed when a major development or change to a company's business operations or financial conditions occurs. Excluding disclosures applicable to new securities offering and listed companies, disclosure for significant event include large share ownership, disclosure for corporate insiders, tender offer, and short-swing profit.

(b) Unfair Trading and Enforcement

Although unfair trading covers wide-ranging unlawful activities in the securities markets and is not specifically defined in the FSCMA, it comprises three general types: the use of material nonpublic information, market manipulation, and other illegal acts.

As authorized under the Financial Investment Services and Capital Markets Act (FSCMA), the Securities and Futures Commission (SFC) is vested with the powers to investigate unfair trading and take appropriate enforcement actions. The powers specified for the SFC in the FSCMA include disgorgement of gains from short-swing profit by corporate insiders, reporting of share ownership by company officers and other insiders, prohibition on the use of material nonpublic information, prohibition on market manipulation, and prohibition on unlawful securities trading. The SFC is also granted the authority to investigate security offerings in the primary and secondary markets.

(c) Accounting Supervision

The legal framework for accounting supervision comprises the Financial Investment Services and Capital Markets Act (FSCMA), the Act on External Audit of Stock Companies (AEASC), and the Certified Public Accountant Act.

The FSCMA provides disclosure measures such as the periodic filing of business report to ensure the accuracy and reliability of financial reporting. It requires audited financial reporting from listed companies that are subject to business reports. The FSCMA also requires companies to continually operate internal controls, evaluate internal audit and the external auditors, and provide detailed assessment in their business report.

The AEASC provides for independent external audit of listed companies and others subject to independent external audit. Listed companies are required to appoint an auditor for a three-year term but may dismiss the auditor before the three-year term ends with the approval of the company's audit committee and reporting to the SFC. The Certified Public Accountant Act governs the qualification, registration, services, rights, and duties of certified public accountants (CPAs) and accounting firms. CPAs and accounting firms must register with the FSC/FSS. Under the AEASC, any group of three or CPAs that operates as a non-business entity must register with the Korean Institute of Certified Public Accountants to carry on audit performance.

Companies subject to external audit are required to present financial statements in accordance with the established accounting standards. With accounting oversight authority delegated from the SFC, the FSS examines listed companies' and unlisted financial services firms' financial statements and the audit performed while it inspects the auditor's report. Companies subject to external audit must also operate with an internal accounting management system for the preparation of accounting information. The auditor must also prepare an evaluation of the actual status of the audited company's internal accounting management system and provide it in the business report.

(4) **Consumer Protection**

The Financial Supervisory Service works to protect financial consumers in collaboration with various government consumer protection agencies such as the Korea Consumer Agency, the Korea Deposit Insurance Corporation, and the Fair Trade Commission.

Consumer protection activities that the Financial Supervisory Service performs can be broadly divided into ex-ante and ex-post measures. Whereas ex-ante measures include activities such as enforcing proper contract provisions for financial products and due disclosures and providing counseling and financial education to consumers, ex-post measures refer to actions that are intended to rectify abuses and malpractices of financial institutions and bring remedy to consumers who have been harmed.

In May 2012, the Financial Supervisory Service consolidated its consumer protection functions and established the Financial Consumer Protection Bureau (FCPB) for enhanced financial consumer protection. The FCPB's main responsibilities and functions are to administer consumer complaints, provide consumer counseling and dispute mediation services, and take supervisory actions on improper business practices of financial institutions. In addition, the FCPB conducts wide-ranging financial education programs to help improve consumer financial literacy.

As part of its consumer protection mandate, the FCPB also evaluates financial institutions' consumer protection practices and consumer complaint administration systems. When deemed necessary, the FCPB reviews complaints filed against financial institutions and conducts on-site inspections. In respect of product and service disclosures, the FCPB works to improve disclosures standards to help consumers make informed decisions. It also provides personal finance counseling services to help consumers exercise responsible and sound personal finance, management debt, and understand financial products. The FCPB also works to expand financial education by fostering partnerships between schools and financial institutions so that students can develop sound personal finance habits and skills.[57]

3.2 Deposit Insurance Corporation

3.2.1 Korea Deposit Insurance Corporation

The KDIC was established on June 1, 1996 after the legislation of the Depositor Protection Act (DPA) on December 29, 1995. The KDIC started as a protector of bank depositors, while there were separate funds for non-bank financial sectors. The coverage was initially KRW 20 million per depositor, but the financial instability that resulted from the 1997 Asian financial crisis led the government to adopting a temporary blanket coverage scheme.

The DPA was revised at the end of 1997, and, accordingly, separate deposit insurance funds were consolidated into the KDIC's Deposit Insurance Fund in April 1998. Not only deposits of banks but also those held by securities companies, insurance companies, merchant banks, mutual savings banks, and credit unions (excluded from the coverage since 2004) became eligible for protection. This created a single, comprehensive, and integrated deposit insurance system designed to enhance financial stability and to ensure the public's confidence in the financial system.

A transition was made to a limited coverage of KRW 50 million in 2001. The higher limit was established to ensure sustainable stability in the financial market. As the system is not immune to the risk of moral hazard, the KDIC closely monitors both financial and non-financial risks of insured financial institutions.

Although Korea's deposit insurance system has only been in operation for a relatively short period of time, it has shown remarkable growth and will continue to make a positive contribution to financial stability through the adoption of various devices and policies designed to further advance the deposit insurance system.

3.2.2 Insured financial institutions

Insured financial institutions include: banks, insurance companies (life insurers and non-life insurers), investment traders and brokers, merchant banks and mutual savings banks. On February 4, 2009, with the enactment of the Financial Investment Services and Capital Markets Act, asset management firms licensed under the said Act for investment brokerage and trading (excluding investment brokers engaged in electronic securities brokerage services as defined under Article 78 of the Financial Investment Services and Capital Markets Act) were included in coverage.

Local branches of foreign banks, the National Agricultural Cooperatives Federation (NongHyup) and the National Federation of Fisheries Cooperatives (SuHyup) are KDIC-insured. (However, local branches of NongHyup and SuHyup, the National Credit Unions' Federation of Korea and the Community Credit Cooperatives are not KDIC-insured. They are protected by their own funds established under the relevant legislation.)

3.2.3 Deposit Insurance Coverage

Korea provided protection of up to KRW 20 million per depositor (or KRW 50 million won for insurance policyholders) when the deposit insurance scheme was first introduced. However, in the wake of the 1997 Asian financial crisis, blanket guarantees were temporarily introduced in order to minimize the impact of the restructuring of the financial system and ensure the stability of financial transactions. In 2001, limited coverage was reinstated. Since January 1, 2001, the KDIC has insured up to KRW 50 million per depositor including principal and designated interest in case an insured financial institution goes bankrupt due to an insurance contingency (e.g. business suspension, license revocation).

For the remaining amount that is not KDIC-insured, depositors can recover all or part of that when they receive bankruptcy dividends from the bankruptcy estate. The bankruptcy estate pays bankruptcy dividends from remaining assets, if any, after repaying senior debts.

The coverage limit of KRW 50 million is the total amount that a depositor can receive per institution. It is not calculated per type of deposit or per branch. "Per depositor" means not only individuals, but also corporate entities. If a depositor of a failed financial institution has an outstanding debt to the institution, the debt will be deducted from the deposit (which is called a set-off) and the remaining amount will be protected.[58]

3.3 Dispute Settlement Organization

The Financial Disputes Settlement Committee (FDSC) is a committee that has been created within the FSS specifically to help mediate and resolve financial disputes between consumers and financial service firms. Upon a consumer petition or in response to a consumer complaint, the FSS verifies the relevant facts and makes impartial recommendations so that both the consumer and the financial institution can mutually come to a resolution with resorting to often time-consuming and costly litigation through the court.

The FDSC is staffed by 30 specialists that include independent outside experts. Each FDSC mediation meeting is attended by seven to eleven members who are selected by the FDSC chairperson on the basis of the specific areas of consumer complaints, which may vary from banking, nonbanking, and financial investments to insurance.

Consumer complaint is referred to the FDSC when the parties involved are unable to reach an agreement within 30 days from the day the request for mediation was submitted. The FDSC then deliberates on the case and proposes a resolution within 60 days with due consideration given to the applicable rules and regulations and information provide by both parties. The FDSC may dismiss a complaint if it does not merit a mediated resolution from the FDSC or if the facts and information provided by the parties involved cannot be substantiated. The FSDC decides on a resolution proposal with the majority vote. Once an FDSC resolution proposal is accepted by the parties involved, no further recourse is available.

Unlike arbitration, the FDSC recommendation is not legally binding, and adjudication through the court is still available to consumers and financial institutions. The FSS may provide litigation support to a consumer if the FSS deems the action of a financial institution improper.[59]

4 Special Financial Consumer Protection Systems

4.1 For the Elderly Group

4.1.1 Long-Term Care Insurance

(1) **Definitions**

This is the social insurance system that provides long-term care benefit to the elderly who have difficulty taking care of themselves for a period of at least 6 months due to old age or geriatric disease. It supports them in their physical activities or housework based on the principle of social solidarity.

Recipients of the long-term care treatment insurance system access long-term benefits such as assistance with excretion, bathing, eating, cooking, washing, cleaning, nursing, treatment or recuperation counseling. Developed countries that are experiencing the aging phenomenon have long since introduced long-term care systems and provided long-term care services

Purpose is to regulate items on long-term care benefit, which supports physical activity or housework for the elderly who have difficulty taking care of themselves due to old age or geriatric disease. It aims at promoting senior citizens'health and life stabilization as well as increasing the quality of people's lives by mitigating the burden of care on family members.

(2) **Insurance Benefit**

Welfare equipment provides assistance in the ADL (activities of daily living) and physical activities of those who have difficulty carrying out their daily routine due to the deterioration of physical and mental function. Welfare equipment can be utilized by purchase or rental by making small copayments.

- Welfare items available for purchase include (9 types): portable toilets, bath chairs, adult walkers, safety handles, non-slip products, toilet pots, canes, bedsore prevention matresses, posture conversion tools.
- Welfare items available for rental include (8 types): manual wheelchairs, motorized beds, manual beds, bedsore preventing matresses, movable tubs, bath lifts, ramps, wandering detectors.[60]

4.2 For the Poor Group

4.2.1 Microinsurance

This is the protection of low-income people against specific perils in exchange for regular premium payment proportionate to the likelihood and cost of the risks involved. This definition is exactly the same as one might use for regular insurance except for the clearly prescribed target market: low-income people.

The government has been driving policy efforts to reduce financial burden of low-income borrowers and enhance their access to financial services through various microfinance programs. The Happiness Fund, launched in March 2013, purchased delinquent loans of 2.8 million low-income borrowers to reduce their debt repayment burden and supported debt-restructuring of 410,000 borrowers as of May 2015. Four major government-backed microloans have also provided a total of KRW 11 trillion to more than 1.1 million low-income borrowers since 2013.

In order to expand microfinance support in a sustainable way, the FSC came up with its plan focused on increasing the amount of policy microloans, while reducing debt servicing burden of low-income borrowers. Policy incentives will be also devised to give more benefits to those who faithfully repay their debt. Microfinance policy will be pushed forward to support the self-sufficiency of low-income families and individuals through comprehensive assistance for debt restructuring, job seeking and micro-savings.

4.3 For the Young

4.3.1 Financial Literacy Pilot Program

The Financial Supervisory Service announced that a total of 667 primary and secondary schools nationwide have been selected for the Financial Literacy Pilot (FLP) program, an educational initiative aimed at advancing financial literacy of students in elementary, middle, and high schools.

With growing interest in the FLP program and rising demand for finance education, the number of schools applying for FSS-supported financial education has surged 62% from the previous year. The FSS noted that more than 90% of the selected schools are located in provincial districts.

A total of 49 institutions that are members of the Financial Education Total Network (FETN)—a partnership formed between the FSS and financial institutions to promote financial literacy—are expected to take part in the FLP program. Of the participating institutions, banks have been assigned a total of 293 schools, the largest number, for the program. This year, the FSS expects to more than double the number of schools it covers under the FLP program to demonstrate its commitment to the FLP program and encourage financial institutions to step up their contributions to the program.[61]

5 Market Issues

5.1 Financial Consumer Informatiom Portal "FINE" (Financial Information Network)

The Financial Supervisory Service established a system which enables consumers to search financial products from all areas and compare their characteristics at a single platform.

This one-stop service for search and comparison has been operated and considered favorable for financial consumers. The FSS decided to provide additional information regarding loans, bank deposits/installment savings, tax-saving investment products and credit/debit cards.

It is expected that the expanded service will help users rationally choose financial products which are suitable for their purposes and also prevent them from wasting times and costs. Furthermore, the service will encourage competition in a free market and contribute to improving information asymmetry.[62]

Notes

1. The Financial Supervisory Service (FSS) which is the main body of the integrated supervisory agency was established on January 2, 1999, under the Act on the Establishment of Financial Supervisory Organizations, Act No. 5490, enacted as of December 31, 1997. This Act is the general statue governing the current organizational structure of financial regulation in Korea.
2. One of the central issues in the debate on how to reform the regulatory structure, is whether or not to create and reassign the consumer protection function to a separate regulator, and reform the current structure where the FSS oversees both prudential regulation and consumer protection functions.
3. The Financial Services Commission ("FSC") a governmental commission that oversees the FSS regarding financial supervision, has made a legislative notice on June 28, 2016 (Notice No. 2016-197), and finalized the government bill on April 25, 2017. The FSC prospects the Bill to be submitted to the National Assembly in May 2017. (http://www.lawmaking.go.kr/lmSts/govLm/2000000168047?gnb=2&snb=3&lnb=1&lmPlnSeq=1000000127310).
4. Article 2 Para. 8 of the Proposed Bill.
5. Article 2 Para. 9 of the Proposed Bill.
6. Article 2 Para. 10 of the Proposed Bill.
7. Article 62 of the Proposed Bill.
8. Articles 51–52 of the Proposed Bill.

9. Articles 16–22 of the Proposed Bill.
10. Articles 54, 62 of the Proposed Bill.
11. Article 18 of the Proposed Bill.
12. Articles 45–47 of the Proposed Bill.
13. Article 3 of the Proposed Bill.
14. Article 6 of the Proposed Bill.
15. Criticism that consumer protection issues were treated in a fragmented ad hoc manner has elicited several unsuccessful legislative bills, the most recent bill being the Proposed Bill discussed in Part 1.
16. Act No. 8635, enacted on August 3, 2007 (effective on February 4, 2009).
17. Act No. 139, enacted on May 5, 1950.
18. Act No. 973, enacted on January 15, 1962.
19. Act No. 5374, enacted in August 28, 1997.
20. Use and Protection of Credit Information Act, Act No. 4866, enacted on January 5, 1995.
21. Fair Debt Collection Act, Act No. 9418, enacted in February 6, 2009.
22. Article 52-2 Para. 2 of the Banking Act; Article 24-4 Para. 1 of the Enforcement Decree of the Banking Act.
23. Article 52-2 Para. 2 of the Banking Act; Article 24-4 Para. 2. of the Enforcement Decree of the Banking Act.
24. Article 52-2 Para. 2 of the Banking Act; Article 24-4 Para. 2 of the Enforcement Decree of the Banking Act; Article 89 of the Regulation on Supervision of Banking Business; Articles 70–76 of the Detailed Regulations on Supervision of Banking Business.
25. Article 52-2 of the Banking Act; Detailed Regulations on Supervision of Banking Business Article 78.
26. Article 52-3 Para. 2 of the Banking Act.
27. Article 52-2 Para. 1 of the Banking Act; Article 24-4 of the Enforcement Decree of the Banking Act.
28. Article 34-2 of the Banking Act (Enacted under the amendment of March 29, 2016, Act No.141290).
29. Article 34-3 of the Banking Act (Enacted under the amendment of March 29, 2016 Act No.141290).
30. Act No. 972, enacted on January 15, 1962.
31. The Capital Market Act abolished and replaced the previous major capital market laws such as the Securities and Exchange Act, Futures Trading Act, Korea Securities and Futures Exchange Act, Indirect Investment Asset Management Act, Trust Business Act and Merchant Banks Act.
32. A technical term defined under Article 8 of the Capital Markets Act, which includes securities brokers and dealers, investment banks and investment advisory companies that are licensed or registered with the FSC.
33. A technical term defined under Article 9 Para. 6 of the Capital Markets Act; generally meaning a retail or unsophisticated investor.

34. A technical term defined under Article 3 of the Capital Markets Act which includes securities and derivatives.
35. Articles 47 and 58 of the Capital Market Act; Article 53 of the Enforcement Decree of the Capital Market Act.
36. Article 47 Para. 2 of the Capital Markets Act.
37. Article 57 Para 2 of the Capital Markets Act.
38. A technical term defined by Article 6 Para. 5 of the Capital Market Act, which is similar to a mutual fund.
39. Article 57 Para 3 of the Capital Markets Act.
40. Article 4-37 of the Regulation on Financial Investment Business.
41. Article 46-2 Para. 1 of the Capital Markets Act.
42. Article 46-2 Para. 2 of the Capital Markets Act.
43. Article 49 of the Capital Markets Act.
44. Article 55 of the Capital Markets Act.
45. Article 71 Paras. 1 and 2 of the Capital Markets Act.
46. Article 71 Para 3 of the Capital Markets Act.
47. Part 4 (Articles 638 to 739-3) of the Commercial Act (Act No. 1000, enacted in January 20, 1962).
48. Article 95 of the Insurance Business Act.
49. Article 95-2 of the Insurance Business Act (Added by amendment on July 23, 2010).
50. Article 95-4 Para. 2 of the Insurance Business Act (Added by amendment on July 23, 2010).
51. Article 95-4 Para. 3 of the Insurance Business Act (Added by amendment on July 23, 2010).
52. Article 95-3 Para. 1 of the Insurance Business Act (Added by amendment on July 23, 2010).
53. "Ordinary policyholder" is defined under Article 2 Para. 20 of the Insurance Business Act, generally meaning a retail policy holder that lacks expertise on insurance contracts. A "professional policyholder," on the other hand, are entities such as the government or financial institutions that are capable of understanding insurance contracts based in their expertise.
54. Article 95-3 Para. 3 of the Insurance Business Act (Added by amendment on July 23, 2010).
55. Article 95-5 of the Insurance Business Act (Added by amendment on July 23, 2010).
56. Article 97 of the Insurance Business Act.
57. FSS Annual Report 2016, Financial Supervisory Service.
58. KDIC Annual Report 2016, Korea Deposit Insurance Corporation.
59. Consumer Complaint Mediation, Financial Supervisory Service.
60. Long Term Care Insurance, National Health Insurance Service.
61. FSS Press Release March 25, 2015, Financial Supervisory Service.
62. Financial Consumer Information Portal.

Hongjoo Jung has been teaching at SungKyunKwan University since 1991, right after obtaining his Ph.D. degree in the area of Risk Management and Insurance at the Wharton School, University of Pennsylvania. His research interests include financial convergence, financial consumer protection, social security system, in addition to the RMI. In the year 2010 and 2015, Dr. Jung played a key role in organizing the Korean Academy of Financial Consumers and the International Academy of Financial Consumers respectively.

Misoo Choi has been teaching at Seoul Digital University since 2003, right after obtaining Ph.D. degree in the area of Insurance at SungKyunKwan University. Her research interests include financial consumer protection, dispute cases of finance and insurance. Dr. Choi is a member of the board of directors of Korean Academy of Financial Consumers and the International Academy of Financial Consumers respectively.

Youkyung Huh is a doctoral candidate (Doctor of Juridicial Science; SJD) at the University of Virginia School of Law and a member of the Korean Bar Association. Her research interests include financial regulation, consumer protection, financial regulatory structure and securities regulation. Her work experience includes serving as legal counsel at the Korean Financial Supervisory Service, South Korea's financial regulatory agency. She earned LL.M. degrees from Harvard Law School (2013) and Seoul National University (2012) and a Bachelor of Laws from Ewha Womans University.

Chapter 11
Financial Consumer in Malaysia: Regulators Efforts and Measurements for Consumer Protection

Ahcene Lahsasna

Abstract The public (or retail) consumer is a very important aspect in any financial market. Although they do not provide the bulk of the financing income compared to business consumers or corporations, they make up in terms of quantity and is an essential contributor to the performance of any financial institution. However, financing retail consumers are very much fragile and volatile in nature due to their inability to gasp their own financial capability as well as the tendency to overextend their credit limit which may create problems in the future and affect their ability to pay their financing. This in turn, creates problems for the financial institutions making the recovery process very lengthy and expensive. With that in mind, it is imperative that the retail consumers are educated and taught the proper ways to manage their credit and protect themselves against the inability to pay their financing. Thus, the purpose of this chapter is to highlight the importance of consumer protection and the means that have been put in place by the central bank of Malaysia, Bank Negara Malaysia (BNM) to help increase customer awareness and financial literacy in Malaysia. This chapter will also highlight the challenges that are faced in consumer protection and efforts that have been made to improve consumer protection. This chapter found that the highest percentage of loan approved in Malaysia are loans from the household sector and despite the measures to increase financial literacy and consumer awareness that have been put in place by BNM, there has been a steady increase of bankruptcy cases and scam victims for the past years in Malaysia. It would be interesting to see the impact of the measures put in place by FSA 2013 and IFSA 2013 on financial institutions and retail consumers and it is recommended that a more stringent regulative framework be put in place to address the increase in bankruptcy and scam scandals among the working population.

Keywords Financial inclusion · Financial consumer · Consumer protection Financial literacy

---

A. Lahsasna (✉)
Malaysian Financial Planning Council, Kuala Lumpur, Malaysia
e-mail: lahsasna@gmail.com

© Springer Nature Singapore Pte Ltd. 2018

T.-J. Chen (ed.), *An International Comparison of Financial Consumer Protection*,
https://doi.org/10.1007/978-981-10-8441-6_11

1 Introduction

The average consumer or the retail consumer is the backbone of any country. The prosperity of the people can be used as a yardstick to measure the economic condition of any country. If there are a flurry of activities in the market, be it the financial markets or even the local wet market, it is a sure sign that businesses are doing well and the local (or retail) consumers are able to proactively engage in the economy. Despite the importance of the financial consumer as part of the economy, it could be seen that the path of the financial consumer is paved with risks. The average consumer faces many challenges when making financial decisions, and even savings decisions (one part of an financial decision that a retail consumer will make other than financing, investment, retirement decisions etc.) the requirements before an individual can make an informed decision is very demanding (Lusardi 2008). The consumer is expected to have collected various information and be able to make forecasts on factors such as interest rates, projected inflation, dividend payments, opportunity costs involved if he or she were to save in one particular bank compared to another bank and many others. Thus, an individual faces many challenges and risks when trying to make and commit to financial decisions which will affect their daily lives. And without proper knowledge and exposure towards financial awareness and protection, a consumer might fall into financial pitfalls such as over-extending their credit limit and capacity, bankruptcy, and scams making poor financial decisions, lack of financial planning, lack of awareness of financial protection and many others. With that in mind, this chapter aims to explore the avenues that are put in place by the Malaysian government and its central bank, Bank Negara Malaysia to help improve consumer awareness and financial protection as well as the reasons why a consumer would fall into financial distress and the current trend in bankruptcy in Malaysia.

This chapter is structured into four (4) sections; the first section provides an introduction towards financial literacy and, also looks into the background of the country. The second section describes the current Malaysian financing spectrum focusing especially on retail financing and the third section explores the mechanisms that have been put in place by the Malaysian government. The fourth section then looks into the improvements that have been made by the Malaysian government on the regulations in the financial sector. Finally this chapter concludes on the worrying fact that despite the efforts made by the government and BNM, there has been a steady increase in bankruptcy and financial scams among Malaysians and efforts should be taken to look into the matter and identify the underlying reasons as well as develop measures to address them.

1.1 Background of the Country: Malaysia

Malaysia is a federal constitutional monarchy located in Southeast Asia. It consists of thirteen states and three federal territories. Malaysia is well known to the global financial sector as the center of Islamic finance. In addition to this, the country is also known for its application of a dual financial system where both Islamic and conventional financial systems are running concurrently (Table 1).

Malaysia currently has a population of roughly about 32 million people, with a sustainable GDP growth rate of about 5.8%, a low inflation and unemployment rate of about 4.3 and 3.4% respectively (BNM, Malaysia). The country is also currently ranked on the 18th spot under the Ease of Doing Business by the World Bank Group (2014). This indicates that Malaysia is one of the countries where it would be easy for foreigners and foreign institutions alike to do business in the country. This in itself is a positive indication that Malaysia is an attractive destination for foreign investors to do business and make investments and this would have a positive trickle-down effect to the people and the economy as a whole. A report by the International Monetary Fund (2014) found that Malaysia currently has a sound financial system which is supported by strong supervision and regulation. However, the institution in their country report of Malaysia state concerns on the increase in credit growth and household debt and advices close monitoring of the effectiveness of the country's macro-prudential policies in addressing the risks that are likely to arise due to the increase in credit and debt. The report also mentions on the plans that Malaysia has in place to transform the developing country to becoming a high-income nation by the year 2020 and notes that though several efforts are on track, there are also several activities that needs to be realigned to ensure the success of the whole transformation program.

Malaysia has transformed from a country that is heavily reliant on agricultural exports, to a manufacturing country to now an emerging multi-sector economy. It is now focusing on becoming a high-income nation by the year 2020 (Performance Management & Delivery Unit 2013) and the country aims to achieve this goal via a multi-faceted approach through involvements and investments in various areas such as Islamic finance, high technology industries, biotechnology, and services. A New Economic Model (NEM) was unveiled in 2010 and to achieve the goal in transforming Malaysia as a high-income nation, a National Transformation Programme (NTP) which follows a two-pronged approach consisting of the Economic Transformation Programme (ETP) and Government Transformation Programme (GTP) was unveiled to put the NEM in place (Fig. 1).

Table 1 Key economic facts: Malaysia

Real GDP	5.6% (2017 est.)
GDP growth	5.8% (2017, 2Q)
Inflation rate	4.3% (2017 est.)
Unemployment rate	3.4% (2017 est.)
Population	31,600,000 (Nov. 2017 est.)
Ease of doing business ranking	24th

Source Bank Negara Malaysia

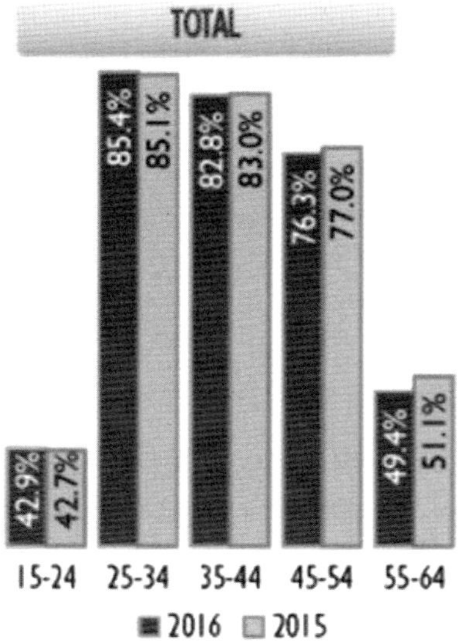

Fig. 1 Demographic population in Malaysia. *Source* Ministry of Statistics Malaysia (2017)

Looking at demographic factors such as age, it can be seen that the majority of the population in Malaysia is the working population. It is a growing nation, and a big number of the population (42.9%t) are those below 25 years old while those who are nearing retirement and already retired are less than 49.4% of the population. There is a demographic shift in Malaysia where majority of the population has shifted from the rural areas to the urban areas. Urban population consists of 72.8% of the population and the rate of urbanization is changing at a rate of 2.49% annually. This is similar to what is published by the World Bank Group (2014) where they recorded that the urban population is rising, with the number of people living in urban areas increasing from 71% of the total population in 2009 to 74% in 2013.

1.2 Retail Financing in Malaysia

The Malaysian financial sector had recently experienced advancement in the system where the country introduced a new law converging the financial system into a single legislative framework. The financial sector is undoubtedly one of the main contributors to the growth of the country's economy. Two new acts, the Financial Services Act 2013 (FSA 2013) and the Islamic Financial Services Act 2013 (IFSA 2013) were enacted as a measure to further strengthen the regulatory framework of the country's financial system. Further advancement and continuous growth of both the Islamic and conventional sector assisted by the development in technology has positioned the Malaysian financial consumer with vast opportunity in financial involvement. At the same time, the risks associated with this involvement creates vulnerability and puts the consumers in need of protection due to the sophistication of today's financial products. Financial consumer protection thus becomes of vital importance to protect both the individual consumers as well as to ensure economic growth. The Malaysian corporate sector financing activity was predominantly bank-based in the early 2000s has now transitioned into more market-based. The development of the Malaysian capital market has opened up a new funding medium for the corporate sector in Malaysia and this shifted the lending environment from bank-based towards a more market-based lending. The banking sector's lending structure has since evolved from offering corporate loans towards retail-based loans in which the loans are distributed to household consumers and to small-and-medium enterprises (SMEs). It has been reported that the share of outstanding loans to the household sector has increased.

The initiative of the government is to move the country into value-added market has placed the financial sector as one of the biggest contributing market to the economic development of the country. The financing activities in Malaysia play an important role in strengthening the consumers' purchasing power. The financing activities in Malaysia are categorized into various sectors. The different segments of contributors under the Malaysian financing spectrum are as depicted in Fig. 2.

Based on financing purpose (Fig. 3), it is apparent that the bulk of the financing is due to the purchase of residential property and non-residential 25 and 9% respectively, working capital 23%, and the purchase of vehicles transport and passenger 10 and 9% respectively. This is consistent with the demographics of the country, as a country that is populated mainly by the younger generation, there is a need for the younger population to commit to huge purchase decisions such as purchasing a property and a car to fit their current needs. Unfortunately, the act of borrowing results in dire consequences, especially for borrowers. Borrowers face

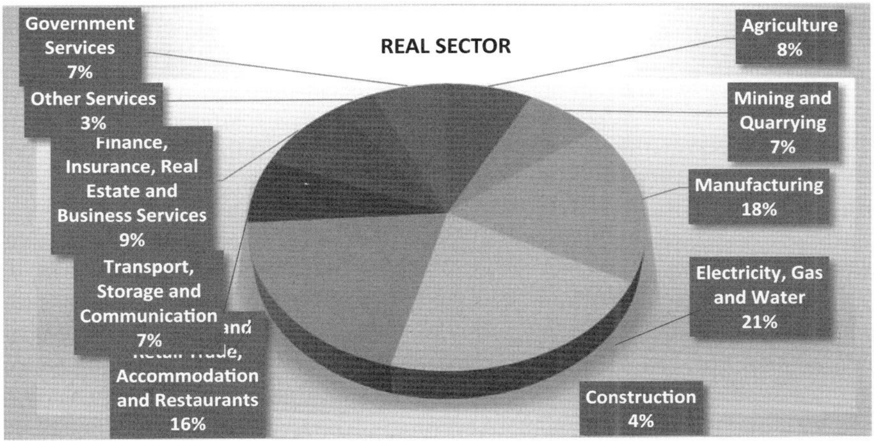

Fig. 2 Financing activities based on sector (November 2017). *Source* Bank Negara Malaysia (2017)

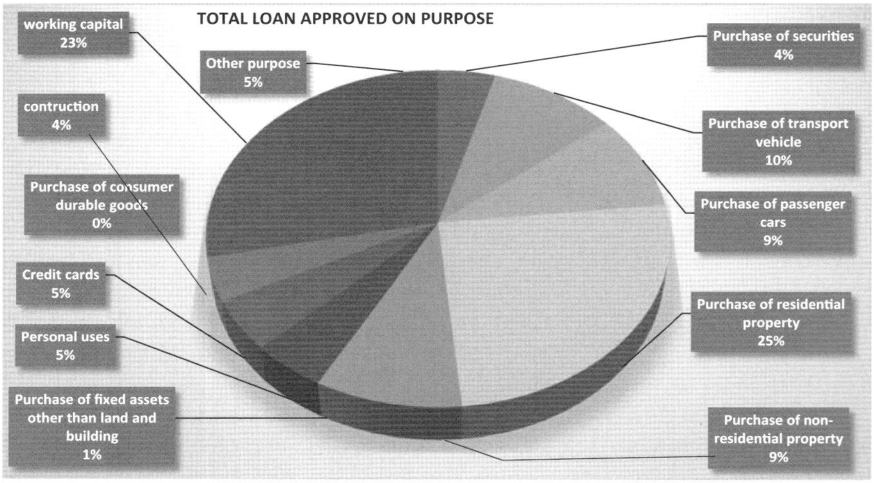

Fig. 3 Total loan approved based on purpose. *Source* Bank Negara Malaysia (2014)

certain risks when they make a decision to borrow and those risks may be contributed by their own naivety and ignorance on prudent credit management or it can also be due to successful marketing campaigns and persuasive, experienced personnel who are able to charm the public into excessive borrowing. Among the consequences are the inability to meet the payments of their monthly loans, getting into more debt just so that they are able to pay their previous loans, and later it turns into a vicious cycle where the borrower face the possibility of being blacklisted by financial institutions and also bankruptcy.

Numbers provided by the Credit Counseling and Debt Management Agency (AKPK) reveals an alarming increase in bankruptcy cases in Malaysia over the past few years (Fig. 4), where in a period of five (5) years between 2008–2012. The bankruptcy cases in 2012 is more than 40% higher than those in 2008.

Among those who are declared as a bankrupt, majority are in the 35–44 age group (Fig. 5). This is coincidentally is also the biggest age group in the Malaysian population. The Department of Statistics Malaysia recorded that in 2012 alone 36% of the total bankruptcy cases are from the same age group. According to another report by BNM, 50% of those who were bankrupt due to credit card debt are those below 30. These figures inarguably illustrate a worrying trend that Malaysians are facing a frightening debt crisis.

Considering that the largest pool of the Malaysian financial consumer are household consumer and those from the working age group have a high propensity for spending, the call for customer awareness and protection is a top priority. Fortunately, the Malaysian government is very committed on improving customer awareness and financial protection is very strong and this was translated through the Financial Sector Blueprint 2011–2020. As emphasized by Bank Negara Malaysia (2011), it was highlighted that the "*financial integrity and consumer protection will*

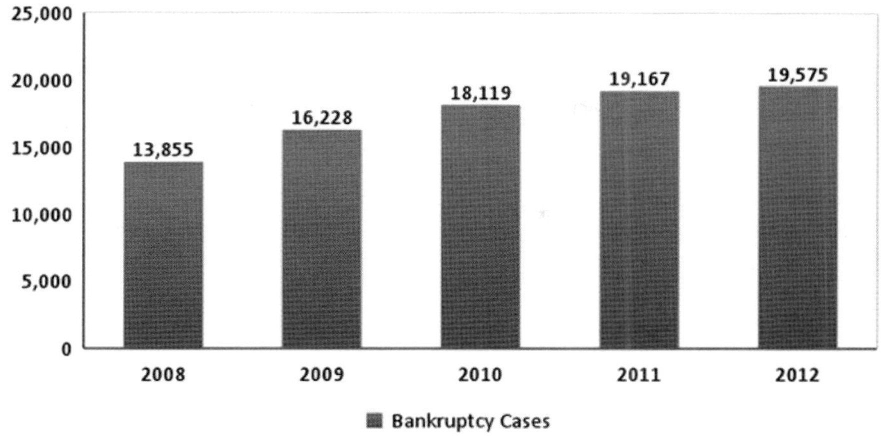

Fig. 4 Bankruptcy cases, 2008–2012. *Source* Credit Counseling and Debt Management Agency (2014)

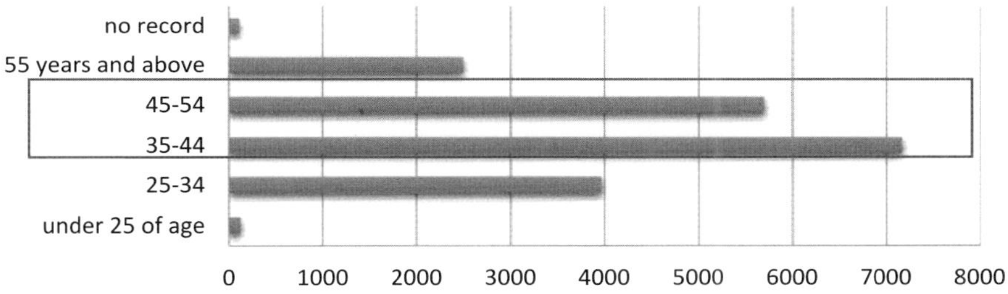

	under 25 of age	25-34	35-44	45-54	55 years and above	no record
Number of people	130	3970	7164	5698	2499	114

Fig. 5 Bankruptcy cases based on age. *Source* Department of Statistics Malaysia (2014)

also be further emphasized with enhanced arrangements for the investigation of financial crimes, regulation of all consumer credit activities and coordination of financial capability initiatives".

2 Improving Consumer Awareness and Financial Protection

In light of the worrying statistics, the Malaysian government is looking into a national strategy to help Malaysians improve the level financial literacy and develop the necessary skills to keep their personal financial matters in order.

In 2004, the central bank governor, Tan Sri Dr. Zati Akhtar Aziz proposed that financial education be made as part of the school curriculum in view of its importance in the nation's economic activities. In addition, various steps and initiatives have been taken by both BNM and the government to strengthen financial literacy and protection among retail consumers in Malaysia (Fig. 6).

Four (4) initiatives were established to enhance financial awareness and consumer protection. The initiatives are: (1) the Financial Mediation Bureau (FMB); (2) the Credit Counseling and Management Agency (AKPK); (3) a BNM Integrated Contact Centre and (4) Perbadanan Insurans Deposit Malaysia (PIDM). Table 2 lists a brief overview on the incorporation, purpose, scope and audience of the four (4) initiatives.

In addition to the above agencies, other agencies contribute the same objectives of safety of the financial system and consumer protections. They are as follows:

A. Ombudsman for financial services

OFS, is Ombudsman for financial services, it is a set up as an alternative complaint/dispute resolution body to assist financial consumers to resolve their complaints/disputes with the Financial Service Providers (FSPs). They accept all complaints/disputes that are within our jurisdiction subject to our Terms of Reference (TOR).

As for the OFS mandate it is as follows:

- To provide financial consumers an avenue for effective and prompt resolution of complaints/disputes arising from products and services provided by our Members on "free of charge" basis
- To resolve complaints/disputes in an independent, impartial and fair manner
- To collaborate with our Members in resolving complaints/disputes
- To create awareness on matters of common interest to financial consumers and the financial industry

B. Financial Technology Enabler Group (FTEG)

The Financial Technology Enabler Group (FTEG) was established by Bank Negara Malaysia (BNM) in June 2016 to support innovations that will improve the quality,

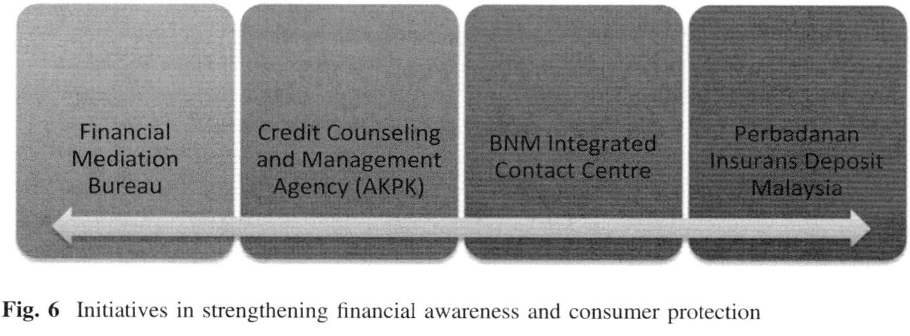

Fig. 6 Initiatives in strengthening financial awareness and consumer protection

Table 2 Initiatives established by Bank Negara Malaysia to improve financial awareness and consumer protection

	Financial Mediation Bureau (FMB)	Credit Counseling and Management Agency (AKPK)	BNM Integrated Contact Centre	Perbadanan Insurans Deposit Malaysia (PIDM)
Incorporation	30th August 2004. Officially commenced operations on 20th January 2005	April 2006		2005
Purpose	A non-profit organization set up under the initiative of BNM as an alternative dispute resolution channel to resolve complaints between the Financial Service Providers (FSPs) and their customers	An agency set up by Bank Negara Malaysia to help individuals take control of their financial situation and gain peace of mind that comes from the wise use of credit	An integrated contact centre provided by BNM which consists of the BNMLINK for walk-in customers, BNMTELELINK for calls, faxes, emails or SMS and a Complaint Management and Advisory Unit	A government agency that administers the Deposit Insurance System (DIS) and the Takaful and Insurance Benefits Protection System (TIPS)
Scope	Covers cases involving conventional/ Islamic banking product and services; and insurance/takaful product and services. However, there are certain exclusions that fall outside their scope as stated in their terms of reference such as underwriting issues, delays, appeals for restructuring or variation of loans, fraud cases etc.	Covers financial education, debt management and financial counseling activities	To handle and facilitate public complaints and enquiries	(1) Protects depositors against the loss of their insured deposits place with member banks in the unlikely event of a member bank failure. (2) Protects owners of Takaful certificates and insurance policies from the loss of their eligible Takaful or insurance benefits in the unlikely event of an insurer member failure
Audience	Financial consumers and Financial Service Providers (FSPs)	Financial consumers	Members of the public	Depositors and Takaful certificate and insurance policy owners

efficiency and accessibility of financial services in Malaysia. Comprising of cross functional group within BNM, the FTEG is responsible for formulating and enhancing regulatory policies to facilitate the adoption of technological innovations in the Malaysian financial services industry.[1] The aim of the FTEG is to ensure safety of the system and ensure financial consumers.

One of the key concern of the regulator is the market conduct, which aim Promoting fair and equitable market practices, and Promoting financial capabilities of consumers.

The key scope provided to the financial consumer covers important aspects as follows:

- Assist financial consumers involving conventional/Islamic banking product and services; and insurance/takaful product and services
- Underwriting issues, delays, appeals for restructuring or variation of loans, fraud cases etc.
- Provide financial education
- Debt management advise
- Financial counselling activities
- Handle and facilitate public complaints and enquiries
- Protects depositors against the loss of their insured deposits place with member banks in the unlikely event of a member bank failure
- Protects owners of Takaful certificates and insurance policies from the loss of their eligible Takaful or insurance benefits in the unlikely event of an insurer member failure
- Promoting fair and equitable market practices
- Promoting financial capabilities of consumers.
- Etc.

In addition to the above other initiative have been undertaken by the regulators such as Bank Negara Malaysia, Securities Commission Malaysia, and other government related agencies: among that:

- Online public platform for insurance and Takaful information for information and education
- Online public platform in banking, which provide online learning portal and other related banking information
- Online public platform for Financial fraud alert for financial consumers protection, to be protected again fraud and scams
- Online public platform for education for kids between 7 and 12, and kids between 13 and 17 to improve the level of the financial literacy within the financial consumers community.

2.1 Challenges in Consumer Protection

The increased sophistication in the Malaysian financial market has induced a need to modify the medium for consumer protection. With the evolution of the financial market, the risks that are faced by financial consumers have also increased and the regulators would need to cope with the evolution of challenges in consumer protection. With new advancements in information technology, the evolution of consumer needs, demographic shifts and rapid urbanization, and the increased acceptance of online shopping would create new challenges that would affect how consumers spend. With the new changes and advancements in how consumers spend, there are numerous risks that the consumers will be facing.

2.1.1 Advancements in Information Technology

Advancements in information technology have changed the way how financial products and services are packaged, sold and delivered. Information technology has undoubtedly contributed a large proportion to the development of today's business conduct, nevertheless the risks associated with it is also inarguable high which would actually influence the final purchase decision of the customers. Customers are bombarded with numerous advertisements everyday be it online or offline and the various advertisements that the consumers are exposed to might subconsciously affect the consumers perception of a particular product or service. Customers might also unknowingly agree to their personal data being used by merchants for promotional activities and this could lead to the customer being lured to purchase a product which would is beneficial to the customer. Thus, it is important for the customer to be educated and knowledgeable on how the advancements in information technology would affect how merchants interact with consumers and, also be taught how to identify the ways in which a merchant uses information technology to influence the customer's purchase decision.

2.1.2 Evolution of Consumer Needs

As the country paves its way into a well-developed country the need of the financial consumer needs to be given more precise attention. The country's vision to become a high-income nation continues to drive the nation into a developed nation by way of placing various sectors to drive economic development. With that vision in mind, the socio-economic needs of the consumer will affect their individual financial needs and consumption. Product innovation will continue to be introduced by the financial sector with the aim to fulfill customers' needs. Besides having to cater to the specific needs of the customer, new regulations and protection schemes will need to be enforced and further enhances. Regulators need to consistently update themselves and be aware of any market changes in order to fulfill those needs.

2.1.3 Demographic Shifts, Rapid Urbanization

Rapid urbanization in Malaysia makes it necessary for regulators to provide a strong regulative framework conceding the increase in urban population and the sophisticated evolution of the financial market. The World Bank reported that there is a rapid increase in urbanization and this will indirectly build a barrier on financial education between the regulators and educators. Increase in urbanization will indirectly contribute to a rise in financial product consumption by various financial consumers who may or may not be equipped with financial literacy. Due to the vulnerability of the financial consumers, the educators and regulators have to increase financial awareness and education to attend to the need for consumer protection.

2.1.4 Online Shopping

The rapid evolution of information technology and the ease of going online has created a new market medium, online shopping. This new medium has created a new consumerist society and in line with the current trends, the banking sector also came on board with online banking as a new medium of payment. This has caught regulators attention as the risks associated with online shopping are higher compared to normal offline shopping and consumers should be aware of the risks that they are exposed too.

3 Improvements in Regulatory Framework for Financial Consumer Protection

Due to concerns over consumer protection, BNM has collaborated with the Ministry of Education (MOE) to incorporate financial education into the school curriculum. In 2013, AKPK and BNM collaborated in ensuring the delivery of financial education programmes at the workplace through public-private sector partnerships which includes government agencies such as Amanah Ikhtiar Malaysia, Institutit Pendidikan Guru Malaysia, Jabatan Kemajuan Islam Malaysia (JAKIM), the Royal Malaysian Police and the Royal Malaysian Navy.

There has been improvement in the regulatory framework that has been put in place by regulators as a means to keep up with the rapid changes that financial consumers are facing. The recent enactment of FSA 2013 and IFSA 2013 have strengthened business conduct and consumer protection requirements and this move is seen to enhance consumer confidence in the use of financial services and products. Given the importance of financial capability in promoting the financial well-being of an individual, financial literacy and education initiatives continue to form a crucial component of BNM's consumer protection framework.

3.1 *Financial Services Act 2013 (FSA 2013) and Islamic Financial Services Act 2013 (IFSA 2013)*

When both new laws, the FSA 2013 and the IFSA 2013 came into force, it repealed a number of separate laws, namely; the Banking and Financial Institutions Act 1989 (BAFIA 1989), Insurance Act 1996, Islamic Banking Act 1983 (IBA 1983), Takaful Act 1984, Payment Systems Act 2003 and Exchange Control Act 1953. The new law was enacted to promote a more robust regulatory framework for the financial market. Both the FSA 2013 and IFSA 2013 were enacted to strengthen the Malaysian banking, insurance and takaful sector, the financial market and payment systems and other financial intermediaries in line with the country's vision in promoting a sound financial structure. The new regulation hopes to promote clarity and transparency in the implementation of the law, focus on Shariah compliance and governance, provide provisions in regulating both financial and non-financial holdings, strengthen business conduct and consumer protection, strengthen enforcement and provide supervisory intervention, and contain provisions towards the differentiated regulatory requirements in order to cater to the overall financial system. It is evident that the new regulations are intended to provide a sound consumer protection framework by having specific provisions towards safeguarding the consumer's right.

Among the provisions included under consumer protection are:

- FSA 2013 provides a specific provision on the prohibition of business conduct (under Schedule 7 of the FSA) where contravention may result in imprisonment, fine or both. The act also prohibits financial institutions from exerting undue influence and pressure on consumers to make debt repayments and to accept unsolicited offers for financial products and services.
- IFSA 2013 contains a prohibition of business conduct (additional to the one mentioned in Section 7) which includes examples of misleading and deceptive conduct, exerting undue pressure in relation to the provision of any financial service, demanding payments from a financial consumer for unsolicited financial services or colluding with any other person to fix or control the feature or terms of any financial service or product to the detriment of a financial customer, other than any tariff or premium rates or policy terms which have been approved by BNM.

3.2 *Personal Data Protection Act 2010*

Personal data is defined as any data or information that relates directly or indirectly to the individual, including any sensitive personal data that may represent the individual (Department of Personal Data Protection 2015). This act applies to any person who collects and processes personal information regarding commercial transactions (Price Water House Coopers 2015). Examples include the individual's name, identity card number, date of birth, mobile number etc. In the event that the personal data needs to be outsourced to a third party, the data user (the institution that originally obtained the data) have to ensure that the third party provides sufficient guarantee to protect the individual's personal data.

The Personal Data Protection Act (PDPA) was enforced in November 2014 to protect the public's personal data. The act was gazetted in June 2010 is an act which regulates the processing of personal data regarding commercial transactions. Considering that financial institutions in Malaysia are involved in storing and managing a huge amount of consumers' personal information, the financial sector in Malaysia will inevitably be affected with the enactment of this act. The needs and risks faced by financial consumers in Malaysia will continue to evolve and this will create more challenges and obstacles in the future for regulators in protecting consumer's interests. The enactment of this act is in line with the evolution of the Malaysian business sector and aims to reduce the risks that are faced by financial consumers. The need to improve consumer protection is of vital importance. Through this enactment, Malaysia has achieved another milestone in developing a viable platform in protection the financial sector's main stakeholder; the consumers.

4 Conclusion

Financial consumers in Malaysia will continue to evolve and will face greater challenges in the future. As the country's backbone, it is in the interest of future regulators to protect the consumers' interest. Without adequate consumer awareness and protection, consumers would be inclined to do injustice to themselves, especially when they are influenced by the media, peers and, also business entities to further spend to enrich their lifestyles, when in actual fact their spending will be the cause of their own economic downfall. Although the Malaysian government have put several measures into place to address and minimize the risks that consumers will be facing, however, it would seem that the measures have not been effective to curb financial mismanagement among retail consumers based on the numbers of bankruptcy and scams being on the rise and the fact that a huge number of those who are bankrupt are those from the working population. Thus, it would be recommended for BNM and the government to test the impact of the programs that has been put in place to reduce the financial and economic risks that consumers might face and also to try and introduce other new measures such as an informative portal or program where consumers get to evaluate their recent financial decision or spending activity and identify which financial decision is the actual planned decision and which one was influenced by a third party such as a friend, family member, advertisement, television, movies or others so that they will learn to identify the steps in which they are exposing themselves to external financial risk. It is hoped that the continuous positive growth of the financial sector in Malaysia will further spur the nation's economic growth and that a sound regulative framework is put in place in line with the needs of the sector.

Notes

1. https://www.myfteg.com/about. Retrieved 1/12/2017 (official website).

References

Bank Negara Malaysia. (2011). *Financial Sector Blueprint 2011–2020*. Kuala Lumpur: Bank Negara Malaysia Retrieved from http://www.bnm.gov.my/index.php?ch=en_publication_catalogue&pg=en_publication_blueprint&ac=7&lang=en.

Bank Negara Malaysia. (2014). Monthly Statistical Bulletin. Kuala Lumpur: Bank Negara Malaysia.

Bank Negara Malaysia (2017).

Credit Counseling and Debt Management Agency. (2014). Bankruptcy in Malaysia - A Reality Check *Department of Insolvency Malaysia*. Kuala Lumpur: Credit Counseling and Debt Management Agency.

Department of Personal Data Protection. (2015, 13 January). Department of Personal Data Protection. Retrieved 12 January, 2015, from http://www.pdp.gov.my

Department of Statistics Malaysia. (2014, 31 December). Department of Statistics Malaysia, Official Portal. Retrieved 11 January, 2015, from http://www.statistics.gov.my/portal/index.php?lang=en

Financial Services Act (2013 30 June).

International Monetary Fund. (2014). IMF Country Report No. 14/80 (P. Services, Trans.). Washington D. C. : International Monetary Fund.

Islamic Financial Services Act (2013 30 June).

Lusardi, Annamaria. (2008). Financial literacy: an essential tool for informed consumer choice?: National Bureau of Economic Research.

Ministry of Statistics Malaysia (2017).

Performance Management & Delivery Unit. (2013). Economic Transformation Programme. Retrieved 13 January, 2015, from http://etp.pemandu.gov.my/About_ETP-@-Overview_of_ETP.aspx

PriceWaterHouse Coopers. (2015). Personal Data Protection Act 2010 (PDPA). Retrieved 11 January, 2015, from http://www.pwc.com/my/en/services/what-is-pdpa.jhtml

World Bank Group. (2014). Doing Business: Measuring Business Regulations. Retrieved 12 January 2015, from http://www.doingbusiness.org/data/exploreeconomies/malaysia

http://www.bnm.gov.my/index.php?ch=mone&pg=mone_opr_stmt

Ahcene Lahsasna is currently Vice President, Research and Publication, Malaysian Financial Planning Council (MFPC) (Malaysia), prior to that he was an Associate Professor at the International Centre for Education in Islamic Finance (INCEIF) Malaysia, Ahcene Lahsasna received his Master's and Ph.D. degrees in Islamic law and Islamic jurisprudence from International Islamic University Malaysia (IIUM). Prof. Ahcene Lahsasna has industry experience acting as Shariah advisor for Islamic banking, Islamic capital market, Talaful, and Re-Takaful in Malaysia. Prof. Ahcene Lahsasna is certified training and certified examiner, In 2016 Dr. Ahcene Lahsasna received the Distinguished Scientist Award (Specialization: Islamic Finance) for the contribution to Islamic finance. Research Awards-VIRA. Venus International foundation. India. In 2017 he received the Global Responsible Business Leadership Award in 2017, for Islamic Financial Excellence. By Asia Pacific CSR council, and supported by United Nations Global Compact. Prof. Ahcene Lahsasna has authored articles, research papers and books on various topics and issues in Islamic finance. He has authored more than 22 Books in Arabic and English, Published in Lebanon, Egypt, Singapore and Malaysia.

Chapter 12
Financial Consumer Protection in Spain

Montserrat Guillen and Jorge M. Uribe

1 Financial Consumer

1.1 Official Definition of Financial Consumer

In Spain the notion of *consumer* does not coincide with the legal definition of the individual protected by domestic financial regulation. That is, while a consumer (or user) refers to *a physical or legal entity, which operates in an area outside a business or professional activity*; the individual in financial regulation is *a client*. The client can be an active or passive user of banks' services, or a retail consumer (investor) in the capital market. The concept of client is more general than the concept of consumer. For instance the non-financial firms are also included in the former, while they are not in the later.

Nevertheless, as explained by Zunzunegui (2013), in practice there exists a tendency to limit the protection of the financial client to the one implied by the narrower definition of "financial consumer". This later concept is indeed related to *physical persons that in payments services, distance contracts or credit to consumption, act with purposes different to her business or professional activities.*

1.2 Economic Situation of the Financial Consumer

In what follow with present key statistics related to the Spanish population, age structure, gender distribution and income. Those statistics provide a clear picture of the demographic dynamics that impact the dynamics of financial markets, and

M. Guillen (✉) · J. M. Uribe
University of Barcelona, Barcelona, Spain
e-mail: mguillen@ub.edu

© Springer Nature Singapore Pte Ltd. 2018

T.-J. Chen (ed.), *An International Comparison of Financial Consumer Protection*,
https://doi.org/10.1007/978-981-10-8441-6_12

constitute the individual subject to regulation and protection by financial authorities in Spain and in the European Union. They also help to foresee future tendencies in both, financial markets and the legal status of the financial consumer, which certainly will require considering changes in the age structure and the type of financial services required (Fig. 1).

The total population in Spain reached a peak in the years 2011–2012 and afterwards has started to decrease. The average yearly growth rate of 1.71 that featured the population dynamics from 2005 to 2008 was replaced by an annual growth of 0.44 between 2009 and 2012, and then by an annual reduction around −0.25 from 2013 to 2015. This pattern is explained by the demographic transition, typical of high-income economies, during the later decades, which consists in a sustained reduction of fertility rates, accompanied by a reduction in mortality, both at early and late ages. The population-aging phenomenon that characterized the financial consumer in Spain is better shown in the next two figures; which describe the age structure of the Spanish population (Figs. 2, 3).

As can be observed in the two figures above, the age structure of the Spanish population has slightly changed during the last decade. In particular the share of population above 65 years has increased from 16.63% in 2015 to 18.80%, 10 years later. The population bellow 14 years has shown instead a rather stable participation in the total (14.32% in 2005 against 14.88% in 2015), while the working age population, between 15 and 64 years has decreased from being a 69.03% of the total in 2005, to a 66.3% in 2015. This tendency is expected to be reinforced in the future, while the phenomenon of population aging is still in place. In the pyramid plot may be seen that this dynamics implies a significant reduction of the Spanish labor supply and considerable increments in the size of old population for the year 2064, and even as soon as for 2029. The expected demographic changes in the near future are remarkable for both males and females.

The patterns described above explain a notable interest by academics and politicians in the issues related to population aging and longevity risk in Spain, an in European countries in general, during the last years. This interest is completely

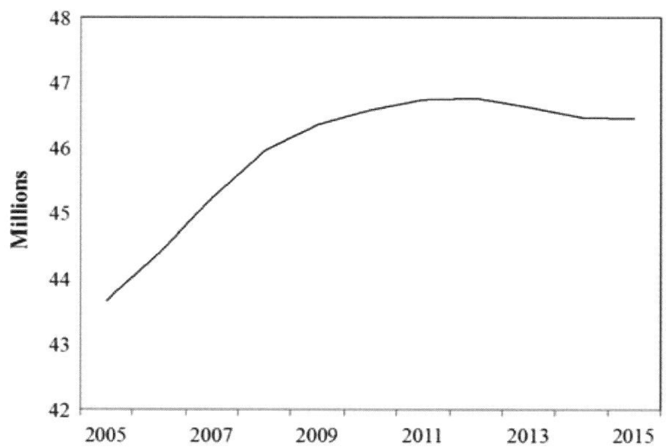

Fig. 1 Total population in Spain, 2005–2015. *Source* National Statistics Institute of Spain

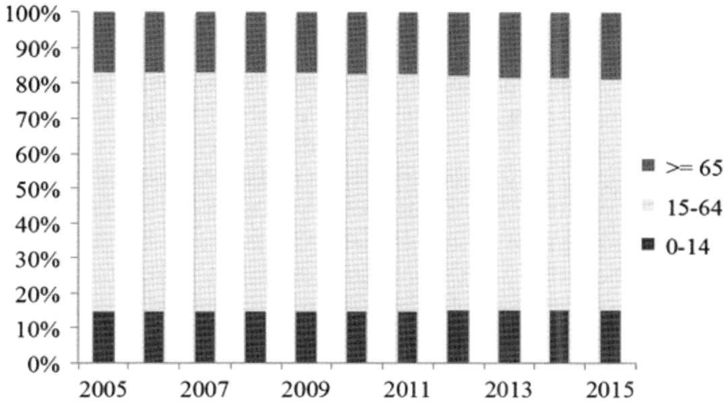

Fig. 2 Age structure of population in Spain, 2005–2015. *Source* National Statistics Institute of Spain

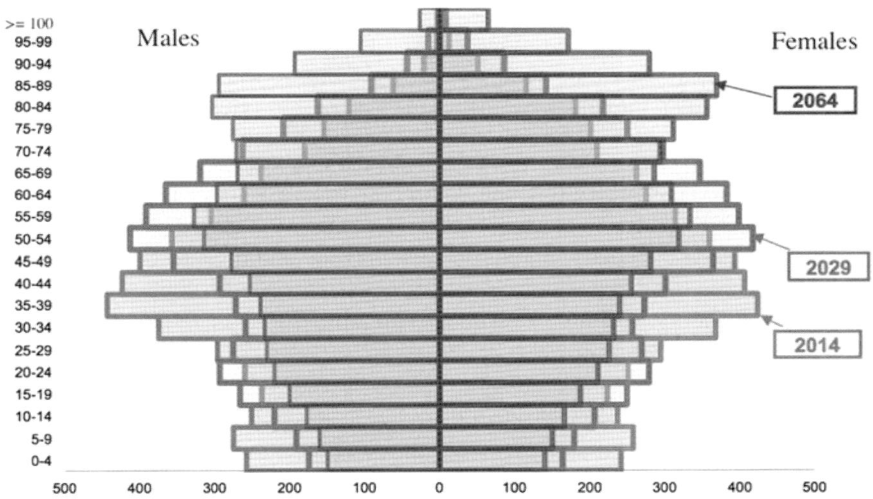

Fig. 3 Expected changes in the population structure, 2014–2064. *Source* Press Bulletin October 24 2014, National Statistics Institute of Spain, Page 7

justified, given the fact that this phenomenon affects different products and contracts involving public and private sector agents alike in the financial markets. For instance, it has an impact on immediate and deferred annuities, enhanced and impaired annuities, guaranteed annuity options, lifetime mortgages and, more importantly, defined benefit pension schemes. Therefore it threatens current agreements in financial markets and imposes huge challenges for regulators in the near future. Among these, the ones related to pension schemes are by far the most worrying ones. To foresee and restructure regulation is relevant not only for insurance companies or private employers, who promise a pension on retirement based on the employee's final salary, but also for institutions within the public sector, which typically offer generous final salary benefits, albeit largely unfunded.

We turn now to statistics related to economic standards of the Spanish populations, which bound the financial consumer investment opportunities in Spain by saving, or its debt capacity with financial institutions (Fig. 4).

The analysis of the man indicators shows a remarkable reduction in the Spanish income from 2007 to 2013. The reduction, which accounts for above 8.9% in real terms, was the consequence of the global financial crisis that spanned the years 2007–2009, and the subsequent European debt crisis from 2010 to 2013. Both events affected greatly the Spanish economy and impacted the generation of income negatively, with important consequences for financial markets and therefore for financial consumers. Indeed, as we will be explore in the next sections, these two crises made evident the priority of addressing relevant issues of the European common regulation of banks and insurance companies, and the necessity of progressing towards a more general and solid framework to resolve bankruptcies of multinational financial institutions, while preserving the domestic financial stability of the countries within the Union.

The figure also shows a partial recovery of the national per capita income from 2013 to 2015. In the last year it reached levels similar to those in 2009, before the European debt crisis (around USD 3400). Yet it has not returned to the pre-crisis levels in 2006–2007. It must be noticed that the economic recovery of the European economies, among them Spain, has been considerably slower than in other countries, including United States itself where the crises begun. This has warned politicians and financial authorities, which have recently started to acknowledge drawbacks in the monetary union implementation, and the necessity of more flexible and coordinate fiscal policy stances in the European Union.

In what follows we show the recent evolution of the securities and banking markets in Spain (Figs. 5, 6).

As can be observed in the two figures above, the global financial crises implied a remarkable reduction of Spanish stock market capitalization and banks credit to the

Fig. 4 GNI per capita in Spain, 2005–2015. *Source* National Statistics Institute of Spain

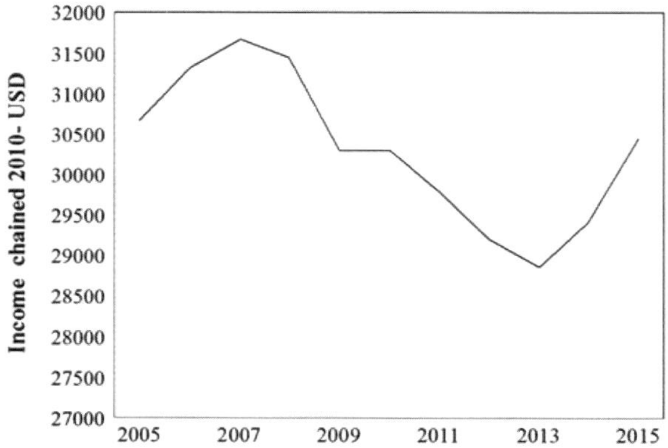

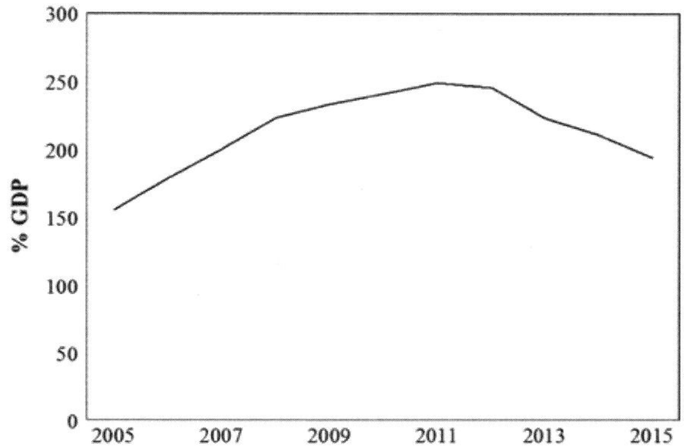

Fig. 5 Domestic credit provided by the financial sector (% of GDP). *Source* National Statistics Institute of Spain

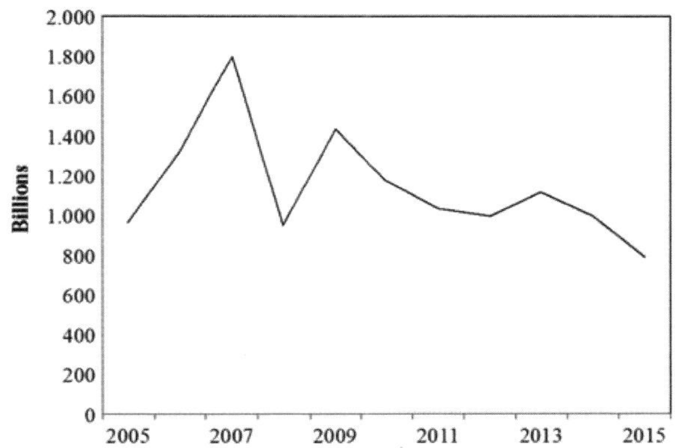

Fig. 6 Market capitalization of listed domestic companies (current US $). *Source* National Statistics Institute of Spain

private sector. This was particularly notorious during the years 2007–2008 in the stock market, and 2012–2013 for the credit market.

2 Financial Consumer Protection Institutions (Hardware)

Regulation of financial institutions in Spain, and therefore protection of the financial consumer are subject to the guidelines of the European Union (EU). Indeed, there exist since the decade of 80s, transnational regulatory committees around Europe, which oversee financial activities across the European Union members and other countries that have whished to align to the same principles. In Frankfurt one can find the European Insurance and Occupational Pensions Authority (EIOPA); in Paris the European Securities and Markets Authority (ESMA), and in London the European Baking Authority (EBA).

Moreover, very recently, in an attempt to foster coordination across its members especially for managing crises episodes, the European Union has established the European Systemic Risk Board (ESRB), which consists of the members of the European Central Bank's (ECB) council, the chairpersons of the EIOPA, EBA and ESMA, and one member of the European Commission. There are also chairs of an Advisory Scientific Committee and an Advisory Technical Committee. In the figure bellow we present the general organization of the supervisory authorities in the EU (Fig. 7).

In Spain, the issues related to restructuring and resolution processes of credit institutions are in charged of the Fund for Orderly and Bank Restructuring (FROB) established in 2012. The issues related to the insurance market are under the supervision of the Directorate General for Insurance and Pension Funds and finally, regarding the securities markets, there is the Spanish National Securities Market Commission and the Ministry of Economy. Above all of the former and in charge

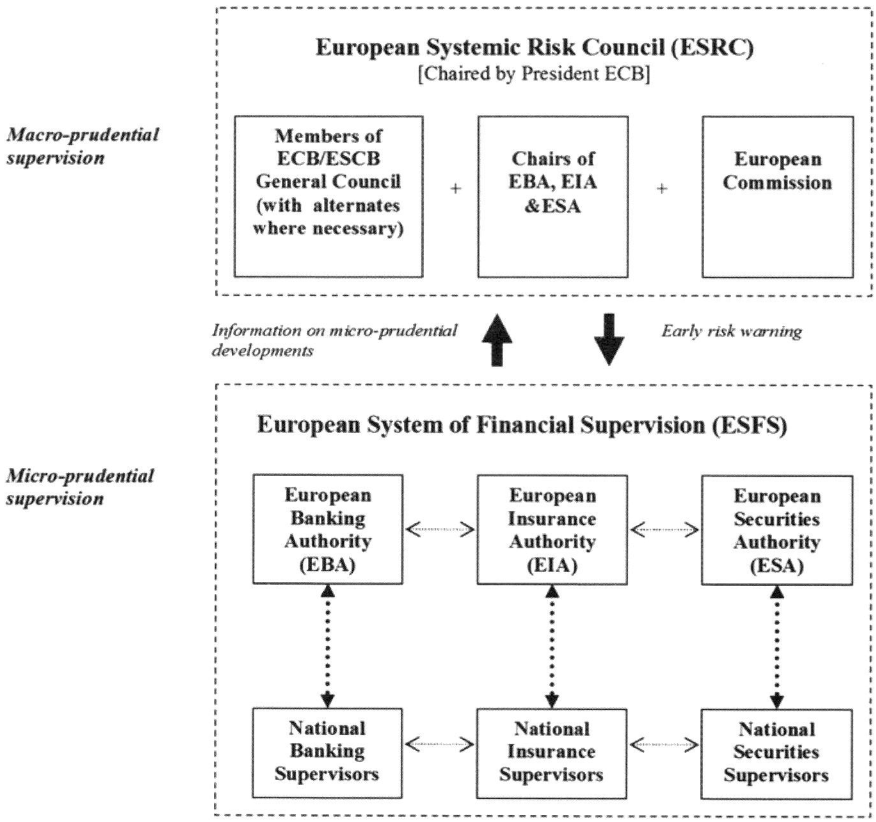

Fig. 7 Supervision European regulatory framework. *Source* (Larosière 2009, page 56)

of conducting macroprudential policy in the country is the Bank of Spain (BOE), which acts as a supervisor in the three markets.

3 Financial Consumer Protection System (Software)

In what follows we describe the general features of securities, banking and insurance markets regulation, and the principles that underlie financial consumer protection in each case.

3.1 Banking Regulation

In the first half of the 80s the European Union aimed at creating a unified market for financial services. Nevertheless, at that time, instead of opting for the creation of a unified framework in terms of regulation, monitoring and financial structure; their members opted for harmonizing some issues that they perceived as strictly necessary. For example, they unified the definition of a credit institution, and defined business activities that these institutions were allowed to conduct. However the supervision and treatment of bankruptcy, restructuring and resolution of banks, so as the supervision of these financial institutions, remained under the jurisdiction of each country, ruled by its own laws and legal principles.

The global financial crisis that started at the end of 2007 in the United States changed this situation. European banks faced an impossible dilemma in which every attempt to increase capitalization was perceived by the market as a sign of financial fragility that confirmed ex ante doubts about their solvency (Garrido 2016). Suddenly the financial crisis evidenced the lack of a regulatory framework that allows coordination among the European Union members, which were forced to make extraordinary individual efforts to preserve domestic financial and payment systems. Consequently, in 2010, following the recommendations by the Larosière Report (Larosière 2009), the ESRC was established, by the EU regulation 1092/2010 (see Fig. 7), and the former committees (EBA, ESA, EIOPA) were transformed into actual regulatory supranational authorities. Macroprudential regulation continued under the guidance of national authorities (for example the Bank of Spain (BOE), in the case of Spain), but micropudential supervision from now on would be under the rule of the European institutions. The Bank Recovery and Resolution Directive (BRRD) directive was also approved by the European Commission, which provides a general framework for national authorities to manage bank bailouts effectively, and especially in a timely and coordinate fashion [In the case of Spain the BRRD was effectively approved by the Spanish Parliament in June 11 2015 (Law 11/2015)].

A Single Resolution Mechanism (SRM) has been approved, starting to operate in January 2016. The SRM applies to banks covered by the single supervisory mechanism, which in the case are about 90% of the total. It is the second pillar of the banking union. If a bank fails despite stronger supervision, the SRM allows bank resolution to be managed effectively through a single resolution board and a single resolution fund that is financed by the banking sector. The purpose of the SRM is to ensure an orderly resolution of failing banks with minimal costs for taxpayers and to the real economy. The SRM regulation establishes the framework for the resolution of banks in EU countries participating in the banking union, among them Spain.

A bank resolution occurs when authorities decide that a failing bank cannot go through regular insolvency proceedings, at least not without harming public interest and causing financial instability to the whole economy. To manage banks' failure in an organized fashion, authorities within the European Union use resolution tools that ensure continuity of the affected bank critical functions, while preserving financial stability and restoring the viability of parts (or all) of the bank. Any bank's division that cannot be made viable again goes through regular insolvency procedures. The BRRD requires banks to prepare recovery plans to overcome possible situations of financial distress. The directive includes rules to build up a national resolution fund, which has to be established by each EU country. All financial institutions have to contribute to these funds. Contributions are calculated on the basis of each institution's size and risk profile. The EU's bank resolution rules aim to ensure that the banks' stockholders and creditors pay their share of the costs via a "bail-in" mechanism. If that was still not sufficient, the national resolution funds set up under the BRRD can provide the resources needed to ensure that a bank is able to continue operating, while it is being restructured.

In the case of Spain the BRRD substituted the former Spanish resolution framework (Law 9/2012) implemented in the context of the Financial Assistance Program led by the Troika in 2012.[1]

3.1.1 Deposit Insurance

In November 2015 the European Commission proposed to set up a European deposit insurance scheme (EDIS) for bank deposits in the euro area. EDIS constitutes the third pillar of the banking union (joint to the Single Supervisory Mechanism and the Single Resolution Mechanism described before). This proposal was adopted as a part of a broader package of measures to foster the economic and monetary union. The EDIS has been built on the system of national deposit guarantee schemes (DGS) regulated by Directive 2014/49/EU. This later system already ensures that all deposits up to €100,000 are protected through national DGS across the countries that conform the EU.

The EDIS provide a stronger and more uniform degree of insurance cover in the euro area and it is expected to reduce vulnerability of national DGS to large local shocks, by ensuring that the level of depositor confidence in a bank would not depend on the bank's location. EDIS apply to deposits below €100,000 of all banks in the banking union.

3.2 Insurance Regulation

On 1 January 2016, a new supervisory framework for insurance and reinsurance companies in the European Union, and therefore pertinent for insurance companies and pensions funds in Spain, known as Solvency II, has became applicable. Solvency II is a coherent (and integrated) prudential supervisory regime, which consists of the three pillars: (i) *Calculation of capital reserves*: It outlines the standard formula that insurance companies across the European Union have to employ for the calculation of capital reserves, (ii) *Management of risks and governance*: It outlines the requirements for management of potential risks and for governance. (iii) *Reporting and disclosure*: It describes the information and reporting insurance companies across the European Union have to offer to the national supervisor and also to disclose publicly.

Solvency II enriches protection of financial consumers of insurance products, by introducing risk and governance management, as well as by demanding a market-consistent valuation of insurers' assets and liabilities. All in all, financial consumers in Spain should be better protected and be able to get the benefits of the insurance contracts they have signed. It is the contention of the European regulators that an adequate management of risks and governance enable insurance companies to keep the promises they made to their clients and the contracts that have been signed with them.

As a regulator EIOPA's powers include issuing guidelines and recommendations and developing draft regulatory and implementing technical standards. It is also allowed to provide opinions to the European Parliament, the Council of the European Union and the European Commission on insurance related issues. EIOPA also provides input into the European Commission's policy-making with regards to Insurance Guarantee Schemes (IGS) seeking to contribute to the assessment of the need for a European network of national Insurance Guarantee Schemes, adequately funded and sufficiently harmonized.

Solvency II is not the unique European regulation that affects the insurance market in Spain. There is also the Packaged Retail and Insurance-based Investment Products (PRIIPS, Resolution 1286/2014), which introduces the simplified information document, in which the contract characteristics are explained; the Insurance Distribution Directive (IDD) (former Insurance Mediation Directive), which contains requirements for EU Member States' regulation of insurance intermediaries. It has a view on a level playing field between participants in insurance sales, in order to improve consumer protection, market integration and competition. The new directive constitutes a minimum harmonization framework, so Member States can adopt stricter provisions if they wish.

In Spain, there exist indeed a national fund that complements the private sector in the insurance market, known as *Consorcio de Compensanción de Seguros*. Its main objective is to satisfy extraordinary claims by insurance clients, who after having paid their insurance policy continued exposed to extraordinary risk, or after having contracted an insurance policy, the insurance company could not comply with the contract, because of bankruptcy or insolvency. It performs many functions within the insurance field. Amongst those are: coverage of extraordinary risk, compulsory vehicle insurance, combined agricultural insurance and liquidation of insurance companies.

The reforms in the context if the European Union were aimed to foster financial consumer protection, with an especial view on financial literacy and on providing enough elements to the financial consumer, as for her to understand the kind of risk retained after signing an insurance contract.

3.3 Securities Regulation

European regulation on securities markets seeks for a harmonized treatment of financial consumers across the member states. As mentioned before, ESMA is the competent authority in this case. It contributes to the work of the ESRB, by providing data and undertaking stress tests in close co-ordination with the other ESAs and the ESRB (i.e. EBA and EIOPA). It was established by the European Parliament in 2010, to protect the public interest, preserve financial stability by effective regulation and supervision, to contribute in the search for transparency and to the well functioning of financial markets, and to protect investors and financial consumers, all of the above, within the context of the European system, aiming to reduce at its minimum the possibility of regulatory arbitrage.

The European laws that affect in a more significant fashion the Spanish institutions, and thus the financial consumers, are the Financial Instruments Directive I and II (MiFID). The main objective of MiFID was to improve financial investors protection and to harmonize legislation across the EU's member states. Market transparency must guarantee that the information disclosure to the investors is trustworthy and that there is not inside information. Thus, a proper price formation mechanism should be able to avoid market abuses. In every case a maximum protection is provided to the retail investors, because of both their lower amount of resources and their considerable minor expertise dealing with the complex nature of financial markets.

In Spain the regulation and supervision of the security markets follows an institutional approach, supported on three organisms that supervise the full spectrum of institutions (the Ministry of Economy, the National Securities Market Commission and the Bank of Spain). On top of the supervision of the financial institutions that operate in the market, the National Securities Market Commission (CNMV) is also in charged of fostering consumer protection. In case that a financial client considers that a financial institution has negatively affected her, she can look for assistance by the CNMV.

Finally there exist as well FOGAIN (General Fund of Investment Guarantees), which is the Investors Compensation Scheme for clients of Spanish investment firms and clients of Spanish UCITS Managers (in this latter case, only where a discretionary portfolio management relationship has been established by the investor with the firm). The FOGAIN has been established to compensate, with some quantitative bounds legally established, to those clients regarding to the following: (i) the relevant firm becomes insolvent, and (ii) as a consequence of that, the investor is not able to recover securities that he delivered to the investment firm.

All Spanish investment firms, including portfolio managers, brokers and broker-dealers are mandatory members of the FOGAIN. Becoming a member of the FOGAIN is also mandatory for branches in Spain of foreign investment firms incorporated in a non-EU country. Branches in Spain of foreign investment firms incorporated in another EU country may also join the FOGAIN if they decide to do so.

On top of the aforementioned, those Spanish UCITS Managers and Managers of Alternative Investment Funds closed-ended type authorized to provide discretionary portfolio management service to individuals, must also join the FOGAIN. In the last case, only those clients obtaining that service will be covered by the FOGAIN. As a consequence UCITS portfolios are not covered by the FOGAIN. The FOGAIN is founded principally with contributions made, on an annual basis, by all its members. Moreover, FOGAIN is allowed to organize credit transactions with commercial banks and with the CNMV in the event it was necessary to cover payment needs.

3.4 Main Related Laws

Banking:

- BRRD- establishment in Spain—Law 11/2015.
- EDIS- Deposit Insurance—Directive 2014/49/EU.

Insurance:

- Solvency II. Guidelines on the supervision of branches of third country insurance undertakings EIOPA. https://eiopa.europa.eu/GuidelinesSII/GL_Third_Country_Branches_EN_ORI_FINAL.pdf
- Package retail and insurance-based investment products, PRIIPS, Resolution 1286/2014
- Insurance Distribution Directive (IDD) 2016/97
- Consorcio de Compensanción de Seguros. Decreto Legislativo 7/2004

Securities:

- Markets in Financial Instruments Directive (MiFID I)—Directive 2004/39/EC
- Markets in Financial Instruments (MiFID II)—Directive 2014/65/EU
- Markets in Financial Instruments (MiFIR)—Regulation (EU) No 600/2014

Notes

1. The Troika is a decision group formed by the European Commission, the European Central Bank and the International Monetary Fund.

References

Garrido A. (2016) "La Regulació Bancaria a la Zona Euro", in Revista Econòmica de Catalunya, No 72, 2016, pages 80–87.

Larosière Group (2009) "The High-Level Group on Financial Supervision in the EU", available at http://ec.europa.eu/internal_market/finances/docs/de_larosiere_report_en.pdf

National Institute of Statistics. (2014) Press Bulletin October 28 2014.

Zunzunegui, F. (2013) Derechos del consumidor de servicios y productos financieros como derechos básicos. Revista de Derecho del Mercado Financiero, Madrid November 29 2013.

Montserrat Guillen is Chair Professor of the Department of Econometrics at the University of Barcelona (Spain) and director of Riskcenter research group. She received a MSc in Mathematics in 1987 and a Ph.D. in Economics from UB in 1992. She received a MSc in Data Analysis from the University of Essex (United Kingdom). She is currently Honorary Visiting Professor in the Faculty of Actuarial Science and Insurance at City University London. She was Visiting Research faculty at the University of Texas at Austin (USA) and Visiting Professor at the University of Paris II. She was awarded the ICREA Academia distinction.

Jorge Mario Uribe is a Ph.D. in Economics, and a visiting researcher at the University of Barcelona (Spain). He is a lecturer at the University del Valle (Colombia). He received the M.Phil in Economics at the European University Institute (Italy) in 2012 and MA in Economics at the Universidad de los Andes (Colombia) in 2009. He is associate researcher at Riskcenter and leader of the Research Group in Applied Macroeconomics and Financial Economics, Universidad del Valle since 2015. He got his degree in Finance and International Business with honors at Santiago de Cali University (Colombia) and BA in Economics at Universidad del Valle.

Chapter 13
Financial Consumer Protection in Taiwan: Systems and Market Issues

Jan-juy Lin

Preface

Traditionally, a customer of financial products or services in Taiwan shall be protected mainly under the Consumer Protection Act (CPA), associated with the relevant legislations providing different functions of protection such as the Personal Information Protection Act, Securities and Futures Investors Protection Act, and the remedy from the financial safety net (*e.g.* deposit insurance, insurance guarantee fund) in case of default of financial institutions. After the financial crisis in 2008, many investors of the Lehman-Brother structured products suffered a lot and many disputes due to banks' mis-selling have emerged. Due to the segregation of investment and consumption by the judicial sector and administrative sector, the investors who purchases financial products or services are not legitimate to argue for the protection under the CPA.

With the global trend of financial consumer protection, the competent authority, the Financial Supervisory Commission (FSC) introduced the legislation of the Financial Consumer Protection Act (FCPA) in 2011 as the foundation to provide a comprehensive mechanism to protect financial consumers. Based on the fundamental and the relevant legal systems, the government bodies can undertake the mandate to conduct regulations and operations to protect financial consumers, with the assistance of certain non-government organizations, such as the Financial Ombudsman Institution (FOI) and the Securities and Futures Investors Protection Fund (SFIPF).

This article addresses the controversy in the definition of financial consumers, scrutinizes the current legal systems of financial consumer protection, the government competent authorities, the non-government organizations with special purposes of protection in this perspective, and reviews the recent development and enhancement in financial consumer protection and certain financial market issues in Taiwan.

J. Lin (✉)
National Chengchi University, Taipei, Taiwan
e-mail: jjlin@nccu.edu.tw

© Springer Nature Singapore Pte Ltd. 2018

T.-J. Chen (ed.), *An International Comparison of Financial Consumer Protection*,
https://doi.org/10.1007/978-981-10-8441-6_13

1 Financial Consumers

1.1 Definition of Consumers

Due to social changes, in order to satisfy various living needs such as food, clothing, housing, transportation, education, and recreation, people are constantly engaging in various consumer activities with business operators. Because of the reasons such as the technologizing and mass production of goods and services, the transformation of production and distribution channels, as well as the enterprization and collectivization of manufacturers and sellers, consumer protection has become a vital issue in accordance with the development and transition of economy.[1]

To protect consumers' interests, the Consumer Protection Act (hereinafter the CPA) was enacted in 1994 and official consumer protection agencies were established. A comprehensive system of consumer protection that encompasses of consumer education, establishment of consumer protection measures, administrative supervision to enterprises, and handling of consumer disputes has been instituted.[2] For the purpose of the CPA, the "Consumer" means any person who in relation to a commercial practice, is acting for purposes of consumption to make transactions in exchange for goods or services.[3] "Consumer relationship" means the legal relationship arising between consumers and traders for the sale of goods or provision of services.[4]

In the viewpoint of judicial sector and the behavior of investment is conducted to acquiring products or services for monetary gains or profits, not for necessary living, therefore cannot be construed as a kind of consumption. Under such a scenario, the provisions of the CPA cannot be applied in the cases of investment products or services.[5] Taking similar rules to the judicial practice, the competent authority have explained that investment conduct is an aleatory transaction by taking high degree of risk to accumulate one's wealth, neither finance for ordinary living, nor final consumption of goods or services, therefore is not consumption at all.[6] Based on the segregation of investment and consumption in the judicial sector and administrative sector, the investors who purchases financial services are not legitimate to argue for the protection under the CPA. Instead, they can only fight against financial services enterprises based on traditional civil laws and respective financial regulation, with higher burden of proof in resolving their complaint or disputes of the provision of financial services.

1.2 Definition of Financial Consumers

After the occurrence of financial crisis in 2008, many investors of the structured products issues by the Lehman-Brother suffered a lot and many disputes due to banks' mis-selling emerged in Taiwan. Many investors of such as financial products who suffered significant losses brought litigation suits against the banks, while others resolved the disputes with the banks to share the losses through mediation or compromises. In the litigation, subject to relevant laws and regulations, the investors must bear the burden of proof on banks' negligence and damages, therefore situated on a more disadvantaged position. To further advocate their interests, the investors claimed themselves consumers and the purchase of such financial products is a kind of consumer behavior in order to seek for the protection under the CPA. However, such assertion was not accepted by the court and the competent authority as mentioned above.

In the rapidly changing financial market, purchasers of financial products, compared to financial services providers, due to the asymmetry of information and knowledge become more and more vulnerable transaction disputes. This is the reason globally recognized why a fair and thorough protection system should be in place to protect the investors of such kind of financial products and services. Under such scenario, the concept of financial consumer protection has been introduced and the legislation for this purpose has been codified in many jurisdictions. The "financial consumer" is a collective term to describe the clients who purchase or acquire financial products or services provided by financial institutions. It covers depositors, policyholders, investors, credit card holders, the users of electronic payment and many other financial services users to meet the innovation and dynamic change in the global financial market.

With the global trend, the term "financial consumer" was first introduced in the legislation of the Financial Consumer Protection Act (FCPA 2011) in Taiwan. It means the parties that receive financial products or services provided by a financial services enterprise provided. It does not include qualified institutional investors nor those natural persons or juristic persons with a prescribed level of financial capacity or professional expertise.

1.3 Economic Situation Relevant to Financial Consumers

The total population in Taiwan is around 23.5 million in 2016. Although the population growth is still positive, the annual growth rate has been less than 0.05% since 2005. The age structure of the population is shown in Fig. 1, which indicates Taiwan also faces an aging society, with 13.2% of population older than 65 in 2016.[7]

The economic environment in general is stable with slow growth during the past ten years, except for the short period after the global financial crisis of 2008, as shown in Table 1. The unemployment rate is low in Taiwan, compared with the western countries. However, the income level is low and unsatisfactory, especially combined with a very high cost of housing. Probably due to cultural reasons, Taiwanese people work hard and live thriftily. As a result, the savings rate remains constantly high at around 30%. The composites of GDP in 2016 can be categorized as agricultural sector (1.7%), industrial sector (35.13%), and service sector

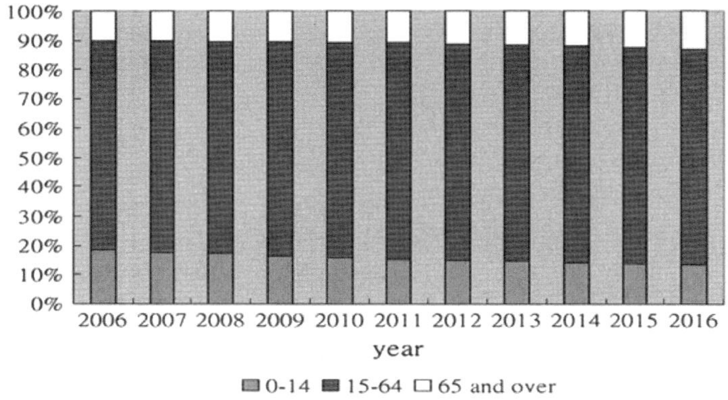

Fig. 1 Age structure of the population in Taiwan. Source: Accounting and Statistics, Executive Yuan, Taiwan

Table 1 A summary of the economic environment in Taiwan

Year	GDP growth (%)	National income per capita (US$)	Savings rate (%)	Unemployment rate (%)
2006	5.62	14,974	31.05	3.91
2007	6.52	15,401	31.46	3.91
2008	0.7	15,388	29.62	4.14
2009	−1.57	14,398	29.29	5.85
2010	10.63	16,650	33.14	5.21
2011	3.8	17,982	31.46	4.39
2012	2.06	18,125	30.45	4.24
2013	2.2	18,872	32	4.18
2014	4.02	19,724	33.58	3.96
2015	0.72	19,540	34.7	3.78
2016	1.48	19,626	33.91	3.92

Source: Accounting and Statistics, Executive Yuan, Taiwan

(63.17%). Among these statistics, the contribution of financial service sector to GDP is about 6.56%.[8]

The development of the financial service sector in Taiwan during the past ten years is fast and strong, especially the life insurance industry. Currently the total assets of financial industries are around NT$ 92 trillion (US$3 trillion), where the banking industry accounts for around 70% and insurance industry accounts about 25%. There are 40 domestic banks, 29 foreign banks, and 29 credit unions and cooperatives. Besides, there are 23 life insurance companies, 20 non-life insurance companies, 3 reinsurance companies. The number of securities companies is 116. The total number of employees in financial industries is around 810,000 (including 168,000 in banking industry, 367,000 in insurance industry, 233,000 in insurance agency & brokerage, and 46,000 in securities industry).[9]

2 Legal Systems of Financial Consumers Protection

The legal systems of financial consumer protection in Taiwan can be categorized into legislations as below to provide protection and regulation to meet respective legislative purposes. The most significant one is the Financial Consumer Protection Act (FCPA) 2011 which covers core rules of protection, dispute resolution, financial education, regulations. The Consumer Protection Act (CPA) 1994 protects general consumers for their final consumption, including many financial consumers such as insurance policyholder and credit card holders. Securities and Futures Investors Protection Act (SFIPA) 2002 protects the investors in security and future markets particularly. The Personal Information Protection Act (PIPA) 1995 covers the protection of the personal information of financial consumers. In addition, many other financial laws and regulations, such as the Banking Act, the Insurance Act, also contain protection functions therein as the supplement.

2.1 Consumer Protection Act

2.1.1 Legislative Purpose

On January 11, 1994, the Consumer Protection Act (CPA) was promulgated in order to protect the interests, facilitating the safety, and improving the quality of life of the consumers.[10] It also represents that Taiwan enters into a new milestone on making efforts to promote consumer protection work. The CPA is the basic law of consumer protection. This Act is composed of the following chapters: general principles, consumer interests, consumer advocacy groups, administrative supervision, handling consumer disputes, penalty and supplement provisions.

For the purpose of this Act, the term of "consumer" means any person who in relation to a commercial practice, is acting for purposes of consumption to make transactions in exchange for goods or services. "Trader" means any person who in relation to a commercial practice, is acting for purposes relating to his business in designing, producing, manufacturing, importing or distributing goods, or providing services.[11]

2.1.2 Major Coverage

To achieve the legislative purpose of this Act, the competent authority shall implement the following measures by periodically reviewing, coordinating and improving upon their relevant regulations and enforcement:[12]

1. Maintaining the quality, safety and sanitation of the goods or services.
2. Preventing that the goods or services do not cause damages to consumer's life, body, health, property or other legitimate interests.

3. Ensuring that the labeling of goods or services is compliant with laws and regulations.
4. Ensuring that the advertising of goods or services is compliant with laws and regulations.
5. Ensuring that the weights and measures of goods or services are compliant with laws and regulations.
6. Facilitating the price for goods or services remain reasonable.
7. Promoting the fair packaging of goods.
8. Encouraging fair trade in goods or services.
9. Funding and fostering consumer advocacy groups.
10. Coordinating the handling of consumer disputes.
11. Promoting consumer education.
12. Providing consumer consulting services.
13. Other protective measures necessary for the development of consumer life.

2.1.3 Miscellaneous Duties of Traders

For the goods or services provided, traders shall emphasis on the importance of consumer health and safety, offer proper instructions, provide adequate and accurate information to ensure fair transaction, and take measures necessary to protect consumers.[13] Government, traders and consumers shall endeavor together to enrich consumer information which could assist consumers to take appropriate and reasonable decisions accordingly in the protection of their safety and interests.[14]

2.2 Securities and Futures Investors Protection Act

2.2.1 Legislative Purpose

Although there has an abundance of measurements and regulations to protect investors, it seems not good enough for investors to fight against malicious behaviors of listed companies and securities firms. According to the judiciary rules in Taiwan, malicious business practices can be treated as a criminal charge rather than a civil responsibility, in which the integrity of the company owner is hardly defined by legislation. Therefore, once owners of either listed companies or securities firms illegally transfer the companies' assets to their own accounts, which cause investors' financial damages, the capacity of "the protection funds" is not full enough to cover whole compensation of investors' loss. In order to be more thoughtful to protect investors, the competent authority has, for years, been working on the legitimacy of Investor Protection Act (hereinafter referred as the Protection Act), a bible of protecting *bona fide* investors. The draft of the Protection Act was formalized in 1999, and, finally passed, in May 2002. It was specially promulgated to safeguard the rights and interests of securities investors and futures traders and promote the sound development of the securities and futures markets.[15]

2.2.2 Major Contexts

The Protection Act contains 56 provisions, which can be categorized into several focuses as follows:

1. A specific administrative body is established to serve investors. The entity is organized as a trustee with financial supports from contributions of each securities related institution. A board of trustee is formed and board of directors should be assigned by contributors and appointed by the Authority from scholars, professionals and fair-minded people.
2. A maximum of NT$ 5 billion protection fund is reserved to protect bona fide investors whose losses are not covered by the securities settlement fund or other compensations. The sources of the fund are from the primitive contributors and securities related sectors.
3. A service of consultation is imposed to advance investors' claims and help negotiating with troubled securities companies.
4. Litigation of class actions is proceeded for investors to fight against the fraud. Class action, which is referred from the promulgation of Securities Investor Protection Act of U.S.A., 1970, provides investors with a channel of group appeal to the court. The action is legally represented by the trustee and free of charge.

2.2.3 Enhancement of Corporate Governance

Additionally, the Protection Act mandates independency of corporate governance of public as well as listed companies that at least two independent directors must be on company board, with specialization and non-relevance to the companies. The Act also requires that documentation of securities related firms particular to business operation and financial statement must be saved properly for investigation uses, with no rejection whatsoever.

2.3 Personal Information Protection Act

2.3.1 Legislative Purpose

The collection and use of personal data in Taiwan is primarily regulated by the Personal Information Protection Act (PIPA). It was enacted in 1995 to govern the collection, processing and use of personal information so as to prevent harm on personality rights, and to facilitate the proper use of personal information. The PIPA implements a number of core principles of Directive 95/46/EC on data protection (Data Protection Directive) including: minimal collection, fair and lawful processing, deletion of data, sensitive data protections, direct marketing opt-outs. However, the PIPA has weak data transfer restrictions and does not provide for a single data protection authority.[16] The Ministry of Justice (MOJ) is responsible only for planning Taiwan's legal framework for data protection and interpreting the PIPA.[17]

In addition to the PIPA, the Taiwanese legislature has enacted sector-specific laws that impose specific data protection requirements or enhanced enforcement powers. Most sectoral laws regulate the financial services sector and health care sector. In general, they empower regulators to impose fines higher than those permitted by the PIPA. Central government agencies are also authorized by the PIPA to issue regulations setting the standard of care for the protection of personal data in particular industries. For example, in the financial services sector, the Financial Holding Company Act imposes enhanced fines on financial holding companies and their subsidiaries who fail to keep personal data confidential. The Act Governing Electronic Payment Institutions prohibits third party payment processors from using customers' personal data for marketing on behalf of third parties.

2.3.2 Definition of Personal Information

The personal information is defined under the PIPA as the information that can identify a natural person directly or indirectly. This includes the natural person's name, date of birth, national Identification Card number, passport number, physical characteristics, fingerprints, marital status, family, education, occupation, medical records, information pertaining to medical treatment, genetic information, sexual life, health examination information, criminal records, contact information, financial information and social activities. Certain of the personal information are defined as sensitive information, which may not be collected, processed, or used unless an enumerated exception applies, such as medical records, genetic information, Information pertaining to medical treatment, sexual life, health examination information and criminal records.

2.3.3 Information Collection, Processing and Use

The PIPA regulates the collection, processing, and use of personal data. "Collection" means obtaining personal data by any method. "Processing" means the recording, input, storage, editing, correction, reproduction, searching, deletion, output, linking, or internal transfer of information for the purposes of building or using a personal information file. Processing includes digital processing as well as the use of traditional paper filing methods. "Use" of personal data means any utilization of collected personal data with the exception of processing. The transfer of personal data by a data controller to a third party is an example of use.

The PIPA does not apply to the collection, processing, and use of personal data by a natural person in the course of personal or domestic activities. The PIPA also does not apply to the collection, processing, and use of sound and image data in public places or in relation with public activities where the sound and image data is not linked to other personal data. This exemption generally permits closed-circuit television (CCTV) monitoring in stores or the recording of public conversations at ticket windows.

2.4 Financial Consumer Protection Act (FCPA)

2.4.1 Legislative Purpose

The purpose of the Financial Consumer Protection Act (FCPA) is specifically enacted in 2011 to protect the interests of financial consumers, and to fairly, reasonably, and effectively handle financial consumer disputes, thereby reinforcing the confidence of financial consumers in markets and promoting sound development of financial markets. Under such scenario, the FCPA contains two major parts: i.e. the rule and regulation for enhancing the protection of financial consumers, associated with those current existing in relevant financial regulation, and the resolution system to deal with all kinds of financial consumer disputes.

Under the FCPA, the term "financial consumer" means parties that receive financial products or services provided by a financial services enterprise; provided, however, that it does not include qualified institutional investors or professional investors, i.e. those natural persons or juristic persons with a prescribed level of financial capacity or professional expertise.[18]

In respect of the coverage of the financial services, the term "financial services enterprise" as used in the FCPA includes banking enterprises, securities enterprises, futures enterprises, insurance enterprises, electronic stored value card enterprises, and enterprises in other financial services as may be publicly announced by the competent authority[19]. The terms "banking enterprises," "securities enterprises," "futures enterprises," and "insurance enterprises" shall take the definitions set out in the Organic Act Governing the Establishment of the Financial Supervisory Commission. Meanwhile, the term "electronic stored value card enterprises" as used in the FCPA means issuers as defined in the Act Governing Issuance of Electronic Stored Value Cards.

2.4.2 Fair Treatment to Financial Consumers

The FCPA applies the fundamental principles of fairness, reasonableness and good faith as the core function to protect financial consumer. When a financial services enterprise enters into a contract with a financial consumer for the provision of financial products or services, it shall act in conformance with the principles of fairness, reasonableness, equality, reciprocity, and good faith. Clearly unfair contractual provisions entered into by a financial services enterprise and a financial consumer shall be invalid. If there is a disagreement over the meaning of any contractual provision, the provision shall be interpreted in favor of the financial consumer. A financial services enterprise, in providing financial products or services, shall exercise the due care of a good administrator; for any financial product or service it provides that has the nature of a trust or mandate arrangement, the financial services enterprise shall also bear such fiduciary duty as may be required by applicable legal provisions or contractual stipulations.[20]

In the occasions of advertisement or solicitation of financial services, a financial services enterprise, in publishing or broadcasting advertisements or carrying out solicitation or promotional activities, shall not engage in falsehood, deception, concealment, or other conduct sufficient to mislead another party, and shall verify the truthfulness of the content of its advertisements. The obligation it bears to financial consumers shall not be less than that indicated in the content of the aforementioned advertisements or in the materials or explanations provided to financial consumers in the aforementioned solicitation or promotional activities. All the advertisements and solicitation or promotional activities shall be prescribed by the competent authority. A financial services enterprise shall not take advantage of education and awareness programs to introduce individual financial products or services.[21]

2.4.3 Know Your Customers

Knowing your customers (KYC) before providing services becomes significant for financial services industry all around the world. Before a financial services enterprise enters into a contract with a financial consumer for the provision of financial products or services, it shall fully understand the information pertaining to the financial consumer in order to ascertain the suitability of those products or services to the financial consumer. Regulations governing—what "information pertaining to the financial consumer" must be fully understood and what matters relating to "suitability" must be taken into account, as mentioned in the preceding paragraph, and other matters requiring compliance, shall be prescribed by the competent authority.[22]

2.4.4 Risk Disclosure and Explanation

In respect of the "know-your-product" (KYP), the risk disclosure and explanation for the financial products or services to consumers is also significant information to facilitate in making right decision. Before a financial services enterprise enters into a contract with a financial consumer for the provision of financial products or services, it shall fully explain the important aspects of the financial products or services, and of the contact, to the financial consumer, and shall also fully disclose the associated risks. While engaging in the collection, processing, and use of personal information, a financial services enterprise shall fully explain to the financial consumer about his or her rights regarding the protection of personal information, and the possible negative consequences of any refusal to provide consent. While engaging in lending business, a financial services enterprise shall also carefully consider the borrower, the intended use of the funds, the source of repayment, the security for its claim, the perspective risks and benefits of the loan, and other such lending principles, and it shall not decline to provide a loan to a financial consumer solely on the grounds that the financial consumer has refused to authorize it to submit a query about his or her credit information to an enterprise that conducts inter-institutional credit information services.[23]

The explanations and disclosures that the financial services enterprise provides to the financial consumer shall be in text or use another method that is fully understandable to the financial consumer; and the content thereof shall include, without limitation, aspects of material significance to the interests of the financial consumer, such as transaction costs, and possible gains and risks.

When financial products provided by a financial services enterprise are complex, high risk products, the aforementioned explanations and disclosures should be recorded or filmed unless it is an automatic channel transaction or the consumer does not agree.

2.4.5 Damages to Financial Consumers

A financial services enterprise which, by violating any provision in either the duty of know-your-customer (KYC) or the duty of risk disclosure and explanation as aforementioned, causes harm to a financial consumer shall bear liability for damages; provided, however, that this shall not apply if the financial services enterprise can prove that occurrence of the harm was not due to: its failure to fully understand the suitability of a product or service to the financial consumer; its failure to provide an explanation, or provision of an explanation that was untrue or incorrect; or its failure to fully disclose risks.[24] In addition, the court may, in response to a claim by a financial consumer, award punitive damages up to three times the amount of actual damage for damage caused by a willful act of misconduct by a financial services enterprise; however, if such damage is caused by negligence, a court may award punitive damages up to one the amount of the actual damage.[25]

2.4.6 Establishing an Ombudsman Body

In order to handle financial consumer disputes fairly, reasonably, quickly, and effectively, thereby protecting the interests of financial consumers, an ombudsman body shall be established.[26] In exchange for handling financial consumer disputes and conducting financial education and awareness program,[27] the ombudsman body may charge financial services enterprises annual fees and dispute handling service fees. Schedules for the annual fees and service fees, and related requirements, shall be prescribed by the competent authority, i.e. the Financial Supervisory Commission (FSC).

2.4.7 Filing a Complaint by Consumers

Financial consumers shall deal with a financial consumer dispute by first filing a complaint with the financial services enterprise. The financial services enterprise shall appropriately handle the matter within 30 days of the day the complaint is received, and shall inform the financial consumer that filed the complaint of its disposition. If the financial consumer does not accept the disposition or the financial services enterprise fails to handle the matter before the aforementioned time limit, the financial consumer may, within 60 days of either the day he receives notification of the disposition or the day the time limit expires, apply to the ombudsman body to institute an ombudsman case. To apply to institute an ombudsman case, a financial consumer shall fill out an application form that expressly indicates the names and basic identifying information of the parties to the dispute, the claims, the facts, the reasons, the related documents or information, and details regarding the inappropriate handling of the complaint.[28] When a financial consumer files a complaint with the ombudsman body, the financial consumer contact division of the ombudsman body shall refer the complaint to the financial services enterprise for handling.

2.4.8 Ombudsman Committee

In order to handle an ombudsman case, the ombudsman body shall establish an ombudsman committee comprising 9–25 members, and may as necessary appoint additional members. One member shall be the chairperson. All members shall be selected from among scholars, experts, and fair and impartial persons who possess relevant learning or professional experience, and shall be hired after their selections have been submitted to and approved by the competent authority. An ombudsman committee member shall serve a term of three years, and may be reappointed upon the expiration of the term. The chairperson shall serve in a full-time capacity, while the other ombudsman committee members may serve part-time. All ombudsman committee members shall exercise their authority in a fair and impartial manner.[29]

2.4.9 Principles of Fairness and Reasonableness

After the ombudsman body entertains an application to institute an ombudsman case, it shall consider factual evidence related to the case and conduct an impartial and independent hearing in keeping with the principles of fairness and reasonableness. In order to handle a financial consumer dispute, the ombudsman body may, as reasonably necessary, ask the financial services enterprise to provide assistance or submit documents and related materials. If the financial services enterprise that receives such a request fails to provide assistance or submit documents and related materials, the ombudsman body may report the matter to the competent authority for handling.[30]

2.4.10 Enforcement of an Ombudsman Statement

After the ombudsman statement delivered to the parties in dispute, they shall notify the ombudsman body in writing, before the time limit prescribed in the ombudsman statement, whether they accept or reject the ombudsman decision. Once both parties accept it, the ombudsman case is resolved. Where the financial services enterprise has expressed prior written consent, or in the contracts for its products and services or in other documents has expressed a willingness to abide by the dispute handling procedures of the FCPA, it shall accept any decision by the ombudsman committee that requires it to make payment below a "certain amount" to a financial consumer or convey thereto property valued at less than a certain amount.[31] This shall also apply where the decision exceeds a certain amount but the financial consumer has expressed a willingness to reduce the amount of the payment or the value of the property to a certain amount.[32]

A financial consumer may, within a peremptory period of 90-days counting from the day on which the ombudsman case achieves a resolution, apply for the ombudsman body to send the ombudsman statement to a court for approval. Except the circumstances where the content of the ombudsman statement violates laws or regulations, contravenes public order or good morals, or its compulsory enforcement is not possible for some other reason, exist, the court shall approve the ombudsman statement. An ombudsman statement that has been approved by a court of law shall have the same force as a final and irrevocable civil judgment.[33]

3 Financial Consumer Protection Institutions

Based on different governing legislation, the institutions for financial consumer protection may include certain government entities, such as the Financial Supervisory Commission (FSC), Department of Consumer Protection (DCP) in the Executive Yuan, the Ministry of Justice (MOJ). As for those non-government organization or special institutions in this aspect, the entities might include the Financial Ombudsman Institution (FOI), the Securities and Futures Investors Protection Fund (SFIPF), the Central Deposit Insurance Corporation (CDIC) and the Taiwan Insurance Guarantee Fund (TIGF). Except the MOJ, the functions and operations of these entities and institutions will be introduced respectively in the followings.

3.1 Department of Consumer Protection

3.1.1 Missions

On January 11, 1994, the Consumer Protection Act (CPA) was promulgated in order to protect consumer interests and to improve the quality of consumer life. It also represents that Taiwan enters into a new milestone on making efforts to promote consumer protection work. The CPA is the basic law of consumer protection. The other laws and regulations related to consumer protection include Commodity Inspection Act, Commodity Labeling Act, Act Governing Food Sanitation, Pharmaceutical Affairs Act, etc. They are administered and enforced by the authorities of the central government respectively. Furthermore, the local governments could also enact municipal laws and regulations relevant to consumer protection.

The task of consumer protection in Taiwan is an affair carried out jointly by agencies at both the central and local government levels. At the central government level, in addition to the Department of Consumer Protection (DCP) responsible for conducting the enhancement of consumer protection duties nationwide, ministries in the central government, in their respective areas of governance, make relevant laws and policies to carry out consumer protection works. As for the local governments, they are responsible for implementing. Through the supervision and coordination, DCP establishes horizontal integration of various administrative agencies responsible for consumer protection works, and enacts consumer protection policies and plans. Besides, through the regular performance evaluation of consumer protection works done by agencies of the central and local governments, DCP could review and decide improvement actions.

3.1.2 Responsibility

DCP's primary duties include: to draft/amend basic consumer protection policies and plans, to coordinate and supervise the execution carried out by the agencies of the central and local government, to draft/amend consumer protection laws, to mediate and handle significant consumer disputes. And it is responsible for staff works of the Consumer Protection Committee (predecessor of the DCP), Executive Yuan. For the purpose of the CPA, the "Consumer" means any person who in relation to a commercial practice, is acting for purposes of consumption to make transactions in exchange for goods or services. "Consumer relationship" means the legal relationship arising between consumers and traders for the sale of goods or provision of services. Under such scenario, certain financial services with investment features won't be covered under the CPA. It means certain financial consumers won't be protected by the CPA.

3.2 Financial Supervisory Commission (FSC)

The Financial Supervisory Commission (FSC) was established on 1 July 2004, a central government agency established under the Executive Yuan, as the competent authority responsible for development, supervision, regulation, and examination of financial markets and financial service enterprises in Taiwan. The FSC seeks to ensure safe and sound financial institutions, maintain financial stability, and promote the development of our financial markets. Since its establishment, the main goals of the FSC have been to create a sound, fair, efficient, and internationalized environment for financial industry, strengthen safeguards for consumers and investors and help financial industry achieve sustainable development.

3.2.1 Missions

Subject to the "FSC Organic Act," the Executive Yuan hereby establishes the Financial Supervisory Commission ("the FSC") to promote sound business management at financial institutions, maintain financial stability, and facilitate the development of financial markets. Pursuant to Article 2 of the "FSC Organic Act," the FSC is the competent authority for development, supervision, regulation, and examination of financial markets and financial service enterprises. The term of "financial markets" includes the banking market, bills market, securities market, futures and derivatives market, insurance market, and their respective settlement systems. The term of "financial service enterprises" includes financial holding companies, the Financial Restructuring Fund, the Central Deposit Insurance Corporation, banking enterprises, securities enterprises, futures enterprises, insurance enterprises, electronic financial transaction enterprises, and other financial service enterprises. However, the Central Bank shall be the competent authority in charge of the bank payment system.

3.2.2 Organizational Structure

The FSC is a central government agency established under the Executive Yuan as the competent authority responsible for financial supervisory policies and businesses, and it carries out its duties independently in accordance with the law. The chairperson of the FSC is a minister appointed by the President on the recommendation of the premier. The FSC has two vice chairpersons, both appointed by the President on the recommendation of the Premier, and 6 to 12 commissioners.[34] The FSC comprises four bureaus (banking, securities and futures, insurance, financial examination), four departments (planning, international affairs, legal affairs, and information management), four offices, a government-owned business (the Central Deposit Insurance Corporation) and two Representative Offices (in New York and London).

3.2.3 Responsibility

Pursuant to Article 3 of the "FSC Organic Act," The FSC shall be in charge of the following matters:

1. Financial systems and supervisory policies.
2. Prescribing, amending, and repealing financial laws and regulations.
3. Supervising and regulating the following matters in connection with financial institutions: establishment; voidance; revocation; change; merger; business suspension; dissolution; and approval of business scope.
4. Development, supervision, and regulation of financial markets.
5. Examination of financial institutions.
6. Examination of matters relating to public companies and securities markets.
7. International financial matters.
8. Protection of financial consumers.
9. Enforcement of financial laws and regulations, punishment of violators, and handling of matters related thereto.
10. Collection, processing, and analysis of statistical information relating to financial supervision, regulation, and examination work.
11. Other matters relating to financial supervision, regulation, and examination work.

4 Special Institutions for Financial Consumers Protection

4.1 Financial Ombudsman Institution (FOI)

The FOI is positioned to resolve financial services disputes in a fair, reasonable, quick, and effective manner to protect the rights and interests of financial consumers. Its first mission is to build the confidence of financial consumers in financial institutions. It does so by acting as a filter to eliminate inappropriate business practices while promoting positive development and influence so as to prevent financial services disputes. In addition, financial institutions can also take advantage of the FOI's well integrated and categorized educational materials to establish correct business conduct and training methods for employees in the financial industry, and enhance the quality of their services.[35]

4.1.1 Missions

The financial products and services that financial consumers purchase from financial services enterprises are becoming increasingly diverse and ever more complex and specialized. This has resulted in a real asymmetry between financial consumers and financial service enterprises in terms of financial strength, information, and expertise. In the event of a financial consumer dispute, the consumer may find that seeking a remedy through litigation is not worth the cost in time and money. For this reason, it is necessary to provide financial consumers with a professional dispute resolution scheme other than litigation, and that further is fair, reasonable, quick, and effective. In the past, financial consumer disputes in Taiwan were handled by the competent regulatory authority, an industry association, or a financial industry self-regulatory organization. There was no single, integrated entity with statutory authorization to handle financial consumer disputes, so it was necessary to enact a special law for the handling of civil disputes involving financial products and services.

The Government enacted the Financial Consumer Protection Act (FCPA) in 2011 to protect the interests of financial consumers and to fairly, reasonably, and effectively resolve disputes on financial consumer services, thereby reinforcing the confidence of financial consumers in markets and promoting sound development of financial markets. In doing so, the FSC took into reference the operational scheme of the United Kingdom's Financial Services and Markets Act, the FOS of the UK, and Singapore's Financial Industry Disputes Resolution Centre Ltd (FIDReC), as well as related domestic legislation.

The Financial Ombudsman Institution (FOI) was established in 2011 pursuant to the Financial Consumer Protection Act (FCPA) as an independent incorporated foundation to fairly, reasonably, and effectively resolve disputes between financial consumer and financial services enterprise, with the funding from the government.[36] The FOI formally began operating on 2 January 2012 as a scheme with particular duty of handling financial consumer disputes and strengthening financial consumer protection.[37]

4.1.2 Ombudsman Committee

To resolve financial services dispute, the FOI has established an Ombudsman Committee in accordance with the FCPA, as an alternative system for financial services dispute resolution with credibility. All members are selected from among scholars, practitioners, and other impartial persons who possess relevant expertise or professional experience, and are appointed after their nominations have been submitted to and approved by the FSC.[38] The Committee's procedures for handling disputes can be divided into three stages: i.e. filing complaints, mediation, and ombudsman service. All stages are designed to resolve disputes fairly, reasonably, quickly, and effectively to protect the interests of financial consumers.[39]

4.1.3 Financial Education and Awareness

In addition to handling financial consumer disputes, the ombudsman body shall also conduct education and awareness programs for financial services enterprises and financial consumers to ensure that financial services enterprises and financial consumers all have a full and correct understanding of financial consumption principles as well as the rights and obligations that arise in connection with a financial consumption relationship, thereby effectively averting the occurrence of financial consumer disputes.

4.1.4 Features of Ombudsman Scheme

The financial consumer ombudsman scheme has the following features:[40]

1. Efficiency: The Regulations Governing Ombudsman Procedures provide that the FOI must render an ombudsman decision within 3 months after accepting an ombudsman case. The deadline may be extended by 2 months at most. This is faster than ordinary civil litigation procedure.
2. Low Cost: The FOI emulates the scheme of the UK's Financial Ombudsman Service (FOS) in that all services to financial consumers are free of charge. This allows consumers to make extensive use of its alternative dispute resolution scheme to resolve financial consumer disputes.
3. Effectiveness: Pursuant to Article 29 and 30 of the FCPA, as the financial services enterprise has expressed through prior written consent of its intention to be bound by the ombudsman decision which involves disputes incurred from an investment product with the amount of NTD 1 million or less, and disputes incurred from a non-investment product with the amount of NTD a hundred thousand or less, once the ombudsman decision rendering the pecuniary award within the above-mentioned amount has been accepted by the consumer, the ombudsman decision becomes binding and the case is deemed resolved. The consumer may request the FOI to submit the ombudsman decision to the court and for its approval. Once the approval is rendered, the ombudsman decision will have the same effect as a final court decision. Thus, despite being fairly streamlined, the ombudsman procedure does not lack effectiveness.
4. Fairness and Reasonableness: The principle of fairness and reasonableness set out in Article 20 of the FCPA is one of the important features of the FOI's ombudsman scheme. According to this principle, after weighing the rights and obligations of both parties to a case, the FOI may render an ombudsman decision that is more flexible than a court judgment, or, in the absence of applicable legal provisions, a decision based on the principles of equity and jurisprudence.

4.1.5 Future Outlook

At present, the FOI has a dispute resolution rate of greater than 50 percent. This initial result shows that the government is progressively achieving its policy goals in promoting financial consumer protection. In the future, it seems that the role of the FOI will grow in importance, in line with the aspirations of the financial industry, consumer groups, and the relevant government authorities. If the FOI can continue to improve its efficiency and effectiveness in operation, the policy goals initiated by the FCPA can be expected to achieve in respect of protecting financial consumers, reinforcing their confidence in the markets, and facilitating the sound development of the financial markets

The robust functioning of its alternative dispute resolution scheme has enabled the FOI to resolve average over 2000 financial disputes (including complaints, mediations, and ombudsman cases) annually since its establishment in 2012. This number exceeds the number of cases resolved by courts at any level, highlighting the performance of the FOI while also demonstrating a maturing awareness amongst financial consumers that they can turn to the financial consumer ombudsman scheme to resolve disputes.

4.2 Securities and Futures Investors Protection Center (SFIPC)

4.2.1 Missions

Rapid changes in the capital market have steadily led to new innovations to securities and futures, making investor protection a vital facet of the system. The Securities and Futures Investors Protection Center (hereinafter referred to as "the Center") was established in January 2003 under the Securities Investor and Futures Trader Protection Act (hereinafter referred to as Investor Protection Act"). Throughout the years of its existence, the Center has been devoted to accomplishing the missions that the Investor Protection Act has vested upon it, from resolving investors' securities/futures related complaints and disputes, providing mediation service, urging companies to exercise disgorgement claims, to completing any investor protection-related and market development tasks assigned by the competent authority.

4.2.2 Major Business Operations

In recent years, the major business operations of the Center can be categorized as below:[41]

1. Ensuring fulfillment of civil liabilities through class action suits
   The Investor Protection Act has introduced a class action suit mechanism that relieves investors of the financial and mental stress involved.[42] The Center has made significant progress in representing class action suits. At current stage, there have already numerous precedent judgments ruled in investors' favor, whether the disputes involved misrepresentation of financial reports,

misstatements in the prospectus, manipulation of share prices, insider trading or other major misconducts in the securities market. Civil court judgments accumulated through class action suits over the years have been defining and enforcing the notion of civil liabilities under the Securities and Exchange Act, while in the meantime enabling the court decisions to constantly review the application of relevant laws. Under such scenario, the framework of civil liabilities in the securities market can be further enhanced and explicitly established to protect investors' interests, thus these court judgments prompted TWSE/TPEx listed companies to insure against directors' and supervisors' liabilities, and CPA firms to exercise greater risk awareness and due diligence when auditing financial statements.

2. Negotiating settlement for faster compensation of investors' losses
   In order to give investors faster access to their claims over the course of class action, the Center would negotiate settlements with criminal defendants, directors, supervisors, accountants, and underwriters. Pursuant to the Investor Protection Act, the Center is a shareholder of all TWSE/TPEx listed companies. To ensure the corporate governance and protect the investors' rights and interests, the Center has taken the initiative to promote shareholder activism, corporate governance and investors' protection with help from the competent authority and other government agencies.[43]
3. Monitoring corporate governance and shareholder issues
   In cases of private placement, capital decrease, excess compensation for directors and supervisors, disproportionate dividend policy, major reinvestments, significant losses from reinvestments, large-sum endorsement/guarantee and loans to others, which have material influence on the rights and interests of TWSE/TPEx listed companies and shareholders, the Center will send an inquiry letter in the capacity of a shareholder, asking the company concerned to provide explanations or improvements. If necessary, the Center can assign staff to express opinions in the interest of shareholders at various shareholders' meetings.
   The Center also intervenes whenever companies have major cases that are of great concern to investors' rights and interests or whenever dispute arises regarding a company's management/control right. The Center would help devise solutions if these cases pose any concerns to shareholders' rights and interests. In recent years, there have been cases of inappropriate measures taken to fight control over a TWSE/TPEx listed company. Some of these measures involved exploiting technicalities to stop shareholders from exercising their rights, which therefore gave rise to disputes over the shareholder proposal right and nomination right.
4. Filing derivative suit and discharge suit
   The Center has been taking actions for the purpose of enhancing corporate governance and protecting shareholders from misconducts such as breach of trust, misappropriation of assets, and breach of fiduciary duty that involve a company's management, directors or supervisors. Since 2009, the Center has

been empowered by the Investor Protection Act to file derivative suit and/or discharge suit against directors or supervisors when discovering conduct by a director or supervisor of a TWSE/TPEx listed company in the course of performing his or her duties that is materially injurious to the company or is in violation of laws, regulations, and/or provisions of the company's articles of incorporation.

4.2.3 Future Outlook

In the future, ongoing changes of the market will undoubtedly give rise to new forms of securities and futures related dispute in the future. The Center will continue to protect investors' interests and focus on the following tasks:

1. To assist investors in class action suits. Accumulate civil court judgments made on securities and futures related disputes to fulfill the civil liabilities and compensate investors' losses, as stated in the Securities and Exchange Act.
2. To protect investors by actively working with supervisory authorities for material cases with social attention that involve securities or futures before the cases are prosecuted.
3. To promote shareholder activism and urge the development of sound corporate governance practices within TWSE/TPEx listed companies. Raise constructive suggestions as to how policy execution and practical difficulties can be resolved to ensure more efficient corporate governance.
4. To assist investors in obtaining compensation for their losses by compulsory enforcement or settlements. Improve the efficiency at which settlement payments are distributed, and use the media to remind class plaintiffs of unclaimed payments.

4.3 Central Deposit Insurance Corporation (CDIC)

4.3.1 Missions

In many jurisdictions, provision of a financial safety net for banks and other financial institutions has been a key element of the policy response to the financial crisis. As part of financial safety net to protect depositors, the government-owned Central Deposit Insurance Corporation (the CDIC) was established in 1985, with capital jointly invested by the Ministry of Finance and the Central Bank. The CDIC is the only institution in Taiwan exclusively in charge of managing the deposit insurance system and serves as an integral part of the country's financial safety net. The board of directors consists of seven members who are appointed by the Financial Supervisory Commission and three supervisors are appointed by the

Central Bank. The CDIC has strengthened its functions of providing policy insurance since 1999, as all deposit-taking institutions were obligated to join the deposit insurance system. In January 2007, the Deposit Insurance Act had been amended in a large scale; the mandate and functions of the deposit insurance system in Taiwan have been further enhanced.

Before 1980's the government in Taiwan took elaborate measures of regulation and protection of local financial institutions to maintain stable growth of the financial industry. Therefore, the operations of financial institutions had been steady and smooth at that period of time. When local and international financial environments started to experience rapid changes brought about partly by the trend of liberalization and globalization, the government responded by sequential liberalization of the financial businesses and relaxation of relevant financial regulations. As a result, the industry itself was empowered with higher operations freedom, though accompanied by increasing competition and higher business risk.

In consideration of the far-reaching impact of business failure of financial institutions on wide facets of the economy, the government undertook to devise a deposit insurance system to safeguard the benefits of small depositors on the basis of Article 46 of the Banking Law. In 1983 the Ministry of Finance joined by the Central Bank invited representatives from the financial industry and drafted the Deposit Insurance Act. After the approval by the Parliament, the Act was promulgated and implemented on January 9, 1985, which has become the origin of Taiwan's deposit insurance Act. Stockholder's right management of the CDIC was transferred from the Ministry of Finance to the Financial Supervisory Commission (FSC) in 2013. After shares of all original domestic commercial banks (less than 0.01% shares of CDIC) were transferred to the FSC in 2014, the FSC and the Central Bank are the only two shareholders of the CDIC now.

4.3.2 Deposit Insurance System

In Taiwan, all the financial institutions duly approved under the law to accept deposits are required to take part in deposit insurance provided by the CDIC and to pay premiums therefor. Beginning from January 1, 2011, if an insured financial institution terminates its business or is unable to pay off its deposits, CDIC compensates depositors up to NT$ 3 million, including principal and interest. This system is designed to ensure the rights of depositors and maintain the stability of the financial system.[44] Within the insured institutions, not all deposits therein are covered by the CDIC, the facts illustrated in Table 2.[45]

4.3.3 Coverage Provided to Depositors

All depository institutions must apply for deposit insurance by submitting the application form to CDIC, but the CDIC has the right of determination to approve or disapprove the membership. Pursuant to Article 13 of the *Deposit Insurance Act*,

Table 2 Fact sheet on Taiwan deposit insurance system

Launched	September 1985
Administered by	Central Deposit Insurance Corporation (CDIC)
Participating institutions	Domestic Banks (including the postal savings bank), Credit cooperatives, Credit departments of farmers' and fishermen's associations, Foreign bank branches in Taiwan (Foreign bank branches whose deposits are protected in their home countries may not participate.), Agricultural Bank of Taiwan
Premiums	Paid by member institutions
Premium rates	Risk-based premium system and five-tiered rates instituted
Coverage	Apply automatically to all eligible deposits; depositors do not need to apply for deposit insurance.
Maximum coverage	NT$3 million, including principal and interest of deposit in New Taiwan Dollar or non-New Taiwan Dollar per depositor per insured institution.
Types of depositor covered	All depositors including resident/non-resident individuals and organizations
Insured deposits	The following domestic deposits in Taiwan: checking accounts, demand deposits, time deposits, deposits required by law to be deposited in certain financial institutions, and other deposits which the Financial Supervisory Commission has approved as insurable.
Uninsured deposits	Negotiable certificates of deposit, Deposits from government agencies, Deposits from the Central Bank, Deposits from banks, postal savings bank (Chunghwa Post Company), credit cooperatives, Agricultural Bank of Taiwan and credit departments of farmers' and fishermen's associations, Deposit exceeding the per-institution maximum insurance coverage established for each depositor, Other deposits which the Financial Supervisory Commission has approved as non-insurable (e.g. structured deposits)

the maximum insurance coverage that the CDIC offers to each depositor of any insured institution shall be determined by the Financial Supervisory Commission in conjunction with the Ministry of Finance and the Central Bank. Beginning from January 1, 2011, the maximum insurance coverage is set at NT$ 3 million. The new maximum coverage covers around 98.6% of the depositors and 59% of insured deposits.

4.4 Taiwan Insurance Guaranty Fund (TIGF)

In order to efficiently integrate the resources of insurance stabilization funds, set up and implement the exit mechanism, conduct off-site monitoring, strengthen the early warning system, have a good grasp of the performance of the insurance industry and help the regulator supervise and control the risks of insurance companies in a timely manner, the Fund is set up as an dedicated institution to actively carry out the functions mandated by the Insurance Act. On April 15, 2009, the Fund held its first donors' meeting. The Articles of Taiwan Insurance Guaranty Fund were finalized on May 8, 2009, and the Fund was established on July 3, 2009 accordingly.

4.4.1 Missions

The missions of the TIGF are to protect the interests of policyholders (i.e. proposers, insured and beneficiaries), and maintain financial stability of insurance market in Taiwan. In respect of its duties and responsibilities, the TIGF shall handle the following matters:

1. The Fund may extend loans to insurance enterprises experiencing business difficulties.
2. The Fund may provide low-interest loans or subsidies to insurance enterprises that incur loss by merging with troubled insurance enterprises or assuming their contracts.
3. When an insurance enterprise is placed into receivership, ordered to suspend business and undergo rehabilitation, or ordered to dissolve, or when a receiver applies to a court for reorganization, pursuant to the Insurance Act, the Fund shall, as necessary, advance funds on behalf of the insurance enterprises to settle claims which policyholders are entitled to make under in-force contracts, and with respect to the amount thus advanced shall succeed to and exercise the rights of policyholders to claim against the insurance enterprise.
4. In order to safeguard the interests of policyholders and help expedite reorganization proceedings, when an insurance enterprise undergoes reorganization pursuant to the Insurance Act, the policyholders shall, unless they object in writing, be deemed to have granted consent for the Fund to act as their agent in attending meetings of related parties and exercising rights related to the reorganization. The Fund shall adopt procedures for actions they take when serving as agent, as well as other compliance matters, and shall file them with the competent authority for recordation.
5. The Fund shall act as receiver, rehabilitator or liquidator upon appointed by the competent authority.
6. The Fund shall assume, upon approved by the competent authority, the insurance contracts of insolvent insurance companies.
7. The Fund shall undertake other matters, as approved by the competent authority, to stabilize the insurance market or safeguard the interests of insured parties.

4.4.2 Bailout of Insolvent Insurance Companies

In August 2009, the TIGF was entrusted by the government to take charge of Kuo Hua Life for the protection of the company's clients and employees. Kuo Hua is the first Taiwanese life insurer to be brought under government receivership for incurring huge losses and failing to meet capital increase requirements. The TIGF held an auction in 2010 to find a buyer for Kuo Hua Life, but the effort failed. The fund later engaged in talks with Taiwan Financial Holding Company to assume control of Kuo Hua Life, but the negotiations fell apart.[46] In November 2012, the TransGlobe Life signed an agreement with the Taiwan Insurance Guaranty Fund to take over Kuo Hua after winning a bid for the insurer by offering to accept less in government subsidies (NT$88.37 billion) to cover Kuo Hua's losses than other contenders.

In March 2015, Cathay Life Insurance won the auction for insolvent Global Life Insurance and Singfor Life Insurance with an offer of administrative forbearance by the FSC. Cathay Life took over the assets, liabilities and operations of the two companies, with the TIGF, offering compensation totaling NT$30.3 billion for its takeover of the two insurers, including NT$8 billion in reserve assets.[47] In Dec. 2017, similar to the previous auction, Nan Shan Life Insurance won the TIGF bailout auction of troubled Chaoyang Life Insurance for NT$200 million (US$6.3 million),[48] allowing Nan Shan to take over Chaoyang's assets and debts, and retain the rights of existing policyholders unaffected.[49]

4.4.3 Future Outlook

In the future, it is expected that TIGF shall assist the competent authority to handle the following regulatory affairs:

1. To establish a complete early warning system, help the regulator grasp the performance of the insurance industry, and assist the insurers to manage their operational risk.
2. To develop and implement an exit mechanism for the insurance companies to protect the interests of policyholders and maintain financial stability.
3. To assist the insurance industry understand about domestic and international financial trends, gain insight to the changes of the business environment and manage business risks.

5 Recent Enhancement and Development

In recent years, the FSC undertook the enhancement and development in respect of financial consumer protection in the following aspects:

5.1 Amendment of the Financial Consumer Protection Act[50]

Parts of the Financial Consumer Protection Act were amended on February 4, 2015, and the Act went into effect on 3 May the same year. The FSC also amended relevant regulations. The primary amendments of the Act included the following:

1. With respect to assisting disadvantaged financial consumers, a group ombudsman mechanism has been added;
2. When a financial institution infringes financial customer rights against the law, the FSC may impose an administrative penalty, such as giving warning, imposing prohibition on its sales activities, etc., depending on the seriousness of the breach. Moreover, the FSC may revoke the business license in the case of serious violation;
3. When a financial institution infringes financial customer rights against the law, there is no amount limitation for imposition of a fine, which will be imposed within the scope of income or interests gained in the case of serious violation;
4. In order to enhance the responsibility of the Board of Directors, both the salesperson remuneration system and the initial sale of complex and high-risk products by financial services enterprises shall be reported to and approved by the Board of Directors or the Executive Board of Directors.

5.2 Standard Operation Procedure for the Consumer Disputes[51]

In order to enhance the handling consumer disputes by financial services enterprises, elevate the efficiency and quality of handling disputes, protect the rights and interests of the financial consumer, and to avoid the punishment by the FSC due to regulation violation, the FSC promulgated that all financial services enterprises shall set a consumer dispute handling policy and related standard operating procedure in May 2015. In addition, the procedure shall be reported to and approved by the Board of Directors and truly implemented by financial services enterprises. The above policy shall include at least the scope of the consumer dispute, framework, application method, handling procedure, timeline, searching the process of application case, tracking and auditing the case, education and training, and regularly review, etc., The FSC will review the financial services enterprises implementation situation when the annual financial examinations are conducted. To strengthen the protection of financial consumer rights and interests, the FSC conducted 114, 200, and 235 consumer-protection related examinations in 2013, 2014 and 2015 respectively.

5.3 Principle of Fair Treatment of Customers[52]

In order to achieve the goal that all financial consumers are treated equitably and fairly at all stages of their relationship with financial service enterprises, with reference to the UK, Singapore and Hong Kong model and reviewing relevant financial consumer protection laws, the FSC formulated the Principle of Fair

Treatment of Customers by Financial Services Enterprises, as the guideline of consumer protection for the financial industry. In addition, the FSC held the "Financial Services Enterprise Treating Customers Fairly Principle Symposium" and Signing Ceremony in November 2015, showing the determination to attach importance to consumer protection. Moreover, all financial service enterprises shall establish its own Principle of Fair Treatment of Customers policy and method, and have them approved by the Board of Directors by April 30, 2016.

5.4 *Online Application for Personal Credit Reports*[53]

In response to the FSC's policy of building a digital financial environment and to provide the public with better access to personal credit reports, the Joint Credit Information Center (JCIC) has put in place an online channel for obtaining such reports. Any person over age 20 may file an application on the JCIC website using his/her citizen digital certificate issued by the Ministry of Interior.

5.5 *Mitigation of Insurance Service Complaints*[54]

To urge the executive managers of insurance companies to address importance consumer rights and interests, the FSC, based on the figures provided by the FOI as a reference for administrative supervision of insurance business, the FSC posted "the combined complaint rate" for individual insurers, which was comprised of "non-claim complaint rate", "claim complaint rate" and "number of claim handling days" and announced the rates in the "Public Petition and Financial Consumer Disputes Management System" on March 30, 2015, and September 30, 2015.

5.6 *TRF Trading Malpractice and Disputes*

TRF stands for Target Redemption Forward, an option type of complex high-risk derivative with a better rate of return but also higher risks, become popular in Taiwan as investors pursue greater profits in recent years. However, the sale of such financial derivative product sparked an outcry after the Chinese yuan (RMB) plunged against the U.S. dollar, resulting in massive losses for investors who bought TRFs, which bet on a higher yuan. To enlarge trading size, some banks have even falsified financial statements for corporate customers to hide their TRF trading losses. Many cases show that banks failed to comply with the KYC and disclosure rules and violated regulations requiring strict internal controls and comprehensive operational processes while selling TRFs. For example, they failed to inform customers about possible risks associated with TRF trading, consider customer financial backgrounds or loss tolerance.[55]

The dramatic depreciation of the Chinese yuan (RMB) has resulted in a series of disputes between banks and their customers, resulting in the FSC instructing banks to settle such cases as soon as possible, through the arbitration by the Arbitration Association and the mediation of the Financial Ombudsman Institutions (FOI).[56]

As for the regulatory measures, the FSC has imposed fines on 16 banks so far for their malpractices in the sale of TRFs to local investors. In June 2015, the FSC announced new regulations to provide the definition of complex high-risk products, establish a disbursement query mechanism at the Joint Credit Information Center (JCIC) and stipulate the maximum losses on complex high-risk products. Nonetheless, since the Chinese yuan (RMB) depreciated massively in August 2015, and the TRF investors suffered heavy losses. In order to strengthen the supervision of complex high-risk derivatives, the FSC eventually announced the amendment of the regulation in January 2016, particularly in respect of redefining qualified professional investors under the FCPA and applying the principle of fair treatment to customers. In the Legislative Yuan (the Parliament), it has been argued that certain individual professional investors and small and medium enterprises (SME) shall be treated as financial consumers and protected under the FCPA. In the contrast, some people with counter-arguments asserted that it may create inequity in the trading between financial services enterprises and such "professionals" and therefore result in an abuse-using the resources for protecting legitimate financial consumers.

5.7 Steering Taskforce for Financial Consumer Protection

In order to implement the financial consumer protection policy, and strengthen communication and coordination mechanism among relevant entities and institutions, grasp the latest development of financial consumer protection systems around the world, undertake a timely research and development of financial consumer protection measures, and promote comprehensive protection of the financial interests of consumers, the FSC specifically set up the "Steering Taskforce for Financial Consumer Protection" in Nov. 2016. The Steering Taskforce meeting every season is convened by the chairman of the FSC, has the members including two vice chairpersons, the director generals of four business bureaus, the directors of four departments under the FSC, the chairman of the FOI and the chairman of the SFIPC. The Taskforce's mission covers the following:

1. Research and development on financial consumer protection policy, relevant regulations, protective measures and the review mechanism;
2. Enhancement of current financial consumer protection policies, relevant regulations and the operation mechanism of practice;
3. Statistical analysis and strategy on the cases financial consumer disputes;
4. Division, collaboration and coordination of financial consumer protection policies and measures.

6 Conclusion

By reference to the advanced models in other jurisdictions and observation on global trend, Taiwan has constructed a comprehensive mechanism to protect consumers in the financial markets. It provides well designed legal systems to delegate the power to the competent authority, the Financial Supervisory Commission (FSC), to execute its functions under the FCPA, accompanied with the supplemental functions provided by other government entities such as the Department of consumer protection (DCP), the Ministry of Justice (MOJ).

In respect of financial consumer disputes resolution, the ombudsman scheme provided by the Financial Ombudsman Institution (FOI) may cover all kinds of disputes and redresses in the retail financial services market, while the Securities and Futures Investors Protection Center (SFIPC) also handle certain dispute resolution for the investors.

With the safety net of financial service sector, the financial consumers can be compensated in the amount under the threshold when a financial crisis or insolvency cases occurs. Not just as the safety net, the Central Deposit Insurance Corporation (CDIC), the Taiwan Insurance Guarantee Fund (TIGF) and Securities and Futures Investors Protection Fund (SFIPF) can assist the respective competent authorities to enhance the regulations for consumer protection.

In the rapidly changing financial market, due to the asymmetry of information and the lack of professional knowledge, financial consumers are vulnerable in most transactions. In recent years, Taiwan encountered many troublesome cases and suffered from the disputes of the complex high-risk such as Lehman Brother structure note and the Redemption Forward (TRF) product. It has been argued that certain individual professional investors and small and medium enterprises (SME) shall be treated as financial consumers and protected under the FCPA. Counter-arguments asserted that it may result in the inequity in the trading and an abuse-using of resources for protecting legitimate financial consumers. In addition, with the global development in financial technology and cyber risks, many innovative financial services and business models may trigger various kinds of potential financial services disputes. It is expected that the current protection mechanism in Taiwan would be reviewed and reinforced promptly by the competent authorities to cope with the evolution of financial market and truly provide comprehensive protection to all kinds of financial consumers.

Notes

1. Department of Consumer Protection (DCP), Introduction to the Department of Consumer Protection, Executive Yuan, Republic of China (Taiwan) 2012.
2. *Id.*
3. Consumer Protection Act (CPA), Article 2.
4. *Id.*
5. The Shou-Sheng-Chi No. 5 of the High Court Decision in 2000.

6. Consumer Protection Commission (predecessor of the DCP), Executive Yuan, Shou-Pao-Chi No. 09700076831, 2008/9/4.
7. Directorate-General of Budget, Accounting and Statistics, Executive Yuan, R. O.C. (Taiwan).
8. *Id.*
9. Source: Financial Supervisory Commission, R.O.C. (Taiwan); Directorate-General of Budget, Accounting and Statistics, Executive Yuan, R. O.C. (Taiwan), and Taiwan Insurance Institute.
10. CPA, Article 1.
11. The CPA also covers the definition of the following terms, such as consumer relationship, consumer litigation, consumer advocacy group, standard terms and conditions, individually negotiated terms, standard contracts, distance sales, door-to-door sales, installment sales and so on.
12. CPA, Article 3.
13. *Id*, Article 4.
14. *Id*, Article 5.
15. The relevant provisions of the Securities and Exchange Act, the Futures Trading Act, the Securities Investment Trust and Consulting Act, and other applicable acts shall apply with regard to any matters not provided under the Protection Law.
16. Chen Hui-Ling & Michael R Fahey, Data Protection in Taiwan: Overview, Data Protection Global Guide 2016/17, Thomson Reuters 2016.
17. The MOJ has issued the Enforcement Rules of the Personal Information Protection Act, the Specific Purposes and the Classification of Personal Information under the Personal Information Protection Act (a comprehensive guide to officially recognized legitimate purposes for processing personal data and types of personal data) and more than 600 letters of interpretation.
18. The meanings of the terms "qualified institutional investors" and "prescribed level of financial capacity or professional expertise" as used in the FCPA shall be prescribed by the competent authority (FSC).
19. Securities exchanges, over-the-counter securities exchanges, central securities depositories, futures exchanges, and enterprises in other financial services have been publicly announced by the competent authority are not included within the meaning of these terms.
20. FCPA, Article 7.
21. *Id*, Article 8.
22. *Id*, Article 9.
23. *Id*, Article 10.
24. *Id*, Article 11.
25. *Id*, Article 11-3.
26. The ombudsman body is an incorporated foundation with total contributed capital of NT$1 billion, which, in addition to private donations, mostly contributed by the government from funds budgeted for that purpose over a period of five years. The ombudsman body at the time of its establishment had contributed capital in the amount of NT$200 million, currently have accumulated

more than NT$ 1 billion. The ombudsman had established a fund, the funding sources of which included properties donated, annual fees and service fees collected from financial service enterprises, interest and investment gains earned by the fund and other donation income. *See* FCPA, Article 13 & Article 14.

27. In addition to handling financial consumer disputes, the ombudsman body shall also conduct education and awareness programs for financial services enterprises and financial consumers to ensure that financial services enterprises and financial consumers all have a full and correct understanding of financial consumption principles as well as the rights and obligations that arise in connection with a financial consumption relationship, thereby effectively averting the occurrence of financial consumer disputes.
28. Any of the situations listed in Article 24 of the FCPA applies with respect to a financial consumer who applies to institute an ombudsman case, the ombudsman body shall decide not to entertain the application, and shall provide written notification to the financial consumer and the financial services enterprise; provided, however, that if the situation can be corrected, the ombudsman body shall notify the financial consumer to make correction within a reasonable time limit.
29. FCPA, Article 17.
30. *Id*, Article 20.
31. *Id*, Article 29.
32. The "certain amount" shall be set by the ombudsman body and submitted to the competent authority for approval and public announcement. Currently the amount announced by the FSC is NT$ 1 million for most financial products and services.
33. FCPA, Article 30.
34. The Minister of Finance, the Minister of Economic and Energy Affairs, and the Minister of Justice shall serve as *ex officio* commissioners. The other commissioners shall be appointed (or retained) by the Premier from among the heads of related government agencies as well as persons with academic expertise or work experience in a relevant field, to serve in a concurrent capacity.
35. Financial Ombudsman Institute (FOI), *Message from the Chairman*, in 2015 Annual Report.
36. The FOI is totally funded by the government with NTD 1 billion (€25,000,000) and governed by the Financial Supervisory Commission (FSC). The institution has officially started operation on 2nd January 2012. All the services provided to financial consumers are free of charge.
37. FOI, *About us*. https://www.foi.org.tw/Article.aspx?Arti=32&Lang=2&Role=1.
38. Currently, the Committee currently comprises 21 Committee members, one of whom is the Committee Chair. Ombudsmen are divided into three groups in line with their expertise, namely, banking, insurance, and securities and futures.

39. When the Committee receives a case, it shall consider factual evidence related to the case and conduct an impartial and independent hearing in keeping with the principles of fairness and reasonableness. If reasonably necessary, the Committee may ask the financial services enterprise to provide assistance or submit documents and related materials.
40. FOI, *Message from the Ombudsman Committee Chair and President*, in 2015 Annual Report.
41. SFIPC, *Operation Report,* in 2015 Annual Report.
42. As of the year-end 2015, the Center has assisted investors in 201 class action suits (including cases transferred from Securities & Futures Institute) with claim amount exceeding NT$44.6 billion and involving 115,000 claimants.
43. At the end of 2015, the Center had helped investors claim a total of NT$3,010 million in settlements and NT$82.11 million of which were claimed in settlement in 2015.
44. All the financial institutions that may, pursuant to the law, accept deposits whose principal and interest are guaranteed and with uses designated by the financial institutions, including banks, the Agricultural Bank of Taiwan, the branches of foreign and mainland Chinese banks in Taiwan, credit cooperatives, credit departments of farmers' and fishermen's associations, and postal savings bank (the Chunghwa Post Company), are required to participate in the deposit insurance system as insured institutions. Accounts and products of securities firms, insurance companies, bills finance corporations and other financial institutions that do not accept deposits are not covered under the deposit insurance system.
45. Source: the CDIC Taiwan, 2017.
46. The China Post, *TransGlobe Life completes takeover of troubled Kuo Hua,* Sunday, March 31, 2013, CNA.
47. Taipei Times, *Cathay wins bid for insolvent insurers*, Tue, Mar 24, 2015.
48. Apart from the compensation, the Financial Supervisory Commission will grant Nan Shan amnesties so it can better emerge from Chaoyang's financial burdens. Chaoyang had about 100,000 clients with 123,000 policies, total assets of NT $34.52 billion and long-standing negative net worth prior to the receivership that came after the company failed to remedy capital inadequacy. Insurers with risk-based capital (RBC) ratios of lower than 50 percent might be taken into government control to safeguard the interests of customers and employees. Taipei Times, *Nan Shan wins Chaoyang bailout bid*, Tue, Jan 17, 2017.
49. Taipei Times, *Nan Shan wins Chaoyang bailout bid*, Tue, Jan 17, 2017.
50. 2015 Annual Report, FSC.
51. *Id.*
52. *Id.*
53. *Id.*
54. *Id.*
55. Focus Taiwan, *FSC fines two more banks over TRF trading*, News Channel (CNA) Dec. 1 2016.

- The United States population is equivalent to 4.34% of the total world population.
- The population density in the United States is 36 per square kilometer (92 people per square mile).
- 82.9% of the population is urban (270,683,202 people in 2017)
- The median age in the United States is 38.1 years.

The next set of figures are included to illustrate the various aspects of the financial situation of the U.S. population. To begin, Fig. 3 illustrates the trend in real (inflation adjusted) per capita disposable income and the corresponding average annual personal saving rate.

Real per capita disposable income has generally increased, with the exception of 2009–2010 and 2012–2013. The increase indicates a greater amount available for savings or consumption. The personal saving rate also declined in the same periods, but shows an overall increasing trend over the past decade.

Figure 4 provides an alternative look at consumer savings. From the figure, we can see that the total amount of savings by families, in 2013 dollars, has declined since 2007. Families with retirement savings, however, do show an increase from 2010 to 2013.

The U.S. Social Security (Old Age, Survivors, and Disability Insurance) Program was established by the Social Security Act in 1935. Social security payments to current retirees are financed by a payroll tax on current workers' wages. Over time, provisions have been changed and the method of funding continues to be a concern. Amendments have included increased funding for the Aid to Dependent Children, establishment of Medicare and Medicaid health insurance programs, cost of living increases, and the addition of Supplemental Security Income (SSI). An amendment in 1983 modifies the full retirement benefit age. When established, the full benefit age was 65, and early retirement benefits, at an 80-percent reduction in the benefit amount, could be received beginning at age 62. The full retirement benefit age is now 66 for people born in 1943–1954, and rises to 67 for those born

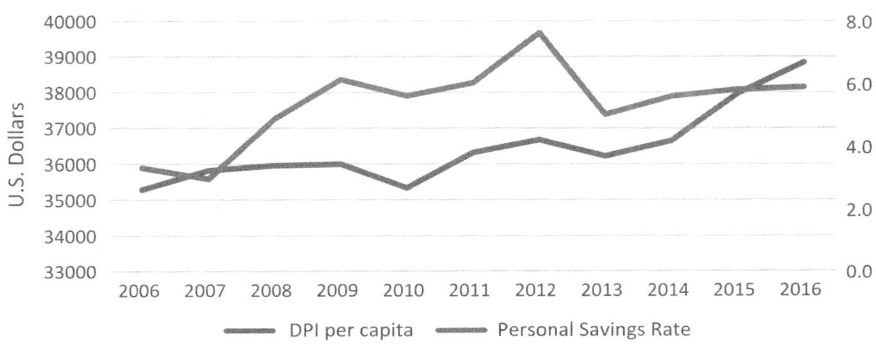

Fig. 3 Real disposable personal income per capita and personal saving rate (*Source* U.S. Federal Reserve Economic Data)

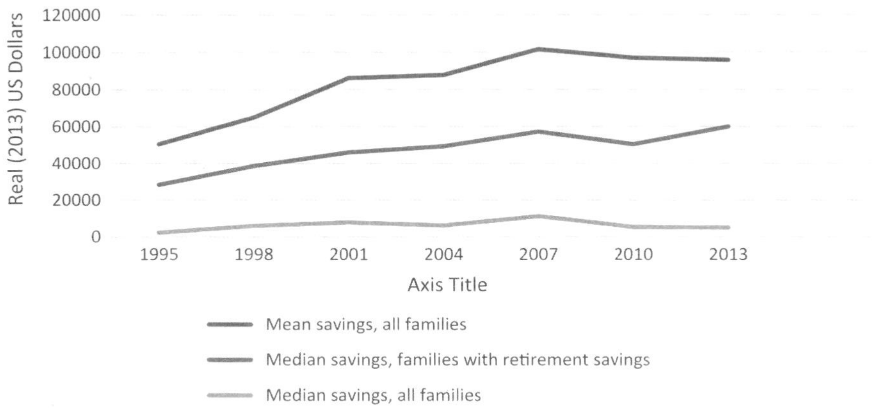

Fig. 4 Distribution of family savings in the U.S. (*Source* Economic Policy Institute Survey of Consumer Finances)

in 1960 or later.[1] Also, retirement benefits are increased an additional 8% for each year one delays collecting benefits.

Table 1 below shows the total enrolments by the type of benefit received by major categories.

Figures 5 and 6 illustrate the growth in the number of males and females, respectively, that receive Social Security Benefit payments. Each figure also illustrates the average age of the population receiving benefits.

Figure 7 shows the development of the OASDI Trust Fund over the past decade. The figure shows that the balance in the trust fund is rising at a decreasing rate. Annual changes in the trust fund balance are projected to be negative beginning in 2017 and will continue to be eroded as the population continues to age. Trustees of the Social Security and Medicare trust funds currently project that the combined funds (OASI and DI) will be bankrupt by 2034, if no further changes are made.

Other major sources of retirement income include pension plans (defined benefits) and defined contribution plans offered by employers. Figure 8 shows that, although the total number of plans has been relatively steady over the past decade, the number of enrollees has increased steadily.

The number of defined benefit plans has dropped considerably over the past thirty years, but has been fairly stable over the last decade. The shift from defined benefits to defined contribution plans transfers the risk of adequate retirement earnings to the employee. Recent evidence suggests that this shift has resulted in a slight decline in the percentage of salary going towards retirement but, after considering returns and other various adjustments, the amount people have accumulated for retirement has not dropped significantly.[2]

Consumer financial resources also include homeownership and investments in various securities. Figure 9 shows the homeownership rate and the proportion of U.S. adults investing in the stock market since 2000.

Table 1 Enrolments in OASDI programs, by category of beneficiary

Year	Total enrollees receiving benefits[a]	Retired workers	Disabled workers	Wives and husbands of—		Children of—			Widowed mothers and fathers	Widow (er)s
				Retired workers	Disabled workers	Retired workers	Deceased workers	Disabled workers		
2000	4,290,080	1,960,649	621,650	341,503	43,941	115,358	297,686	363,632	40,491	505,021
2001	4,161,971	1,779,228	691,309	314,547	43,412	110,680	302,445	383,049	41,323	495,848
2002	4,335,714	1,812,551	750,003	317,685	45,600	116,186	310,395	419,780	40,829	522,537
2003	4,321,778	1,791,316	777,461	305,831	47,183	111,992	305,409	434,953	39,206	508,306
2004	4,458,816	1,883,060	795,775	319,430	48,016	115,391	309,472	433,699	40,030	513,839
2005	4,672,152	2,000,157	829,687	329,225	50,187	123,494	314,786	469,267	38,248	516,949
2006	4,621,110	1,999,019	798,675	328,430	49,521	126,860	321,155	449,020	35,981	512,320
2007	4,710,830	2,035,780	804,787	316,782	47,583	126,678	322,326	453,292	33,597	569,862
2008	5,134,644	2,278,997	877,226	344,003	50,756	140,581	329,397	490,895	32,717	589,940
2009	5,728,086	2,739,966	970,696	375,123	54,112	156,412	319,127	532,132	32,878	547,495
2010	5,697,011	2,634,439	1,026,988	354,947	53,987	155,193	320,293	569,020	31,797	550,223
2011	5,567,020	2,577,647	998,979	345,821	53,276	152,427	310,926	553,157	30,117	544,542
2012	5,654,668	2,735,007	960,206	369,410	50,165	142,114	304,199	512,706	28,618	552,135
2013	5,533,395	2,794,285	868,965	373,933	46,183	136,934	288,474	451,427	26,669	546,435
2014	5,361,293	2,771,933	778,796	385,394	42,609	134,070	282,492	393,513	25,319	547,090

Source Social Security Administration

[a]The total includes all individuals receiving at least one form of benefit. Some beneficiaries fall into multiple categories

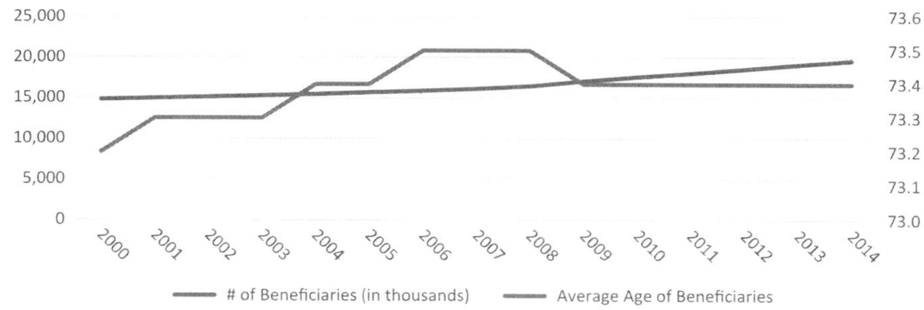

Fig. 5 Number of male SS retirement beneficiaries and average age (*Source* Social Security Administration)

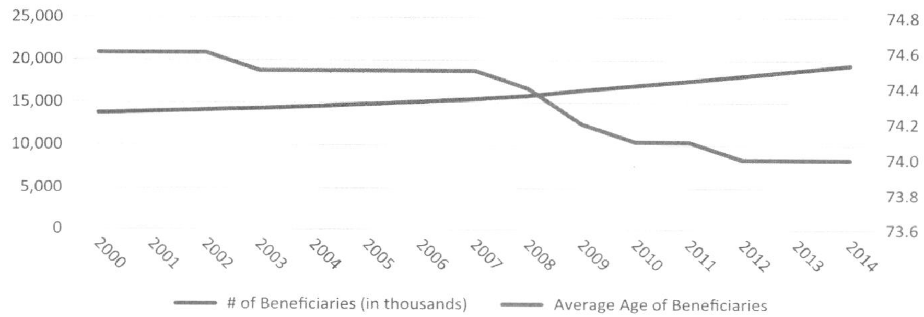

Fig. 6 Number of female SS retirement beneficiaries and average age (*Source* Social Security Administration)

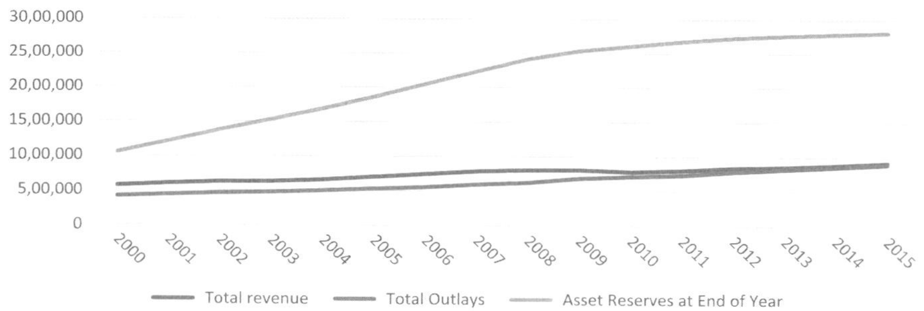

Fig. 7 Old-age, survivors, and disability insurance trust funds (in $millions) (*Source* Social Security Administration)

The homeownership rate, defined as the proportion of households that are owner-occupied, has been declining steadily since 2005. The proportion of adults investing in the stock market rose to 65% in 2007 and has dropped to just over 50%.

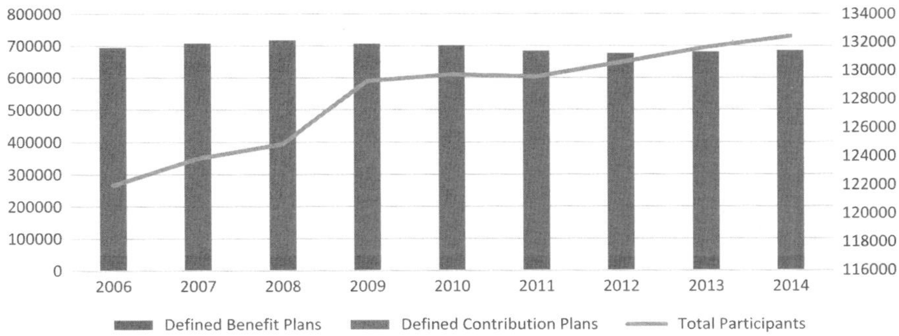

Fig. 8 Number of private retirement plans and total participants (*Source* U.S. Department of Labor)

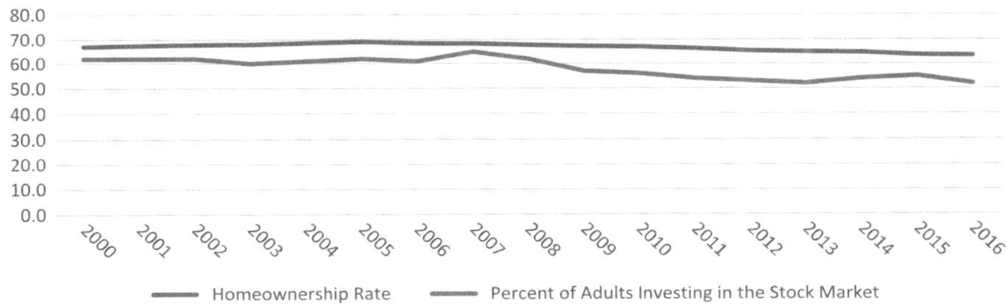

Fig. 9 Homeownership and percent of adults investing in the stock market (*Source* Federal Reserve Economic Data and Gallup Annual Economy and Personal Finance Survey)

U.S. consumers largely finance home purchases with conventional mortgages. This is illustrated in Fig. 10. The use of adjustable rate mortgages declined from 2006 to 2010. Mortgage consumer protections have become especially important following the 2008–2009 financial crisis. Data from the Federal Reserve suggests that the default rate on first-lien mortgages peaked at 1.4% in 2009 and dropped steadily to about 0.2% at the end of 2014.[3]

Table 2 illustrates the relative importance of all sources of household wealth in 2011. It shows the median values for overall net worth (including and excluding home) and median values for 13 classes of assets. The variety of assets illustrates why a variety of different consumer protections may be needed, as discussed in the next sections.

Figure 11 illustrates how consumer credit has evolved since 2011. While revolving credit balances have been relatively stable, the amount of credit outstanding on non-revolving products (e.g., student loans and motor vehicle loans) has increased from 1.9 trillion to 2.6 trillion over the past 5 years.

The figures thus far provide an overview of the U.S. financial consumer's condition, and how it has evolved over the past decade or so.[4] An understanding of the U.S. financial consumer's condition is not complete without understanding the

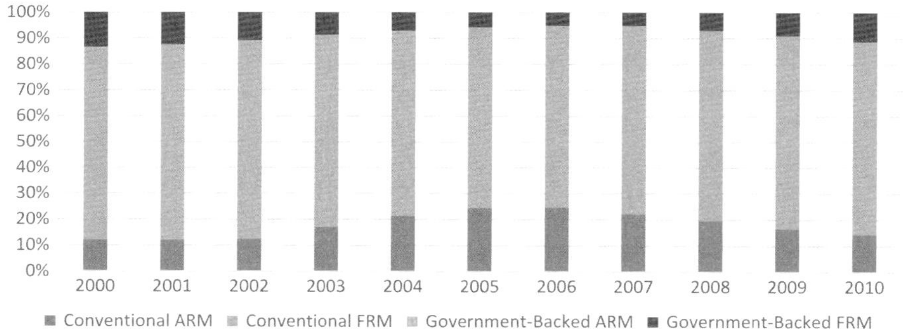

Fig. 10 Single-family mortgages outstanding, 2000–2010 (*Source* Federal Housing Finance Agency)

Table 2 Net worth and asset ownership of households, 2011

Characteristic	Total Amount
Net worth	68,828
Net worth (excluding equity in own home)	16,942
Interest earning assets at financial institutions	2450
Other interest—earning assets	18,181
Regular checking accounts	600
Stocks and mutual fund shares	20,000
Equity in business or profession	8000
Equity in motor vehicles	6824
Equity in own home	80,000
Rental property equity	180,000
Other real estate equity	80,000
U.S. saving bonds	1000
IRA or KEOGH accounts	34,000
401K & thrift savings plan	30,000
Other assets	22,000

Source U.S. Census Bureau

degree to which they are protected by private insurance products. Figure 12 shows total insurance premiums for the three major types of insurers in the U.S.[5]

The U.S. insurance industry is well-developed and competitive. Market characteristics will be examined further in a later section. While U.S. consumers are able to purchase a wide range of insurance products, penetration is not consistent across all forms for many reasons. Penetration for homeowners and automobile coverage are high due to mandates for purchasing. Health insurance penetration has increased more recently due to the enactment of the Affordable Care Act in 2010. The factors affecting demand for coverage are also discussed in more detail in a later section.

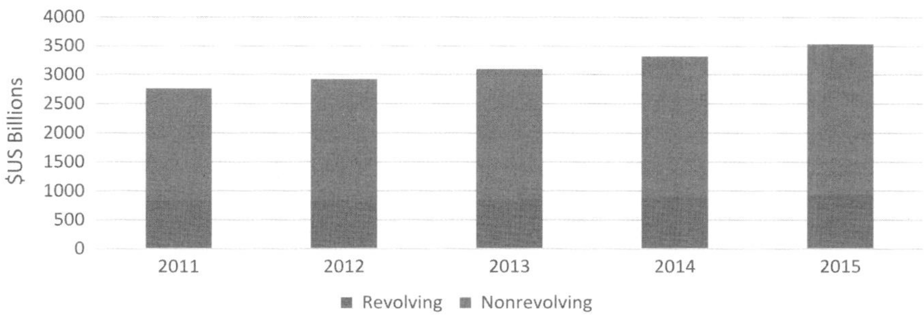

Fig. 11 Consumer credit outstanding (*Source* Board of Governors of the Federal Reserve System)

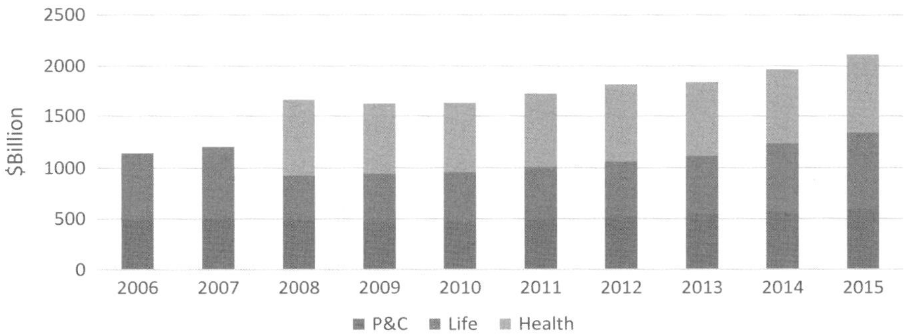

Fig. 12 Insurance premiums by insurer type (*Source* National Association of Insurance Commissioners)

2 Financial Consumer Protection System

2.1 *Relevant Laws and Rules*

Thousands of companies operate in the financial services market, providing U.S. consumers a wide range of financial products. As noted above, financial consumers in the U.S. receive some degree of protection through a wide range of regulations and activities at the federal, state, and local levels. The specific forms of protection depend, to some extent, on the types of financial products and the regulator that has authority over the companies providing the product. For example, because insurance activities are regulated at the state level, insurance protections are offered through state agencies and promulgated through state regulations. On the other hand, banks are federally regulated, and thus certain consumer protections are addressed in federal law, with federal agencies having monitoring and regulatory authority.

2.2 *Changing Needs and the Direction of Financial Consumer Protection*

The complex structure of financial products, generally, creates information asymmetry between providers and consumers and opens up opportunities for consumers to become targets of fraud or scams which can be financially devastating. As the array of products available to U.S. consumers continues to grow, so does the number of schemes to take advantage of these consumers.

The variability in products, markets, and distribution methods presents a challenge for coordinating financial consumer protection activities. Thus, it is not surprising that laws and activities addressing financial consumer protection come from a wide range of sources including federal laws and regulations, state laws and regulations, industry members, industry associations, and community/non-profit groups. Among the broadest options for general improvement are improving informed choice through ex ante activities—disclosure, transparency and education —as well as ex post opportunities for remedy and advocacy.

2.3 *Ex-ante Protection*

In the U.S., *ex-ante* protections to financial consumers include price controls, agent licensing requirements, disclosure requirements, educational resources, anti-competition laws, and efforts to promote literacy. These protections are derived primarily from a variety of federal and state regulations, but are enhanced through additional efforts by members of the financial services industry and consumer groups.

2.3.1 Product and Price Regulation

The Fair Credit Reporting Act (1970) provides important protections in three areas: credit reports, consumer investigatory reports, and employment background checks. It establishes the requirement that credit reporting agencies protect the confidentiality, accuracy, and relevance of individual credit information. It also establishes Fair Information Practices for personal information. These practices address data quality (access and correct), data security, limitations on use, data destruction, notice, user consent, and accountability. This rule was revised by the Fair and Accurate Credit Transactions Act of 2003.

The Fair Housing Act, enacted in 1968, addresses discrimination in mortgage lending. The provisions of the act address various industry practices, such as imposing different terms of conditions for groups based on race or national origin. The Act is enforced by the Office of Fair Housing and Equal Opportunity, a division of U.S. Housing and Urban Development.

The Fair and Accurate Credit Transaction Act (FACTA) (2003) establishes the right for consumers to request and obtain a free credit report once per year. Also, it allows a consumer to place an alert on his or her credit history if identity theft is suspected. FACTA also established the Financial Literacy and Education Commission (FLEC), which is responsible for developing a national financial education strategy along with a national financial education web site, http://mymoney.gov. The Commission is chaired by the Secretary of the Treasury and includes the heads of 19 additional federal agencies.

In 2011, the FLEC produced a report containing their strategy entitled, "Promoting Financial Success in the United States: National Strategy for Financial Literacy."[6] The report establishes goals to increase financial literacy and improve individual financial well-being. The goals included:

- Increase awareness of and access to effective financial education.
- Determine and integrate core financial competencies.
- Improve financial education infrastructure.
- Identify, enhance, and share effective practices.

The Fair Credit Reporting Medical Information Regulations Act (2005) addresses the use of medical information in determining a consumer's eligibility, or continued eligibility, for credit. The Act allows creditors to obtain or use medical information for determining credit eligibility only where necessary for legitimate purposes.

2.3.2 Fiduciary Duties

Because consumers' access to financial products often involves an intermediary, several laws address fiduciary duties, i.e., they govern the behaviors of those who provide financial advice, or make financial decisions for another person.

One of the earliest Acts to address fiduciary duties was the Employee Retirement Income Security Act of 1974 (ERISA). This Act requires pension and health benefits plans to provide consumers with information about plan features and establishes the responsibility for managing and control of pension plan assets. Further, the Act contains various measures to address grievances and provides for the right to sue for benefits and breaches of fiduciary duty, including breaches of privacy. Three organizations share the responsibility for the interpretation and enforcement of ERISA measures: The Department of Labor, the Department of the Treasury, and the Pension Benefit Guaranty Corporation.

Securities and brokerage transactions are governed by several rules that encourage suitable investment advice. Together, FINRA Rule 2090, "Know Your Customer", and FINRA Rule 2111, "Suitability", require that brokerage firms and their financial advisors use all relevant information on an investor's financial situation, including age, employment status, and risk tolerances, to determine the suitability of a particular investment.

2.3.3 Privacy Protections

Financial consumer protections also include rights to privacy, which are addressed in many federal regulations. For example, the Privacy Act of 1974 prohibits the disclosure of personally identifiable information maintained by government agencies and gives individuals increased rights of access to records maintained on themselves. More recently, the Health Insurance Portability and Accountability Act (HIPAA) established national standards for the privacy of health information.[7] The Act assures individual rights in health information and restricts how this information may be used or disclosed. Violation of the standards can result in civil and criminal penalties. The Act also established several notification rules that require vendors of personal health records (PHRs) and related entities, including business associates, to notify individuals when their individually identifiable health information is breached.

The Right to Financial Privacy Act (1978) requires financial institutions to protect information collected about individuals. Financial institutions must provide customers with privacy notices and give them the opportunity to control how personally identifiable information is shared, e.g., with outside companies. The Act does not provide consumers with the right to stop sharing among affiliated companies. The Act is enforced by four different agencies: The National Credit Union Administration, the Secretary of the Treasury, the Securities and Exchange Commission, and the Federal Trade Commission.

2.3.4 Antitrust Laws

Consolidation in the U.S. financial services industry raises some concerns with respect to its effect on competition and, consequently, consumer choice. In 2016, the American Antitrust Institute released a report addressing competition in the U.S. banking and financial services sectors with the conclusion that "the economic and political consequences of increased consolidation and decreased competition are particularly grave."[8]

Three federal laws have established U.S. consumers' protection from antitrust activities: The Sherman Act (1890), the Clayton Act (1914), and Federal Trade Commission Act (1914). At the time the Sherman Act was enacted, interstate commerce was expanding. The goal of the Act was to prevent restraints of free competition, as such restraints may affect the cost and availability of products. The Clayton Act provided further clarification on pricing practices, such as price fixing and price discrimination, and the Federal Trade Commission Act created the Federal Trade Commission (FTC), which is the agency charged with promoting competition in U.S. markets and protecting consumers from anticompetitive mergers. Along with the Department of Justice, the FTC is responsible for enforcing federal antitrust laws. Although the McCarran-Ferguson Act, enacted in 1945, confirmed the power of states to regulate the activities of insurers, insurers are not exempt from federal antitrust laws.

Consumer protection laws and antitrust laws may be in conflict. On the one hand, both types of laws seek to maximize consumer welfare; antitrust policy addresses market failures associated with the creation of market power, while consumer protections address the potential for information asymmetries and deception despite ample competition. However, where consumer protection laws presume consumers cannot make rational decisions (and hence, standardization is needed), antitrust law has generally held that consumer choices, which reflect consumers' true preferences, should be preserved.[9]

2.3.5 Good Faith and Fair Treatment

Bad faith refers to a variety of deceptive and improper practices in the insurance industry. To promote good faith and fair treatment, many states have enacted statutes that specifically prohibit certain bad faith practices on the part of insurers including, for example, failing to disclose policy limits, the use of abusive tactics to settle a claim, and unreasonable delay in resolving a claim. In other states, however, bad faith insurance practices are largely governed by court-made law. A majority of states have granted policyholders the right to file private lawsuits against insurers alleging unfair claim settlement practices. Today, statutes addressing bad-faith and unfair insurance claims settlement practices exist, in some form, in every state.[10] These laws are largely a product of model legislation drafted by the National Association of Insurance Commissioners (NAIC) in the early 1970s. Furthermore, all states have departments of insurance which, among their other duties, investigate bad faith and fraudulent practices committed by insurance companies.

2.3.6 Information Disclosure

Information disclosure is one of the most important areas in which regulators can protect consumers. In the financial industry, disclosure of information has important consequences in many places. Therefore, most financial services firms face requirements to disclose certain information to consumers so that they are able to make informed financial decisions.

Inadequate or incomplete information can lead consumers to select unsuitable products. Regulation DD, established by the Federal Reserve in 1993, was enacted to implement the Truth in Savings Act of 1991. The regulation requires banks to disclose the following information to their customers upon opening up an account: interest rates, credit and compounding policies, service fees, method of computing the balance, and minimum balance requirements. Additional disclosures are required if the terms of the account are changed.[11] Disclosures themselves must meet certain requirements, such as being clear and conspicuous, in writing, and identifiable for different accounts. Research suggests that the cost of implementing the Act was not trivial, as it required all banks to change their practices, not just the banks that were making use of a particular practice.[12]

In the insurance industry, disclosures are addressed through states' Unfair Trade Practices Acts, generally found in state insurance statutes.[13] In the life insurance context, these state regulations have the avowed purpose of improving consumers' ability to select the most appropriate insurance form of life insurance to meet their needs. More generally, disclosures that are required include policy summaries which clearly indicate assumptions and guaranteed values, where relevant.

Disclosure of information for securities prices serves to make firms more efficient and productive.[14] Disclosure of securities prices has important implications for investors in financial markets. The potential for managers to selectively disclose information to particular investors and analysts can have severe consequences for the investors that do not have the same information. This selective disclosure could make current and/or potential investors unwilling to trade in financial markets. In light of such concerns, the U.S. Congress enacted Regulation Fair Disclosure (Reg FD) in 2000. Reg FD states that any material information disclosed by managers must be publicly available and accessible to all investors at the same. The regulation is enforced by the Securities and Exchange Commission (SEC), which specifies that such material information includes any information "that a reasonable shareholder would consider … important in making an investment decision."

2.3.7 Financial Literacy, Insurance, and Retirement Savings

Evidence suggests that the U.S. Population is not adequately protected against a variety of risks. The take-up rate on insurance for flood risks,[15] for example, is surprising low, as is the take-up for annuities.[16] Studies indicate that a large portion of the population is not adequately preparing for retirement. This can be seen in the number of people remaining or returning to the workforce in their 70 s (graphic).

Many of the organizations mentioned above provide educational resources to financial consumers in an effort to promote better financial decision making. As noted above, FLEC has a National Strategy for Financial Literacy. These types of activities extend the mission of protecting financial consumers by increasing awareness of potential scams and fraudulent activity.

Consumers seeking financial information via the internet will encounter an overwhelming number of organizations willing to provide advice. Those providing investment advice include, for example, Investopedia, The Street, Morningstar, NerdWallet, Money Crashers, and Bank Rate. Tips for getting out of debt can be found on a variety of banking and credit card websites.

Consumer Reports, established over 80 years ago, is a nonprofit organization that promotes consumer safety and economic awareness through a range of educational resources.[17] Their mission is to provide evidence-based protect testing and ratings, backed by research and investigative journalism. Their reviews of financial products include car and home insurance, banks and credit unions, credit cards, prepaid cards, rewards cards, brokerage services.

Take Charge America is one of the largest nonprofit credit counseling and debt management agencies in the U.S. It is an organization that works with individuals and families facing financial challenges. The resources provided include tips for managing credit card debt, paying off student loans, and avoiding bankruptcy.[18]

2.4 *Ex-post Protection*

One of the first federal Acts to address financial consumers is the Federal Trade Commission Act (1914). This act established the bipartisan Federal Trade Commission (FTC), designed to promote a competitive marketplace for both consumers and businesses. It develops policy and research tools through hearings and conferences, and in collaboration with law enforcement agencies across the U.S. The FTC protects consumers in a number of ways. First, it monitors marketplace practices and intervenes when such practices are deemed unfair, deceptive or fraudulent. They collect complaints on a wide range of issues, including complaints involving financial practices, deceptive advertising, and identity theft. The information is shared with law enforcement agencies for further investigation. The FTC can bring lawsuits against companies and people that violate the law. Since it was established, the FTC's role in consumer protection continues to expand, as noted below.

The Fair Debt Collection Practices Act (Revised 2006) provides consumers with a right to dispute the accuracy of debt information. It creates guidelines for organizations conducting debt collections and establishes penalties for violations.

The Federal Trade Commission Identify Theft Rule, aka the "Red Flags Rule" was enacted in 2007 requires certain financial institutions and creditors to implement a written identity theft program that identifies and detects the relevant warning signs—or "red flags"—of identity theft in their day-to-day operations. The program should explain steps that are taken to prevent the crime and mitigate any potential damage. The rule is enforced by the FTC along with several other agencies.

U.S. consumers can file complaints against financial services organizations or financial services agents with a variety of organizations. Most state financial services departments have online forms for submitting complains against financial institutions. Also, consumers have a variety of options for suing financial services firms, e.g., for bad faith. A ruling by the U.S. Supreme Court in the case of *Merrill Lynch, Pierce Fenner & Smith,* et al., *v. Manning,* et al., affirmed that investors may use state courts to bring grievances against financial services firms.

2.4.1 State Fraud Bureaus

State insurance fraud bureaus are state agencies that provide various services including detection and investigation of insurance scams. Most bureaus are located within the state department of insurance, department of financial services, or the office of the state attorney. They generally deal with all types of insurance fraud, and operate online or phone-in hotlines by which consumers can report suspected scams. A list of state insurance fraud bureaus is available at http://www.insurancefraud.org/fraud-bureaus-directory.htm.

The Coalition Against Insurance Fraud is an alliance of insurance organizations, government agencies, and consumers that promotes enactment of anti-fraud laws and regulations. It was founded in 1993 following a dramatic increase in automobile scams in New Jersey. The original 17 members has grown over time to over 90 members. It provides education services and coordinates and disseminates research on specific areas of fraud. Some of the areas addressed include medical identity theft schemes and auto repair scams. http://www.insurancefraud.org/about-us.htm

2.4.2 The Dodd-Frank Act

In the years leading up to the 2008 financial collapse, there were reports of a variety of practices that were harmful to consumers. One such practice was predatory mortgage lending, whereby consumers were steered into inappropriate loan situations. Research suggests that both fraud and confusion played a role in this activity, which resulted in a significant increase in foreclosures.[19] Other practices include tricks to entice individuals to accept new credit cards and unfair overdraft policies used by banks.

The Dodd–Frank Wall Street Reform and Consumer Protection Act was signed into law in 2010. This major Act, enacted in the aftermath of the financial crisis of 2008–2009, made changes in the U.S. financial regulatory environment that affect almost every part of the US financial services industry. Title IX of the Act, entitled "Investor Protections and Improvements to the Regulation of Securities," includes measures that revise the powers and structure of the Securities and Exchange Commission and credit rating organizations. It also establishes new rules addressing relationships between customers and broker-dealers or investment advisers. While Title IX contains ten subtitles, the provisions in subtitle A specifically address financial consumer protections. These provisions include:

- The creation of the Office of the Investor Advocate, an Investor Advisory Committee, and an ombudsman appointed by the Office of the Investor Advocate.[20] These organizations are designed to prevent regulatory capture within the SEC and increase the influence of investors.
- Authority for the SEC to issue "point-of-sale disclosure (POS)" rules. POS disclosure items include key product features, information on costs and risks, and conflicts of interest.
- Authority for the SEC to establish standards and impose regulations that require "fiduciary duty" by broker-dealers to their customers. As of the end of 2016, the SEC has still not proposed a uniform fiduciary rule. One proposal is a rule that would allow non-governmental, or third-party, examinations of investment advisers. This rule would increase the number of adviser exams that are conducted annually. Currently, only about 10% of registered advisers are examined each year.

The remainder of Title IX includes measures that address a range of regulatory and monitoring issues including the regulation of credit rating agencies and the establishment of a Public Company Accounting Oversight Board with the authority to establish oversight of certified public accounting firms. Title X creates the Consumer Financial Protection Bureau (CFPB), which provides education and research to improve consumers' interactions with financial products. Recent research studies by the CFPB address the benefits of financial coaching and fees paid by online payday loan borrowers. The CFPB maintains a website, YouTube, and Twitter accounts by which consumers may post comments and suggestions. Although the Bureau has authority over retirement and savings plans, it has not taken an active role in helping consumers managing savings.

2.4.3 Better Business Bureaus

Better Business Bureaus (BBB) are accrediting agencies that set standards for ethical business behavior and then monitors compliance with these standards over time. In 2016, almost 400,000 accredited businesses meet and commit to their standards. Some of the areas in which they set standards is in advertising and the use of donations by charitable organizations. Services are offered online and in person at locations across the country. The Council of Better Business Bureaus (CBBB) is the network hub for the local locations across the US and Canada.

A BBB does not have any regulatory authority. It collects complaints and information on scams through an online system and provides this information to local, state and federal law enforcement agencies. The Bureau asserts that they are "often the first organization to know about a developing scam and alert authorities and the public. When a scam develops in one part of the country, the news travels quickly between BBBs in the U.S. and Canada that in turn alert the public in their communities."

3 Financial Consumer Protection Institutions

3.1 Financial Regulation

Banks and banking operations in the U.S. are largely regulated by federal entities, but some state regulation also applies, in addition to federal regulation, to certain types of banks, e.g., state-chartered banks which are not members of the Federal Reserve System. The three primary federal regulators include the Federal Reserve Board, the Federal Deposit Insurance Corporation (FDIC), and the Office of the Comptroller of the Currency.

The Federal Reserve System, commonly referred to as "The Fed," is the primary regulator for large and complex financial institutions. It was created by the Federal

Reserve Act in 1913, and has responsibilities that include: (1) conducting U.S. monetary policy,[21] (2) supervising and regulating banks and other important financial institutions to ensure solvency and promote consumer protections, (3) maintain stability of the U.S. financial system, and (4) providing financial services to the U.S. government and various other financial institutions. The Fed provides consumer information and education resources via the website at https://www.federalreserve.gov/consumerinfo/default.htm. Resources cover mortgages and foreclosures, frauds and scams, identity theft, and vehicle leasing. It regularly monitors fraudulent activities, but does not communicate directly with consumers.

In the U.S., insurance operations are regulated at the state level. A state department of insurance or department of financial services, headed by a state insurance commissioner, has regulatory authority that extends from monitoring solvency, reviewing and approving premium rates, and providing insurers and agents with licenses to operate in the state.

Financial exploitation is a criminal offense in most states, and each state's definition of exploitation and the associated penalties differ. A database of state laws on financial exploitation is available on the Department of Justice website.[22] Many of the state laws specifically address exploitation of the elderly or adults with a disability and will be discussed further below.

Many states have addressed consumer protections through licensing standards. Agents and brokers receive training in ethical practices and insurers are responsible for the compliance. As an example, in 2003, the NAIC adopted a model law with standards addressing suitability in annuity transactions. It establishes that an insurer or insurance producer "shall have reasonable grounds for believing that the recommendation to purchase an annuity or exchange an annuity is suitable for the consumer based on the facts disclosed by the consumer as to his or her investments and other insurance products and financial situation and needs, including the consumer's suitability information." If a violation occurs, the state insurance commissioner may order an insurer to "take reasonably appropriate corrective action for any consumer harmed by the insurer's, or by its insurance producer's, violation."[23]

As noted above, consumers may file complaints against financial services organizations and their agents. In addition, U.S. consumers have access to a legal system that allows for both civil torts and criminal complaints against financial institutions for a variety of reasons including bad faith, fraud, and breach of contract. The Federal Bureau of Investigation (FBI) is responsible for investigating allegations of financial fraud, theft, or embezzlement within the U.S. financial community.

3.2 Deposit Insurance

The FDIC was created by the Banking Act of 1933. It is an independent federal agency that was created by Congress to promote stability and maintain public confidence in the U.S. financial system. The activities of the FDIC include monitoring financial institutions for "safety and soundness and consumer protection."[24] It serves as the primary regulator of federally-insured state-chartered banks—e.g., most community banks—that are not members of the Federal Reserve System.

3.3 Dispute Settlement Organizations

The avenues for settling disputes with financial services firms depends on the industry. Most financial services actively advertise complaint services directly to customers, e.g., through customer service lines. If these avenues are not successful, consumers can turn to a range of consumer-oriented groups (such as the Better Business Bureau) as well as state and federal regulators for assistance. Consumers can also obtain legal counsel and file a lawsuit against the firm.

Increasingly, U.S. investors are using class action lawsuits as a means for settling disputes with financial services firms. In 2008, the value of securities class-action settlements was about $3.09 billion, while the total value for the preceding six years was just $45.6 million. The increase in the dollar value of settlements suggests that consumers have found this to be a key method for achieving redress. The total number of filings has not dropped, but the nature of the cases has shifted to include more merger objection cases.[25]

4 Special FCP Systems

4.1 For the Elderly

Senior adults are often targeted by financial scams for two main reasons. On the one hand, they will have generally accumulated wealth for their retirement, which may include substantial home equity. On the other hand, aging comes with cognitive decline, which can complicate decision making, especially for complex financial products.[26]

Title 12 of the U.S. Code § 5537, enacted 2010, pushes significant senior investor protections to the states. The code describes a financial product as "a security, an insurance product (including an insurance product that pays a return, whether fixed or variable), a bank product, and a loan product."[27] Most importantly, it authorizes the Office of Financial Literacy to establish a program under which it may make grants to states or other eligible entities (e.g., an insurance department) for enhanced protection of seniors from being misled by false designations and fraudulent marketing.

As noted above, most states have financial exploitation laws designed to protect vulnerable or incapacitated populations, e.g., aged adults and adults with a disability. The laws vary widely across states, most specifically establish the penalties for financial exploitation (versus physical neglect). Florida law, for example, defines "exploitation of an elderly person or disabled adult" as "knowingly obtaining or using, or endeavoring to obtain or use, an elderly person's or disabled adult's funds, assets, or property with the intent to temporality or permanently deprive the elderly person or disable adult of the use, benefit, or possession of the funds, assets, or property, or to benefit someone other than the elderly person or disabled adult," by a person who holds a position of trust, or has a business relationship, with the elderly person or disabled adult.[28] It further establishes penalties that depend on the value of the assets involved in the exploitation: "if the funds, assets, or property involved in the exploitation of the elderly person or disabled adult is valued at $50,000 or more, the offender commits a felony of the first degree.

A variety of federal, state, and private/non-profit organizations provide services to protect elderly consumers. In addition to the general consumer protection services discussed above, the Federal Trade Commission provides some specific resources for spotting elder financial abuse. Through the Division of Consumer and Business Education, they sponsor a "World Elder Abuse Awareness Day" to promote talking with others about elder abuse and financial exploitation. The FTC's "Pass It On" campaign similarly encourages consumers to talk with friends, family, and other loved ones about avoiding common scams, like identity theft.

The Gramm-Leach Bliley Act (GLBA), mentioned above, encourages that financial institutions report suspected financial exploitation of older adults. Because many provisions in the Act address privacy concerns, further guidance was provided by federal agencies to clarify that "reporting suspected financial abuse of older adults to appropriate local, state, or federal agencies does not, in general, violate the privacy provisions of the GLBA or its implementing regulations."[29]

As noted earlier, many states have specific continuing education modules for agents that address ethical issues in the sales of insurance products. The requirements for obtaining continuing education in ethics may address specific forms of care owed to seniors.

The American Association for Retirement Persons (AARP) is a non-profit and non-partisan organization that was founded in 1958.[30] Initially formed in response to the need for retired teachers to obtain health insurance, its founding principles include promoting independence and the quality of life for elderly persons. The organization provides educational resources and advocacy that serves all retired persons. Members of AARP receive additional benefits, such as special rates on hotels and travel services. The financial services offered to members—exclusive home, auto, and life products, for example—are "trusted providers" that are researched and evaluated by AARP.

The National Committee for the Prevention of Elder Abuse (NCPEA) is a national association established in 1988 to address elder abuse, neglect, and exploitation. Members include practitioners and researchers from a wide range of social services areas including healthcare, law, and finance. The Committee provides training and advocacy materials on their website.[31]

4.2 For the Poor

The protections noted thus far are available to all U.S. financial consumers. However, individuals in the lower-income groups may be more vulnerable to losses due to financial fraud or misleading marketing, especially as they do not have the resources to recover financially from an adverse event. Educational programs and resources for lower income populations are generally offered through community programs.

Individuals meeting certain income eligibility requirements can receive health insurance through the U.S. Medicaid program and may receive additional financial assistance through the Temporary Aid to Needy Families Program. Both programs are managed at the state level, and are designed to ensure that individuals can support themselves and their families.

One area in which specific protections have been sought is protecting this population from the high fees associated with cashing government benefits checks. These consumers are often charged as much as 4-5% to cash a payroll check because they do not have a bank account in which to deposit the money.[32]

4.3 For the Young

The younger population, which may be characterized by low income and low wealth, primarily receives financial protection in two places: through restrictions on the marketing of credit cards to college students and through efforts to increase financial awareness in high schools. Credit card companies, in particular, have been accused of preying on college students. Prior to the enactment of the Credit Card Accountability, Responsibility, and Disclosure (Credit CARD) Act of 2009, these companies routinely offered free gifts for applying and allowed students to get cards without parental approval. The Act sets high barriers to credit approval and outlaws the practice of "freebies" near college campuses.[33]

Forbes reported in 2014 that the gap in financial literacy costs college graduates thousands of dollars through college and beyond.[34] Some problems arise through student loan opportunities that are not well understood and a lack of fundamental budgeting skills. Several organizations actively promote early education in financial literacy, recognizing that poor financial decisions among the younger population can follow them throughout their lives. The High School Financial Planning Program, sponsored by the National Endowment for Financial Education, provides a personal finance curriculum relevant to teens, ages 13–19. The U.S. Department of Education maintains a website devoted to financial student aid, which includes resources for students and parents applying preparing for college.

Some states have specifically enacted laws that require instruction in the principles of the U.S. economic system. Virginia code, for example, requires this instruction in the middle and high schools "to promote economics education and financial literacy of students and to further the development of knowledge, skills, and attitudes needed for responsible citizenship in a constitutional democracy."[35]

A 2016 survey by the Council for Economic Education reports that 20 states require high school students to take a course in economics and 17 states require high school students to take a course in personal finance.[36]

5 Market Issues

5.1 *Financial Technology and Bitcoin*

Advances in financial technology are creating new risks to financial consumers.[37] The risks to consumers come from a range of online activities and include phishing emails, data breaches, and identity thieves. In the insurance arena, for example, the complexity of underwriting and risk classifications has resulted in large datasets of personal information, and raises concerns about consumer privacy and ownership of data. Financial institutions collect large amounts of personal data, making them valuable targets of cybercrimes. Generally, U.S. financial consumer protections from cyber risks have evolved with changing technology. However, one more recent advance deserves further discussion: bitcoin transactions.

Recent advances in the use of the Internet for financial transactions include the ability for users to perform transactions without the need for a credit card or a central bank. Users perform transactions through Bitcoin addresses with private keys that are designed to ensure security, and there are generally no fees unless the transactions is very small or involves many addresses. Concerns regarding bitcoin use include using the currency for illegal transactions, include fraud schemes. Transactions in the Bitcoin network are continuously logged in a blockchain, a public ledger.

The introduction of bitcoin has opened up a new avenue for scams. These include bitcoin Ponzi schemes, wallet scams, exchange scams, phishing scams and mining investment scams. The use of bitcoin is still largely unregulated because it operates independently of any government or central bank and allows for exchanges without passing through any financial intermediary. In 2015, New York developed BitLicense, which extends regulation of financial services institutions to financial operators (known as wallet providers).[38] The licensing approach used in New York may not be the optimal way for addressing bitcoin issues; providers complained that the process of obtaining the license is slow and the regulations are overreaching. Nevertheless, other countries are actively regulating bitcoin transactions, and the U.S. may eventually follow suit.

5.2 *Marketing of Debt, Not Savings*

In the period before the financial crisis of 2008–2009, the U.S. went through a period of financial deregulation. The assumption was that competitive market forces would keep risk-taking in check. The crisis proved that shocks to the financial sector become magnified due to the interconnectedness of the financial services firms. The Dodd-Frank financial reforms, described above, implemented a range of new measures and these policies have helped to restore stability to the financial market. From a consumer's point of view, the Act has improved both efficiency and fairness in financial markets.

There is ongoing debate over the many causes of the crisis. One more contentious issue is whether consumer credit was too cheap. The Federal Reserve notes that there was a run-up in consumer debt between 1999 and 2008, and most views suggest that the crisis began in the residential mortgage market, due to a large increase in delinquencies leading to foreclosures.[39] Consumer debt has declined since the crisis, and financial services firms are increasingly advertising the importance of saving. More recent advertisements have emphasized the importance of knowing your credit score. The Fair Credit Reporting Act allows consumers to obtain a free credit report once per year.[40] Most commercial banks are also offering free credit scores to consumers on a regular basis.

5.3 The New Administration

Lastly, the election of President Trump in 2016 has introduced considerable uncertainty into the financial regulatory systems in the U.S. The new administration has proposed significant changes to the Dodd-Frank Act and other financial regulatory reforms, with the aim of reducing the financial burden of the Act on banks. Congressional Republicans have proposed repealing and reducing provisions of the Dodd-Frank Act and making changes to the structure and responsibilities of several federal agencies, including the CFPB, the Office of the Comptroller of the Currency (OCC), and the National Credit Union Administration (NCUA). In June, 2017, the Financial CHOICE ("Creating Hope and Opportunity for Investors, Consumers and Entrepreneurs") Act was passed by the U.S. House of Representatives. This Act would abolish most of the Dodd-Frank Act and the CFPB would lose much of its power. At the time of this writing, the future of the Financial CHOICE Act, and the outlook for at least some components of the current system of U.S. financial consumer protections remains uncertain.

Notes

1. The early retirement benefit age is still 62, but the early benefit amount is reduced further.
2. Munnell, A., J.P. Autry, and C. Crawford (2015) "How Has Shift to Defined Contribution Plans Affected Savings?" Center for Retirement Research at Boston College. September. No. 15–16. Available at: http://crr.bc.edu/wp-content/uploads/2015/09/IB_15-16.pdf.
3. Federal Reserve Economic Data, "Delinquency Rate on Single-Family Residential Morgages, Booked in Domestic Offices, All Commercial Banks."

4. This chapter does not address the many areas of inequality across population groups—e.g., age, gender, race. In some cases, inequalities may require different approaches to consumer protection. This is considered further in a later section.
5. Total health insurance industry premiums were not reported by the NAIC in 2006 and 2007.
6. Report is available at https://www.treasury.gov/resource-center/financial-education/Documents/National%20Strategy%20for%20Financial%20Literacy%202016%20Update.pdf.
7. HIPAA rules provide a federal floor of health information privacy protection. State laws that may provide additional protections also remain in force.
8. AAI President Diana Moss. Statement available at http://www.antitrustinstitute.org/content/aai-releases-competition-policy-recommendations-banking-and-financial-services-sector.
9. For further discussion of this paradox, see Wright, J. "The Antitrust/Consumer Protection Paradox: Two Policies at War with Each Other," *The Yale Law Journal* 121: 2216-2268.
10. Mississippi and Wisconsin do not appear to have statutes specific to insurance bad-faith or unfair claims settlement practices, but do generally prohibit unfair or deceptive insurance practices and set forth time periods in which claims must be paid. See Schwartz, V. and C. Appel (2009). "Common-Sense Construction of Unfair Claims Settlement Laws: Restoring the Good Faith in Bad Faith," *American University Law Rev*. 58: 1477.
11. Further, the regulation establishes rules for any persons who advertise accounts to ensure fair and accurate disclosure of information, such as interest rates.
12. Elliehausen, Gregory, and Barbara R. Lowrey. "The costs of implementing regulatory changes: The Truth in Savings Act." *Journal of Financial Services Research* 17.2 (2000): 165–179.
13. See Carter, Carolyn, "A 50-State Report on Unfair and Deceptive Acts and Practices Statutes," National Consumer Law Center. Available at https://www.nclc.org/images/pdf/udap/report_50_states.pdf.
14. See Leuz, Christian and Robert E. Verrecchia, 2000, "The Economic Consequences of Increased Disclosure." *Journal of Accounting Research* 38, 91–124.
15. See Michel-Kerjan, E. and C. Kousky (2010) "Come Rain or Shine: Evidence on Flood Insurance purchases in Florida," *Journal of Risk and Insurance* 77(2): 369–397.
16. See Benartzi, S., A. Previtero, and R. Thaler (2011). "Annuitization Puzzles," *Journal of Economic Perspectives*, 25(4): 143–164.
17. Resources are available at http://www.consumerreports.org/.
18. Resources are available at http://www.takechargeamerica.org/.
19. Bond, Philip, David K. Musto, and Bilge Yilmaz. "Predatory mortgage lending." *Journal of Financial Economics* 94.3 (2009): 412–427.

20. The Investor Advisory Committee was actually established in 2009, but the Dodd-Frank Act gives the committee specific authorization.
21. This includes, for example, influencing money and credit conditions through activities of the Federal Open Market Committee (FOMC), which is the monetary policymaking body of the Fed.
22. See https://www.justice.gov/elderjustice/prosecutors/statutes.
23. National Association of Insurance Commissioners, Suitability in Annuity Transactions Model Regulation. Available at http://www.naic.org/store/free/MDL-275.pdf.
24. The FDIC 2015-2019 Strategic Plan is available at https://www.fdic.gov/about/strategic/strategic/mission.html.
25. See Noked, N. (2013) "2012 Trends in Securities Class Actions," available at https://corpgov.law.harvard.edu/2013/01/15/2012-trends-in-securities-class-actions/.
26. See Blanton, K., (2012) "The Rise of Financial Fraud," Center for Retirement Research at Boston College. Available at https://pdfs.semanticscholar.org/4227/7bf5a2f18fcca90a0c2c5128dc25b6a643f0.pdf.
27. U.S. Code § 5537, Title 12, Chapter 53, Subchapter V, Part C—Senior Investor Protections.
28. Fla. Stat. § 825.103. Title 46. Crimes. Chapters 775–896.
29. See "Interagency Guidance on Privacy Laws and Reporting Financial Abuse of Older Americans," available at https://www.federalreserve.gov/newsevents/press/bcreg/bcreg20130924a2.pdf.
30. Information about AARP is available at http://www.aarp.org.
31. Information about ACPEA is available at http://www.preventelderabuse.org/.
32. See Sprague, A. (2013) "In California, New Consumer Protections for TANF Families," available at https://www.newamerica.org/asset-building/the-ladder/in-california-new-consumer-protections-for-tanf-families/.
33. For more information on the CreditCARD Act, see http://www.creditcards.com/credit-card-news/college-student-credit-card-law-1279.php.
34. See http://www.forbes.com/sites/robertfarrington/2014/07/16/the-financial-literacy-gap-costs-college-graduates-thousands/#13053c0365a9.
35. Code of Virginia §21.1-200.03.
36. Survey of the States, 2016, Economic and Personal Finance Education in Our Nation's Schools, 2016. Available at http://www.councilforeconed.org/wp/wp-content/uploads/2014/02/2014-Survey-of-the-States.pdf.
37. See Arner, Douglas W., Jànos Barberis, and Ross P. Buckley. "The evolution of Fintech: A new post-crisis paradigm." *Geo. J. Int'l L.* 47 (2015): 1271.
38. For a discussion of regulatory and legal actions related to Bitcoin, see Greebel, Evan L., et al. "Recent key Bitcoin and virtual currency regulatory and law enforcement developments." *Journal of Investment Compliance* 16.1 (2015): 13–18.

39. See Brown, M., A. Haughwout, D. Lee and W. van der Klaauw (2013) "The Financial Crisis at the Kitchen Table: Trends in Household Debt and Credit," Current Issues in Economics and Finance, Federal Reserve Bank of New York 19(2). Available at https://www.newyorkfed.org/medialibrary/media/research/current_issues/ci19-2.pdf.
40. 15 U.S.C. § 1681.

Patricia (Patty) Born received her Ph.D. in Economics from Duke University and is currently the Midyette Eminent Scholar of Insurance in the Department of Risk Management/Insurance, Real Estate and Legal Studies at Florida State University. She is a research associate in the FSU Center for Innovative Collaboration in Medicine and Law, the FSU Institute for Successful Longevity, the Florida Catastrophic Storm Risk Management Center, and the Munich Risk and Insurance Center. She serves as the Insurance Expert on the Florida Hurricane Loss Projection Methodology Commission. She is also the Director of the Risk Management/Insurance PhD program in the College of Business and holds a courtesy appointment at the FSU College of Law.

Her research interests include the regulation of insurance, medical malpractice, health insurance, annuities, and the modeling and management of catastrophic risks. She has published in leading insurance academic journals including Journal of Risk and Uncertainty, Journal of Risk and Insurance, Journal of Regulatory Economics, Columbia Business Law Review, Insurance: Mathematics and Economics, and the Journal of Business and Economic Statistics. She is currently President of the Risk Theory Society and is a former President of the American Risk and Insurance Association. Recent consulting clients include the Florida Department of Transportation and the National Association of Mutual Insurance Companies. She also serves as a Long Term Care Ombudsman for the Panhandle District in Florida.

Introduction to the IAFICO (International Academy of Financial Consumers) www.iafico.org

Raison d'etre of the IAFICO

- In spite of their increasing importance, financial consumers are still under-presented in economy.
- Existing forums are focusing on the consumers from business or regulatory perspectives, but little from academic viewpoint.
- We need to conduct cross-country comparison of experiences, ideas, or best practices from financial consumers' standpoint.

History and Mission

- The IAFICO was established in Seoul Korea at the end of 2014 by some Asian Scholars.
- The academic society exist in order to create and share knowledge on Finance in the following 4Is
  - **Internationalization** (Globalization)
  - **Inclusion** (Development Cooperation)
  - **Innovation** (Technological Advancement)
  - **Integrity** (Ethics, RBC, Sustainability)

Conference

- The IAFICO has held an annual conference every year since its birth:

  2015 Jeju University, Jeju, Korea

  2016 SKK University, Seoul, Korea

  2017 Fudan University, Shanghai, China

  2018 Waseda University, Tokyo, Japan

  2019 University of Gajah Mada, Yogyakart, Indonesia (scheduled)

Journal (IRFC)

- The International Review of Financial Consumers is published twice a year - in April & October.

- The editorial board of the journal is composed of world class academicians in variety of areas including economics, business, law, and so on.

- The IRFC is Co-edited by professor Man Cho & Tsai-Jyh Chen.

Membership & Governance

- By its bylaw, the IAFICO has individual (regular) membership as well as institutional membership.
- Individual members consisting of **professors,** researchers, consumer activist, experts, or regulators serving public interest.
- As of August, 2018, the IAFICO keeps 107 Individual Members and 3 Institutional Members - The Institute of Actuaries of Korea, Korea Deposit Insurance Corporation, International Association of Consumer Law.
- Nevertheless, guests are also welcomed to attend the conference without any voting right, subject to a non-member fee for participation .

- Board of Directors (2 year Term) make major decisions while President (1 year Term) hosts and organizes an annual conference. Secretary Office (SKKU, Seoul) administers membership and financial management and the journal publication.

Finance

- The IAFICO is mostly financed by membership fee, conference attendance fee and qualified donation.

- As a legal entity recognized by Korean government, it maintains a highly transparent financial management and reporting system (every detail is to be disclosed at its website).

2019 Venue (August 23/24)

The University of Gadjah Mada (UGM), Yogyakarta, Indonesia is hosting the 2019 IAFICO (Global Forum for Financial Consumers). Please join us (See for the details and membership at www.iafico.org).